Mass Media and the Popular Arts

Mass Media

Fredric Rissover
Associate Professor of English
St. Louis Community College at Meramec

David C. Birch
Instructor in English
Formerly of St. Louis Community College at Meramec

Second Edition

and the
Popular Arts

McGraw-Hill Book Company
New York St. Louis San Francisco Auckland Bogotá Düsseldorf
Johannesburg London Madrid Mexico Montreal New Delhi
Panama Paris São Paulo Singapore Sydney Tokyo Toronto

MASS MEDIA AND THE POPULAR ARTS

1 2 3 4 5 6 7 8 9 0 D O D O 7 8 3 2 1 0 9 8 7

This book was set in Vega Light by National ShareGraphics, Inc.
The editors were Donald W. Burden and David Dunham;
the designer was Anne Canevari Green;
the cover photos were taken by John Pinderhughes;
the production supervisor was Charles Hess.
The photo editor was Juanita James.
R. R. Donnelley & Sons Company was printer and binder.

See Acknowledgments on pages 481–484.
Copyrights included on this page by reference.

Photos on part-opening pages which have not been credited
within the text are from the following sources:

Part Four, Popular Print, photo by John Pinderhughes.

Part Five, Radio and Television, photo of ''Mary Hartman'' copyright
TAT Communications Company. All rights reserved.

Part Six, Photography and Films, photo by John Pinderhughes.

Part Seven, Popular Music, photo by John Pinderhughes.

Part Eight, Education, Mad magazine cover, copyright © 1966
by E. C. Publications, Inc.

Library of Congress Cataloging in Publication Data

Rissover, Fredric, comp.
    Mass media and the popular arts.

    Bibliography: p.
    Includes index.
      1.   Mass media—Addresses, essays, lectures.
2.   Popular culture—Addresses, essays, lectures.
I. Birch, David C., joint comp. II. Title.
P90.R56   1977   001.5   76-51744
ISBN 0-07-052950-7

CONTENTS

SELECTIONS WHICH CONCERN MORE THAN ONE OF THE MASS MEDIA AND POPULAR ARTS ARE LISTED HERE IN THE ADDITIONAL UNITS TO WHICH THEY RELATE

■ THEMATIC CONTENTS

Violence and War *(Also see the Index)*

Women in the Media

■ PREFACE

The purpose of this second edition of *Mass Media and the Popular Arts,* like that of the first edition, is to encourage students to investigate, evaluate, and appreciate more fully the workings of the mass media and popular arts and to recognize how these media and art forms daily influence them and their society. When the first edition of *Mass Media and the Popular Arts* was published in 1971, few books of this kind were available, which is why this book was compiled in the first place. Since its appearance, other much-needed books on this subject have followed. Few of them, however, seem to have been designed specifically for the use of college freshmen and sophomores, or even of advanced high school students, as the first edition of this volume was. Because sales of the first edition have indicated that there is still a need for such a book, the second edition has been prepared to meet the needs of these same kinds of students for whom the study of mass media and popular arts is a new and, we hope, interesting challenge.

In this second edition, we have retained those elements of the first edition which we believed, and others have told us, were of particular value. These include the general format, the study questions at the ends of selections, the discussion and project suggestions at the ends of chapters, the alternate tables of contents, the bibliography and the index, and some of the original selections.

The new edition also embodies many modifications and changes. The new introduction is written in the form of an essay which provides a background or context for the material to follow. Most of the selections are new, and there are more of them. They have been chosen to illuminate various facets of the mass media and popular arts—production, aesthetics, psychology, sociology, rhetoric, economics, and others. The short introductions to chapters have been replaced by quotations from selections which appear in the chapters. The list of general themes and the list of media sources for the classroom have been moved from the teacher's manual into the volume itself. So have some of the suggestions for projects. These changes are intended to make the present edition more timely, more complete, more interesting, and more convenient for both the student and the instructor.

We hope that *Mass Media and the Popular Arts* will continue to prove useful in communications and mass media classes. For such courses, it remains our hope that this book will serve as a stimulus, a guide, and a supplement to the examination of mass media and popular arts, both in and outside the classroom. No book on this subject, we believe, can substitute for direct examination of the current media and art forms themselves. We also hope that this volume will remain useful in other related courses—composition, journalism, sociology, and popular culture, for example—where it can suggest topics for discussion and writing, provide a variety of relatively current writing models from popular sources, and offer insights into an important area of contemporary life. However this anthology may be used, in whatever courses, we hope that students and teachers will find it stimulating and enjoyable.

The modifications and changes in this second edition were the product not only of our own observations and those of our students but also of the many helpful suggestions offered by other instructors who have used the first edition in their classes. We are grateful for all the good advice we have received.

We would like to express our special thanks to the library staff of the St. Louis Community College at Meramec, and particularly to Martha Newman, for help in locating material and tracking down sources. We are also grateful to Elliott and Juleta Blevins, Dorothy Carlson, Laverne Curtis, Dale Dufer, David Kopp, Denise Lapp, Jan Pine, Professor Marion Reis, Dr. Lee Thayer, and Professor Clyde Tracy for suggesting material and helping with typing, correspondence, proofreading, and other tasks necessary for the preparation of this edition. And we thank Diane Birch and Jean Rissover for their patient encouragement. Again, we dedicate this book to all our friends, colleagues, and students who have contributed so much to our education in this exciting subject.

Fredric Rissover
David C. Birch

Introduction

Mass Media and the Popular Arts: Previews and Viewpoints

If we're a mature people, and we know what our freedom is about, and we remain aware that this great choice of opinion is a good thing, then we're free to make our own judgment without bitterness or hate.

—Alistair Cooke

The man or institution which has the greatest political, military or economic power today is the one with access to the greatest amount of relevant information in the most usable form in the quickest time; and, in institutions or societies where popular understanding and support are relevant, the greatest access to the mass media.

—Nicholas Johnson

Ideas in a mass society are transmitted in the mass communications media. . . . Admission to them assures notoriety and public response. Denial assures obscurity and, apparently, frustration.

—Jerome A. Barron

As extensions of our psychic and sensory powers, the media have a way of shaping us even as we are shaping them. Understanding media has a lot to do with understanding *me.*

—John Culkin

. . . The late Alfred North Whitehead . . . said: "The process is the actuality."
In other words, if you want to understand any phenomenon, study it in motion.

—Pete Seeger

AN INTRODUCTION TO MASS MEDIA AND POPULAR ARTS

Fredric Rissover

I. WHAT ARE MASS MEDIA AND POPULAR ARTS?

Mass communications media, usually called simply "mass media," may be defined as the tools, instruments, or materials by means of which senders can record information or experiences and transmit them to large numbers of receivers in a short period of time.

The human voice is a communications medium; so is a hand raised to wave "hello" or "goodbye." Pencil and paper are also communications media. But these tools, instruments, or materials are not considered mass media because, without the aid of other media, they can communicate to relatively few people at a time. The traditional mass media commonly employ mechanical or electronic means to produce multiple copies of their information. Printing presses, for example, turn out thousands of copies of books, newspapers, magazines, pamphlets, and posters so that many people can receive the same information at just about the same time. Broadcasting equipment facilitates the almost instantaneous sending of information to hundreds, thousands, or even millions of listeners and viewers. Sometimes various media function together to deliver their information. Printing presses can transmit the information recorded by a photographer's camera. Television frequently transmits information recorded on film by motion picture cameras. Radio, more often than not, broadcasts information stored on disc or tape recordings.

Because mass communication, transmitted via the mass media, is intended for large numbers of receivers, it is necessarily general and impersonal. The larger the number of receivers for whom the communication is intended, the more general and impersonal it becomes. Consequently, mass communication can be thought of as information addressed: "To Whom It May Concern." When an individual receiver becomes saturated with "To Whom It May Concern" messages, he learns to ignore most of them because most of them do not concern him. To make the most of mass communication messages which come his way, he must become both selective and vigilant. While he disregards the flood of information which does not serve his needs, he must be able to identify and concentrate on the information which does.

The impersonal and general nature of mass communication is reinforced by the fact that mass media are usually designed to facilitate information flow in one direction only—from the one or few senders to many receivers. A person speaking to his friends or colleagues can receive immediate feedback in the form of reactions and questions. But a person communicating by means of a magazine article or a television broadcast cannot know how his message is being received at the time he is presenting it. Of course, magazine readers and television viewers can write letters of comment or inquiry to publishers and broadcasters, but few readers or viewers take the time and effort. And even if they do, their feedback is delayed, and they cannot be certain that their letters will reach the appropriate source or that they will receive a satisfactory reply. It is not surprising, therefore, that senders of information via the mass media often must do a lot of guessing about what their receivers want and that the receivers often feel powerless to inform the senders about their desires and needs.

The information transmitted via the mass media often takes the form of carefully structured messages which we call "popular arts." The arts, in general, are kinds of communications which may be informative but which principally provide pleasure for the participants and which are designed to be meaningful experiences in themselves. The popular arts are simply those art forms which appeal to large numbers of people who share similar experiences, interests, values, or tastes.

In the large realm of the arts, "popular arts" are sometimes contrasted with "fine arts"—the forms of expression which traditionally appeal to relatively small and elite segments of the public. Poetry, painting, sculpture, drama, symphonic music, and ballet, for example, are usually considered "fine arts," whereas movies, photographs, cartoons, television shows, and dance music are usually considered "popular arts."

Such a distinction between "fine art" and "popular art," however, is difficult to maintain. Some works of art were popular when they first appeared—some of Shakespeare's plays, for instance, which were well attended by people in various levels of society, or some of Charles Dickens's novels which appeared in serialized form in magazines. Now that they have stood the test of time, these plays and novels are considered examples of "fine art." The same process has occurred with some good movies—products of our own century—which were once considered "merely" popular entertainment but which have subsequently been recognized as enduring works of art, as "fine" in their own way as many plays and novels. Photography, once considered merely a way of recording reality, is now recognized as art, and superior photographs are displayed in museums which once exhibited only paintings and sculpture.

Conversely, the music of Bach, Mozart, Beethoven, Rossini, and Richard Strauss was long considered less than "popular" in its appeal. But when Bach's music was "switched on" by the Moog synthesizer and recorded, and when the music of Mozart, Beethoven, Rossini, and Strauss became part of the soundtracks of such movies as *Elvira Madigan, A Clockwork Orange,* and *2001: A Space Odyssey,* the appeal of this music was no longer confined to the musical elite.

Wide exposure to the public, therefore, is really what makes the popular arts popular. And wide exposure is possible only through the mass media. Exposure to the public via movies and television has returned some of Shakespeare's plays to the realm of popular art while not detracting from their status as fine art. The music of Scott Joplin, popular when first performed but for many years appreciated only by a handful of ragtime music fans, has lately returned to popularity because it was featured on the soundtrack of a movie, *The Sting,* reproduced on records, and broadcast on the radio. Of course, not all popular art is as good or enduring as the best drama of Shakespeare or the best ragtime of Scott Joplin. The mass media, in their efforts to keep us constantly entertained, popularize much art which is mediocre. They also provide exposure for some trivial and shoddy art which is quickly forgotten except, it seems, by worshippers of "nostalgia." But to claim that all popular art is inferior simply because it is popular is to engage in a kind of snobbery which, like other kinds of snobbery, isolates the snob from many potentially enriching and enjoyable experiences.

The mass media are what make the popular arts popular. But, on a more basic level, the mass media are what make the popular arts possible. Photography would not exist as an art form if there were no cameras or film. Neither, of course, would movies. Furthermore, photographs do not become popular until they are reproduced by mechanical and electronic means—the means that made such paintings as "Mona Lisa," "The Dutch Masters," and "American Gothic" familiar to millions of people who have never visited art galleries in Paris, Amsterdam, or Chicago. Even best-selling novels, written in the solitude of the author's study, would exist only as manuscripts in the libraries of a few wealthy book lovers unless there were printing methods to make them available to the reading public.

The mass media make the popular arts possible and popular, and the popular arts create demands for new mass media and necessitate their development and refinement. The printing press came into being when a demand arose for a large number of copies of the all-time best seller—the Bible. As the relatively crude printing presses and typesetting of centuries past continued to give the reading public a taste for the printed word, new technologies were developed to meet the growing demand. Today, sophisticated electronic presses turn out millions of hardback and paperback volumes, millions of magazines, and millions of newspapers every year. They also turn out millions of brochures and catalogs, millions of pieces of direct-mail advertising, and millions of pieces of sheet music. The demand for

DNESBURY   by Garry Trudeau

accurate visual records of historical events led to the development of photography, and the desire for more and better photographs stimulated the development of increasingly sophisticated photography apparatus. As the crude phonographs and cylinders of the early twentieth century stimulated the market for reproduced music, both old and new, the listening public, over the years, began to enjoy their music on increasingly longer-playing phonograph discs, on hi-fi and stereo and quadraphonic record players, and on multiple-track stereo tape cassettes.

The mass media and the popular arts, therefore, are inseparably bound to each other. The mass media make the popular arts both possible and popular while continuing to provide new and improved channels for creative expression. The popular arts, in their many forms, create a demand for new media and for more sophisticated media. And we, the public, benefit from the interworking of both.

II. HOW DO MASS MEDIA AND POPULAR ARTS SERVE US?

The first step in understanding how extensively the mass media and popular arts serve us is to recognize just how many communications channels and how many kinds of informative and pleasurable "messages" can be included under these two headings.

Usually, mass media are thought of as being of two major types—print media and electronic media. The so-called print media are devices which record and reproduce words, photographs, and other two-dimensional visual art forms such as drawings and paintings. Originally, the print media were only mechanical; now they are both mechanical and electronic. They include cameras, typewriters and typesetters, printing presses, and various other devices which produce multiple copies of words and pictures. By extension, the term "print media" is commonly applied to the widely circulated products of the printing press—newspapers, magazines, catalogs, posters, and books. The so-called electronic media are devices which record and reproduce auditory and visual events which involve time and change—speech, music, visual images in motion, or any combination of these. Such devices include microphones, sound recorders and amplifiers, television and motion picture cameras, videotape equipment, broadcast transmitters, phonographs and audio tape players, motion picture projectors, radios, and television sets.

Along with the media listed above, we also make use of other channels of communication which can be said to function as mass media. If we think of mass media as those means by which information and experiences are made accessible to large numbers of people, we will recognize that most of our social institutions serve as mass media. Schools, health and social welfare agencies, police departments, government offices, professional associations and unions, clubs and recreational organizations, and even religious institutions serve to disseminate information and to facilitate the sharing of experiences. So do the local trading post or market, the high school or college hangout, and the neighborhood store or tavern. So do libraries, museums and galleries, theaters and concert halls, fairs, exhibits, window displays, billboards, and bulletin boards. Private individuals make public statements—"to whom it may concern"—by wearing messages on pins, buttons, sweatshirts, and T-shirts, as well as by placing decals and bumper stickers on their cars. The postal service can be considered a mass medium because it serves to disseminate information. All forms of transportation, which provide for the distribution of goods and the interaction of people, may be classified, in the broadest sense, as mass media.

When people speak of the popular arts, they are usually referring to widely read fiction and nonfiction in books and magazines, news stories and other features in magazines and newspapers, cartoons and comics, photographs, motion pictures, popular music, all kinds of radio and television programs, and all the many forms of advertising. All of us come in contact with these art forms regularly, often with several at a time.

But the popular arts can include other forms of expression which are appreciated and enjoyed by large numbers of people. Some are clearly products of the traditional print and electronic media, such as greeting cards, wall posters, and comedy routines on phonograph records. Others do not relate to the traditional media. Architecture, for example, helps to shape our environment and can provide pleasurable surroundings in residential neighborhoods and in public areas devoted to shopping and business, health services, government, education, religion, and the arts and recreation. The design of public buildings is sometimes enhanced by such other art forms as murals, mosaic, and sculpture. (The walls of public buildings also serve as places where individuals write short "to whom it may concern" messages known as "graffiti.") Out of doors, our environment may be enhanced by landscaping with plantings, fountains, monuments, and the like.

On a more personal scale, our automobiles are designed to provide pleasure as well as transportation. Why else would the styles of cars change so often, or why would automobile owners spend so much money on custom paint jobs, vinyl roofs, wire wheel covers, and leather upholstery? Like our cars, our clothes fill a practical function, but they also serve as forms of expression. Uniforms are clothes with "built-in" messages. Other kinds of clothes change style often, and people buy new clothes and jewelry to satisfy their desires to wear something attractive, self-enhancing, and socially prestigious. Fashion is big business.

Another big business is the organization and promotion of sports. Our many different individual sports and team sports, ranging from the noncompetitive to the violently competitive, are often practiced with all the vigor and style of ballet or drama. Sports occupy many hours of our attention on sandlots and playgrounds, on golf courses and tennis courts, at gymnasiums and stadiums, and, of course, in movies, in newspapers and magazines, and on radio and television. The various symbols of our favorite sports, including the star players, confront us on billboards, bumper stickers, T-shirts, notebooks, packaging, bubble gum cards, and beer glasses. Who can doubt that sports are among the most popular of our popular art forms?

What, then, do all these various mass media and popular art forms do for us? In what ways are we affected or served by the mechanisms and messages of mass communication to which we are continually exposed, willingly and unwillingly, by choice and by chance?

Undoubtedly, one of the major ways we are affected is economically. Huge quantities of wood, paper, metals, glass, plastics, and other processed materials are needed to produce all of the media and their products. This provides jobs for millions of people. Additional millions are employed as artists and designers, photographers, writers, editors, composers, performers, producers, and directors. Still others make their livings as administrative personnel, promoters, exhibitors, retailers, engineers, technicians, and maintenance experts. As consumers, we buy the products and services of the media and the additional products and services they promote, thereby keeping the economy going and helping to maintain the high standard of living to which we have grown accustomed.

The services, other than economic or material, which the mass media and other popular arts provide for us may be thought of as falling into three closely related and sometimes overlapping categories: information, socialization, and compensation.

Information is probably the function which comes to mind first when we think of the mass media and popular arts. One kind of information is "news"—reporting of events that have happened, are happening, or are likely to happen in our world, our country, our region, and our immediate community. To the extent that these events are of interest or importance to us, we pay attention to information about them and are affected by this information. In addition to news, the mass media and popular arts also inform us of other people's knowledge, ideas, opinions, feelings, and experiences. This information comes not only from newspaper and magazine articles, nonfiction books, radio and television editorials and talk shows, and our educational, religious, and other social institutions, but also from fictional novels and stories, television "entertainment" shows, movies, photographs, cartoons, and popular music. A third very influential kind of information that comes to us in a large number of forms and with great frequency is advertising. Advertising constantly informs us of new products, new uses for familiar products, and the availability and costs of products and services.

The availability of all this information affects us in many ways. We acquire facts and ideas. We learn and improve skills, including our abilities to use language and express ourselves. We share feelings and experiences. We participate in an economy that offers us a high material standard of living. Because of the huge volume of information to which we are steadily exposed, we have to learn to be selective—to choose the information we want and to ignore the rest. Still, we often cannot help but pick up lots of pieces of unrelated information—unrelated to other information or to our other experiences—which we store away but fail to develop or use. If we mistake this collection of fragments for a fund of knowledge, we may do ourselves the disservice of substituting trivia for education. In other words, we may clutter our attics while failing to furnish our homes. Similarly, be-

THE GIRLS   By Franklin Folger

"I know I don't like television but it keeps me from doing
a lot of things I don't want to do."

"The Girls" by Franklin Folger, courtesy of Field Newspaper Syndicate.

cause the popular arts often try to catch our attention by frequent changes in their styles and subjects of focus, we are regularly encouraged to become faddish. If we succumb to fads in our ideas and life styles, we may become too impatient to finish what we begin before moving on to something else. We may tend to want constant change without considering the value of each change before we make it or without following through on each change thoroughly enough to achieve a satisfying result.

If we think of information as meaning "in-formation," we can recognize its close relationship to another major function of the mass media and the popular arts—socialization. "Socialization" is the continuing process by which we learn how to interact with and be participants in our society. It is the process by which we are formed to fit in. As socializing agents, the mass media and the popular arts provide us with goals and values, with roles and models, and with the "rules of the game" for our social interactions. Schools, churches, newspaper columns, and the like often communicate these things explicitly. They tell us what to believe and how to act. Television shows, movies, popular music, fiction, and the like often communicate these things implicitly. They suggest or show us what to believe and how to act. In addition, the mass media and the popular arts facilitate socialization by providing experiences and topics of conversation which we can share. Together we watch television, attend football games, see movies, and go to concerts. When we have finished talking to our families about our children, to our colleagues about our jobs, to our friends about our other friends, or to new acquaintances about the weather, we talk about a book or an article we have read, about last Sunday's sermon at church, about a television show or commercial we have seen, about a song we have heard, about a movie star we admire, or about who we think will win the World Series.

Socialization through the mass media and the popular arts helps our society to run smoothly by adding substantially to the things which people hold in common. Socialization, on a large scale, helps people in a variety of different societies and cultures to know and understand each other better. It helps to make our world into what Marshall McLuhan has called "the global village." We should recognize, however, that the mass media and the popular arts also tend to homogenize and standardize people. If we permit this process to go so far that individual variety or diverse cultures and forms of expression are standardized or assimilated into obscurity, we will be the poorer through our loss.

An additional complex function of the mass media and the popular arts is that of compensation. "Compensation" is making up or substituting for too much or too little reality, certainty, order, or human interaction. When we are tense from problems and pressures, we can be tranquilized with a good dose of romantic fiction, easy-listenin' music, or TV comedy. When we feel bored, we can inject some excitement into our lives with a rock radio station, a TV detective show, a disaster movie, or a hockey game. Downers and uppers—the mass media and the popular arts provide both.

Mass media and the popular arts offer compensation for our inability to experience some things directly. They provide us the opportunity to witness a moon landing or a visit by our president to a foreign country, the chance to hear a noted surgeon talk about heart transplants or a famous actress comment on her third marriage, or the means to explore marine life in a Caribbean bay or human life in the wilds of Australia.

They also provide us with ways to structure or schedule our lives when other ways are lacking. We get up in time to read the morning paper, we go to school when our classes begin, we do our ironing during the afternoon soap operas, we eat dinner when the network news broadcast is on, we go out in the evening in time to arrive at our union meeting, and we go to bed after we finish reading the newest issue of our photography magazine or after watching the late movie on television.

The mass media and the popular arts often compensate for human interaction when other human beings aren't available. They serve as company for the lonely and as baby-sitters for our children. Although mass media and popular arts bring people together by providing common experiences and topics for conversation, they also substitute for direct interaction. People may choose to watch bowling on television instead of playing themselves. People may choose to see a movie together instead of talking. Moreover, mass media and popular arts often reassure us, in ways that even our families and friends cannot, that the world is steadily going about its business, that we inhabitants of this interesting world amount to something, that human expression sometimes can be inspired or even beautiful, and that we individuals are not so very different from one another.

The compensations offered by the mass media and the popular arts can relax or stimulate us, can broaden our experiences, can help us to structure our time, can provide some relief from loneliness, and can even reassure us about ourselves and our world. But we should realize that if we let outside forces gain too much control over our feelings and our life styles, we may lose some of our desire or ability to control these things for ourselves. We should recognize that frequent indulgence in vicarious experiences can distance us from real people and direct experiences and can lead us to become passive spectators instead of active participants.

The mass media and the popular arts are our regular companions which serve us in many ways. Whether they serve us well or serve us ill is really up to us. But one fact is undeniable: the better we understand them and the ways they operate, the more control we will have over them and over ourselves, and the better able we will be to use the enormous resources they offer us to our advantage.

For examining or evaluating mass media and popular arts, some questions such as these can serve as a kind of critical checklist:

1.   To what audience does the communication or work of art seem to appeal? How well does it succeed?
2.   What seems to be the apparent purpose of the work? What immediate effect does it achieve?
3.   What basic human needs or desires are appealed to? What image is appealed to? Is any fixed response called for?
4.   What persuasion or propaganda devices are employed? How well?
5.   What attitudes toward the subject and the audience are expressed openly or implied?
6.   What social, moral, or artistic value does the work have?
7.   What is the relationship between the form or style and the subject? What is the relationship between the medium and the subject? How effective are these relationships?

SOME GENERAL THEMES RELATED TO MASS MEDIA AND POPULAR ARTS

The following are ideas and problems that apply to the entire range of the mass media and popular arts. These themes appear again and again in the study of the individual media and art forms and can serve to lend unity to such studies.

1.   *Popular art as a reflection of social concerns.* To what extent does art that is popular, that finds favor with a large proportion of a particular society, tell us something about the needs and desires of those who enjoy this art? What insights can it give us into the values and tastes of society?
2.   *Standardization and the loss of identity.* What roles do the mass media and the popular arts play in the homogenization of our culture and the standardization of the individual and of minority cultures? Which media and

arts help the individual or the minority culture to preserve and build a sense of identity? How do they do this? Which media and arts tend to destroy a person's or a minority culture's self-awareness and sense of worth? How? What can be done to change this situation?

3. *Specialization versus homogenization.* Among all the media it is possible to see the tension between attempts to reach (and sell to) the largest possible audience, and the counter tendency to concentrate on an audience with a single special interest. In some media, such as magazines, both tendencies are accommodated. Such mass-appeal publications as *Time* and *Reader's Digest* can be found on the newsstand side by side with such specialized publications as *Hot Rod Magazine* and *The New York Review of Books.* In other media, such as television and movies, special interests are largely ignored. What factors allow one medium to specialize and prevent another from specialization? What effects does specialization or homogenization have on the quality of the material presented?

4. *Youth culture.* What is "youth culture"? Is it a myth or a major social force? What role do the mass media and popular arts play in this culture? Which media in particular are important to the youth culture? Why?

5. *The depersonalization of art.* To an ever-increasing degree the mass media seem to separate the artist from his audience. Almost all our entertainment comes not directly from people but out of machines: phonographs, movie projectors, television sets, and so forth. What effect does this have on our attitude toward the artist and on the role art plays in our lives? What effect does this depersonalization have on the artist and on his art?

6. *The "star system."* Why is a particular performer rocketed to unprecedented fame and financial success rather than any of a hundred other performers equally talented? Do we need stars? Does our society require individuals to idolize and adore regardless of their actual merit or achievements? Do the media, then, fill a psychological need that already exists, or do the media create that need?

7. *Psychological effects of the media.* Just how valid are Marshall McLuhan's assertions that media significantly affect the perceptual abilities of those exposed to them? Are those who grew up with TV, for instance, fundamentally different psychologically from those who grew up without TV? Do the illiterate perceive things in a substantially different manner from those who read?

8. *Commercial aspects of the mass media and popular arts.* Almost without exception, the mass media and the popular arts are run to make money. Nearly always, the first and foremost question is, "Will it sell?" How does this bias affect what is offered to the public? In what few areas of the popular arts and mass media is profit *not* the paramount concern? With what results? How might the bad effects of the profit incentive be mitigated for the good of the public?

9. *Trends in media.* How are the media changing with respect to the roles they play in our lives? Are the mass media and the popular arts becoming more or less important to our society? What is the outlook for the future? Are we, for instance, headed toward a nonliterate police state such as described in Ray Bradbury's *Fahrenheit 451?*

10. *The interdynamics of the media.* A change in one medium always affects the other media. The advent of television, for instance, has profoundly affected all the other media. Similar smaller complexes of actions and reactions can be seen throughout the mass media and popular arts.

THE GIRLS   Franklin Folger

"Tell the doctor, never mind — that last commercial told me what to take for what I've got."

"The Girls" by Franklin Folger, courtesy of Field Newspaper Syndicate

Part One

Advertising: Previews and Viewpoints

Our character is geared to exchange and to receive, to barter and to consume; everything, spiritual as well as material objects, becomes an object of exchange and of consumption.

—Erich Fromm

. . . There would appear to be, in modern love, a mysterious disembodiment of emotion: it is not so much the *beautiful person* who is loved, but the *beautifying instrumentality.*

—Morton M. Hunt

[TV] commercials stress . . . a host of negative images, particularly feelings of fear, guilt, and uncertainty. And inane as they may appear, these commercials are one of the stronger social forces keeping women in line.

—Patricia O'Brien

The general raising of the standards of modern civilization among all groups of people during the past half century would have been impossible without the spreading of the knowledge of higher standards by means of advertising.

—Franklin D. Roosevelt
As quoted by David Ogilvy

The destiny of our Western civilization turns on the issue of our struggle with all that Madison Avenue stands for.

—Arnold Toynbee
As quoted by David Ogilvy

Advertising

■ PERSONALITY PACKAGES

Erich Fromm   *The Art of Loving,* 1956

. . . Modern capitalism needs men who co-operate smoothly and in large numbers; who want to consume more and more; and whose tastes are standardized and can be easily influenced and anticipated. It needs men who feel free and independent, not subject to any authority or principle of conscience—yet willing to be commanded, to do what is expected of them, to fit into the social machine without friction; who can be guided without force, led without leaders, prompted without aim—except the one to make good, to be on the move, to function, to go ahead.

What is the outcome? Modern man is alienated from himself, from his fellow men, and from nature. He has been transformed into a commodity, experiences his life forces as an investment which must bring him the maximum profit obtainable under existing market conditions. Human relations are essentially those of alienated automatons, each basing his security on staying close to the herd, and not being different in thought, feeling or action. While everybody tries to be as close as possible to the rest, everybody remains utterly alone, pervaded by the deep sense of insecurity, anxiety and guilt which always results when human separateness cannot be overcome. Our civilization offers many palliatives[1] which help people to be consciously unaware of this aloneness: first of all the strict routine of bureaucratized, mechanical work, which helps people to remain unaware of their most fundamental human desires, of the longing for transcendence and unity. Inasmuch as the routine alone does not succeed in this, man overcomes his unconscious despair by the routine of amusement, the passive consumption of sounds and sights offered by the amusement industry; furthermore by the satisfaction of buying ever new things, and soon exchanging them for others. Modern man is actually close to the picture Huxley describes in his *Brave New World:* well fed, well clad, satisfied sexually, yet without self, without any except the most superficial contact with his fellow men, guided by the slogans which Huxley formulated so succinctly, such as: "When the individual feels, the community reels"; or "Never put off till tomorrow the fun you can have today," or, as the crowning statement: "Everybody is happy nowadays." Man's happiness today consists in "having fun." Having fun lies in the satisfaction of consuming and "taking in" commodities, sights, food, drinks, cigarettes, people, lectures, books, movies—all are consumed, swallowed. The world is one great object for our appetite, a big apple, a big bottle, a big breast; we are the sucklers, the eternally expectant ones, the hopeful ones—and the eternally disappointed ones. Our character is geared to exchange and to receive, to barter and to consume; everything, spiritual as well as material objects, becomes an object of exchange and of consumption.

The situation as far as love is concerned corresponds, as it has to by

---

[1] Palliatives are ways of reducing the painful consequences of a problem without really solving the problem.

necessity, to this social character of modern man. Automatons cannot love; they can only exchange their "personality packages" and hope for a fair bargain. . . .

■ POINTS TO CONSIDER

1. Why do modern people often feel alienated from themselves and from other people as well as from nature and from society as a whole?

2. In what ways do you feel that the modern individual is transformed into a "commodity"? Do you agree with the author's assertion that this process leaves people "utterly alone"? Explain.

3. In what kind of behavior do modern people engage to help them feel more secure? What kinds of security are offered by society?

4. What is the difference between "having fun" and "being happy"?

5. What are "personality packages"? Consider as you read the selections in this book on various mass media and popular art forms how they often tend to fill up personality packages rather than communicate to individual personalities. Why do you think this is so? Do you note any exceptions? What are they?

■ THE ADVERTISER'S BAG OF TRICKS

Marjorie Burns   *Scholastic Voice*, November 8, 1973

Ask the average man or woman on the street what he or she thinks of advertising and you'll probably hear, "Oh, that stuff! I never pay any attention to it." But don't you believe it. People not only pay attention to advertising, they let it influence their behavior. That's because the creators of ads know many subtle tricks for outflanking a person's intellectual resistance and getting their sales messages into his skull.

Here is a bagful of those tricks. For convenience, we've divided them into three categories: Claims, Appeals, and Techniques. Claims focus attention on the products and what they can do for you, the buyer; they are, or appear to be, rational. Appeals zero in on your emotions; they hit you where you are the weakest—in your fears, desires, and cherished beliefs. Techniques are specific ways of expressing or presenting claims and appeals in printed advertisements and in radio and television commercials.

The three compartments aren't watertight. For instance, you may find that some of the Claims seem to be leaking in among the Appeals. But that's not important. The important thing is for you to have a variety of advertising methods to choose from so you can do a good job for your client. If the public is able to recognize these Claims, Appeals, and Techniques, they will become more intelligent consumers.

One note of warning: Some of these tricks are really tricky. That is, they're on the borderline between honesty and dishonesty. However, we do not label any of them "ethical" or "unethical." All of them are widely used in the advertising industry. Whether or not they should be used is for the ad agency and the consumer to decide.

CLAIMS

C-1 Product Benefit

The first thing an ad man looks for in the product he's trying to sell is some definite benefit to the consumer. Perhaps it gets dishes clean without water-spotting, helps to prevent tooth decay, or makes the buyer's work easier. If it offers any kind of concrete advantage, the ad man's troubles aren't over, but at least he has something to start with. He can say:

> Trident sugarless gum. The gum most dentists recommend for their patients who chew gum.
> Bounty—the quicker picker-upper (paper towels).

Of course, he won't stop with the concrete product benefit; he'll try to combine it with some kind of emotional appeal. Have you seen the recent TV commercials for the two products mentioned above? After you read the section on Appeals, you should be able to tell how each tries to involve the viewer's feelings as well as his reason.

The ad man's dream is the product that's first, or among the first, of its kind. When detergents first came on the market, one claim was enough: "Detergent cleans better than soap." (Of course, detergent also pollutes better than soap, but we didn't find that out until later.)

C-2 New, Improved

If your product isn't the first in its category, maybe the manufacturer can do something to change it. Then you can claim that it's "new." If the change makes it better, you can even claim it's "improved."

But be careful how you toss that word "new" around. The Federal Trade Commission, which sets standards for truth-in-advertising, says that for an old product to become legally "new," it has to undergo a "material functional change." Don't ask what that means, exactly; the meaning differs from case to case.

Suppose you decide that you can't honestly or legally claim your product is new. Never mind; there are ways you can imply newness. You can "introduce" or "announce" the product. You can say "Now," or "Meet," or "Today's Fresh Idea," etc.

> *Introducing No-Fry Doughnuts. Doughnuts that are different from any other kind. Because you don't fry them. You bake them. (With Gold Medal Flour)*
> *Announcing: the end of city skin! (Pond's Creamy Lemon Facial Cleanser)*

C-3 Exclusively Ours

If your product has a secret ingredient or an important feature that none of its competitors have, you're in luck. But if it doesn't, don't give up yet. Maybe you can invent a claim to exclusivity, or exaggerate a trivial difference.

a. Single out an ordinary ingredient or feature and give it a special name.

> **Mobil detergent gasoline** *(All petroleum products have cleansing properties.)*
> **Colgate with MFP** *(MFP is a fluoride formula.)*
> **RCA Accutron** *(One-button color tuning is offered by most makers of TV sets.)*

b. Take some feature shared by all products in the category and imply that it's exclusively yours.

> **Fly the Friendly Skies of United.** *(You thought all airlines used the same sky, didn't you?)*

c. Simply state that your product is different and leave it at that. If the difference is too small to mention, don't mention it.

> **This is color television as only Sylvania makes it.**
> **There are lots of shirts. There's only one Van Heusen.**
> **No other shortening has Crisco's formula.**

C-4 Tests Show

To be convincing, a test must be conducted by someone who is both impartial and an expert in the field. Usually, the ad states that an independent clinic or laboratory has made the test and found that the product is "58 per cent more effective," or "lasts twice as long as the other leading brand," or some such factual-sounding claim.

Occasionally, however, the "test" is a survey of customer reaction. This can be impressive.

In a test *(of 6 color TV's),* **50.1 per cent** *(of 2,707 persons participating)* **said Zenith had the best picture.** *(Only 21.1 per cent voted for the second best, etc.)*

C-5 Take It From Me

Sometimes a simple assertion, if made firmly and confidently, will convince people that your client's product is good.

> **You can be sure if it's Westinghouse.**
> **At Zenith, the quality goes in before the name goes on.**

Often an assertion of this type is circular. It says, in effect, "This product is what it is."

> **Savarin—the coffee-er coffee**
> **Coke—the real thing**
> **Peter Pan Peanut Butter is the P-nuttiest.**

If your client has been doing business for many years, that may be considered a recommendation.

> **We know what we're doing at Big Yank. We've been making cotton jeans for America's families for 75 years.**

C-6 Careful Words for Careful Claims (Weasel Words)

You can't promise positively that your product will cure nasal congestion, or never leave a single spot on glassware—no product is perfect. But you can convince the buyer that it'll do great things for him if you choose your words carefully. You can say, for example, that your product *helps* clear up nasal passages, acts *like* a cyclone to get rid of dirt, *works* to kill *virtually* all dangerous household germs, or *can* give every girl a clearer, smoother complexion. If the shirt you're selling isn't made of silk, you can still say it *looks like* or *has the look of* silk. Your shampoo may not be guaranteed to get rid of dandruff, but you can promise that it'll *fight* dandruff. If your bread has had most of the nutrients processed out of it, but the manufacturer has put some vitamins back in, you can label it *enriched.*

> **Get the Cascade look . . . virtually spotless.** *(dishwasher detergent)*
> **Helps your hair stay outdoor-fresh** *(Breck instant shampoo)*

Speaking of freshness, that's one of those qualities that depend on personal taste and subjective judgment. One person's idea of robust flavor, smart styling, provocative fragrance, or warm, creamy goodness may make another say, "Yechh!" So you can claim as many of these qualities for your product as you want to, and no one will argue.

APPEALS

If the product you're trying to sell offers no special benefit to the consumer; or if it is essentially like every other product in its category (a sugar or an airline, for example), you'll have to fall back on some kind of emotional appeal. But even if you can make lots of rational claims for your product's superiority, your pitch will be more effective if you add an emotional appeal. The makers of Pampers (disposable diapers) learned that lesson.

When Pampers were ready to be put on the market, the ad men decided to "play it straight." After all, the product was new, and it offered definite advantages over old-fashioned cloth diapers. So the agency created ads that simply stated the advantages. What happened? Nothing. Nobody bought Pampers. Store owners started calling the supplier and begging him to remove the space-wasting merchandise from their shelves.

Then the agency got busy and created a new ad campaign. This one consisted of a little slice-of-life drama, with some cute gurgling babies, proud mamas, and perhaps an awkward, fumbling papa or two. The ad showed the product as part of a loving family situation—and it sold Pampers by the carload.

A-1 The Family

Most Americans regard the close-knit, loving family as the foundation of a healthy society. Therefore, if you can suggest that your product is a part of family life, or can contribute to family life, you may not need to make any further claims.

Since the woman of the house makes most of the buying decisions in this area, your pitch for home and motherhood will be directed at her. You'll suggest that if she cares about her family she'll buy your product.

> **You discovered Profile, Mom.** (Father and the children say this gratefully to a beaming mom as they all munch on Profile bread.)
> **Stop Vitamin Shortage in Children!** (St. Joseph's vitamins for children)
> **The boy by Mrs. Whitehead. The boy's shirt by Kaynee.** (The photo shows a woman and her young son posing together, obviously proud of each other.)

A-2 It's You! (Image Appeal)

This type of appeal focuses on the user instead of on the product. What aspect of the user's personality should you aim for? Motivational researchers suggest that the best place to hit a prospective customer is in his self-image. They say we tend to buy products that harmonize with the way we would like others to see us.

Take, for example, the full-time housewife who thinks of herself as a conscientious homemaker, a fine cook and gracious hostess. You'll have a hard time selling her an instant coffee, or one of those "just-heat-and-serve" dinners. Your job will be to convince her she can have convenience and her self-image too.

Instant Maxwell House. We tested against perked . . . and we won! *(In other words, if instant coffee pleases people more than "regular" does, a good cook will use it.)*

Morton. You don't have to cook to care. *(Packaged spaghetti and meat sauce)*

It's easier to get where you'd like to be if you dress like you're already there. *(Mavest sportcoats for men. The appeal is to the buyer's wish to be successful.)*

Live-it up outfit from Bobbie Brooks *(Women's clothing. Aimed at those who see themselves as active, fun-loving, and youthful.)*

A-3 Snob Appeal

When you say your product is "for the discriminating few," you're using snob appeal. Actually, of course, you'd like those "few" to be as numerous as possible.

Our $20 an ounce Make-up. Because a beautiful face is priceless. *(Countess Isserlyn Make-Up)*

Town & Travel. It looks a little more expensive. It is. *(Ladies' suede coat)*

Our 'British Clubs'. They don't run with the rest of the crowd. *(Neckties by Rooster. Notice that even the punctuation is British style.)*

A-4 Bandwagon

This is the exact opposite of A-3. Here you tell the customer, "Don't be left out. Everybody else is using this product, so you should, too."

Would millions of women use it if it didn't work? *(One-Wipe Dust Cloths)*

A-5 Youth

In this country, it sometimes seems that everybody would like to have eternal youth. That's impossible, of course, but it gives you the chance to offer the next best thing: eternal (or at least life-long) youthfulness. Perhaps your product will help the user to feel or appear youthful. If it's not that kind of product, then simply try to associate it with youthful people and activities.

A little Morgan's pomade every day/Turns your hair back from gray.

Would your husband like a younger-looking wife? *(Oil of Olay. Note the appeal to fear, too.)*

It's Pepsi, for those who think young.

A-6 Love

Here the trick is to suggest that anyone who uses your product will instantly become more attractive to the opposite sex.

Brush up your sex appeal with Ultra Brite. *(toothpaste)*
Arrow introduces the shirt women love to touch.

A-7 Patriotism

Sometimes you can make a little of the customer's love-of-country rub off on your product.

Chevrolet: Building a better way to see the USA.
The great American wool *(Burlington Woolens)*

A-8 Good Citizenship

If you can show that your client is a generous contributor to charities or is working to improve the environment, you will enhance his "institutional image" in the public eye. Eventually some of this approval will probably be transferred to the client's product or service.

TECHNIQUES

T-1 Straight Delivery

The most direct way to approach the customer is to say, "You should use Product X because. . . ."

T-2 Drama

But if you'll remember, the direct approach didn't work for Pampers, while the dramatic approach did. On radio and TV you'll find many examples of commercial drama. Notice that sometimes there's a "tag" at the end—a statement by the announcer that repeats the name of the product and perhaps the reason people should buy it. In other cases, the "sell" is worked into the drama itself, or delivered along with the drama by a voice-over commentator.

T-3 Personification

You can dramatize your pitch in another way by turning the product into a human or partly human character. Examples are the SOS soap pad, the Jolly Green Giant, the Wonder Bread Fresh Guys, and Rice Krispies' Snap, Crackle, and Pop.

T-4 Demonstration

One advantage of TV is that it gives you a chance to show your product in action. For example, watch Josephine the Plumber get a sink clean with Comet. Notice that Josephine combines Drama and Demonstration.

T-5 Testimonials and Endorsements

This technique can be divided into several sub-types. There's the Expert Testimonial, in which medical men, engineers, laboratory scientists, or other knowledgeable persons say that the product really works. However, since there are rules against in-person endorsements by medical professionals, such endorsements have to be worded carefully. You can't say, "Dr. So-and-so prescribes our pain-reliever for all his patients." But you can say, "Our product contains more of the pain-relieving ingredient that most doctors recommend."

> **Dentists want to save teeth, not pull them. That's why a dentist designed the PY-CO-PAY brush.**
> **1,694 hospitals use Pampers.**

Then there's the Celebrity Testimonial. Find an athlete, actress, or other accomplished and well-known person who will say in public that he uses and likes your product. Then hope the audience will follow his example.

Customer Testimonials can also be very effective. You set up interviews with a number of ordinary citizens who've used your product, and then publicize the comments of those who say they like it. Naturally, you ignore those who say it's terrible.

Finally, there's the Employee Testimonial. This involves identifying some of the workers who make the product or offer the service you're advertising. You present them as interesting, friendly human beings with whom it's a pleasure to do business. Thus you suggest to the customer that if X Company has all these nice people working for it, it must be reliable.

> **Come to Gramercy Park** *(a men's clothing store in N. Y. C.).* **Rosie-with-the-cigar or Flatbush Phil will be glad to help you.**
> **We don't have to work for Pan Am—but we want to.** *(The accompanying photo shows smiling crew and office personnel.)*

T-6 Names, Slogans, and Jingles

Some years ago, National Biscuit Company introduced a cookie called Snickerdoodles. With that name, it just crumbled away from old age on grocery shelves. Then the company changed the name to Cinnamon Sugar Cookies, and sales rocketed past $4 million.

Probably you won't get a chance to name the product; your job will be to make an already established name a household word. To do this, mention it often in your ad copy, perhaps making it part of a memorable slogan or musical jingle.

One observer has called advertising catch-phrases "a good old American substitute for the facts." Yet no one can deny that they stick in the mind. And, after all, getting into the customer's skull is what these Claims, Appeals, and Techniques are all about.

> **Try it—you'll like it.** *(Alka-Seltzer)*

I can be *very* friendly. *(Sunoco service stations)*
We go to a lot of pains. *(Bayer Aspirin)*

■| POINTS TO CONSIDER

1. What is the difference between claims and appeals? What kinds of products tend to use claims and what kinds of products tend to use appeals?

2. Using the ads on pages 26–53 or other ads, find as many of the "tricks" described in the article as you can. Which ads do you find especially effective as trickery? Why?

3. Do you believe, as the article suggests, that people actually pay quite a bit of attention to ads? Is it possible that people let advertising "influence their behavior" by *not* paying attention or by paying the wrong kind of attention? Explain, using as examples some of the "tricks" described in the article. Do you pay quite a bit of attention to ads? Why, or why not?

4. Do you think that "trick" is the right word for what ads attempt to do? Can you suggest a more accurate word? Explain.

■ A PORTFOLIO OF ADS

■| POINTS TO CONSIDER

1. To whom does this ad appeal? How can you tell?

2. Why does the ad feature "mother"?

3. With what image or feeling does the ad attempt to associate the product? What words and phrases particularly stress this appeal?

4. Although the ad obviously implies the superiority of home/mother-baked breads and cakes, why would it have been a mistake for the ad to say, or even to suggest, something negative about store-bought baked goods?

5. Do you think that this ad, with its very obvious "home and mother" approach, is completely serious, or do you think it is employing a bit of "tongue in cheek" humor? How do you react to the appeal? Why?

HOME.

Remember the rich, warm feeling you got in your mother's home every time she baked? The smell? The taste?

It seemed to tell you just how much she cared.

There's nothing stopping you from giving your own family the same good feeling.

All it takes is fine ingredients like Fleischmann's Yeast, a little imagination and love.

You too, can bake beautiful breads and cakes like these the first time you try. It's that easy.

To start, why not try an Apple Cake, some Rye Bread Sticks, a basketful of Breakfast Bow Knots, Cheese Bread or any one of the seven tempting baking ideas pictured above.

You'll find the recipes for these, as well as a host of others, in Fleischmann's Bake-it-Easy Yeast Book.

For your copy, send 50¢ (no stamps) to the following address: Fleischmann's Yeast, Box 1396, Elm City, North Carolina 27822.

Allow 4-5 weeks for delivery. No orders accepted without Zip Code. Offer good only in U.S.A. while supply lasts. Void where prohibited or restricted.

Another fine product of *Standard Brands*

FLEISCHMANN'S YEAST. BAKE SOMEONE HAPPY.

(McCalls, June 1974)

POINTS TO CONSIDER

1. On what advertising "trick" does this ad chiefly rely? Can you find other "tricks"?

2. Who conducted the "recent survey" and "clinical test" referred to in the ad's copy? Where are the results of the survey and test published? What reasons do you think the writers of this ad had for neglecting to give this information? (See ad for Vantage Cigarettes on page 33.)

3. Compare this ad with the ad for Fleischmann's Yeast. Which makes the stronger appeal to the emotions and which the stronger appeal to reason? Explain.

Fleischmann's is the margarine most recommended by doctors!*

(*Better Homes & Gardens,* November 1974)

■ **POINTS TO CONSIDER**

1. Which of the propaganda techniques (see Martin Quigley's article, p. 100) are most apparent in this ad? What other ads or commercials have you seen that use similar techniques?

2. Do you think this ad would be more effective or less effective with the illustration and headline alone, without the copy? Explain. Would the ad be more effective or less effective if the cigarette pack were smaller? Explain.

3. What is your "gut reaction" to this ad? If you smoke, does this ad encourage you to buy L&Ms?

The proud smoke

Product of a proud land.

Tobacco. It's as proud a part of the
American tradition as the Statue of Liberty.
At Liggett & Myers, we've made tobacco into a
cigarette worthy of that tradition. The rich,
mellow, distinctively smooth L&M.
Smoke it proudly.

For color poster of New York Harbor without commercial identification, send 2 L&M pack
bottoms and 75¢ to P.O. Box 60-1904, Minneapolis, MN 55460. Offer void to persons under
21 years of age. Good in U.S. only, except where prohibited, licensed, taxed or restricted
by law. Offer expires December 31, 1976. Allow four to six weeks for delivery.

RICH, MELLOW, DISTINCTIVELY SMOOTH

L&M
FILTER KINGS

20 CLASS A CIGARETTES

L&M
FILTER KINGS

Warning: The Surgeon General Has Determined
That Cigarette Smoking Is Dangerous to Your Health.

Filter King: 18 mg. "tar", 1.2 mg. nicotine av. per cigarette, by FTC Method.

(*Sports Illustrated,* January 26, 1976)

■ **POINTS TO CONSIDER**

1. Why are there no pictures in this ad except for the pictures of the cigarette packages?

2. With what image, concept, or feeling, if any, does this ad attempt to associate its product? Can you find key phrases that stress this appeal?

3. What reasons do you think the writers of this ad had for declining to advance arguments in favor of smoking? In what ways might this approach be more likely to persuade people to continue smoking than attempts to argue the point?

4. Why does this ad include tar and nicotine levels?

5. Of the two cigarette ads in this section, which do you consider the more effective? Why?

Smoking.
What are you going to do about it?

Many people are against cigarettes. You've heard their arguments.

And even though we're in the business of selling cigarettes, we're not going to advance arguments in favor of smoking.

We simply want to discuss one irrefutable fact.

A lot of people are still smoking cigarettes. In all likelihood, they'll continue to smoke cigarettes and nothing anybody has said or is likely to say is going to change their minds.

Now, if you're one of these cigarette smokers, what are you going to do about it? You may continue to smoke your present brand. With all the enjoyment and pleasure you get from smoking it. Or, if 'tar' and nicotine has become a concern to you, you may consider changing to a cigarette like Vantage.

(Of course, there is no other cigarette quite like Vantage.)

Vantage has a unique filter that allows rich flavor to come through it and yet substantially cuts down on 'tar' and nicotine.

We want to be frank. Vantage is not the lowest 'tar' and nicotine cigarette you can buy. But it may well be the lowest 'tar' and nicotine cigarette you will enjoy smoking.

Vantage. It's the only cigarette that gives you so much taste with so little 'tar' and nicotine.

We suggest you try a pack.

MENTHOL
11 mg. 'tar'
0.7 mg. nicotine

FILTER
11 mg. 'tar'
0.7 mg. nicotine

FILTER, MENTHOL: 11 mg. "tar", 0.7 mg. nicotine, av. per cigarette, FTC Report SEPT. '75.

(*McCalls*, June 1974)

POINTS TO CONSIDER

1. What is the idea or image this ad tries to associate with the product it is selling? What does the ad suggest Viceroys will do for you?

2. Why do you think this ad doesn't publish its cigarette's tar and nicotine levels as does the ad for Vantage Cigarettes on page 33?

3. In what ways does the girl in the ad fit Harvey Cox's description of "The Girl"? (See page 225.) In what ways is she different?

"Why Viceroy Super Longs? Because I'd never smoke a boring cigarette."

Warning: The Surgeon General Has Determined That Cigarette Smoking Is Dangerous to Your Health.

Viceroy Super Longs
Where excitement is now a taste.

Enjoy Viceroy flavor–now in a bold new pack.

(*Ms.*, December 1974)

POINTS TO CONSIDER

1. What various appeals are used in this ad to sell Dewar's Scotch? (See "The Advertiser's Bag of Tricks," page 18.)

2. The ad claims that Dewar's Scotch is "authentic." What does this mean to you? How does the picture of the Scottish Highlander in full regalia reinforce the idea of authenticity?

3. What connection is implied between the characteristics of the woman who is profiled and the Scotch she is said to drink? How is this implied connection intended to promote the sale of Dewar's Scotch?

4. This ad is one of a series of similar "Dewar's Profiles" that have appeared over a period of time in a number of popular magazines. Do you think that the repeated appearance of these ads produces a cumulative effect that will sell Dewar's Scotch better than a single ad of this kind, or of any other kind, might do? If you have seen this series of ads, what is your reaction to them?

DEWAR'S PROFILES

(Pronounced Do-ers "White Label")

BLENDED SCOTCH WHISKY • 86.8 PROOF • © SCHENLEY IMPORTS CO., N.Y., N.Y.

RAQUEL RAMATI

HOME: New York City

AGE: 34

PROFESSION: Architect/Urban Designer

HOBBIES: Graphic art, tennis, people.

MOST MEMORABLE BOOK: Tolstoy's "Anna Karenina"

LAST ACCOMPLISHMENT: Headed the urban design group which devised a plan to preserve and revitalize New York's Little Italy.

QUOTE: "The built environment is a reflection of our culture. A cityscape reveals where we are at, how we feel about our community and how much we respect ourselves. To an urban designer, a good urban environment is one which gives us a sense of place, joy, and freedom of choice."

PROFILE: Sophisticated. Persuasive. Concerned about how the urban environment affects the people who live in it.

SCOTCH: Dewar's "White Label®"

(Time, March 29, 1976)

Authentic. There are more than a thousand ways to blend whiskies in Scotland, but few are authentic enough for Dewar's "White Label." The quality standards established in 1846 have never varied. Into each drop go only the finest whiskies from the Highlands, the Lowlands, the Hebrides. *Dewar's never varies.*

■ POINTS TO CONSIDER

1. What image does this ad attempt to identify with its product? How do the style of the illustration and the details concerning the 1935 auto show contribute to this image?

2. Why do you think this ad repeats the phrase "was there"?

3. What similarities and differences do you observe in the techniques employed by this Ballantine's Scotch ad and by the preceding Dewar's Scotch ad? Do you find one of the ads more appealing or more persuasive than the other? Which one? Why?

4. Compare these ads with some ads for Bourbon whiskey. What similarities and differences do you find?

Ballantine's Scotch was there.

The 1935 Auto Show

Chicago. At the International Amphitheatre, a crowd waits to see what delights Detroit has offered this year. "Ashtrays in the backseat? Fingertip control? A radio? How marvelous!"

Ladies in polo coats look longingly at a LaSalle and talk about moving to the country. Those who already owned cars try not to look smug as they whisper about a new kind of restaurant called a "drive-in."

A line forms to try out the speaking tube in a Packard limousine. Couples sigh over a gift-wrapped Pierce-Arrow. America was having a love affair with the automobile.

Ballantine's was there. A stylish sort of scotch. Like those grand cars, a scotch for people who prefer classics.

Taste the scotch that was there- Ballantine's

(Time)

POINTS TO CONSIDER

1. What various "tricks" or techniques does this ad use to sell its product?
2. Do you find the endorsement in this ad convincing? Why, or why not? What is the purpose of the information included in the box at the bottom of the large illustration?
3. What does the ad seem to say about the qualities of a good wife and mother?
4. To whom is this ad meant to appeal? What features of this ad help to make the appropriate appeal? (Notice, among other features, the language used in the ad copy.)

Q. Does Norge pack a coupon for Tide in every new automatic washer?

A. Do pirates dig for treasure?

This Norge washer has a giant 20 lb. capacity that's powered by a commercial grade heavy-duty Transmission. In addition, Norge offers an exclusive lint filter that works at every water level and an Energy Sentry Control System.

Tide has agreed with washer makers to supply Tide coupons packed by them and to feature their washers in Tide advertising.

The makers of 17 washers pack Tide coupons in every top-loading automatic.

Searching for buried treasure can be a very dirty job. But to help you get out the dirt your buccaneer might get into, Norge packs a 40-cents-off Tide coupon in every new automatic washer.

Now 40-cents off may be a good reason to try Tide, but there's a better reason to keep on using it. 'Cause Tide was made to handle the different kinds of dirt you see so much of, like the tough ground-in dirt that actually goes through the pants legs to the inside. And even stuff like grape jelly and catsup. On tough problems like those, Tide gives you the kind of cleaning you need.

The dirt you see the most, is the dirt Tide cleans the best.

(*McCalls*, June 1974)

POINTS TO CONSIDER

1.   What techniques does this ad employ to sell its product? Can you spot the "careful claim" in this ad?

2.   How do you interpret the expressions on the faces of the luncheon guests?

3.   What is the effect of having the drinking glass loom so large in the foreground of the illustration?

4.   In what ways is the hostess in this ad similar to the mother in the Tide ad? In what ways is she different? Why do you think she appears on the very edge of the illustration instead of in the center or some more prominent position?

5.   Why do you think detergents are given names like Tide and Cascade? What qualities are suggested by such names?

If your luncheon guests looked this close at your glasses, would you worry about spots?

Not with Cascade.

You'll feel sure of your glasses, knowing that even up close they have the Cascade look...virtually spotless! Cascade's sheeting action fights water drops that spot. It actually makes water rinse off in sheets. Leaves glasses looking just the way you want them—for your guests, your family, yourself. You can count on Cascade. Try it and see.

Cascade...for virtually spotless dishes.

(*Good Housekeeping,* June 1976)

1. What is your immediate reaction to this ad? Do you think it is a a reaction that the maker of these products would like you to have?

2. What techniques, claims, and appeals does this ad use to sell its product? To whom do you think this ad will principally appeal? Why? Do you think this ad appeals more to men or to women? Why?

3. Why do you think that there is so much "copy" (verbal message) in this ad while the illustrations are relatively small? Why do you think the illustrations are round rather than the more common square or rectangular shapes?

4. Examine the language used in this ad. Do you understand such expressions as "private sanctum," "enduring fusion," "soul and psyche"? Why are such expressions employed? Does it really matter whether you understand the precise meanings of all the words?

5. What do you think would be the reaction to this ad if it appeared in such magazines as *Family Circle? Field and Stream? TV Guide?*

The bath
that draws you
closer together.

You have come to your senses now. Tonight, in your own perfumed and private sanctum, there are just the two of you. The only two who matter at this perfect moment.

Tonight, you who have shared so much pleasure and pain together, so much passion, so much tenderness, will partake of yet another sharing, another mutual joy, another fragile but enduring fusion.

And how inevitable that this basic communion between you should be inspired by one of the most basic elements in the world: water. Water: to warm you, to gentle you, to caress you—singularly and together. Water: to make you float through time—towards each other. Water: to enfold and hold you, to be as sensuously tactile as your hands upon each other.

You touch in a new way. For this bath is a touching experience. Your fingers trace a delicate pathway across a silken shoulder, down a responsive spine. The fragranced soap runs in rivulets down the beautifully balanced globe of a breast, down a tapered thigh.

And suddenly, the walls of your bathroom fragment, fall away and dissolve.

And you have traveled backward to other times, other places. And become a sybaritic duality, sharing a bath together within the templed walls of ancient Egypt, amidst the marble arches of The Roman Empire, synthesized in the ritualistic and grave sensuality of a bath house in fourteenth century Japan. Other times, other places, where bathing was a daily renewal

of soul and psyche, part of the art of social intercourse, as well as a bodily awakening.

You speak to each other with your hands, your eyes, your mouths. You bring to each other the understanding of shared silences, as well. You cleanse each other scrupulously, fastidiously, as if performing a lovely rite that makes you one. And it all happens with three new and natural adjuncts to this intimacy of caring and sharing: Benandré Soap, Benandré Bath Crystals, and Benandré Bath Gelée. To draw a bath that draws you closer together.

Benandré:

**to recapture the sensuous past
in the beautiful present,
turn on the taps,
turn on Benandré,
then just turn on.**

ben rickert, inc.
100 asia place, carlstadt, n.j. 07072

(*Vogue*, July 1976)

POINTS TO CONSIDER

1. How does the large picture in this ad attempt to evoke interest? Does it succeed in catching your interest? Explain. What do you think is happening in the picture?

2. What is the purpose of the small picture of the woman? How does it tie in with the large picture and with the ad copy (the written material)?

3. How does this ad use "The Girl" to sell its product? (See Harvey Cox, "The Playboy and Miss America," page 225.)

4. What qualities do you think that the man who wears clothes by Curlee is supposed to have? How do you know? What do you think is the "certain kind of clothes a woman likes to see a man in"?

Men like to be noticed by women.
 But there's a certain kind of clothes a woman likes to see a man in.
 Clothes that don't get in the way of the man.
 A woman likes that.

Curlee

(*Esquire,* March 1975)

POINTS TO CONSIDER

1. At what audience is each of the three ads aimed? How does each ad appeal to that audience and its particular image? How well do the ads reflect the personalities of the magazines in which they appear?

2. What differences do you find between the language and style of the *Good Housekeeping* ad and that of the *Field and Stream* ad? How do these differences reflect the differing appeals of the ads?

3. To what extent do all three of the ads reflect the values and practices discussed by Harvey Cox in "The Playboy and Miss America" (p. 225)?

If you guys don't buy
these new Drummond sweaters,
we'll go right back
to male models.

D

FROM $17 TO $35, IN LOTS OF COLORS. OF PURE WOOL, SUEDE AND WOOL, OR MOHAIR-AND-WOOL BLEND. AT GOOD STORES, OR WRITE DRUMMOND, EMPIRE STATE BUILDING, NEW YORK, N.Y. 10001.

(*Playboy*)

What sportsmen like about Lochlana® shirts by Hathaway

A Lochlana feels like no other shirt in the world. Warm as wool but a lot lighter. Soft as cashmere but much hardier. You can wear a Lochlana shirt next to your skin and never feel the urge to scratch.

In cooler weather, wear *two*—a buttoned Lochlana over a knitted Lochlana (as shown in our picture). This is called the "layered" look. Plenty warm—but still lightweight.

And for the sportsman who wants more—Hathaway designs Lochlanas so they're good *looking*, too.

Lochlana is woven exclusively for Hathaway in Switzerland of 50% wool "tops" blended with 50% cotton. ("Tops" are the long, smooth strands of wool that you get after you've combed out all the short, scratchy hairs.)

Hathaway shirts are still being hand-tailored. So they cost a little more than most. $21 for these button-down shirts in checks—$18 in solids—$15 for the turtlenecks. For store names, write C. F. **Hathaway®** Hathaway, Dept. F, Waterville, Me. THE ▓▓WARNACO GROUP

(Field and Stream)

Even if he's running for class president there's no need to pay a fancy price for his underwear and shirts...not if they're Fruit of the Loom.

When a man dresses up for something special, he wants to feel special. You can give him that feeling for a lot less than you think. For just 79¢ you can get him long-wearing Fruit of the Loom Sanforized® wash-and-wear cotton shorts. With extra seat room, extra leg room, extra give and take in the waist. Even new Golden Fruit of the Loom underwear is just 99¢. And it's no-iron Dacron* polyester and cotton. Same savings go for Fruit of the Loom permanent press shirts. Trim, tapered, fine quality dress and sport shirts, just $2.99 to $4.99. See, there's no need to pay a fancy price for his underwear and shirts. Not if they're Fruit of the Loom. Why not get him some for school.

The price is so low, the value so high . . . you can't afford not to buy Fruit of the Loom.

Fruit of the Loom, 1290 Avenue of the Americas, N.Y.
Prices subject to change without notice.

Men's Underwear-59¢, 79¢ & 99¢ / Men's Shirts-$2.99, $3.99 & $4.99 / Boys' Underwear-39¢ & 59¢ / Infants' Underwear-39¢ to 89¢

*DuPont's reg. T.M.

(Good Housekeeping)

POINTS TO CONSIDER

1. In what ways does this ad "grab" the reader's attention?

2. Do you find this ad informative? Does it tell you anything you didn't know about malpractice insurance? Do you find the statement well-written and convincing?

3. To whom do you think this ad is primarily directed? Why? How does this ad affect you?

4. What do you think is the purpose of this ad? Is it intended for selling insurance, or does it have some other aim? Have you seen other ads—by oil companies, or by manufacturers of industrial products or by public utilities, for example—that seem to have a similar purpose?

You might die if he doesn't operate.
You might sue if he does.

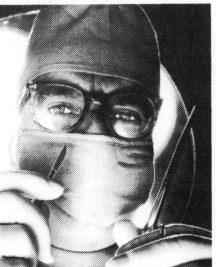

In 1975, there were twice as many medical malpractice suits as there were in 1970.

Why has this happened?

For one thing, the new operations and miracle drugs that save lives also bring new risks. And no matter how careful a doctor or hospital may be, more and more unsatisfied patients are seeking compensation for their misfortunes.

So they sue.

And sympathetic juries are making bigger awards. In the last 10 years, the average award has jumped over 6 times.

In order to deal with these bigger awards, insurance companies must charge doctors and hospitals more for malpractice insurance.

Insurance, after all, is simply a means of spreading risk. Insurance companies collect premiums from many people and compensate the few who have losses.

The price of insurance must reflect the rising cost of compensating those losses and the work that goes into doing that.

And that's why everyone's premiums have been going up.

No one likes higher prices. But we're telling it straight.

(*Time*, March 1, 1976)

■ THE MAESTRO OF MOTIVATIONAL RESEARCH

August Gribbin   *National Observer,* November 13, 1971

You know Ernest Dichter, don't you? The short, rusty-haired psychoanalyst? The one who lives on a mountaintop north of New York City? Well, he knows *you.*

At least he says that he knows which of your emotions to tweak to make you buy a certain carpet, tooth paste, automobile—or almost anything. And to Dichter and the advertising industry, knowing how to make you buy is what makes factories hum and cash registers ring.

Dichter calls himself a "behavioral engineer." He's *the* maestro of mass psychoanalysis, the founder of "motivational research." Manufacturers, businessmen, and advertising people consult him in seeking ways to use psychology to break down buyers' resistance.

Vance Packard made Dichter the foremost antihero of his book on advertising, *The Hidden Persuaders,* and Dichter is a friendly villain to consumer activists and, indirectly, to numerous regretful impulse buyers who don't even know his name.

Dr. Dichter, a native of Vienna, earned his Ph.D. from the University of Vienna in 1934 and later obtained a second degree from the Sorbonne in Paris. He practiced psychoanalysis in Vienna until his name appeared on a Nazi blacklist and he fled to France. There he sold woolen goods and began developing his theories for applying psychological methods to advertising and sales. Finally he emigrated to America, where he quickly got into advertising.

In the United States Dichter struggled at first. He got a major assist in 1946 when Frank Stanton, president of CBS, gave him a one-year consulting contract—his first account. Since than he has earned "a couple of million."

His success had come from his ability to determine scientifically consumers' feelings about various products. Dichter and his associates don't ask the buyer to tell how he feels about products, as most pollsters do. He says that people can't give an unbiased answer. So he finds out surreptitiously.

"YOU ARE A SHAMPOO"

In a 30-room mansion overlooking the river here at Croton-on-Hudson near Ossining, N. Y., the institute has a "behavioral theater." It's equipped with video cameras and a one-way mirror so Dichter and his staff can watch unseen as children react to new toys and adults to new products and packages.

Frequently consumer volunteers come to the theater to act out their feelings about products. But they do not use words. Dichter says they might be told: "You are a cake. Or you are a shampoo." The "actors" endeavor to

portray these obj... ...
drama. In acting the part of a product, the consumer revealed emotions and not some logical, superficial, spoken viewpoint, Dichter contends.

Mostly, though, Dichter relies on "depth interviewing." It works this way: Given a problem about promoting television, say, Dichter and his staff of psychologists and anthropologists will meet and propose numerous "working hypotheses" about the public's attitude toward TV, TV ownership, and anything else that might relate to their client's problem. Then they test these hypotheses by staging conversations with 200 or 300 individuals.

SEEKING OUT HIDDEN BELIEFS

In these interviews they try to elicit information indirectly and by free association of ideas. They may not even mention at first the product that they wish to discuss. Explains Dichter:

"The interviewer might ask: 'What did you do last night?' The person answers: 'Nothing much. Ate supper and watched the stupid TV.'

" 'TV?'

" 'Yeah. I don't really pay much attention to it. It bores me; I fall asleep.' But then the person goes on and recalls a couple of TV shows in detail. This reveals a lot," Dichter adds.

If those attitudes crop up in a significant number of interviews, the researchers might conclude that people love to watch television but feel guilty about it. Thus the promoter must assuage the guilt in his commercials. Often Dichter and his staff can tell the advertiser what appeals will accomplish this.

One section of his newest book deals with the sale of "sinful products." Dichter shows how he might go about it, recommending:

✔ Make people feel that they "deserve" the object. "Make the user believe he has the right to enjoy, that he deserves to pamper himself at times: 'My life is tense,' 'I need a pick-me-up. . . .' Many products that suggest indulgence and luxury can thus become 'needs.' "

✔ Make consumers believe that everybody's doing it. "Sinning in groups is less sinful. . . . Eating candy from a box by yourself is wrong, but pass it around, and everything's fine."

✔ Note that "sin is in style. . . . It is currently fashionable to emphasize one's individuality. This makes it easy to enhance a 'sinful' product with an aura of creative distinctiveness. . . . A person who enjoys rich, fattening foods gets away with it if he eats with the gusto of a gourmet. . . . Give people an excuse for enjoying themselves."

THE BABY-FOOD CAPER

Not so new? Perhaps. But Dichter sells old appeals that he gives new scientific support as well as new twists. And his clients pay well for them. A one-day brainstorming session in which Dichter and his staff "ask irreverent, challenging questions, toss out ideas, and attempt to get the client to look at his product in a new way" costs about $500 to $1,000. A survey involving depth interviewing costs $2,500 to $5,000 or more, depending on the research required.

Dichter explains that clients may feel his services are cheap if he can tell them something useful that they wouldn't otherwise have discovered. Consider his baby-food findings.

Dichter discovered that mothers weren't really attracted by the pretty baby pictured on the baby-food labels; actually, they were jealous because their children didn't resemble the picture. Besides, mothers basically don't seek to grow a picture-healthy baby; they want to get through with the job of feeding the kid as quickly as possible, Dichter says. He and his staff advised the manufacturers to change tactics. The client did so, and his baby-food sales went up.

Not all Dichter's undertakings succeed. American Motors utilized the institute when pitting its Ramblers against the competition's fancier, tail-finned cars in the '50s. The Ramblers didn't sell dramatically.

Hubert Humphrey turned to Dichter in the stretch of the 1968 run for the Presidency. Humphrey lost.

What's more, Dichter and his institute aren't universally admired. Many in industry and business have no faith in psychology or for research based on it. Many in advertising take the approach of Joseph Callo, president of Callo and Carroll, a small but respected New York agency. Callo insists:

"I don't think you can establish creative approaches with any kind of research. You generate evidence and new vistas that might help, but little more. As for manipulation of consumers—that's a bunch of garbage."

CONSUMERS AND DEVILS

On the other hand, a psychologist at the Menninger Clinic in Topeka, Kan., says of Dichter's work: "Sure his techniques work: That's the trouble. I don't believe manipulating people to buy things they can't afford and don't need is best for mankind. It borders on the unethical."

Consumers Union of the U. S., Inc., the product-testing foundation, and Ralph Nader's consumer groups also oppose the work of Dichter and all who utilize the research techniques he pioneered.

Dichter and his institute are thriving nonetheless. So far the institute has run 4,500 studies for hundreds of U. S. companies ranging from General Motors on down. The end isn't in sight. And Dichter, in his own defense, says that he too is against dishonest advertising, but that the consumer who gives in to advertising and buys what he can't afford isn't blameless.

"The truth is that the consumer isn't dumb," says Dichter. "He wants what we're selling. However, when he buys he's just like Flip Wilson. You know Flip's excuse: 'The devil made me do it.' "

1.   What is meant by "depth interviewing"? How does it find the "hidden beliefs" of the consumer? What other techniques do Dichter and his associates use to discover what consumers feel about the things they buy?

2.   What are "sinful products"? Can you think of any examples? What advice does Dichter give for selling these products? Does it seem to you that the approaches he suggests would be effective? Explain.

3.   Who, according to Dichter, is ultimately responsible when consumers buy what they can't afford or don't really need? Do you agree? Explain. Have you as a consumer ever felt the "need" to buy something you didn't need? Do you know why you felt this need?

■ LOVE ACCORDING TO MADISON AVENUE

Morton M. Hunt   *Horizon,* November 1959

In studying the love life of the ancient Romans, I have been struck by the fact that some of the sharpest and most illuminating evidence comes not from weighty works of history but from wayward and trivial sources. A lustful *graffito*[1] scratched on a marble column, palpitating for the scarred arms of a gladiator; indecorous decorations on the bedroom walls of a seaside villa; a versified book of cosmetic recipes; a sentimental funeral oration carved on a huge tombstone—these are the real voices of the past.

It occurs to me, therefore, that in our own time the sociologists with their ponderous surveys, the psychologists with their dissecting analyses, and the cultural historians with their masses of documentation may be missing the truth and the essence of modern love. Perhaps those who write the contemporary equivalent of *graffiti* come closer. I suggest that the persons who do so are those who scribble on Madison Avenue—not on the building fronts, to be sure, but on typewriter paper, in air-conditioned cubicles in the well-carpeted offices of B. B. D. & O., K. & E., Y. & R., E. W. R. & R., and so on.[2]

Certainly they see a number of truths about American love that have never been reported in the scientific literature. For one thing, the ad men apparently perceive more clearly than anyone else just how deeply love has penetrated and colored the ordinary routine of American life until a number of formerly nonerotic objects have become associated with the most tender scenes and the most romantic moments. Eating utensils, for example, are not thought by most cultural historians to have any love-value, and even the

---

[1] Graffito is a statement written or scratched on the wall of a public place.

[2] These are the initials of some well-known national advertising agencies.

Freudians see symbolism only in the knife. But the ad men for Oneida silverware are more acute reporters of the local scene. In a recent ad in *Mademoiselle* they recorded the spontaneous love-dialogue of two young people examining a teaspoon at a store counter:

She: It's a dream come true, Bob. . . . I thought we'd *never* find it. Now we could almost choose blindfolded—just by following out hearts.

He: Looks as if *both* our hearts are set on "Lasting Spring"—it's a "forever thing," like our marriage!

Paolo and Francesca were moved by a poem, Tristan and Iseult by a potion, but with young lovers in America it is the sight of a four-piece place setting at $18 (plus Federal tax) that unlocks the gates of the heart.[3]

Similarly, it is the writers of fashion copy who see through the shadows and mists of native puritanism and recognize that the shoe, which traditionally has played no recognized part in American lovemaking, has recently acquired an aura of erotic value such as it has not had since Solomon, or whoever wrote the *Song of Solomon,* sang the finest bit of advertising copy yet: "How beautiful are thy feet with shoes, O prince's daughter!" In a comparably rapturous vein, the Wohl Shoe Company of St. Louis offered young women, via the February 15, 1959, issue of *Vogue,* a pump described as a "dream of a shoe," and spelled out the dream visually: a lovely young miss leaned upon the manly chest of a masked *caballero.* No prosaic considerations of arch support or hygienic insole for her; the shoe is no longer a piece of utilitarian clothing, but a *laissez-passer*[4] to the wondrous fantasy world of romance. Underwear, too, according to the testimony of the Madison Avenue confraternity,[5] has an equally transporting effect. A case in point is a message some of them produced for Seamprufe, Inc. in a recent issue of *Seventeen.* In this instance, the journey took place in time as well as in space: the ad showed a medieval knight in chain mail, mounted upon a white charger, in the act of sweeping up with one arm a damsel improbably clad only in a lace-trimmed slip of nylon tricot. If, indeed, lingerie produces such reveries in American women, one can only be struck with admiration at the strength of character they show in getting past the state of deshabille and actually arriving at their jobs or starting their housework.

Like shoes and slips, it would seem that many liquids which formerly were thirst quenchers have also picked up amorous overtones in recent years. Coca-Cola was for decades a drink that made merely for a refreshing pause; nowadays, we learn, it is also an accoutrement[6] of teen-age love trysts. In the April issue of *Seventeen,* for example, a Coke ad shows lad

---

[3] Paolo and Francesca: young lovers in Dante's *Divine Comedy* who were aroused by a poem and later punished in hell for their lust. Tristan and Iseult: in a medieval legend Tristan was delivering Iseult to be the bride of a man she didn't want to marry. In despair, she attempted to poison both Tristan and herself, but her servant substituted a love potion for the poison and Tristan and Iseult fell in love with each other.

[4] *Laissez-passer* is a permit to enter.

[5] A confraternity is a group of men united in a single profession, in this case advertising.

[6] An accoutrement is an accessory; a tryst is a meeting in some secretive or private place.

once to fall tenderly upon each other's bosom, preparatory to nuzzling.

Even more noteworthy is the instance of beer. This drink was once the hearty, indelicate, eructative refreshment of the hard-working plebeian male.[7] It has apparently undergone a marvelous metamorphosis in recent years, becoming not only suitable for delicate lips, but acquiring an aura of enchantment and romance. A series of Schlitz advertisements in several major magazines has shown young couples parked by a lakeside at twilight, alone on a snow-capped mountaintop, and so on. Young, attractive, and clearly drawn to each other, they are always drinking beer out of one glass; these lovers, and their circumstances, exemplify the hedonistic[8] exhortation under the picture: "Know the real joy of good living." This, to be sure, could refer either to the romance or the beer; the ad is not explicit. Nor can one be sure whether romance inspired a desire for beer or beer a desire for romance. One thing *is* indisputable: the distinctive odor of hops, now found upon the attractive female, must have been reclassified in the national aesthetic system, becoming a scent rather than a smell.

Other procedures, once gustatory, have likewise become amatory, or so it would seem.[9] The smoking of tobacco, long thought appropriate to manly work or solitary reflection, has become almost obligatory at times of flirtation or intimacy. From the ubiquitous scenes of nubile young people igniting their little white tubes, one gains the impression that drawing in a lungful of soot and carcinogens has an amorous value as great as once did the reading aloud of Byron or the strumming of a banjo.[10] Amatory smoking does present one awkward problem, however, since countless ads (not by cigarette makers) report that love is inconceivable unless the mouth and breath are totally unsullied. Once again the problem is solved by reshuffling of the national stimulus-response bonds, until smoke, on the breath, becomes exciting; the old proverb should really be altered to read: "Where there is smoke, there will soon be fire." Let no one find fault with this or make mock of it. Do not lovers in the Trobriand Islands extract and eat lice from one another's hair, becoming mightily inflamed with love by the procedure? If, in the liberal spirit of cultural relativism, one accepts this and refuses to find it revolting, should he not do the same in the case of the reeking Americans?

Still, Americans themselves have not yet altogether succeeded in eroticizing[11] the by-products of smoking, as Madison Avenue itself admits. A remarkably candid ad for Parliament cigarettes recently came right out

---

[7] Eructative means causing belching; a plebeian is a member of the lower class.

[8] Hedonistic means believing that life should be lived for pleasure.

[9] Gustatory means pertaining to eating or drinking; amatory means pertaining to love.

[10] Ubiquitous means being everywhere; nubile means available for marriage; carcinogens are irritants which cause cancer.

[11] To eroticize something is to cause it to be romantically stimulated. Eros was a Greek god of love.

about the risk to amorous aesthetics: man and girl were shown, heads thrillingly close together, match lit for their cigarettes, while the copy, drawing attention to the recessed filter, promised in a throaty aside, "No filter feedback on your lips . . . or hers." Love in America in 1959 is evidently not for the oaf, but for the thoughtful practitioner of methodology. Ovid himself, that dedicated professor of tasteful dalliance, would have recognized in the Parliament copy writer a kindred spirit, a fellow toiler in the vineyards of impeccable passion.

Again and again the ad men indicate how easily Americans are aroused to lust or moved to tenderness by formerly nonerotic consumer products. Consider the vitamins offered in *Cosmopolitan* by the Vitasafe Corporation: their effect is plainly amorous, for the middle-aged couple are snuggling happily while the woman confesses, from an overflowing heart, "He made me feel like a bride again." Consider the electric portable offered by Smith-Corona: a book-laden youth passing a pretty girl looks down at her typewriter with a mooncalf expression, but it is clear that the machine has made him tender towards the girl as well. Consider fudge, of all things: Carnation Evaporated Milk shows a lass plastering it on cupcakes, while a crewcut lad eats one out of her hand, the plain implication being that fudge is an important component of her sex appeal.

The point is not spelled out in so many words, but sometimes obscurity is in itself a species of truth. The Marlboro people have been portraying rugged middle-aged sporting types lighting cigarettes for lovely young things; in small type under each such picture is the cryptic text, "The cigarette designed for men that women like." The Delphic Oracle[12] herself might have written it; parse it and puzzle over it as one will, he cannot be sure whether the "that" liked by the young thing is the cigarette designed for men, or the men themselves. But the truth lies not in deciding which one; the answer is that it means *both* of them, for they are blended in her mind and emotions. *That* is the truth the copy writer was conveying—in the prevailing romantic American landscape, the erotic object and the erotic person have become indistinguishable.

Precisely the same conclusion may be drawn from Pan American World Airways' appeal to businesswomen in *Mademoiselle.* "Look what Jet Clippers can do for your dreams," it reads, and illustrates what it means: the young businesswoman is seated on a hillside with a morsel of Roman ruin behind her and a dark-haired handsome man beside her. What is the dream referred to—the man or the *mise-en-scène?* Possibly the text gives a further clue. "The fun of new experiences comes faster on Pan Am wings," it says. No help there; that still fits either one. But does it really matter? Not in the least: the trip abroad, the Roman ruin, the handsome man are all inseparable and indivisible. Love and the product are two aspects of a single essence; that is all they know on Madison Avenue, and all they need to know.

Within this general picture of American love, as set down by the creative men in the copy and art departments of the major agencies, no detail is more intriguing than the observation that contemporary Americans, though

---

[12] The Delphic Oracle in Greek legend was the priestess of Apollo at Delphi whose prophecies were difficult to interpret and often had more than one meaning.

It is, of course, no secret to anyone that the normal exudates of the human body, the wrinkles that come after youth, and such other common characteristics as dull hair, small breasts, plumpness, and blackheads are totally incompatible with affection and sex, and that no person with any of these defects can possibly find happiness in life. Luckily there is available today a splendid armamentarium[14] of lotions, oils, paddings, pills, cleansers, and paints the use of which obviates the fault and admits the user to the arena of love.

But this is only the surface of truth. A closer inspection of advertising art and copy reveals a far subtler message being set down for all to read who are not willfully blind. If I read it rightly, there would appear to be, in modern love, a mysterious disembodiment of emotion: it is not so much the *beautiful person* who is loved, but the *beautifying instrumentality.* Observe the statement made repeatedly in ads for Coty's "L'Aimant": "Nothing makes a woman more feminine to a man. . . ." What exegesis[15] can there be, except that the femininity is in the bottled liquid, and not, basically, in the woman? And the same brand of metaphysics must lie behind the Lanvin ad which shows a small boy kissing a small girl who, though pleased, admits to herself: "He loves me . . . he loves my Mommy's Arpège!" The artful minx knows the truth; only by virtue of the applied balsam is she a nymphet, and he, willy-nilly, a nympholept.[16]

The female of all ages is continually advised that she need only wipe on this unguent, pat on this fragrance, slip on this magical garment, and lo! he sees with new eyes, thinks with a different brain, loses his own purpose and becomes a willing slave. "If he can't make up his mind . . . wear Wind Song," whispers Prince Matchabelli. Lanvin slyly peddles the same kind of bottled powers, offering them with the tag, "How to make him lose the first round!" And let a woman but slip into a marvelous checked suit made by Junior Sophisticates, and, she is advised, "What can he do but surrender. . . ."

All this has a disturbingly supernatural sound, yet a hauntingly familiar one. What *is* it all an echo of? What old, well-known, half-forgotten nightmare? So musing, one may recall that there *were* women once who cloaked themselves in borrowed beauty to steal the love of man—sinful women who compacted with Satan to receive unlawful powers, and in return did his vile work for him. Suddenly, certain words and phrases in advertising copy, seemingly harmless, begin to assume an ominous sound. Danskin, Inc., who make a lounging outfit modeled after ballet costumes, use the telltale phrase, "for your 'at home' *bewitching* hours" (my italics). For being be-

---

[13] Occultism is belief in mysterious or supernatural powers. Philters, amulets, and so forth are objects and drugs with magic powers.

[14] An armamentarium is a collection or an array.

[15] An exegesis is an interpretation or explanation, originally of a Biblical passage.

[16] A minx is an impudent girl; a nymphet is an unusually sexy young girl; and "he, willy-nilly, a nympholept" means he is bewitched by the nymphet whether or not he wants to be.

witching, 30,000 women were burned alive during the fifteenth and six-teenth centuries; let the word not go by unnoticed. And Dawnelle, Inc. frankly (or is it carelessly?) harks back to woman's ancient primal alliance with the Prince of Darkness in both copy and illustration. Says the copy: "You're the temptress who wins him, in Dawnelle's handsewn gloves"; the illustration, meanwhile, shows not one, but four gloved female hands offer-ing a fatuously grinning male four ripe apples. (Has Eve grown more arms, or is the Serpent in an arms race too?)

And now the most damning fact begins to appear more clearly. In dis-tinct defiance of the overtly approved mores, the entrapment or illusion created almost always operates within a context of illicit connection. The ads for a hundred products hint at it, but those of the perfume makers are practically outspoken. The names of perfumes are in themselves an insidi-ous and deadly attack upon Judeo-Christian morality—e.g., "Tabu," "In-discrète," "Conquête," "Temptation," "Surrender," and "My Sin"—while copy strengthens the assault in words such as these:

> "danger in every drop"
> "the 'forbidden' fragrance"
> "provocative as a stranger's smile"
> "dare to wear it only when you seek to conquer"
> "a whispered invitation for a man to be masterful."

One could extract from all this a sinister truth, namely that woman descended of Eve is still borrowing powers and enchantments in order to arouse man's lusts and thereby satisfy her own, and in the process is per-forming Satan's work of dragging man into mortal sin. Six centuries ago the best-educated men in Europe considered the situation a clear and present danger and spoke of it in terms like these:

> In the woman wantonly adorned to capture souls, the garland upon her head is as a firebrand of Hell to kindle men, so too the horned head-dress of another, so the brooch upon the breast [of a third]. . . . Each is a spark, breathing hellfire [and] damning the souls God has created and redeemed at such great cost.

Thus spoke John Bromyard, a typical fourteenth-century English preacher and compiler of sermons, and thus had spoken in earlier times Tertullian, Jerome, and Chrysostom. Today none but advertising men link the same factors in a single picture of woman; but whether the ad men are the Brom-yards and Tertullians of our era or whether they are agents of the Foul Fiend is not altogether clear.

The seductive female is not the only pattern of womanhood about which Madison Avenue furnishes an abundance of information. The other and sharply contrasting pattern is that of the fiancée-wife-mother. The an-cient dichotomy[17] of Woman into Eve and Mary, mistress and mother, witch

---

[17] A dichotomy is a division into two parts.

whenever her smile is secretive and mysterious, she represents the ancient spirit of Profane Love and her mystery is, ultimately, nothing but concupiscence.[18] But when woman is portrayed in the role of fiancée, bride, or wife, she possesses none of these qualities; instead she is feminine in a pure and wholesome sense. The American Gem Society, addressing an ad to the girl about to become engaged, portrays her as a dreaming young thing, chin cupped in hands, wide eyes staring off into the roseate future, guileless face almost completely innocent of make-up, mouth smiling trustfully and a little wistfully. She is Everyman's kid sister or girl friend, but never his passionflower. The Kinsey crowd may publish their revolting statistics on the premarital sexual experiences of American girls, but the advertisements tell a different and lovelier version of the truth: the girl who gets a diamond engagement ring has not been besmirched by sexual experiments or known the indecent hunger of desire.

Even in the embrace of her fiance she preserves a high-minded concentration upon nonsexual matters. A dinnerware ad in *Seventeen* shows a young couple who have ridden in a sleigh out to a secluded field through which runs a purling stream. The lad romantically picks up the girl in his arms and carries her across the virgin snow, while she tenderly and practically murmurs to him, "You get the license . . . I'll get the Lenox." His intentions may have been licentious rather than licensable, but this comment at once purifies and clarifies his mind.

Nuptials and honeymoon make no perceptible change in this side of her character; the bride's mood may be yielding, but her blood runs cool. "Isn't this how you want to live?" asks the Fostoria Glass Company, portraying an ideal young marriage: a young wife, holding a piece of crystal stemware near a single burning taper, seems lost in admiration of the glass and the candle, and only vaguely aware of the handsome husband hovering beside her. She is smiling at him, more or less, with her neat, childish little mouth firmly closed—and a generation trained by Marilyn Monroe does not miss the significance of *that*. Not long ago a Heublein Cocktails ad in *Life* featured what seems merely an amusing line—"A wife's warmest welcome is well chilled"; like so many other jokes, perhaps it says more than it intends to.

After a suitable time, the wife becomes a mother, but despite this presumptive evidence of sexual activity, she remains thoroughly pure. In a Vigoro ad we see her romping on the lawn with her husband and children; she is tanned, healthy, and essentially *friendly*. In a Johnson outboard motor ad we see her roaring along with her husband and children in a speedboat; she is sunburned, tousled, and essentially a *good sport*. In a G-E ad we see her clapping her hands gleefully as her husband and daughter present her with a dishwasher; she is slim, pretty (in a low-heeled way), and essentially *homey*.

We see her in many other situations—cooking, washing, shopping,

---

[18] Concupiscence is lust or sexuality.

playing games—and she is almost invariably clean-looking, hearty, efficient, and brightly lit. Dan River Mills recently devoted a spread in *Life* to the modern American family and showed four typical examples. Every one of the four consisted of a handsome young man, a pretty young woman, and two children (between the ages of four and eight), all dressed in cottons by Dan River. In not one picture is the man touching, holding, or even looking at his wife; in three out of four, he is not even standing beside her, but is separated from her by one of the children. The American wife, it seems reasonable to conclude, is a pal, a helpmeet, a kind of older girl friend; she is emphatically not a lover.

The children have a double function in preserving the mother image: they prove her fecundity, but by their very presence they neutralize or purify the erotic overtones of certain situations. Do she and her husband don Weldon pajamas?—in come the kids, in similar pajamas, making everything sanitary and aboveboard. Does she go off for a ride with her man in a Chrysler product?—she tucks a little girl into her lap, and all is sweet, all is sound. Do she and he park their Chevrolet in a secluded woodland spot?— happily, they brought the dog along, and it is upon the beast that affection is bestowed. Have she and her husband grown cheerfully middle-aged and regained their privacy as the children left home?—the General Motors time-payment plan shows them hugging *two* dogs, one for each. No wonder the dog is called man's best friend—he defends, by his very presence, the purity of the American wife and mother.

Certain other aspects of American love, though not so fully portrayed, are illuminatingly touched upon in magazine advertisements. For it is apparent, from any careful scrutiny of the ads, that Americans require the stimulus of exotic, remote, or uncomfortable surroundings, in order to experience the real transports of delight. Here is an advertisement showing a couple on a wild, chilly-looking beach at sundown (how *did* they get the automobile down there without making tracks in the sand?); here is another couple deep in the forest primeval, smoking cigarettes and hugging each other; here is a third exploring a wild stream bank in their good clothing, undaunted by steep declivity[19] or tangled underbrush. Oasis Cigarettes render continual reports of lovers cozily nestled on a desert cactus, moodily bussing each other in some dim alley of the Vieux Carré of New Orleans, or perching together in a high window overlooking Monte Carlo. They never wax romantic in Middletown, U. S. A.; they never grow fond in a middle-class living room. Wind-swept Alpine crags, the slippery decks of heeled-over yawls, castles without plumbing, streams in the heart of a jungle— these would seem to be the typical loci of love,[20] rather than the sofa, bed, or park bench. How all this may be possible—since most people are forced to spend their lives at or near home—is a nagging question; perhaps the meaning of it all is that love, in the twentieth century, is an actuality for the wealthy, but still only a dream for the poor and the middle class.

Likewise tantalizing are the occasional hints of restiveness and impending revolt on the part of modern man. Ensnared and bewitched by the

[19] A declivity is a hillside or slope.
[20] Loci are places or locations.

luscious female supine at their feet. Can it be mere coincidence that the Cigar Institute of America shows a manly stogy-fancier hefting a caveman's club, while a maiden clad in a leopardskin crouches adoringly at heel? No, it is not coincidence, for here again is Chief Apparel, in *Playboy,* showing us a Bikini-clad morsel sprawled pantingly on the floor before a gentleman clad in dashing sports attire. But perhaps the significant clue is that in all three advertisements the gentlemen are ignoring the females. Woman is a toy (the ad men seem to be saying)—a plaything to be enjoyed when man chooses, and to be scorned when he does not.

Finally, and most challenging of all, is the handful of frivolous and irreverent remarks in recent advertisements that may conceivably portend a general devaluation of love in the near future. Hanes Hosiery in *The New Yorker* shows us a cartoon of a depressed chap clutching a bottle of poison and thinking, "I'd better drink it. All she wants from me is seamless stockings by Hanes." One does not get flippant about God or the Flag; perhaps Love, long the peer of both of these, is losing its position. A Lea & Perrins ad shows a man and woman curled up warmly together, just after dinner; it is the best of all possible times for serious talk, but listen to what she says: "Do you love Lea & Perrins more than me?" Is nothing sacred to woman any longer, that she dares to jest at a time like this?

Whatever may be the ultimate meaning of all these things, one must congratulate the cultural historians of the future; a treasure of evidence is awaiting them, if they will but look away from the scientific studies and scholarly theses and pay attention to the scribblings on Madison Avenue.

POINTS TO CONSIDER

1.   Why do you think the writer uses so many uncommon words like ubiquitous, carcinogens, and concupiscence? What does it reveal about his attitude toward the subject?

2.   Do you agree with Hunt that our ad writers tell us more about our culture than our historians do?

3.   What does Hunt mean when he says about advertising that "the erotic object and the erotic person have become indistinguishable"? What examples can you think of to illustrate this?

4.   What kinds of products are sold as "love-charms"? What is the point of portraying some products as sinister enchantments?

5.   What artificial distinctions do ads make between women as lovers and women as wives and mothers? What kinds of ads illustrate this?

6.   What other unreal or fantasy portrayals of love appear commonly in American advertising? How do you think these approaches help to sell products? How do these approaches affect you?

Drawing by Richter; © 1974 The New Yorker Magazine, Inc.

■ HOUSEWIFE IMAGE TARNISHED ON TV

Patricia O'Brien   *Chicago Sun-Times*

In the never-never land of television advertising, the American housewife's intelligence ranks somewhere between that of a moron and an imbecile. Somehow she never does anything right around the house until she gets help.

It takes Josephine the plumber scolding her for a dirty sink to get her to clean up properly, Mrs. Olsen chiding her for her lousy coffee to get her to improve her cooking. In general, she is treated like a child who doesn't know how to wash her hands.

Despite this TV-nourished image, the American housewife is not a dunce in an apron munching chocolates. She is, as economist John Kenneth Galbraith has pointed out, a vital manager of our economy. Her family is a voracious consumer of products and, with the disappearance of old-time menial servants, it is her job to manage all this consumption. She cleans, shops and organizes. Without her acceptance of this role, says Galbraith, the economy could collapse.

So it is small wonder that the pressures on housewives to conform are fierce. Most television commercials are geared to these women as principal consumers—but not to the positive aspects of their role. The commercials stress instead a host of negative images, particularly feelings of fear, guilt and uncertainty. And inane though they may appear, these commercials are one of the stronger social forces keeping women in line.

poor gardener. All this adds up to a potent message. And although we may scoff at such unrealities, the effect is insidious.

Consider the various themes. One is a play on the hunger for approval and the corresponding fear of disapproval. Guests and mothers-in-law shake their heads and frown over sheets that don't sparkle and plates that don't shine.

Another theme is envy: ("How does she get her furniture so gleaming when mine is so dull?") Another is the fear of losing husbandly love. ("Ring around the collar!" shouts the hula dancer in a detergent commercial. The husband glares, and his wife shrivels. She has failed her duties and must quickly discover the right detergent, or her marriage will be over.)

All of these themes have one purpose: to push the striving housewife to get everything cleaner and shinier than ever before. Maybe the washbowl looked okay with product "A" last week. But now product "B" says it has more bleach, and that means dumping "A" and buying "B". Never, never forget: Mrs. Smith next door may humiliate you at the next coffee klatsch because she switched to "B" before you.

That's the message delivered daily by the white knight and Josephine the plumber. I just wish Prof. Galbraith could get equal time.

POINTS TO CONSIDER

1. According to the author, what negative aspects of the housewife's role are particularly stressed by TV advertising?

2. What does the author mean when she says that ads and the world they create are "one of the stronger social forces keeping women in line"? Do you agree? Explain.

3. What is Professor Galbraith's image of the American housewife? Is it more or less realistic than the housewife of TV land? Explain.

4. Why do you think Professor Galbraith's housewife is not granted "equal time" on TV? Can you think of some ways TV advertising could use the positive aspects of the housewife's role to sell its products?

■ BUGS BUNNY SAYS THEY'RE YUMMY

Dawn Ann Kurth   *New York Times*, July 2, 1972

Do TV commercials take unfair—and even dangerous—advantage of children? Dawn Ann Kurth, 11, of Melbourne, Fla., thinks they do. Miss Kurth was a surprise witness at a recent Senate subcommittee hearing in Washington on the effects of TV advertising. Here is her statement to the committee.

MR. CHAIRMAN:

My name is Dawn Ann Kurth. I am 11 years old and in the fifth grade at Meadowlane Elementary School in Melbourne, Florida. This year I was one of the 36 students chosen by the teachers out of 20,000 5th-through-8th graders, to do a project in the Talented Student Program in Brevard County. We were allowed to choose a project in any field we wanted. It was difficult to decide. There seem to be so many problems in the world today. What could I do?

A small family crisis solved my problem. My sister Martha, who is 7, had asked my mother to buy a box of Post Raisin Bran so that she could get the free record that was on the back of the box. It had been advertised several times on Saturday morning cartoon shows. My mother bought the cereal, and we all (there are four children in our family) helped Martha eat it so she could get the record. It was after the cereal was eaten and she had the record that the crisis occurred. There was no way the record would work.

Martha was very upset and began crying and I was angry too. It just didn't seem right to me that something could be shown on TV that worked fine and people were listening and dancing to the record and when you bought the cereal, instead of laughing and dancing, we were crying and angry. Then I realized that perhaps here was a problem I could do something about or, if I couldn't change things, at least I could make others aware of deceptive advertising practices to children.

To begin my project I decided to keep a record of the number of commercials shown on typical Saturday morning TV shows. There were 25 commercial messages during one hour, from 8 to 9 A.M., not counting ads for shows coming up or public service ads. I found there were only 10 to 12 commercials during shows my parents like to watch. For the first time, I really began to think about what the commercials were saying. I had always listened before and many times asked my mother to buy certain products I had seen advertised, but now I was listening and really thinking about what was being said. Millions of kids are being told:

"Make friends with Kool-aid. Kool-aid makes good friends."

"People who love kids have to buy Fritos."

"Hershey chocolate makes milk taste like a chocolate bar." Why should milk taste like a chocolate bar anyway?

"Cheerios make you feel groovy all day long." I eat them sometimes and I don't feel any different.

"Cocoa Krispies taste like a chocolate milk shake only they are crunchy."

"Lucky Charms are magically delicious with sweet surprises inside." Those sweet surprises are marshmallow candy.

I think the commercials I just mentioned are examples of deceptive advertising practices.

Another type of commercial advertises a free bonus gift if you buy a certain product. The whole commercial tells about the bonus gift and says nothing about the product they want you to buy. Many times, as in the case of the record, the bonus gift appears to be worthless junk or isn't in the package. I wrote to the TV networks and found it costs about $4,000 for a 30-second commercial. Many of those ads appeared four times in each hour. I wonder why any company would spend $15,000 or $20,000 an hour to advertise worthless junk.

The ads that I have mentioned I consider deceptive. However, I've found others I feel are dangerous.

Bugs Bunny vitamin ads say their vitamins "taste yummy" and taste good.

Chocolate Zestabs says their product is "delicious" and compare taking it with eating a chocolate cookie.

If my mother were to buy those vitamins, and my little sister got to the bottles, I'm sure she would eat them just as if they were candy.

I do not know a lot about nutrition, but I do know that my mother tries to keep our family from eating so many sweets. She says they are bad for our teeth. Our dentist says so too. If they are bad, why are companies allowed to make children want them by advertising on TV? Almost all of the ads I have seen during children's programs are for candy, or sugar-coated cereal, or even sugar-coated cereal with candy in it.

I know people who make these commercials are not bad. I know the commercials pay for TV shows and I like to watch TV. I just think that it would be as easy to produce a good commercial as a bad one. If there is nothing good that can be said about a product that is the truth, perhaps the product should not be sold to kids on TV in the first place.

I do not know all the ways to write a good commercial, but I think commercials would be good if they taught kids something that was true. They could teach about good health, and also about where food is grown. If my 3-year-old sister can learn to sing, "It takes two hands to handle a whopper 'cause the burgers are better at Burger King," from a commercial, couldn't a commercial also teach her to recognize the letters of the alphabet, numbers, and colors? I am sure that people who write commercials are much smarter than I and they should be able to think of many ways to write a commercial that tells the truth about a product without telling kids they should eat it because it is sweeter or "shaped like fun" (what shape *is* fun, anyway?) or because Tony Tiger says so.

I also think kids should not be bribed to buy a product by commercials telling of the wonderful free bonus gift inside.

I think kids should not be told to eat a certain product because a well-known hero does. If this is a reason to eat something, then, when a well-known person uses drugs, should kids try drugs for the same reason?

Last of all, I think vitamin companies should never, never be allowed to advertise their product as being delicious, yummy, or in any way make children think they are candy. Perhaps these commercials could teach children the dangers of taking drugs or teach children that, if they do find a bottle of pills, or if the medicine closet is open, they should run and tell a grown-up, and never, never eat the medicine.

I want to thank the Committee for letting me appear. When I leave Washington, the thing that I will remember for the rest of my life is that some people *do* care what kids think. I know I could have led a protest about commercials through our shopping center and people would have laughed at me or thought I needed a good spanking or wondered what kind of parents I had that would let me run around in the streets protesting. I decided to gather my information and write letters to anyone I thought would listen. Many of them didn't listen, but some did. That is why I am here today. Because some people cared about what I thought. I hope now that I can tell every kid in America that when they see a wrong, they shouldn't just try to forget about it and hope it will go away. They should begin to do what they can to change it.

People will listen. I know, because you're here listening to me.

■ POINTS TO CONSIDER

1. What differences did Dawn Ann Kurth find between the number of commercials shown in one hour on Saturday morning and the number shown in an hour of prime "adult" time? What reasons might there be for this disparity?

2. What kinds of commercials did the author find "deceptive"? Can you discover any of the "tricks" described in "The Advertiser's Bag of Tricks" (pages 18 to 26)?

3. What commercials does Miss Kurth consider "dangerous"? Why? Do you agree? Explain.

4. What is the author's idea of a "good" commercial? Do you think that such a commercial would be feasible for a product like Lucky Charms or Kool-aid or toy racing cars? Explain.

5. Do you agree with Miss Kurth's closing statement that "People will listen"? Why, or why not?

COMMERCIAL
Robert F. Nelson, Vice President, Foote, Cone & Belding, Chicago

A television commercial is rarely the result of somebody simply coming up with an idea. The process really begins with a product or service; something to be sold in the marketplace. And only after a careful analysis of facts and objectives about what the commercial is supposed to accomplish, does the imagination of an artist or copywriter take over to shape an idea on film.

PRODUCT AND BACKGROUND

Dial Soap is a good example. It was introduced over twenty-two years ago as the first truly effective deodorant soap. Since then Dial has become the sales leader among all soaps and now ranks as number one in both dollar sales and total ounces sold.

Television has always been a major part of the Dial sales effort. The objective was, and still is, to convince viewers that Dial gets rid of the bacteria on your skin that cause perspiration odor. As a result, you stay fresh and socially secure all day long. Thus the line: "Aren't you glad you use Dial? Don't you wish everybody did?"

Over the years Dial has used various commercial patterns and formats on television to get this story across. But certain key elements were usually retained from one commercial to the next. They were (1) pictures of attractive people involved in social situations or activities that call for deodorant protection; (2) scenes of the main character in the commercial taking a shower; and (3) an announcer voice track to explain why and how the product works. All of this was done in such a way as to reflect a totally positive attitude toward the product while ignoring the existence of other deodorant soaps.

PLANNING AN "INTERRUPTER" COMMERCIAL

In spite of this apparently successful formula, however, a meeting was held between the client, Armour-Dial, and the agency, Foote, Cone & Belding, to discuss a possible change of pace in the regular campaign.

In attendance was the Dial brand manager and his assistant, the management supervisor from the agency and the account executive. Together they reasoned that when a product is in such a strong position of leadership as Dial, perhaps there was an opportunity to build greater awareness for it among television viewers by developing an "interrupter" commercial. In other words, while the current campaign was doing a good job of selling and keeping the present users of Dial, maybe a new approach might attract still more customers.

Once an agreement was reached with the client, the account executive from the agency called a meeting of the creative director in charge of Dial, along with his copywriter and art director. There the reasons for the decision to make an "interrupter" commercial were discussed in detail. They set a date for presenting the commercial idea to the client, and a confirming memo was sent to all concerned.

A second meeting was then held by the creative director with all the creative people involved on the Dial account. Writers, artists, and producers were given the complete background on the assignment. Each person listened and was invited to ask questions. They were told the objective was still to sell deodorant protection. But in no way was the approach to resemble anything Dial had done in the past, except in the matter of good taste. Nothing was to be considered that might offend viewers.

At this point the artists and writers began working individually and in pairs. Producers were invited to contribute their thoughts. Before long literally hundreds of ideas had been considered. Included were new film techniques, special sound effects, unusual musical themes, the use of animated characters as opposed to live actors. No area of creative innovation was overlooked.

Finally, after several weeks of intense discussion and exploration, the creative director had narrowed the selection of ideas, still in script form, down to three approaches. All emphasized the promise of deodorant protection from Dial but each pattern was distinctly different.

THE STORYBOARD

The next step was to take each of the ideas and render them in storyboard form. This meant having the art director draw key scenes, much like a comic strip, to indicate how the commercial would be filmed, what action would take place, and what words or sounds would accompany each scene.

Before presenting the finished storyboard to the client, however, a separate meeting was held; first with the creative director and then, later, with the Dial account management people. The purpose was to confirm the creative recommendation and prepare a presentation to the client.

Of the three ideas to be presented, the consensus was that the "Volkswagen" one seemed to offer the best opportunity for a uniquely effective "interrupter" commercial.

The situation called for five grown men riding in a small car during the commuting rush hours. None of the men was to register a negative reaction but each would be quite obviously cramped and uncomfortable. As far as the copy message was concerned, only two lines were to be spoken: "Aren't you glad you use Dial? Don't you wish everybody did?" The success (or failure) of the commercial would depend entirely on the humorous reactions generated by the actors. The creative people felt confident that it could be accomplished with the right talent and the right film director.

DATE: April, 1968
PRODUCER: N.LeeLacy/Associates
FILM NO.: 01-67A62-30
FILM TITLE: Volkswagen-30
FILM LENGTH: 30 Secs.

1. (SOUND EFFECTS: ENGINE IDLE) ...

2. ...

3. ...

4. ...

5. ...

6. ...

7. ...

8. ...

9. (SOUND EFFECTS: CAR)

10. ...

11. ...

12. ...

13. ...

14. (ANNCR VO): Aren't you glad you use Dial?

15. Don't you wish everybody did?

MAKING THE DIAL "VOLKSWAGEN" COMMERCIAL **73**

CLIENT APPROVAL

Next came a detailed presentation to the client. The commercial idea and its objectives were carefully explained to the Dial brand manager and the Armour-Dial advertising director. They were in general accord with the proposed idea, but they expressed some reservations about whether it would "play" or be understood in 30 as well as 60 seconds. Armour-Dial uses both commercial lengths as part of their overall corporate buy in purchasing network television time. The agency assured them that it would be no problem and approval was given to go ahead with the filming.

This approval gave the agency authorization to secure bids from three different film studios on the cost of producing the commercial. (Bids from studios for doing a commercial may vary anywhere from two to ten thousand dollars.) Of the three studios considered, two in Los Angeles and one in New York, N. Lee Lacy of Los Angeles was chosen to do the job. The choice was based partly on cost and partly on the fact that they had a very fine director who had a reputation for getting the most out of "people" situations.

PRODUCTION PLANNING

After the production bids had been signed by the client a pre-production meeting was scheduled at the agency. This included the agency producer who would be in charge of the commercial, key members of the creative staff, the account executive, and the Dial brand manager.

At this meeting every aspect of the commercial was discussed in minute detail. Any problems that might occur during the shooting had to be anticipated. Questions about characterization, camera angles, and mood had to be answered. Days on location and recording dates had to be assigned. There had to be a time and cost contingency factor in the event of bad weather. Nothing could be left to chance or on-the-spot improvisation once the actual filming began.

To make sure of this, the creative director then had to write a production memo outlining precisely how and when all the elements of the commercial were to be put together.

PRODUCTION BEGINS

With this memo in hand, a copywriter along with a producer from the agency, was assigned to work directly with the studio in Los Angeles to oversee the total production of the commercial. Their combined job was not only to keep the commercial on track but to be responsible for the final choice of actors, the voice-over announcer, and all the minute details involved in the making of the commercial.

commercial. At the same time, since the actors had no script to follow, it was decided to shoot an excessively large amount of film to insure that the proper reactions would be captured. The film could be edited later to get the desired effect.

Probably the greatest single difficulty in the filming was getting the final shot in the commercial which shows the little car standing still in typical rush hour traffic. It had to be staged on the Los Angeles freeway and taken with a long telephoto lens from a nearby overpass.

Another decision had to do with whether or not to use music as a background effect in the commercial. In the end it was felt that natural sounds such as engine noises, birds chirping, and traffic would lend more believability to the commercial. The announcer voice was selected for the same reason.

FINAL STEPS IN THE PROCESS

Producing all the elements of the commercial was one task; putting them together properly became quite another.

The agency's producer and copywriter had to spend long wearisome hours looking over the rough film footage with the studio film editor. They had to choose approximately ninety feet of film out of the more than nine thousand feet that was shot and developed. Deciding on the right sound effects called for listening to hundreds of sound combinations. Even the right delivery of the last two lines of the commercial by the announcer involved much patience and many dozens of takes.

One last but vitally important detail was to film the Dial Soap package so it could be optically matted in over the last scene in the commercial. How soon it should appear in the commercial and how long it should stay on the screen was another decision that had to be made.

SEEING THE RESULTS

The first version of the film was put together at the studio in a rough cut (scenes in the film are spliced together without the final optical effects) and the sound track was played against it. This was sent back to the agency and shown to the creative director and the artists and writers for their comments.

They felt quite strongly that the action was entirely too heavy-handed and not at all in keeping with the Dial image. The way the film had been cut portrayed the men as being unfriendly toward each other and generally disapproving of their situation. The film was sent back to the studio with these comments and once again the agency producer and the writer went

FOOTE, CONE & BELDING

CLIENT: Armour & Co.
PRODUCT: Dial Soap
FILM NO.: 01-67A62-30
FILM TITLE: Volkswagen-30
FILM LENGTH: 30 Secs.

DATE: April, 1968
PRODUCER: N. LeeLacy/Associates

1. (Sound effects: engine idle)...

2. ...

3. ...

4. ...

5. ...

6. ...

7. ...

8. ...

9. ...

10. ...

11. ...

12. ...

13. (Sound effects: car)

14. (Anncr VO) Aren't you glad you use Dial?

15. Don't you wish everybody did?

The second rough cut, along with the sound track, was again sent back to the agency in Chicago. The opinion now was that it did contain the feeling the creative people felt should be in the film when it was originally conceived. Their feeling was shared by the creative director and the producer was told to advance the film to the interlock stage. In this step the film is finished, with camera dissolves and effects, just as it would appear on the screen, but the sound track remains separate.

The next person to see the commercial, in interlock form, was the account executive. He agreed that the commercial was ready to be shown to the client.

FINAL CLIENT APPROVAL

Shortly afterwards the Dial brand manager gave the commercial his approval. This meant the agency could now proceed to the last stage in the production cycle which was to order an answer print, a composite of both the visual and the sound track on a single piece of film. The producer has to check the answer print very carefully for color clarity, film contrast, and sound fidelity before ordering duplicate prints. These duplicate prints are then sent to the various network television stations for showing on the air.

When the films were mailed, the project was complete. The commercial was scheduled to appear in regular rotation on the Armour-Dial network TV spots.

But one little nag persisted in the minds of many people at Armour-Dial and Foote, Cone & Belding. In spite of the many sound marketing reasons for making an "interrupter" type commercial, many still wondered if it would communicate the Dial Soap sales message as effectively as the regular campaign. The new commercial contained no scenes of people using the soap in the shower. There was no copy to explain how the product works or why it is effective. There was not even the usual social scene of active people. In fact, other than the last two lines of the commercial, almost none of the traditional characteristics of former Dial commercials had been retained.

SALES EFFECTIVENESS

One thing, however, was certain. People did seem to like the commercial. It made them laugh. They enjoyed seeing it again and again. But there was as yet no real evidence to prove that the commercial was actually selling the soap.

To answer this critical question Armour-Dial submitted the commercial to a very sophisticated type of research test. The commercial would be measured for awareness or attention-getting value. The test would also give an indication of how strongly the commercial motivated people to buy the product.

When the results were tabulated, the scores showed that "Volkswagen" was probably the most effective selling commercial Dial had ever used on the air. It reached both men and women with a high degree of communication. They were able to play back all of the sales points about the product, even though there were just two lines of copy in the commercial.

This last measure, sales effectiveness, is, of course, the most important accolade a commercial can receive. It is the only reason why companies like Armour-Dial invest hundreds of thousands of dollars in advertising. A special plaudit came to Armour-Dial and Foote, Cone & Belding when the "Volkswagen" commercial won a coveted CLIO award in the American TV Commercial Festival.

■ **POINTS TO CONSIDER**

1. What is the "image" of Dial soap? What for many years had been the key elements of television commercials for Dial? Which were retained and which were changed in making the "Volkswagen" commercial? Why?

2. What were the major steps involved in making the Dial "Volkswagen" commercial? Who were the professional participants involved?

3. What were some of the key decisions which had to be made in the planning and filming of this commercial?

4. What made the Dial "Volkswagen" commercial so effective on TV? Would this commercial encourage you to buy Dial soap? Why, or why not?

5. Have you seen other television commercials that use an approach similar to that of the Dial "Volkswagen" ad? What is your opinion of them?

6. What does this article reveal to you about the making of TV commercials in general? Has this article reinforced or changed any of your ideas or feelings about TV commercials?

Not long ago Lady Hendy, my Socialist elder sister, invited me to agree with her that advertising should be abolished. I found it difficult to deal with this menacing suggestion, because I am neither an economist nor a philosopher. But at least I was able to point out that opinion is divided on the question.

The late Aneurin Bevan thought that advertising was "an evil service." Arnold Toynbee (of Winchester and Balliol[1]) "cannot think of any circumstances in which advertising would not be an evil." Professor Galbraith (Harvard) holds that advertising tempts people to squander money on "unneeded" possessions when they ought to be spending it on public works.

But it would be a mistake to assume that every liberal shares the Bevan-Toynbee-Galbraith view of advertising. President Franklin Roosevelt saw it in a different light:

> *If I were starting life over again, I am inclined to think that I would go into the advertising business in preference to almost any other. . . . The general raising of the standards of modern civilization among all groups of people during the past half century would have been impossible without the spreading of the knowledge of higher standards by means of advertising.*

Sir Winston Churchill agrees with Mr. Roosevelt:

> *Advertising nourishes the consuming power of men. It sets up before a man the goal of a better home, better clothing, better food for himself and his family. It spurs individual exertion and greater production.*

Almost all serious economists, of whatever political color, agree that advertising serves a useful purpose *when it is used to give information about new products.* Thus Anastas L. Mikoyan, the Russian:

> *The task of our Soviet advertising is to give people exact information about the goods that are on sale, to help to create new demands, to cultivate new tastes and requirements, to promote the sale of new kinds of goods and to explain their uses to the consumer. The primary task of Soviet advertising is to give a truthful, exact, apt and striking description of the nature, quality and properties of the goods advertised.*

The Victorian economist Alfred Marshall also approved of "informa-

---

[1] Winchester is a prestigious private school for boys in England. Balliol is a college in Oxford University, also in England.

tive" advertising for new products, but condemned what he called "combative" advertising as a waste. Walter Taplin of the London School of Economics points out that Marshall's analysis of advertising "shows indications of those prejudices and emotional attitudes to advertising from which nobody seems to be completely free, not even classical economists." There was, indeed, a streak of prissiness in Marshall; his most illustrious student, Maynard Keynes, once described him as "an utterly absurd person." What Marshall wrote about advertising has been cribbed by many later economists, and it has become orthodox doctrine to hold that "combative"—or "persuasive"—advertising is economic waste. Is it?

My own clinical experience would suggest that the kind of informative factual advertising which the dons[2] endorse is more effective, *in terms of sales results,* than the "combative" or "persuasive" advertising which they condemn. Commercial self-interest and academic virtue march together.

If all advertisers would give up flatulent puffery,[3] and turn to the kind of factual, informative advertising which I have provided for Rolls-Royce, KLM Royal Dutch Airlines, and Shell, they would not only increase their sales, but they would also place themselves on the side of the angels. The more informative your advertising, the more persuasive it will be.

In a recent poll conducted among thought-leaders, Hill & Knowlton asked, *"Should advertisers give the facts and only the facts?"* The vote in favor of this austere position was strikingly affirmative:

	YES
Religious leaders	76%
Editors of highbrow publications	74
High school administrators	74
Economists	73
Sociologists	62
Government officials	45
Deans of colleges	33
Business leaders	23

Thus we see that factual advertising is very widely regarded as a Good Thing. But when it comes to "persuasive" advertising for one old brand against another, the majority of economists follow Marshall in condemning it. Rexford Tugwell, who earned my undying admiration for inspiring the economic renaissance of Puerto Rico, condemns the "enormous waste involved in the effort to turn trade from one firm to another." The same dogma comes from Stuart Chase:

Advertising makes people stop buying Mogg's soap, and start buying Bogg's soap. . . . Nine-tenths and more of advertising is largely competitive wrangling as to the relative merits of two undistinguished and often undistinguishable compounds. . . .

[2] Professors in English universities.

[3] Flatulent puffery suggests advertising which is puffed up with large quantities of "hot air."

same words, except that they leave Mogg & Bogg to Stuart Crease, substi-
tuting Eureka & Excelsior, Tweedledum & Tweedledee, Bumpo & Bango. Read one of them, and you have read them all.

I will let these dons in on a curious secret. The combative-persuasive kind of advertising which they condemn is not nearly as *profitable* as the informative kind of advertising which they approve.

My experience has been that it is relatively easy for advertising to persuade consumers to try a *new* product. But they grow maddeningly deaf to the advertising of products which have been around for a long time.

Thus we advertising agents get more mileage out of advertising new products than old ones. Once again, academic virtue and commercial self-interest march together.

DOES ADVERTISING RAISE PRICES?

There has been too much sloppy argument on both sides of this intricate question. Few serious studies have been made of the effect of advertising on prices. However, Professor Neil Borden of Harvard has examined hundreds of case histories. With the aid of an advisory committee of five other formidable professors, he reached conclusions which should be more widely studied by other dons before they pop off on the economics of advertising. For example, "In many industries the large scale of operations made possible in part through advertising has resulted in reductions in manufacturing costs." And, "the building of the market by means of advertising and other promotional devices not only makes price reductions attractive or possible for large firms, it also creates an opportunity to develop private brands, which generally are offered at lower prices." They are the natural enemies of us advertising agents. Twenty per cent of total grocery sales are now private brands, owned by retailers and not advertised. Bloody parasites.

Professor Borden and his advisers reached the conclusion that advertising, "though certainly not free from criticism, is an economic asset and not a liability."[4] Thus did they agree with Churchill and Roosevelt. However, they did not support all the shibboleths of Madison Avenue. They found, for example, that advertising does not give consumers sufficient information. My experience at the working level leads me to agree.

It is worth listening to what the men who pay out huge sums of their stockholders' money for advertising say about its effect on prices. Here is Lord Heyworth, the former head of Unilever:

Advertising . . . brings savings in its wake. On the distribution side it speeds up the turnover of stock and thus makes lower retail margins possible, without reducing the shopkeeper's income. On the manufac-

[4] *The Economics of Advertising,* Richard D. Irwin (Chicago, 1942) pages xxv–xxix.

turing side it is one of the factors that make large scale production possible, and who would deny that large scale production leads to lower costs?

Essentially the same thing has recently been said by Howard Morgens, the President of Procter & Gamble:

Time and again in our company, we have seen the start of advertising on a new type of product result in savings that are considerably greater than the entire advertising cost. . . . The use of advertising clearly results in lower prices to the public.

In most industries the cost of advertising represents less than 3 per cent of the price consumers pay at retail. But if advertising were abolished, you would lose on the swings much of what you saved on the roundabouts. For example, you would have to pay a fortune for the Sunday *New York Times* if it carried no advertising. And just think how dull it would be. Jefferson read only one newspaper, "and that more for its advertisements than its news." Most housewives would say the same.

DOES ADVERTISING ENCOURAGE MONOPOLY?

Professor Borden found that "in some industries advertising has contributed to concentration of demand and hence has been a factor in bringing about concentration of supply in the hands of a few dominant firms." But he concluded that advertising is not a *basic cause* of monopoly. Other economists have proclaimed that advertising contributes to monopoly. I agree with them. It is becoming progressively more difficult for small companies to launch new brands. The entrance fee, in terms of advertising, is now so large that only the entrenched giants, with their vast war chests, can afford it. If you don't believe me, try launching a new brand of detergent with a war chest of less than $10,000,000.

Furthermore, the giant advertisers are able to buy space and time far more cheaply than their little competitors, because the media owners cosset them with quantity discounts. These discounts encourage big advertisers to buy up little ones; they can do the same advertising at 25-per-cent less cost, and pocket the savings.

DOES ADVERTISING CORRUPT EDITORS?

Yes it does, but fewer editors than you may suppose. The publisher of a magazine once complained to me, in righteous indignation, that he had given one of my clients five pages of editorial and had received in return

ble.

Harold Ross resented advertising, and once suggested to his partner that all advertisements in *The New Yorker* should be put on one page. His successor exhibits the same sort of town-and-gown snobbery,[5] and loses no opportunity to belittle what he calls "ad-men." Not long ago he published a facetious attack on two of my campaigns, sublimely indifferent to the fact that I have filled 1,173 pages of his magazine with uncommonly ornamental advertisements. It strikes me as bad manners for a magazine to accept one of my advertisements and then attack it editorially—like inviting a man to dinner and then spitting in his eye.

I have often been tempted to punish editors who insult my clients. When one of our advertisements for the British Industries Fair appeared in an issue of the *Chicago Tribune* which printed one of Colonel McCormick's ugly diatribes against Britain, I itched to pull the campaign out of his paper. But to do so would have blown a gaping hole in our coverage of the Middle West, and might well have triggered a brouhaha[6] about advertising pressure on editors.

CAN ADVERTISING FOIST AN INFERIOR PRODUCT ON THE CONSUMER?

Bitter experience has taught me that it cannot. On those rare occasions when I have advertised products which consumer tests found inferior to other products in the same field, the results have been disastrous. If I try hard enough, I can write an advertisement which will persuade consumers to buy an inferior product, *but only once*—and most of my clients depend on repeat purchases for their profit. Phineas T. Barnum was the first to observe that "you may advertise a spurious article and induce many people to buy it once, but they will gradually denounce you as an impostor." Alfred Politz and Howard Morgens believe that advertising can actually accelerate the demise of an inferior product. Says Morgens, "The quickest way to kill a brand that is off in quality is to promote it aggressively. People find out about its poor quality just that much more quickly."

He goes on to point out that advertising has come to play a significant part in product improvement:

Research people, of course are constantly searching for ways to improve the things we buy. But believe me, a great deal of prodding and pushing and suggestions for those improvements also comes from the advertising end of the business. That's bound to be, because the suc-

[5] Town-and-gown snobbery refers to antagonism between businesspeople and intellectuals—in this case "literary" writers and advertising writers.

[6] A brouhaha is an unseemly, often violent controversy.

cess of a company's advertising is closely tied up with the success of its product development activities.

. . . Advertising and scientific research have come to work hand-in-glove on a vast and amazingly productive scale. The direct beneficiary is the consumer, who enjoys an ever-widening selection of better products and services.

On more than one occasion I have been instrumental in persuading clients not to launch a new product until they could develop one which would be demonstrably superior to those already on the market.

Advertising is also a force for sustaining standards of quality and service. Writes Sir Frederic Hooper of Schweppes:

Advertising is a guarantee of quality. A firm which has spent a substantial sum advocating the merits of a product and accustoming the consumer to expect a standard that is both high and uniform, dare not later reduce the quality of its goods. Sometimes the public is gullible, but not to the extent of continuing to buy a patently inferior article.

When we started advertising KLM Royal Dutch Airlines as "punctual" and "reliable," their top management sent out an encyclical, reminding their operations staff to live up to the promise of our advertising.

It may be said that a good advertising agency represents the consumer's interest in the councils of industry.

IS ADVERTISING A PACK OF LIES?

No longer. Fear of becoming embroiled with the Federal Trade Commission, which tries its cases in the newspapers, is now so great that one of our clients recently warned me that if any of our commercials were ever cited by the FTC for dishonesty, he would immediately move his account to another agency. The lawyer at General Foods actually required that our copywriters *prove* that Open-Pit Barbecue Sauce has an "old-fashioned flavor" before he would allow us to make this innocuous claim in advertisements. The consumer is better protected than she knows.

I cannot always keep pace with the changing rules laid down by the various bodies that regulate advertising. The Canadian Government, for example, applies one set of rules to patent medicine advertising, and the United States Government a totally different set. Some American states prohibit the mention of price in whiskey advertisements, while others insist upon it; what is forbidden in one state is obligatory in another. I can only take refuge in the rule which has always governed my own output: never write an advertisement which you wouldn't want your own family to see.

Dorothy Sayers, who wrote advertisements before she wrote whodunits and Anglo-Catholic tracts, says: "Plain lies are dangerous. The only weap-

However, two years later a chemist rescued my conscience by assuring that what I had falsely suggested was actually true.

But I must confess that I am continuously guilty of *suppressio veri.* Surely it is asking too much to expect the advertiser to describe the short-comings of his product? One must be forgiven for putting one's best foot forward.

DOES ADVERTISING MAKE PEOPLE WANT TO BUY PRODUCTS THEY DON'T NEED?

If you don't think people need deodorants, you are at liberty to criticize advertising for having persuaded 87 per cent of American women and 66 per cent of American men to use them. If you don't think people need beer, you are right to criticize advertising for having persuaded 58 per cent of the adult population to drink it. If you disapprove of social mobility,[9] creature comforts, and foreign travel, you are right to blame advertising for encouraging such wickedness. If you dislike affluent society, you are right to blame advertising for inciting the masses to pursue it.

If you are this kind of Puritan, I cannot reason with you. I can only call you a psychic masochist. Like Archbishop Leighton, I pray, "Deliver me, O Lord, from the errors of wise men, yea, and of good men."

Dear old John Burns, the father of the Labor movement in England, used to say that the tragedy of the working class was the poverty of their desires. I make no apology for inciting the working class to desire less Spartan[10] lives.

SHOULD ADVERTISING BE USED IN POLITICS?

I think not. In recent years it has become fashionable for political parties to employ advertising agencies. In 1952 my old friend Rosser Reeves adver-tised General Eisenhower as if he were a tube of toothpaste. He created fifty commercials in which the General was made to read out hand-lettered

---

[7] *Suggestio falsi,* or false suggestion, is a statement which suggests very strongly that something is true without actually saying that it is true. See Marjorie Burns, "The Advertiser's Bag of Tricks" (page 18), for examples of this device.

[8] *Suppressio veri* means suppressing the truth, omitting facts from advertising that would make people less likely to buy the product advertised.

[9] Social mobility means the ability of people to improve their position in life.

[10] Sparta was a city in ancient Greece famous for the strict discipline and rigorous training of its soldiers. Spartan here means a life without physical comforts.

answers to a series of phony questions from imaginary citizens. Like this:

Citizen: Mr. Eisenhower, what about the high cost of living?

General: My wife Mamie worries about the same thing. I tell her it's our job to change that on November 14th.

Between takes the General was heard to say, "To think that an old soldier should come to this."

Whenever my agency is asked to advertise a politician or a political party, we refuse the invitation, on these grounds:

1. The use of advertising to sell statesmen is the ultimate vulgarity.
2. If we were to advertise a Democrat, we would be unfair to the Republicans on our staff; and vice versa.

However, I encourage my colleagues to do their political duty by working for one of the parties—as individuals. If a party or a candidate requires *technical* advertising services, such as the buying of network time to broadcast political rallies, he can employ expert volunteers, banded together in an *ad hoc* consortium.

SHOULD ADVERTISING BE USED IN GOOD CAUSES OF A NONPOLITICAL NATURE?

We advertising agents derive modest satisfaction from the work we do for good causes. Just as surgeons devote much of their time to operating on paupers without remuneration, so we devote much of our time to creating campaigns for charity patients. For example, my agency created the first campaign for Radio Free Europe, and in recent years we have created campaigns for the American Cancer Society, the United States Committee for the United Nations, the Citizens Committee to Keep New York City Clean, and Lincoln Center for the Performing Arts. The professional services we have donated to these causes have cost us about $250,000, which is equivalent to our profit on $12,000,000 of billing.

In 1959 John D. Rockefeller III and Clarence Francis asked me to increase public awareness of Lincoln Center, which was then in the planning stage. A survey revealed that only 25 per cent of the adult population of New York had heard of Lincoln Center. When our campaign was concluded, one year later, 67 per cent had heard of Lincoln Center. When I presented the plans for this campaign, I said:

> The men who conceived Lincoln Center, and particularly the big foundations which have contributed to it, would be dismayed if the people of New York came to think of Lincoln Center as the preserve of the upper crust. . . . It is, therefore, important to create the right image: Lincoln Center is for all the people.

A survey conducted at the conclusion of the campaign showed that this

> *Probably most people living in New York*
> *and its suburbs will visit Lincoln Center at*
> *one time or another*   76%
> *Lincoln Center is only for wealthier people*   4%

Most campaigns for good causes are contributed by one volunteer agency, but in the case of Lincoln Center, BBDO, Young & Rubicam, and Benton & Bowles volunteered to work in harness with us—a remarkable and harmonious quartet. The television commercials were made by BBDO, and New York stations donated $600,000 worth of time to running them. The radio commercials were made by Benton & Bowles, and the radio stations donated $100,000 worth of time to running them. The printed advertisements were made by Young & Rubicam and ourselves; *Reader's Digest, The New Yorker, Newsweek,* and *Cue* ran them free.

When we volunteered to take over the campaign to Keep New York City Clean, the number of streets rated clean had already increased from 56 per cent to 85 per cent. I concluded that those still littering must form a hard core of irresponsible barbarians who could not be reformed by amiable slogans like the previous agency's "Cast Your Ballot Here for a Cleaner New York."

A poll revealed that the majority of New Yorkers were not aware that they could be fined twenty-five dollars for littering. We therefore developed a campaign, warning litterbugs that they would be hauled into court. At the same time we persuaded the New York Sanitation Department to recruit a flying squad of uniformed men to patrol the streets on motor scooters, in search of offenders. The newspapers and magazines donated an unprecedented amount of free space to running our advertisements, and in the first three months the New York television and radio stations gave us 1,105 free commercials. After four months, 39,004 summonses had been handed out, and the magistrates did their duty.

IS ADVERTISING A VULGAR BORE?

C. A. R. Crosland thunders in *The New Statesman* that advertising "is often vulgar, strident and offensive. And it induces a definite cynicism and corruption in both practitioners and audience owing to the constant intermingling of truth and lies."

This, I think, is now the gravamen[11] of the charge against advertising among educated people. Ludwig von Mises describes advertising as "shrill, noisy, coarse, puffing." He blames the public, as not reacting to dignified

---

[11] The gravamen is the part of a charge that weighs most heavily against the accused.

advertising. I am more inclined to blame the advertisers and the agencies—including myself. I must confess that I am a poor judge of what will shock the public. Twice I have produced advertisements which seemed perfectly innocent to me, only to be excoriated for indecency. One was an advertisement for Lady Hathaway shirts, which showed a beautiful woman in velvet trousers, sitting astride a chair and smoking a long cigar. My other transgression was a television commercial in which we rolled Ban deodorant into the armpit of a Greek statue. In both cases the symbolism, which had escaped me, inflamed more prurient souls.

I am less offended by obscenity than by tasteless typography, banal photographs, clumsy copy, and cheap jingles. It is easy to skip these horrors when they appear in magazines and newspapers, but it is impossible to escape them on television. I am angered to the point of violence by the commercial interruption of programs. Are the men who own the television stations so greedy that they cannot resist such intrusive affronts to the dignity of man? They even interrupt the inauguration of Presidents and the coronation of monarchs.

As a practitioner, I know that television is the most potent advertising medium ever devised, and I make most of my living from it. But, as a private person, I would gladly pay for the privilege of watching it without commercial interruptions. Morally, I find myself between the rock and the hard place.

It is television advertising which has made Madison Avenue the archsymbol of tasteless materialism. If governments do not soon set up machinery for the regulation of television, I fear that the majority of thoughtful men will come to agree with Toynbee that "the destiny of our Western civilization turns on the issue of our struggle with all that Madison Avenue stands for." I have a vested interest in the survival of Madison Avenue, and I doubt whether it can survive without drastic reform.

Hill & Knowlton report that the vast majority of thought-leaders now believe that advertising promotes values that are too materialistic. The danger to my bread-and-butter arises out of the fact that what thought-leaders think today, the majority of voters are likely to think tomorrow. No, my darling sister, advertising should not be abolished. But it must be reformed.

■ POINTS TO CONSIDER

1. What two types of advertising does the author describe? Which type is more universally approved of by economists? Why? Which type, according to the author, is more effective? Which is more profitable?

2. What percent of most retail prices is due to the cost of advertising? How, according to the article, does advertising affect consumer prices?

3. What relationship does the author see between advertising and monopoly?

5. Do you agree with the statement that "advertising is a guarantee of quality"? Explain, using examples from your own experience.

6. What are *suggestio falsi* and *suppressio veri*? What apologies does the author offer for each?

7. Why do you think the author considers the selling of statesmen "the ultimate of vulgarity"? (See Joe McGinniss, "Selling the President on TV," page 287.) Do you agree? Explain.

8. With respect to vulgar advertising, what important difference does the author point out between television and the print media?

9. In what areas does the author suggest advertising needs reform? What are some of the reforms that he implies are needed? Can you think of others? Explain.

10. Do you think that advertising should be abolished? Explain.

■ IDEAS FOR INVESTIGATION, DISCUSSION, AND WRITING

1. **a.** Collect half a dozen or so magazine and newspaper ads for the same kind of product or service. What different techniques or appeals are used? Which do you consider effective and which ineffective? Why?
b. Observe several television commercials for the same kind of product or service. What different techniques or appeals are used? How do they compare to or differ from those employed in magazine or newspaper ads? Which do you consider effective and which ineffective?

2. **a.** Examine the advertising in several magazines obviously intended for different types of readers (e.g., *Good Housekeeping, Field and Stream, The New Yorker,* and *Saturday Review*). How do the products and services advertised differ to suit the image of each magazine?
b. Examine the advertising for one kind of product or service in several different types of magazines. How do the ad techniques and appeals differ to suit the image of each magazine?

3. Observe some television commercials broadcast at different times of the day and of the week. How do the subjects and styles of the commercials indicate the different audiences for which they are intended?

4. **a.** Lay out a full-page magazine ad of your own for some original or unusual product or service. Use pictures (you can cut them from magazines or newspapers), headlines, and copy in any proportion you choose. Then write a paragraph explaining the techniques and appeals that you used.
b. Write a twenty-second television commercial for some original or unusual product or service. Indicate what is seen on the screen and what announcements, dialogue, or music is heard. Then write a paragraph explaining the techniques and appeals that you used.

5. Tour a large supermarket, an all-purpose drugstore, or a large variety store. How many different persuasive techniques can you discover that the store is employing? How effective do you feel that each one is?

6. Deal in depth with the question of whether advertising is actually necessary in our society. What evidence is there that advertising is necessary? What arguments can be advanced against advertising? Is it possible that some advertising performs an essential service while other advertising is unnecessary, perhaps even harmful? If so, what criteria can be applied to determine which advertising is useful and which is not?

7. Using the same technique as Morton Hunt uses in his article "Love According to Madison Avenue," derive what seem to be Madison Avenue's images of such things as manliness, sophistication, motherhood, purity, fun. How do ads project these images? How valid are the images?

8. Make a direct survey that attempts to ascertain buying patterns related to a certain product and then compare your results with those of "in-depth" studies published in such motivational research journals as the *Journal of Marketing Research*. A possible point for investigation: Who buys a family's liquor and what determines the brand purchased?

9. Discuss the idea of advertising as an art. Is it possible for an ad to be something more than simply skillful persuasion or clever attention getting?

are there perhaps only parts of the ad, such as its photograph, as its or its use of language that can be enjoyed as art? Find a number of ads which prove your point.

10. Compare television advertising with that of the print media. What difference does the medium make in the kind of images that are presented and how they are presented? The most fruitful approach would probably be to concentrate on ads for one brand of, say, soap or automobile. How do the verbal and visual aspects of the ads vary from one medium to the other? What do these differences suggest about the natures of the media themselves?

11. Look into very specialized advertising such as that found in various trade magazines. (An interesting beginning might be one of the several magazines put out for funeral directors.) What special themes and appeals do these ads use? How are they similar to ads for more common products? How are they different?

12. Investigate the language of ads. What kind of words do ads use, concrete or abstract? Why? Can you find uses of onomatopoeia, simile, metaphor, and other poetic figures? Are the sentences long or short? What kind of paragraph structure is used? (See VW ads.) What effect, if any, do you think ad language could have on the language as a whole?

13. Discuss advertising as a "social force." What evidence is there that advertising significantly affects what we want to look like, what we want to do, and who we want to be? How strong a force does advertising exert on our ideas of what is and what ought to be? Is there any way to measure this?

14. Investigate the structure and function of a typical advertising agency. How are ads developed from ideas to finished products? What people and processes are involved?

Part Two

Journalism: Previews and Viewpoints

Both truth and falsehood are irrelevant to the techniques of persuasion.
—Martin Quigley

The citizen cannot be adequately informed unless his education and, later, his journalism give him some access to that essential part of a public question that lies outside his own immediate sphere of interest and competence.

—Max Ways

The continued absence of . . . coverage of not only the black world but of other minorities as well, the American Indian, for example, is evidence of the lack of perspective of American white-owned journalistic publications. . . .

—Roland E. Wolseley

No matter how powerful the image of war [our] photographers have captured, our fascination tends to outweigh our horror. Photography provides insulation along with access. Pictures don't carry the odor.

—John G. Morris

. . . As a nation (and also as states, as townships, as individuals), we keep getting ourselves into such serious messes—messes that result in good part, anyway, from our having been told the wrong thing or from having an evidently complex situation communicated to us in a simplistic way. . . .

—Michael Arlen

Journalism

What is news? It is the honest and unbiased and complete account of events of interest and concern to the public.

A typical metropolitan daily may receive approximately 8 million words of copy each day from its staff, wire services, feature syndicates, correspondents and special writers. Of this, only about 100,000 can be used in the paper.

Local stories are gathered by staff reporters and correspondents. Each reporter is responsible for certain types of news and some have what are called "beats." One may cover the city offices, another the police court and state police, someone else the society news. Correspondents from neighborhood areas and surrounding towns write or telephone news from their localities.

A reporter on his beat will make notes of various stories he encounters, then return to the office and write them. On a larger paper, or during an emergency when time is precious, he may phone them in to the "desk" where a rewrite man will take them.

Other people also telephone in stories or suggestions for stories. No newspaper has enough reporters to cover every spot where news may break, nor can it possibly keep up with all of the activities in any town. Members of the public and town officials frequently notify a paper when an important issue is coming up in a town meeting, when a deer has wandered into a suburban neighborhood, or when a certain couple is planning to celebrate a golden wedding anniversary.

Public relations and publicity people for all sorts of individuals and organizations regularly send stories to newspapers. Some of these stories are legitimate news, and some are merely designed to keep clients in the spotlight of public attention.

Foreign and out-of-state news stories often carry a set of initials in the dateline which indicates that they were supplied by one of the wire services. AP means Associated Press. UPI means United Press International. Such a story from New York, for instance, was covered by a wire service staff member at the spot where it occurred and phoned in to the New York office. It was handled by a rewrite man, then edited and teletyped to subscribing New York bureaus and to regional bureau offices throughout the country. At each regional office it was again edited before being teletyped to subscribing newspapers in the area. This editing is done to fit the needs of out-of-town papers which will not want as long a story as those near where the event happened. At the local paper, a city editor or news editor evaluated the story and decided where it was to be used in his paper. He then passed it to the copy desk where it was again refined, pared to a specific length, and headlined. It was scrutinized by an editorial board before being sent to the composing room. A newspaper which subscribes to a wire service may edit stories to fit its needs but may not change the content or slant them without removing the wire service identification.

All news stories, once written, are edited and designated for particular spots in the paper. Their length, their position and whether or not news photos accompany them will depend on their importance compared to other news in the same issue.

There is a well-known truism about news that defines it as something out of the ordinary. It says that if a dog bites a man it is not news, but that if a man bites a dog, it *is* news. Anyone who reads the average newspaper will realize that this hardly applies to a large per cent of what is presented to him as news. Much space in all newspapers is devoted to ordinary, expected, and not particularly surprising events.

The Elks have a picnic, the PTA holds a reception for new members, the League of Women Voters offers transportation to the polls, the Little League wins a game, ten speeders are fined in police court—these stories, multiplied a thousand-fold, appear daily in newspapers all across America.

Seemingly even less important and exciting than these are what are called "meet-the-train" items. "Mr. and Mrs. Joseph Smith were dinner guests at the home of Mr. and Mrs. Sam Brown on Thursday, March 19." "Miss Jane Brown has returned home from Chatham College, where she has just completed her junior year." Newspapers value these stories more than you might suppose because they are so important to those whose names are mentioned.

The "big" stories, the hurricane that demolishes a town, the child lost in the woods, the bank robbery, the escaped criminal, do not happen so often, and may well be called "man bites dog" stories.

The type of story that is hardest to get and offers the most potential danger to a paper is the one kept hidden from the public. The good reporter and the good editor are never content with routine news and regular "handouts" from official sources, but are always on the alert for what is not easy to see.

A city plans a huge new park in a residential area. It is much needed to provide recreation facilities for large numbers of children. On the other hand, who now owns the land where it will be located, and when did they buy it? (Did the plans leak from certain city officials so that relatives and friends could buy the land at a low price, to resell later at a profit?) How much will be paid for the land, and who decides on its value? How are contracts for the necessary work to be awarded? Who has written the specifications for construction and will everything be of the best quality? The alert paper seeking this information will have no difficulty if all city officials are honest, but a crooked administration will resent a public scrutiny of its affairs. The paper that battles dishonest public officials is asking for trouble, but many a good paper has brought about great social reforms by doing just that.

News in American newspapers is supposed to be honest, accurate, concise, and easy to understand. It should not be written to serve any special interests, groups, or individuals. Most reporters and editors pride themselves on living up to these standards. It is much more difficult than it might seem to be sure that this is always done.

News which gives a one-sided impression is "slanted." A reporter or editor can, consciously or unconsciously, slant news in many different ways.

The selection of which stories to print may slant the news. Some South-

exist there. Some Northern newspapers have ignored stories of difficulties in the North but headlined those in the South, which may have given the impression that it was a purely regional problem. During a presidential campaign, partisan Republican papers may print countless stories about the huge crowds attending speeches made by the Republican candidate and hardly mention the same sort of crowds present to hear the Democratic candidate. Partisan Democratic papers may run stories showing the popularity of their candidate and select those which show a lack of popularity on the part of his opponent.

When done deliberately, this sort of slanting defeats the purpose of giving the public a clear and balanced picture of current events. It is often done, in a minor way, with no such intention. The editor who is an avid sports fan is apt to have a larger sports section than the one who is uninterested in sports but deeply involved in politics. The reporter who is fascinated by the business growth of the city will see more stories there than in its schools.

Responsible editors are aware that they often "create" news by selecting it for their columns. There are dozens of different departments in any state government, and news is apt to be in the making in all of them most of the time. The highway department is planning new roads, the department of employment is devising new tests for prospective employees, the treasurer has a report on the state's financial condition, the state promotion department is running a contest to choose a state flower, the state police department is reorganizing, the governor is making a speech, the welfare department reports an unusually heavy case load, the state park authority wants to create a new park in land reclaimed by a flood control project. Most of these matters are routine and might ordinarily be handled by routine news treatment.

Suppose that the newspaper editor decides that the matter of reclaimed land is of the utmost importance to the state, either because he thinks it should be a park or because he thinks it should be left untouched and used for a wild life refuge. He can put a good reporter on the story, set him to work digging up background and similar situations in other states, and run a series of front page stories which treat the matter as if it were the only really vital thing going on in the state. He could do the same with any one of the listed stories and give it importance at the expense of other news.

The attempt to make a paper interesting and exciting can slant news. Some newspapers fill their columns with stories of crime, tragedy, and corruption in order to attract readers; this makes it seem that these are the only noteworthy things happening. Other papers, wishing to help their communities by keeping everyone happy, err on the other side and rarely print anything unpleasant.

The position of a particular news story on the page and the page on which it appears, the number of words used for it, whether or not it is illustrated, and the way in which it is headlined can slant news.

Remember our fictitious governor who was involved in a traffic accident? Let us assume that it was snowing, that he was driving down a hill where children were sliding on the sidewalk, and that his car went out of control, narrowly missed another one, and crashed into a tree. He was examined by a doctor but was found to be uninjured. Think of the different headlines that could be written for such a story: "Governor Escapes Death in Accident," "Governor to Face Court Charges on Accident," "Children Uninjured by Governor's Accident, Is Claim"—and so on.

News may be slanted by lack of time and manpower to pursue it thoroughly. A newspaper may get a tip that a Mr. Peter Smith has been victimized by the state highway department. A reporter is sent to investigate the incident.

He finds Mr. Smith, aged 79, living near a new highway but unable to have a driveway built between it and his house. He had previously lived at another location, but his land was confiscated by the highway department to make room for the new highway. Being too poor to hire a lawyer, he had taken the price offered for his land by the state. A neighbor had interceded with the state on his behalf and helped him buy back his original home, which had then been moved to its present spot. Once settled, he had planted a garden, bought a cow, built a henhouse, and *then* had found that the state would not allow him to build the necessary driveway. His only access to the outside world is a path a quarter of a mile long which leads to a secondary road. He cannot afford to turn this into a proper driveway because the only money he has is the amount the state paid him for his former property.

The reporter finds this a heart-rending story and returns to his office to write it. His editor looks it over carefully. It is interesting, the public should know about it if it is a typical incident, and it is true in the sense that it is reported exactly as Mr. Smith told it. If it turns out not to be the complete truth, the paper is not in danger of a libel suit, because the state cannot bring such a suit. (In our country, the government *is* the people, and we cannot sue ourselves. If a story accuses a specific government official of something that may harm his reputation, he can bring suit as an individual on the basis of personal injury.)

The editor suggests that the reporter telephone the proper state official and get the state's side of the story. The reporter makes the call and is connected with a man who has a desk full of important work and no inclination to talk. The official says he is sick and tired of hearing about Mr. Smith and of the way newspaper reporters distort facts. Here is another angle to the story. "State official angered by questions, has no sympathy for Mr. Smith, and accuses newspapers of distorting the truth." It becomes more colorful by the minute.

A good reporter does not stop there. He should insist on his right to know the facts and should explain that the story is going to be printed and he would like to make it as accurate as possible. (Most state officials and others in public life realize it is always better to talk to the press than to refuse to, no matter what they may happen to think of the individual reporter or newspaper concerned.)

A subsequent interview will present new facts. The state is involved in a large-scale operation of highway construction, and the property of Mr. Smith is one of many it has purchased. All such property has been evaluated by professional appraisers to determine its true value. Mr. Smith was

letter, that the property to which he had his house moved would not be allowed access to the new highway. Most new highways, such as this one, have limited side access in order to prevent dangerous cross traffic.

The state official might eventually become more friendly with the reporter and advise him that Mr. Smith is a well-known crank who has caused endless trouble. He may suggest that it would be wise to drop the whole story, since it is obviously not a case of right or wrong, but of a man who can get along with no one.

This changes the story entirely, and the reporter and the paper have now spent considerable time on it—time which would otherwise have gone to other stories. Is this the end?

Not yet. The reporter should check the official records and interview other state officials and those whose property has been purchased for the same highway. Out of all this time and effort may come a story that uncovers wrongdoing on the part of the state or a story that is hardly worth writing and printing. Few newspapers have the facilities for following up every suggested story to this extent. *A story that is incomplete may be slanted because it omits some of the facts.*

Some stories may be both true and important, but misleading. Some years ago the late Senator Joseph McCarthy undertook a crusade to rid the government, schools, and churches of people whom he considered sympathetic to Communism. Speaking in the Senate (where his senatorial immunity made him safe from libel suits), he began to name people whom he said were Communists, Communist sympathizers, or "soft on Communism." Many of them were prominent people whose names were as newsworthy as the senator's.

It is news when any government official makes such statements. Many thoughtful editors did not believe the charges were true but they could not ignore their news value nor express their opinions in the news stories themselves. In order to handle the matter in what they considered the proper perspective, they printed their opinions on the editorial page, made a consistent effort to follow up on all of the accusations and give their readers the facts. Some published interviews with those accused giving their background and stature and with people who opposed Senator McCarthy's project.

To return to our original definition, news is an honest, unbiased, and complete account of events of interest or concern to the public. Professor George H. Morris of Florida Southern University, who was a newspaperman for many years before he became a teacher, characterizes news as "history in a hurry." He says "Read several papers, day after day, and eventually the truth will emerge."

No newspaper, because of the limitations of time and space, can print all of the facts that make the news in any one issue. No reader can understand what is happening by scanning any one issue of any one paper.

It is difficult for even the best newspapers to do a good job of gathering and writing the news. The good reader will evaluate it by reading carefully day after day and comparing the way identical stories are covered in papers with different viewpoints.

1. How can we define news? What are the commonest sources of news for a newspaper?

2. What are "man bites dog" and "meet the train" stories? What other kinds of newspaper stories are of value to the public?

3. What is meant by "slanted news"? What are some of the ways in which newspapers knowingly or unknowingly slant their news? Give some examples of how this may be done.

4. What are some of the qualities of a good newspaper reporter?

5. How can a newspaper story be both true and important and still be misleading?

6. How can the newspaper reader get the clearest and most objective view of the news?

■ ELEMENTS OF PERSUASION AND TECHNIQUES OF PROPAGANDA

Martin Quigley   *The Midwest Motorist,* December 1971

Knowing something about the ancient art of persuasion and some modern techniques and devices of propaganda can be helpful in sifting for the truth in what we read, hear, and see.

All day long, every day of our lives, all of us are bombarded by persuasion. It is an incessant bombardment upon our eyes, ears, feelings, and minds.

None of us can turn on the radio or television, pick up a newspaper or magazine, drive down the street, walk into a store, go to church, chat with a friend, talk with a member of the family, or meet with boss, employee, client, or supplier—not to mention open or devious sex-motivated encounters—without getting involved with some form or degree of persuasion.

In addition to everybody's everyday amateur persuasion, we are all also under constant bombardment from the professional persuaders. This is the skillful and systematic effort to get us to think in certain ways and do certain things. It is directed at us by business, government, labor, and religion, and by political parties, social agencies, and every other organization or individual that wants to influence what we do with our money, our time, and our votes.

There is more professional persuasion going on now than ever before. There are more people to persuade. There are more things to sell and ideas to impart. There are more ways to reach the eyes and ears and minds and

undoubtedly has driven many shaky people to insanity, suicide, and murder. The wonder is that we are all not shakier and flakier than we are.

Persuasion, let us say, is the non-violent, non-coercive effort—amateur and professional—to get people to behave in a certain way. Propaganda, a form of persuasion, has been defined (by Clyde R. Miller, *Propaganda Analysis,* November, 1937) as an "expression of opinion or action by individuals or groups deliberately designed to influence opinions or actions of other individuals or groups with reference to predetermined ends. Thus propaganda differs from scientific analysis. The propagandist is trying to put something across, good or bad, whereas the scientist is trying to discover truth and fact. Often the propagandist does not want careful scrutiny and criticism; he wants to bring about a specific action. Because the action may be socially beneficial or socially harmful to millions of people, it is necessary to focus upon the propagandist and his activities the searchlight of scientific scrutiny. Socially desirable propaganda will not suffer from such examination, but the opposite type will be detected and revealed for what it is."

Before defining some techniques of modern propaganda, let us look at the parental and ancient principles of persuasion upon which they are based.

People through the ages have given a lot of thought to the art of persuasion, and its principles were defined many hundreds of years ago. As you might expect, the earliest and best thought given to the art and ethics of persuasion was by the ancient Greeks.

A few years ago, Dr. Mortimer Adler, the philosopher who helped develop *Great Books of the Western World* and its *Syntopicon,* a guide to the thought and ideas contained in these volumes, summarized the principles and ethics of persuasion as defined and discussed by Aristotle and Plato. What follows is our summary of his summary of ancient Greek thought on the matter.

There are three elements in every successful persuasion—and the Greeks had words for them. These elements, in varying degrees and proportions, were essential to every successful persuasion 2,000 years ago, and they are essential today.

The first element is *ethos* which has to do with the nature, character, and believability of the persuader. It is the Greek word from which our word ethics comes. In order to persuade successfully, you must somehow establish acceptable character and plausibility. It is not necessary to *have* good character, mind you. The successful persuader must merely *seem* to have it. You can be the biggest crook in the world and still establish *ethos,* as some of the biggest crooks in the world have done and are still doing every day. Whether your character is genuine or spurious is irrelevant, as long as you can make people believe that they can take your word for what you are telling them. Without *ethos,* the persuasion cannot succeed.

In order to persuade you to buy its products or invest in its stock, a company may tell you it has been in business since 1776; that its products are the safest, best, and cheapest; that its devoted employees are experienced and honest; that it devotes enormous time and money to research; that its most important product is progress; that its products are favored by discriminating people; and that it supports education and the American way of life. What the company tells you about itself may be true or false, in whole or in part.

As far as the success of persuasion is concerned, what matters is that you have confidence in the persuader. Take the example of the confidence man, the crook. *Ethos* is the name of his game—confidence. The reason he can persuade people to give him their money is because he skillfully and quickly wins their confidence. For the time being, they believe him—and the fact that he is an unscrupulous liar and crook actually helps make it easier for him to establish *ethos*.

The second element, *logos,* the Greek word from which we get logic, is an appeal to the mind or reason. There has to be some appeal to reason in every successful persuasion. Again, it does not have to be a genuine appeal. It can be false. An advertisement that claims a detergent will make your clothes up to three times whiter without telling you three times whiter than what may be a more successful appeal to the mind of the housewife than one that tells her the product is an effective cleansing agent but that it will clog her washing machine and pollute the river.

A genuine appeal to reason—the marshalling of facts and honest reasons for the superiority of a product, an idea, or an institution—can be an effective appeal to reason. But whether the appeal to reason is genuine is irrelevant to the art of persuasion, as long as it is made effectively. The confidence man, for example, makes his victim believe that it is logical to go to the bank and draw out his life's savings in order to match the money the confidence man is willing to put up. People find this a logical arrangement every day, and the persuasion is successful.

The third element, *pathos,* is the word from which we get pathetic, but the Greeks meant an appeal to emotions, desires, and needs. Here again, the appeal need not be to worthy emotions, beneficial desires, or real needs. The appeal can be to greed, lust, snobbery, comfort, love, patriotism, responsibility to family, fear of hunger, fear of failure, desire for success, or almost any other base or worthy emotion, desire, or need of which man is capable. An insurance company, for example, will appeal to your sense of responsibility to your family. A manufacturer of cigars may appeal to a man's desire for female conquest. Our confidence man always appeals to his victim's greed and his desire for easy gain.

Truth and real values are not essential elements of successful persuasion. They can be present and often are. They may be useful. But so can falsehood and spurious values. Both truth and falsehood are irrelevant to the techniques of persuasion. Whether the object of the persuasion is to implant the big lie or to impart the big truth, the elements of persuasion remain the same.

Next time you hear a speech at a meeting or sit down with a car salesman in the boiler room . . . or watch and listen to a TV commercial or a politician or a news commentator . . . or read a newspaper editorial or a print advertisement . . . or listen to a radio commercial or an interview with a bureaucrat . . . keep your three little Greek friends in mind—*ethos, logos,* and *pathos.* They can help keep you from getting gypped or snowed.

Logos—what is the appeal to reason? Are those the facts or are they fake or deceptive statements dressed up to look like facts?

Pathos—what is the emotional appeal? To humor, anger, suspicion, patriotism, love, sex, ambition, security, status?

With these ancient elements of the art of persuasion as a platform, let us take a look at some of the modern techniques and devices of propaganda.

Drawing as freely from Clyde R. Miller and others as from Dr. Adler and the ancient Greeks, we can define and summarize seven of the techniques commonly used by propagandists. They are:

1. THE NAME CALLING DEVICE

This device is used on us (and by most of us) to influence judgment or opinion by appealing to hatred, dislike, fear, distrust, etc. The propagandist gives "bad names" to individuals, groups, nations, races, policies, practices, beliefs, and ideals which he would have us reject or condemn.

2. THE GLITTERING GENERALITIES DEVICE

The propagandist identifies his program or stand on an issue by identifying himself and it with "virtue" words. He appeals to our emotions of love, generosity, patriotism, brotherhood, etc., by using words like truth, freedom, honor, liberty, social justice, public service, right to work, honest toil, loyalty, democracy, the American way, Constitutional rights, etc. He identifies himself and his program—or his race, religion, nation, beliefs, etc.— with the ideals suggested by big fat words of vague meaning. As Name Calling is a device to win rejection or condemnation without evidence, the Glittering Generality is a device to win acceptance and approval without evidence.

3. THE TRANSFER DEVICE

The propagandist uses the Transfer Device to carry over the authority, sanction, and prestige of something we admire, respect, and revere to himself and his program. He frequently does this with the use of symbols, such as the flag, the Cross, the peace symbol, the victory signal, the clenched fist, Uncle Sam, portraits of Washington and Lincoln, etc. A political cartoonist of dovish intent might show Uncle Sam hanging his head in shame over the Vietnam War; a hawkish cartoonist might draw Uncle Sam leading a line of patriots to victory with honor. Both proponents and opponents of a given cause often use the same symbols or Transfer Devices.

4. THE TESTIMONIAL DEVICE

This is a device in which testimonials are used to make us accept a stand, idea, or product. It is currently much in vogue in radio and TV advertising. An ordinary housewife or a glamor girl tells us why she likes a deodorant. A man-on-the-street tells us why he is going to vote for a candidate. A famous comedian does the same. A banker tells us why it is in our best financial interests to vote for toll road bonds. Testimonials are usually used positively to support the propagandist's program.

5. THE PLAIN FOLKS DEVICE

This is a device the propagandist uses to win our confidence by appearing, or seeming to appear, as plain, ordinary people like us. Political candidates show their affection for children, hot dogs, and the common homey things of life. "Just plain folks" are supposed to be good and wise and possessed of down-to-earth common sense and salty humor. A rich, urban-minded propagandist may present himself as a country boy from a poor, hard-working, God-fearing family.

6. THE CARD STACKING DEVICE

The propagandist tries to deceive us by "stacking the cards" against opposing views, stands, and people. By omitting facts, inserting untruths, distorting, over-simplifying, etc., in describing and referring to his opposition, he can then proceed to demolish it with an air and manner of reasonable logic. (This device is in many ways similar to The Straw Dummy Device, in which a false opponent is set up and easily torn to pieces.) Using the same techniques of untruth, part-truth, and simplification, he makes a case for himself and his own program. He makes the real seem unreal, and the unreal real.

7. THE BAND WAGON DEVICE

By this familiar device, the propagandist wants us to have the feeling of following the crowd, joining the majority, being part of an enthusiastic movement, etc. The theme is "everybody's doing it." It is carried out with music, movement, symbols, colors, and all the dramatic arts. It is often specifically applied to groups held together by common ties of race, nationality, politics, religion, environment, sex, vocation, etc. All the artifices of flattery are used to harness fears and hatreds, convictions and ideals, prejudices and biases, etc., of the group appealed to. Emotion is used to push and pull the group on to the Band Wagon.

The persuader tries to make you feel it is "in" to agree with him and "out" to disagree. He tries to get you, at least, to withhold disagreement

"reactionary," "radical," "fascistic," "communistic," square, happy,
etc.

It takes a pretty independent individual to take a stand against the prevailing values of his group, whether it be togetherness in the commune or on the veranda of the country club.

As we strive for independent thought and sift for the nuggets of truth in the daily avalanche of persuasion and propaganda, we have got to be alert to remarkably clever and deceptive present-day applications of the ancient verbal trick of double-talk. In the vogue of our times, it has been identified as "language pollution" and is a device by which the persuader or propagandist either sugar-coats what he means, conceals what he means, or means something other, often the opposite, of what he saying. It is in daily use—by all sides and from every direction.

Grace Hechinger, writing in the *Wall Street Journal* (October 27), describes the "language pollution which is giving the printed and spoken word its own steadily widening credibility gap . . . It obscures problems by making them seem benign."

She reports, as an example, that the word "poverty" has been eliminated from government reports. The U. S. Census has replaced "poverty" with "low income level."

Mrs. Hechinger proceeds:

> *This official effort to eliminate poverty by purging it from the language is part of a long and continuing trend. Poor children have disappeared, if not from the slums, then at least from the language. First, they become "deprived," then "disadvantaged" and finally "culturally disadvantaged," as though they lacked nothing more serious than a free pass to Lincoln Center.*
>
> *Wars always aggravate word pollution. The military of all nations find it necessary to make their task appear more palatable under the cover of verbal camouflage. Pacification may signify anything from fortifying to destroying villages. Vietnamization is intended to suggest ending the war, when it actually means continuing it under different management. An incursion (as in Cambodia) deliberately skirts the poor image of an invasion. A protective reaction strike—a bombing attack that is allegedly undertaken because of what might happen if it were not—is in reality just an orthodox air raid.*

The real danger of this language pollution, Mrs. Hechinger writes, is that it makes "bureaucratic bungling seem harmless, renders antisocial behavior acceptable, gives so benign an image of poverty and social injustice as to lull people into believing that there is nothing to worry about and gives war an antiseptic look."

Richard Barnet, writing in Harpers' Magazine (November, 1971), describes bureaucratic language as "an absolution system." The words bureaucrats use to describe what they are doing—no matter how, stupid, bad or illegal—make their programs seem intelligent, beneficial, and legitimate. Mr. Barnet quotes an assistant secretary of state who in late 1964 proposed bombing and strafing attacks on North Vietnam with these words: "It seems to me that our orchestration should be mainly violins, but with periodic touches of brass." A peculiar danger of this kind of bureaucratic wash, hog and white, is that the people who dish it out slop it up as the truth themselves. As Mr. Barnet states:

> Confusion between what is true and what people would like to be true is an occupational hazard in any institution that spends a great deal of time projecting an image. It is a narcotic that protects people not only from public confrontations but from their own consciences.

On November 15, as another example, Associated Press in New York filed a story to newspapers all over the country pointing out that the "guarantee" of many a manufactured product should have been called a "limitation," since its intent and effect is not to stand behind claims for the product, but is actually "to limit the manufacturer's responsibility to live up to his obligations."

The "phony guarantee," the story goes on, "can be thoroughly disguised in legalese and grammatical convolutions so that what allegedly is an effort to be precise and cover all possibilities is really an effort to be ambiguous and to avoid all eventualities."

I ran across another bad case of word pollution in the *New York Times Book Review* for September 19. A book was described as "the sixth and most accessible novel by, feasibly, our best writer." After puzzling through the review, I realized that by "accessible" the reviewer meant, not that the book was available to readers, but that this novel was less incomprehensible than the author's previous "dense" novels. As far as "feasibly" is concerned, I figured that the reviewer wanted to leave the impression that the author was "possibly" or "potentially" our best novelist, but that he chose "feasibly" as a stylishly dense cop-out. Although this kind of seat-of-the-pants assessment may be regarded as simplistic by the advocates of more precise systems of analysis, I believe that understanding and common sense application of the classic elements of persuasion and modern techniques of distortion, concealment, and evasion can serve as practical protection against getting gypped or snowed.

POINTS TO CONSIDER

1. What is persuasion? How does it differ from propaganda? How are both of these things different from scientific analysis?

2. What are the three elements of persuasion? Can you think of examples of each?

3. What are the seven propaganda devices? Explain how each device fits the definition of propaganda given at the beginning of the article.

danger of language pollution?

5. How can understanding and applying the three elements of persuasion and the devices of propaganda help protect us from getting "gypped or snowed"?

IS THERE A BLACK PRESS?

Roland E. Wolsely   *The Black Press, U. S. A.*, 1971

When a course on the black press in the United States was launched at Syracuse University in the fall, 1968, several professors in other areas of knowledge raised doubts about the existence of such a press.

"How do you tell?" a political scientist asked.

"What determines it?" came from an historian, who went on to inquire: "Is it that the readers are black-skinned?"

Indeed, how does one tell? And is it important that there be a distinction?

This problem was one of the first presented to the students, as it has been in every offering of the course since. For in such a course it is a central point. If there is no black or Negro press there is no point in publishing books about it or scheduling courses concerned with it. The skepticism is not one that springs from ignorance only of this ethnic press; some black publishers also question such a distinction.

The conclusion by the class, at term's end, was that there is such a press and that it definitely is important that a distinction be made between it and other press groups. One graduate student, Kent W. de Felice, selected the problem for deeper investigation and obtained reactions from several leading black journalists. His report concluded that there are certain qualifications which a publication must meet to be considered a unit of the black press. They are:

1. Blacks must own and manage the publication; they must be the dominant racial group connected with it. (In support of that requirement it can be said that if the publication is not black-owned and black-operated, its aims, policies, and programs can be altered by persons unsympathetic to the goals of black editors and publishers. An instance occurred in 1968 when an apparently black-owned newspaper supported George Wallace during the presidential campaigns. Investigation brought out the fact that the paper had been black-owned until shortly before the campaigns began, when whites bought it and altered its policy. The black press otherwise backed Hubert H. Humphrey strongly but included supporters of Richard M. Nixon as well.)

2. The publication must be intended for black consumers. (A science magazine presumably is aimed at scientists or persons interested in scientific matters. A paper about music is directed to persons responsive to its contents. Advertising sales depend upon such identification of reader with subject. Similarly, a magazine or newspaper for black citizens deals with their interests and concerns and is not primarily for whites. So long as there is a cultural and ethnic distinction in society between black and white citizens there will be a place for black journalism. These differences still are acute, especially with the possibility that the present trend toward separatism is only temporary.)

3. The paper or magazine must, the report concluded, "serve, speak and fight for the black minority." It also must have the major objective of fighting for "equality for the Negro in the present white society. Equality means the equality of citizenship rights," de Felice said.

Moses Newson, executive editor of the Baltimore *Afro-American,* one of the major black newspapers, noted that the black press of the United States was "founded for the purpose of serving, publicizing, speaking, and fighting for the colored minority." The late E. Washington Rhodes, publisher of the Philadelphia *Tribune,* a leading semi-weekly, although denying the validity of the use of the word *black* or the existence of a black press and accepting *Negro press* as a term, went on to write that the units of this press are intended "to secure for their readers absolute equality of citizenship rights." And from William O. Walker, editor of the Cleveland *Call and Post,* came the clear view that "Black is a color—Negro is a race; so there is a Negro press. It serves the interests and needs of the Negro people."

A parallel can be drawn with another area of communications: theater. Peter Bailey, writing in *Ebony,* insisted that black theater is one that is written, directed, produced, financed by blacks, located in a black community, and uses the community "as its reference point."

Similarly, some black journalists believe that the black press is that owned, produced, and intended for black readers in a black environment. This third proviso, then, makes the black press a special-pleading institution, one with a cause, goal, or purpose going beyond the basic one necessary for survival in the American economy—the making of a profit.

THE DIFFERENCES DISCERNED

Applying the de Felice specifications to white newspapers and magazines brings out the differences between the black and white presses. Although it usually is owned by whites, the white press need not be. It could be owned by blacks but aimed at whites, for the white press generally hopes to have readers of all hues. The main difference exists in the goals of white publications. Usually they are concerned with the problems of whites, the majority group readers, and only incidentally with those of blacks, Orientals, or other minorities, racial or political. This policy accounts for the complaints

has been indifference to the black minority's problems, if not downright opposition to that race, giving rise to the black press as a corrective force as well as a weapon with which blacks have been fighting for their rights.

It should be noted, however, that by no means are all black publications dedicated to social causes dear to the country's black citizens. Just as with any other business, there are publications whose goal chiefly is financial profit, sometimes to be used in the interest of the race, other times, as with white entrepreneurs, for the personal benefit of the managers and owners.

THE NEED FOR A BLACK PRESS

Whatever they may be called, the black newspapers and magazines and their auxiliaries exist. How they developed is related in subsequent chapters. Why they came into being is part of that history.

The aims of the early publications, from *Freedom's Journal* of 1827 to those issued in Reconstruction days, are clear. The exploitation of slaves, their mistreatment and the limitations placed upon them are examined in the historical perspective. But the black citizen of the United States is a free man or woman, education is available (if not always the best), employment can be had at least by some (even if still mainly in the lower echelons), and civil rights slowly are being won. What, then, is the need for a black press still?

It is needed mainly because all the old battles have not yet been won and because there are so many new ones. "Without the black press, the black man would not know who he is nor what is happening to his struggle for the freedom of citizenship," in the words of Valarie Myers, former editor of Syracuse (N. Y.) *Challenger,* one of the many new community papers of recent years. And perhaps less important now than in the past but still vital is the need for facts about themselves, i.e., coverage of the black society, still neglected by the white press which deals mainly in racial conflict, crime, and news of blacks known to whites from the sports and entertainment worlds.

Also, for many years the black people have mistrusted the white press. As Roi Ottley has explained, the white press and news services earned the suspicion of black citizens in the first half of this century because they could not be trusted to tell the truth about blacks. These white agencies were accused of favoring whites against blacks, i.e., tailoring the news to fit the publications' prejudices or at least those of their owners. Both northern and southern papers followed the practice of race identification of blacks only and of ignoring entirely anything but unfavorable black news.

Complaints about the white press treatment of blacks' news today, however, are no less numerous, perhaps more selective because they single out regions, and merely different in nature from those of the early years of black journalism. Representatives of various types of black organizations, for example, met in Washington in 1969 with editors and reporters from the city's three white dailies to discuss "The Minorities and the Press." The session was typical, in the matter of criticisms of the white press, of others held in various parts of the U.S.A. by newsmen's organizations, schools of journalism, and newspaper unions.

The black critics in Washington objected to the papers' practice of displaying civil rights stories next to crime stories involving blacks. They objected also to all news concerning black citizens being handled as civil rights news instead of being put in appropriate departments, such as financial or women's sections. News about blacks, it also was charged, always is negative and the newspapers tend to deal only with conflict stories about what goes on in the ghetto.

As in the early years, blacks still look to their press to fight their battles. A look at almost any black paper and most magazines dramatizes this point. To the middle-class white or other nonblack reader, such as an Oriental, the black world is a separate realm. The use of "world" in black publication titles, such as *Our World, Bronze World, Black World* magazines or Garvey's paper, *The Negro World,* all indicate this separation. The fault is not all that of white publishers. The general white press does not cover the details of life in most industries or professions or other specialized groups of humans, for that would be impossible; that explains the existence of thousands of special publications to compensate for the lack of their news in the consumer or general press.

Blacks can counter, however, that what they do, day by day, is of more importance for whites to know about and to understand than are the doings, say, of the nation's cost accountants or other specialists who have their own publications. The revolt of the black people at mid-century caught many white Americans by surprise; perhaps adequate coverage of the black community and its problems might have helped solve the problems before they became extreme. Yet the continued absence of such coverage of not only the black world but of other minorities as well, the American Indian, for example, is evidence of the lack of perspective of American white-owned journalistic publications, of which there are about 32,000.

EXTENT OF THE BLACK PRESS

A visitor to the United States from India, whose citizens, being people of color other than white, have a natural interest in and sympathy for the nonwhites anywhere, once remarked to the author that he saw no publications for blacks in his travels around the U.S.A., although he saw many black people. When he was told that at the time the country's black population amounted to 18,870,000, he was astonished.

The experience is a common one for whites as well, although not to be taken too literally. The Indian friend was shown a variety of black periodicals and then recalled having seen several of them on newsstands but of being unaware of their origin. Unless one knows the titles it is not always easy to identify black publications, especially with the greater use by white papers and magazines of black models on covers or the photographs of black celebrities on front as well as inside pages. In general, however, it is

cations, and that the earning power of almost all blacks has kept down the purchase of publications by single copies. Furthermore, it is too expensive to place publications on newsstands, through distribution companies, unless wide sale is likely. Perhaps one stand on a main street may stock a magazine or two.

Library holdings also have been sparse. Exceptions are private and public institutions patronized by blacks, such as college libraries especially interested in black history and culture, only a recent interest in most instances. It is the unusual public library that receives more than one or two magazines and that number of newspapers aimed at black readers.

Most whites and not a few blacks are unaware of the extent of the black press. College people, except those deeply involved in social movements embracing racial problems, rarely can remember seeing a black publication, a situation the author has become aware of through classroom work during thirty years of teaching journalism courses in which some attention has been given to the black press.

As their circulations attest, most black magazines, aside from a few popular ones, seem to exist in secrecy. White scholars have vague impressions of such capably written and well-edited periodicals as the *Journal of Negro History* and the *Journal of Negro Education.* Several dozen other meritorious publications have functioned for years in quiet, surrounded by white indifference. In their effort to understand the black society, some whites now are beginning to look into these publications.

THE SCOPE TODAY

What do these publications tell their readers? What appears in them? The newspapers give their audiences news of the black community as well as of national and international events directly affecting black citizens; a few attempt to offer nonblack news of particular interest. The emphasis is on local or regional news. They also provide entertainment and editorial guidance, although largely the former, as is newspaper habit anywhere in the U.S.A. The magazines also seek to entertain, but more and more are informing and promoting causes. None of this is done with uniform thoroughness or quality. But along with black radio, the black press is still the main source of the black citizen's information and comment about his life. Through their advertising columns these publications fulfill the commercial function. The segment known as specialized magazines serves as a literary outlet, an opinion forum, or a guidebook for business and professional people. As Henry Lee Moon, director of information for the NAACP and editor of its magazine, *Crisis,* has put it: "colored citizens still look to the Negro press for their side of the story and for an interpretation of the news that affects their vital interests." Or as a perceptive white student expressed it: "A black publication actually is one which helps establish the black identity and serves the black community."

These functions and different kinds of content are, of course, not unique to the black press. The newspapers and magazines of any nation or any minority group have more or less the same purposes if not the same content. The black press differs from the white not so much in kind as in message and in quality. It often reports news not covered by other journalism. It interprets that news differently, from an uncommon standpoint. It ventures opinions about matters not dealt with by other presses and its opinions frequently vary from those of other publications treating the same topics. The reporting and writing often are superficial; the editing frequently is careless; the printing, especially of the newspapers, is slovenly in many instances.

By and large, the physical patterns of these papers and magazines are like those of others in the U.S.A. The newspapers, at a glance, look like any to be found on the ordinary display. The main news—or news that will sell papers or hold readers—is on the first page; other news stories are scattered throughout the rest of the paper. An editorial page has all the usual characteristics of such pages: two or three essays on local or national affairs down the left; to their right a cartoon on some national topic or event involving black citizens; and columns and letters to the editor in other areas of the page. The columnists frequently are one or two of the nationally syndicated or otherwise regularly available black leaders such as Louis E. Martin, Roy Wilkins, Bayard Rustin, or Benjamin E. Mays. Local columnists abound.

One or two pages may be devoted each to sports, church, society, and entertainment news. A good deal of this often is obvious publicity material. Occasionally columnists appear on sports and society pages. Syndicated copy, obtained from one of the few black feature companies or, more likely, a regular white-oriented one, and news from United Press International (the latter a white agency), or in some instances radical services such as Liberation News Service, appear sparingly, and chiefly in the larger papers. Some of the little weeklies are hardly more than composites of lifted material, with datelines and the symbol showing the source chopped out before the item is pasted for photo-offset reproduction. The rest is advertising, both classified and display. Space is being bought by large corporations as well as by local enterprises seeking to employ blacks but the bulk of the space is filled by the ads of small firms of service-oriented businesses.

Tabloid size is becoming more common among black newspapers, particularly because many of the new community weeklies use that dimension. A national cross-section study of seventy-nine papers made by the author in 1970 revealed that thirty-five were tabloids. Magazines are mainly of two sizes, eight by twelve inches (or newsmagazine) and the six by nine inches used by scholarly journals. But in the numerous variations are the large, flat *Ebony* and *Sepia* and the pocket-sized *Black World*.

The magazines are too varied for a single description, the *Negro History Bulletin* having little in common with *Soul! Illustrated*. Just as the newspapers resemble the white counterparts, the magazines, type by type, are much like periodicals for whites serving the same function. *Sepia* is like *Look* or *Life*, superficially. *Phylon* resembles the serious literary and public affairs quarterlies of the *Southern Review* type.

The opinions of these publications, since they descended from a press known for its strong protest function, have in common certain positions. But beyond these particular uniform beliefs there is great variety. It goes without saying that pleas and demands for greater recognition of civil rights can be heard from all except a few dissidents and the highly specialized, technical publications, and even they have their say on the subject now and then.

On racial matters the black press is by and large vigorously outspoken. Although the publications have the same goals, they differ considerably in how they propose to achieve them.

By and large, on most national issues aside from race, the bigger publications are socially and politically conservative or moderate but not reactionary. More liberal viewpoints are to be found in the small community weeklies, the publications of militants, and some of the purely opinion publications than in the big-circulation newspapers and periodicals. Although traditionally loyal to the Republican Party, more and more of the black press members in the past decade turned their support to the Democratic Party, led to that viewpoint by President John F. Kennedy, Vice-President and then President Lyndon B. Johnson, Vice-President Hubert H. Humphrey, and Senator Robert F. Kennedy. The newspapers have been the principal purveyors of direct editorial opinion. The magazines, since they are issued on a different frequency, with some exceptions either avoid commitment on current issues or find it impractical to have a timely position on any subject outside the publication's realm.

■ **POINTS TO CONSIDER**

1. What qualifications must a particular publication have in order to be considered a unit of the black press?

2. What differences does the author point out between the black press and the white press? What similarities?

3. What coverage can the black community generally expect in the white press?

4. What need is there for a black press? Can you think of other reasons for a black press? What objections might be raised against the black press?

5. What kind of exposure does the author feel the black press gets in relation to white publications? From your experience would you say his conclusions are valid? Explain. What reasons does the author give for this situation? Can you suggest any possible remedies or improvements?

6. What unities of political opinion does the author find among the various black publications? What differences?

7. Judging from the information contained in the article, what conclusions, if any, can you draw as to the importance of the black press to the black community? To our society as a whole?

THE PRESS REPORTS AND COMMENTS ON THE CONFLICT AT ATTICA PRISON, SEPTEMBER 1971

New York Daily News (September 12): "The Prisoners' Demands"

New York Daily News (September 13): Alton Slagle—"Rocky Rejects Deal with Attica Cons: A Massacre Feared by Negotiators"

Rochester Democrat-Chronicle (September 13): "Wives Will 'Run It Down to the People'"

New York Daily News (September 13): Herman Badillo and James Ryan—Rep. Herman Badillo's Account of His Harrowing Three Days Inside Attica State Prison

New York Daily News (September 14): William Federici—"I Saw Seven Throats Cut"

Buffalo Evening News (September 14): Bob Buyer and Ray Hill—"Attica Death Toll Rises to 41; Transfers Start"

New York Times (September 16): Tom Wicker—"The Animals at Attica"

Black Panther (September 18): "Indict Nelson Rockefeller and Richard Nixon for First Degree Murder at Attica State Prison"

The New Republic (September 25): "Dead End at Attica"

U. S. News and World Report (September 27): "Why U.S. Prisons Are Exploding"

National Review (October 8): "Exploiting Attica"

THE PRISONERS' DEMANDS

New York Daily News, September 12, 1971

Attica, N.Y., Sept. 11 (Special)—Here are the demands presented to state officials by rebellious prisoners at the Attica State Correctional Facility:

Amnesty from prison authorities for the 1,200 inmates who took part. Amnesty from the courts.

Removal of walls that separate p̶r̶i̶s̶o̶n̶e̶r̶s̶
An improved diet.
Better education programs.
No censorship of published materials.
Freedom to engage in political activity.
Better health care.
Freedom to make contacts with the outside world at their own expense.
More religious freedom.
More realistic rehabilitation programs.
Improvement in the quality of guards and social workers, including more black and Puerto Rican guards and social workers.
Improvement in parole procedures.
A federal takeover of the prison.

■ ROCKY REJECTS DEAL WITH ATTICA CONS
A MASSACRE FEARED BY NEGOTIATORS

Alton Slagle   *New York Daily News,* September 13, 1971

Attica, N. Y., Sept. 12—Gov. Rockefeller refused to come to the besieged Attica State Correctional Facility today. He appealed to the rebellious prisoners to release their hostages.

The governor said that even if he had the constitutional authority to grant amnesty to the inmates, as they demanded, he would not do so.

Rockefeller called on the prisoners to cooperate for peaceful restoration of order.

Negotiations to end the four-day rebellion had reached an impasse.

A committee of observers earlier today had called on the governor to meet with them at the prison because—according to one, Rep. Herman Badillo (D–Bronx)—they were "convinced that a massacre of prisoners and guards may take place in this institution."

Rockefeller, replying from his home in Westchester said: "I have carefully considered the request and I am deeply grateful" to the committee members for their effort.

"The key issue at stake, however, is still the demand for total amnesty to any criminal acts which may have occurred," he said.

"I do not have the constitutional authority to grant such a demand and I would not, even if I had the authority, because to do so would undermine the very essence of our free society—the fair and impartial application of the law."

SUPPORTS AUTHORITIES

In rejecting the appeal for him to come to Attica, Rockefeller said: "I do not feel my physical presence on the site can contribute to a peaceful settlement."

Rockefeller said he was "in full support" of the way state and prison authorities have handled the "tragic situation" since the riot started Thursday.

Hundreds of state police were armed for an apparent assault on the prison, where 500 inmates held 33 hostages to back up demands for full amnesty and the removal of prison Superintendent Vincent R. Mancusi.

Four boxes of shotgun shells were carried inside the prison gates at about 2:30 P.M. as the police forces organized for the attack. Four sections of 1½-inch fire hose for high pressure use were later hauled inside the gates and a canister of CS riot control gas was loaded aboard an Army CH-34 helicopter.

Newsmen outside the gates coughed and sneezed as gas filled the air.

The prison flag flew at half-staff in honor of William Quinn, 23-year-old prison guard who died last night of injuries Thursday when he was thrown from a second-story window by rioting inmates.

As gas masks and belt cutters were issued to riot-breakers outside, a typewritten note was passed from the prison, where a citizen committee was trying to solve the crisis. It carried the signature of Jim Ingram, one of the inmate mediators, and read:

"The committee of observers at Attica prison is now convinced that a massacre of prisoners and guards may take place in this institution.

"For the sake of our common humanity we call on every person who hears these words to implore the governor of this state to come to Attica to consult with the observer committee so we can spend time and not lives in an attempt to resolve the issues before us. Send the following telegram immediately to Gov. Nelson Rockefeller of New York State: 'Please come to Attica to meet the observer committee.'"

PLANS PRESS CONFERENCE

Rockefeller was at his Pocantico Hills home this afternoon and planned a press conference at 9:30 A.M. tomorrow in his New York City office to discuss the $2.5 billion transportation bond issue to be placed on the state ballot in November. He was scheduled to leave after the press conference for San Juan, P.R., to attend the National Governors Conference.

Black Panther leader Bobby Seale, whose presence had been requested by the inmates, conferred with State Correction Commissioner Russell G. Oswald and other officials this morning. But no agreement was reached, and Seale left town.

"This morning, the commissioner and his aides basically said I was not going in unless I tried to encourage the prisoners to accept the so-called demands made by the committee," Seale told newsmen. "I am not going to do that."

negotiable and that the removal of the _____ negotiable."

VOWS NO COMPROMISE

Seale said the position of the Black Panther Party was that it would not "compromise" the inmates. He said the Black Panthers believe officials should comply with the request of the rioters that they be transported to a nonimperialistic country.

Seale added: "If the political prisoners are not released then the New York State government will be guilty and must be charged with murder if anything happens to the arrested guards. This is the Black Panther message to the prisoners and the people."

Seale said he had been directed to return to Panther headquarters in Oakland, Calif.

"IN TROUBLE"

Rep. Herman Badillo (D–Bronx), a member of the observer committee, underscored the crisis when he said of Seale's position: "I think we are in trouble. Bobby says 'no.' I don't know what we can do.

Attorney William M. Kunstler, another member of the committee and the lawyer who defended Seale and others on charges growing out of the riots at the Democratic National Convention, said the talks had reached an impasse.

Kunstler said the state should reconsider its attitude on amnesty in light of Quinn's death.

"The state takes the position of nonnegotiability of amnesty," Kunstler said. "The district attorney of this county will prosecute. Then if the prisoners are taken into control again, they—some of them—will face charges of murder which will mean capital punishment. So matters have reached a serious impasse."

11 GUARDS INJURED

Quinn, the father of two girls, was injured in the first hours of riot, which started Thursday when inmates of the maximum security prison refused to report to work and to recreation assignments.

At least 11 other guards were hurt but the remaining hostages—27 guards and 11 civilian employes—were reportedly being well cared for by the rioters.

Later today, Oswald appealed to the prisoners to surrender the hostages. He said he had agreed to 28 prisoner demands, not including amnesty and removal of Mancusi.

WIVES WILL "RUN IT DOWN TO THE PEOPLE"

Marilynn Bailey   *Democratic Chronicle*, Rochester, N.Y., September 13, 1971

Some relatives of inmates at riot-torn Attica prison have huddled together since Thursday night at FIGHT headquarters at 86 Prospect Ave., waiting for word of the prisoners.

Most of the mothers and wives of inmates hadn't had more than a few hours' sleep, since the prison erupted in violence Thursday morning. They've spent their nights at the community organization.

Many of the women have taken extended leaves from their jobs. They take their children "from aunt-to-aunt, grandmother-to-grandmother," one said. One woman has been putting her youngsters to bed in her car parked in front of FIGHT.

The women, who sometimes break into tears, partially from lack of sleep but mostly from worry when they think about the prison, met this weekend and formed a group called Concerned Relatives and Friends of Attica Inmates.

Rev. Raymond B. Scott, head of FIGHT and an observer at Attica, has been telephoning information each night to the group.

The 30-member group, which is headed by Mrs. Annette Thomas and Mrs. Claudette McCuller, both of whose husbands are Attica inmates, will lead a meeting at 7 P.M. tonight at the Memorial A.M.E. Zion Church, 42 Mavors St.

"We want to make the community aware of why the men did what they did. We want them to know how we feel," Mrs. Thomas said. "You hear from the guards and their families, but what about us?"

Group members spent the day in church yesterday, but not just for Sunday morning services. They delivered a sermon of their own.

"Before, I never talked about the conditions at Attica because I was afraid I'd get my husband in trouble. But now that it's all out in the open I'm going to run it all down to the people," Mrs. McCuller said.

REP. HERMAN BADILLO'S ACCOUNT OF HIS HARROWING THREE DAYS INSIDE ATTICA STATE PRISON

Herman Badillo,
As told to James Ryan   *New York Daily News*, September 13, 1971

I received a telephone call from Gov. Rockefeller's counsel, Robert Douglass, at 11 A.M. Friday, the morning after the rebellion began, asking me to join the committee. I agreed at once and canceled my schedule for the rest of the day.

At 1 P.M. I and other members of the committee from this area met a state plane at LaGuardia Airport that carried us to Batavia Airport. State troopers picked us up there and drove us to the prison. We went directly to a room in the administration building and our ordeal began.

It began quietly enough. We were briefed by State Corrections Commissioner Russell G. Oswald and we received printed copies of the prisoners' demands.

NEGOTIATION NEARLY IMPOSSIBLE TASK

Our first meeting with the rebels came late Friday when we filed into a large room and began the nearly impossible task of negotiating with 1,200 men.

We spoke to the prisoners over microphones in response to their increasing list of demands. Our every statement was met by cheers or boos.

It was a most disorganized session. The inmates could not agree on a representative committee and there seemed to be minor differences among them on almost every issue.

It certainly did not seem that it was an organized revolt or that outside forces were involved, as Gov. Rockefeller later suggested.

Saturday morning we discussed the demands. Agreement was easy on the important demands of improved medical attention for the inmates and a team of observers to make sure there were no physical reprisals against prisoners after the insurrection.

GOT WORD SEALE WAS COMING

Then we got word that Bobby Seale was coming in. We could do nothing until he got there. When he arrived Saturday night we told him our position on the demands, that had grown to 28.

He replied that he needed time, that he had to see Huey Newton, that he could only talk to the prisoners for five minutes. We knew we had to wait at least until Sunday.

When Seale did go before the prisoners they were enraged that he only spoke to them a few minutes. When he left the prison I left with him. Some other members of the committee stayed to talk some more with the rebels. But I saw no point to it. Without Seale there was nothing to talk about.

Then Sunday morning Seale came back but refused to enter the prison. "Nothing can be done," he said, and simply disappeared.

This put us in an impossible negotiating position. We were down to the amnesty issue but the most credible man on our side of the table refused to take part in the negotiations. A new approach was necessary.

The committee then decided to ask Gov. Rockefeller to come in person to the prison, not to grant total amnesty but to consult with us and give us additional time to bridge the gap to the rebels.

We first asked him through his aides and there was no response, just a press release. Then I and several other members of the committee asked him personally to step in. He refused.

It seems to me that the governor was at least partially influenced in this decision and the later one to attack the prison by public pressure for stern action.

All Sunday we were pleading for more time. We had tapes of hostages that we wanted to put on TV so the public could see they were unharmed.

But Commissioner Oswald shattered our hopes for time. At 11 P.M. Sunday he said we would have until 7 A.M. the following day to either succeed or get out.

He was as good as his word. At 7 A.M. we were ordered out and when we refused to leave we were locked inside a room in the administration building and guards were placed outside the door.

WE WERE PRISONERS OF THE STATE

We asked for gas masks and were told there were no more. Oswald declared that we were "prisoners of the state."

The attack came and riot gas began to seep into the room. Some among us who had experienced it before told us to hold water-soaked handkerchiefs to our faces. We did.

We were quite concerned that we'd be shot because all during the ordeal the guards had been most hostile toward us.

When it was over, all members of the committee except the elected officials were ordered to leave. Those of us who remained saw the blood, the destruction, the naked prisoners being herded into cells.

We thought ruefully that this terrible tragedy that cost the lives of two score men might have been avoided if only patience had held sway over the rush to violence.

■ I SAW SEVEN THROATS CUT

William Federici   *New York Daily News,* September 14, 1971

Attica, N. Y., Sept. 13—A state police sergeant, the agony of witnessing a massacre etched into his sweating face, described today how an exploding tear-gas canister set off a slaughter of hostages by Attica prison convicts.

tion squad.

CALLED TIMES SQUARE

The sergeant left Times Square, a central area where four prison courtyards meet, covered with bodies and blood. He had led the first assault wave into the convict-held prison yard.

"My knees started to shake," he said. "I could hardly believe what I saw. There were two cons guarding each of eight hostages. They were standing on a concrete platform in the middle of Times Square.

"Each of the hostages was standing straight while a con held a knife to his throat. Another convict stood directly behind each hostage, holding his arms."

ONE OF THEM RAN AWAY

"Officers with bullhorns ordered the 16 cons to drop their weapons and surrender. Then there was an explosion from a tear-gas canister dropped by a helicopter.

"Those cons didn't wait a second. They just slit throats.

"Seven hostages died almost instantly. The eighth broke loose, fought off the cons guarding him, and ran to us like I've never seen a man run before. He ran right into our arms.

"As soon as the sharpshooters realized what was happening, they opened up. There was a barrage of gunfire."

The sharpshooters, stationed at vantage points overlooking Times Square, were armed with .270 caliber rifles with telescopic sights. They killed 15 of the 16 convicts in the square.

The only con who escaped being shot dead was one who was knocked down by the fleeing hostage.

After the sharpshooters' barrage, the order was given for 600 state troopers to enter the prison and restore order. Led by Troop A, they charged through Times Square, stepping on bodies and slipping on pools of blood.

ORDERS WERE TO SHOOT

The rebel cons, now starting to surrender, were told to lie flat on the yard floor.

"Our orders were to shoot any who resisted," the sergeant said, "and we did.

"We were hit with gasoline bombs, make-shift spears, rocks, iron bars, sticks, and other missiles. It's a wonder more of us weren't hurt."

He said that squads of troopers and Essex County deputy sheriffs removed barricades of steel tables that separated Times Square from Cellblock D, where the remaining hostages were held and where rebel holdouts made their final stand.

Troopers then swarmed through tunnels leading into Cellblock D, overwhelmed the rebels and rescued the hostages.

The sergeant, a 15-year veteran of the state force, was one of the first troopers to enter the prison and one of the first out after the revolt was smashed.

Sweat streaming down his face, he groped for words to describe the slaughter of the hostages.

"I can only tell you it was a massacre," he said. "The goddamned fools just wouldn't give up. I hope to God I never have to see a thing like that again."

■ ATTICA DEATH TOLL RISES TO 41; TRANSFERS START

Bob Buyer and Ray Hill   *Buffalo Evening News,* September 14, 1971

Attica, Sept. 14—Autopsies performed today on the eight hostages who were slain Monday in the Attica State Correctional Facility revealed they died from gunshot wounds and not from slashed throats as reported by a State Department of Corrections official.

"They were all shot. Their throats were not slashed," said Richard R. Rintale, chief investigator for the Monroe County medical examiner's office in Rochester, where the autopsies were performed.

He said there were several bullets of different caliber found—raising the possibility that the rioting inmates were either heavily armed or the eight may have been shot accidentally by State Police during the storming of the prison.

But Donald McCabe, director of the Weeks Funeral Home, Warsaw, said the body of one hostage—John G. Monteleone, 42, of Attica—had slashes on the back and side of the throat.

He said he did not know whether these caused Mr. Monteleone's death.

The funeral director said he saw at least two other bodies in Rochester and he believed that the slashes on the throats could have caused the deaths.

On Monday, Deputy Corrections Commissioner Walter Dunbar and Gerald Houlihan, the department's public information officer, told reporters that the convicts slashed the throats of their hostages.

The autopsy performed on the body of William Quinn, 28, who died Saturday of injuries suffered on Thursday when the riot broke our, showed he died of "severe head injuries," Mr. Rintale said.

Surviving hostages, however, deepened the mystery by giving accounts of how their captors threatened to cut their throats.

One hostage told of how his "executioner" told him he didn't "have the heart to do it" and merely cut him.

After the first assault on the prison Monday, Mr. Houlihan emerged and told reporters that throats had been cut. The observation was again made by Mr. Dunbar.

The Associated Press on Monday quoted Mr. Houlihan as saying "several" hostages' throats were slashed.

The autopsy today showed no evidence of this, the medical examiner's office said.

The autopsy also concluded that all of the hostages had died at about the same time.

Corrections Commissioner Russell G. Oswald told reporters on Monday that the killing of captives began before the first assault by police.

There was no evidence found to support claims made Monday by Mr. Houlihan that any of the hostages had been mutilated.

The dramatic and puzzling development came this afternoon as the death toll in the uprising rose to 41, including 10 hostages and 31 prisoners.

The toll rose this morning with the discovery of two prisoners' bodies in a prison tunnel.

Officials also announced the toll of injured was 42 persons.

In Albany, a spokesman for Winn Van Eekeren, the deputy commissioner in charge of the central office of the Department of Correctional Services during Commissioner Oswald's absence, said the department "is trying to check the veracity of the autopsy reports."

"It could be such a serious thing," he said, "that we want to be absolutely sure that the story is true."

The spokesman described the deputy commissioner as being "shocked" by the news from Monroe County about the autopsies.

The spokesman said the autopsy report should be considered "in the light of what surviving hostages have said publicly to all the media about throat slashings."

Mr. Van Eekeren said there were witnesses to the throat-slashings. And he said it was proven the prisoners had zip guns.

"This is definite. These weapons were found," he said.

Dr. Edland said the locations of the gunshot wounds varied. Some had been shot in the head, others in the chest or back, he said.

Judge Robert E. Fischer, the state's "super cop" who was ordered by the attorney general to aid in the probe of the riot, was asked about the medical examiner's report and he replied: "I don't know anything about it."

Dr. Selden Williams, senior prison physician, said the number of persons treated in the facility's infirmary Monday was "close to a hundred."

They were all prisoners and most of them had been shot during Monday's assault by state police.

In the wake of the riot—one of the worst in the nation's history—there were these late-breaking developments:

Dist. Atty. James, assisted by state "super cop" Judge Fischer, has ordered a special Wyoming County grand jury to probe the riot.

Capt. Henry F. Williams of the State Police Bureau of Criminal Investigation, said today that his men have already begun an investigation into "10 homicides."

The 10 included nine hostages killed by their captors, and guard William Quinn, 28, who died Saturday from a beating administered Thursday by convicts who reportedly threw him out a second-story window.

—Buses rolled out of the embattled prison during the night, carrying convicts to other state facilities.

So far, 152 inmates have been moved from the institution.

In Albany, a spokesman for the State Corrections Department said upward of 1000 prisoners will be taken to Dannemora, Great Meadows and Green Haven Correctional Facilities. This will reduce the Attica population to about half of what it was when rioting broke out.

In federal court this morning, Judge Curtin delayed a hearing order until this afternoon to permit Mr. Dunbar to testify about conditions inside the facility.

—Inside the prison, a bizarre search was under way in the vast labyrinth of catacombs under the cellblocks for eight prisoners believed by officials either murdered by fellow convicts or in hiding.

—A group of New York City lawyers and doctors turned up at the prison gates at 3 AM today, armed with a court order signed by U.S. District Judge John T. Curtin allowing them to interview and examine inmates.

They were refused admission, and the state attorney general's office will challenge the order in court today.

The group wants to assure no reprisals against rioters.

"At this stage," argued Asst. State Atty. Gen. Joseph J. Rocotta, "we are in no position to have people wandering around the prison."

William Kunstler, prisoners' counsel and a member of a group of citizens involved in negotiations before the police assault, was in the court this morning but made no representations.

—State Corrections Commissioner Russell G. Oswald, who ordered Monday's assault on the inmate-held prison said today that autopsies on bodies of hostages showed that two of them were killed before the assault by the police began.

Rain fell in Attica this morning, lending to the mood of deep mourning in the town.

Flags flew at half staff, and all schools were closed in observance of a day of mourning.

Mr. Fischer, special assistant state attorney general, remained inside the prison, where an official in Albany described his mission as one that will "adequately prepare for the proper prosecution of the responsible parties."

Workmen labored throughout the night trying to restore normal conditions to the battle scarred institution.

Maintenance men said they have repaired their own shop.

Civilian employees and guards walked quietly into the gates, still guarded by troopers carrying guns.

Most of the paperwork inside the prison concerned the transferring of prisoners to other facilities.

Owing to the riot damage, all of the prisoners—except those being processed for transfer—were being kept in their cells.

At 5:40 AM, a convoy of four buses rolled up to the back gate—an indication that more prisoners will be leaving.

Shortly before 10 AM, two of the buses rolled out of the facility, both carrying prisoners who flashed the peace signs to watching newsmen and police.

State troopers provided an armed escort at both the front and rear of the convoy.

The destination was not known. It's believed they will wind up in another of the state's facilities pending repairs to Attica.

Before noon today, three doctors from Buffalo's E. J. Meyer Memorial Hospital were admitted to the prison to help in the infirmary. But the New York City doctors, along with the lawyers who accompanied them, were denied admission and remained outside.

Dr. Eli Messinger, spokesman for the group of physicians, charged that the refusal to allow the doctors inside was a violation of concessions made to inmates during negotiations aimed at ending the riot.

William F. Hellerstein of the New York Legal Aid Society said the medical-legal group had obtained the order.

"Many of our clients are inmates," he said. "We are concerned about their physical condition and the adequacy of the treatment given them."

He said Judge Curtin's order forbids police and prison authorities from questioning prisoners about the riot.

Dr. Peter Schnall, one of 12 physicians in the group who is connected with Lincoln Hospital, in the Bronx, vigorously condemned Gov. Rockefeller for permitting Monday's assault.

"We want to treat inmates who have not yet been attended and we want to examine inmates who have not been hurt to document their conditions in case of further violence," he said.

■ THE ANIMALS AT ATTICA

Tom Wicker   *The New York Times,* September 16, 1971

Washington, Sept. 15—After the massacre at Attica, Governor Rockefeller issued a statement that began with this sentence:

"Our hearts go out to the families of the hostages who died at Attica."

Much of what went wrong at Attica—and of what is wrong at most other American prisons and "correction facilities"—can be found in the simple fact that neither in that sentence nor in any other did the Governor or any official extend a word of sympathy to the families of the dead prisoners.

True, at that time, it was thought that the deaths of the hostages had been caused by the prisoners, rather than—as is now known—by the bullets and buckshot of those ordered by the state authorities to go over the walls shooting.

But even had the prisoners, instead of the police, been the killers of the hostages, they still would have been human beings; certainly their mothers and wives and children still would have been human beings. But the official heart of the State of New York did not go out to any of them.

That is the root of the matter; prisoners, particularly black prisoners, in all too many cases are neither considered nor treated as human beings. And since they are not, neither are their families. Yesterday, the families of sixteen Attica inmates, gathered outside the medical examiner's office in Rochester, could not find out whether their husbands and sons were dead or alive; since last Thursday night they had not even been able to find out whether the men were involved in the prison rebellion, because the state would not trouble to tell them.

Dead hostages, for another example, were sent to the morgue tagged with their names; dead prisoners went tagged "P-1," "P-2," and so on. That is an almost unbearable fact to those who heard an eloquent prisoner shouting in the yard of D-Block last Friday night: "We no longer wish to be treated as statistics, as numbers. We want to be treated as human beings, we *will* be treated as human beings!" But even in death, they were still just numbers.

Time and again, members of the special observers' group that tried to negotiate a settlement at Attica heard the prisoners plead that they, too, were human beings and wanted above all to be treated as such. Once, in a negotiating session through a steel-barred gate that divided prisoner-held and state-held territory, Assistant Correction Commissioner Walter Dunbar told the prisoner leader, Richard Clark "in thirty years, I've never lied to an inmate."

"But how about to a man?" Clark said quietly.

The physical aspect of a place like Attica—the grim walls, the bare yards, the clanging steel—bespeaks the attitude that prisoners are wild animals to be caged. Entering a tier in Cellblock C, where prisoners were under control, the observers were struck by the pathetic sight of shaving mirrors popping instantly from the window of each steel door; the windows are too small for the cells' occupants to see anywhere but straight ahead, and only the mirrors can show the prisoners what is happening in their "home."

Attica—like most prisons—is not a "correctional facility" at all; the phrase is a gruesome euphemism. No "correctional officer" there has any real training in correcting or teaching or counseling men; rather, they are armed guards set to herd animals. Senselessly, every guard at Attica is white, save one reported Puerto Rican no observer ever saw; but the prisoners are 75 per cent, or maybe 85 per cent—no one seems to know for sure—black and Puerto Rican. There is no Spanish-speaking doctor. All work for 30 cents a day, and one of their grievances claimed that they often were bilked of that.

The emphasis on guns and clubs during the crisis was incredible; it had

yond was packed with so many men bearing clubs, rifles, pistols, and guns and tear-gas launchers. Three or four blocks from the prison, tourists were stopped at roadblocks by as many as four uniformed men, each carrying a club, a pistol, a rifle. So much weaponry was bound to be used sooner or later, and indiscriminately. And it was.

These guns, moreover, were in the hands of men who left no doubt they wanted to use them. Correction Commissioner Oswald's long delay of the assault and his efforts to negotiate were met with impatience and anger by the prison staff; the observers who were trying to prevent bloodshed saw hostility at every turn. A guard bringing them a box of food said as he put it down, "If I'd known it was for you people, I wouldn't have brought it."

The observers, after all, were standing between the men with the guns and the prisoners, who had none. Even the strong belief that an assault on the stronghold in Block D would cause the prisoners to kill their 38 hostages seemed to make little difference to those who had the guns; they wanted to go in.

The observers knew that. They said so to Commissioner Oswald and Governor Rockefeller, forcefully and in every way they could. They predicted a massacre. They said that waiting, while it might not ultimately prevent the slaughter, could hardly cause it; while attacking could result in nothing else.

But time is for men, not for prisoners and animals. Now the dead lie tagged in the morgue, and the men with the guns are counting their kill. They may even be looking forward to the same highly practical form of amnesty American society has already granted to the killers of Kent State and Orangeburg and Jackson State.

INDICT NELSON ROCKEFELLER AND RICHARD NIXON FOR FIRST DEGREE MURDER AT ATTICA STATE PRISON

Central Committee—Black Panther Party

Black Panther, September 18, 1971

The outright murder of more than 50 inmates and guards at Attica State prison on Monday, September 13, 1972, was conspired particularly and specifically by New York State Governor Nelson Rockefeller and U.S. President Richard M. Nixon. There is clear evidence of this fact in that the State's own correctional officers (guards, in the hands of the inmates) and the inmates themselves were shot to death with weapons belonging to nearly 1,700 National guards and State Police, sent in to do the killings. The vicious attack was ordered by and openly congratulated and supported by

Nelson Rockefeller and Richard M. Nixon. The dead guards and dead inmates were filled with holes from 12 gauge shotgun blasts and varying machine guns, rifle and pistol wounds, all the dead bodies having been mutilated by as many as 12 bullet or buckshot holes. Not one such type weapon was in the hands of any of the inmates.

The inhuman tactics of the attack were organized and carried out by a trained militia-man, formerly with the U.S. Army's counter-intelligence division in Washington, D.C., Captain Henry F. Williams of N.Y. State Police. Rockefeller, Nixon, Oswald, et al. willfully ignored all further negotiative guidance and conspired and ordered the murderous attack.

At the request of the inmates at Attica State Prison, Chairman Bobby Seale, of the Black Panther Party, entered the prison grounds on Saturday evening, September 11, 1971. Chairman Bobby explained to the prison brothers that he would leave the prison and return after consultation with other Central Committee members as to the exact nature of practical, political negotiating guidance that the Black Panther Party could and would lend, and that this required returning to the Party's Oakland Headquarters. The prisoners stated to Bobby that no guard would be killed or released, at least until his return with some practical negotiating guidance which the inmates could decide upon. That following Sunday morning, Chairman Bobby was denied permission to reenter the prison. At this point Russell G. Oswald (State Prison Corrections Commissioner) demanded that the Chairman beg the brothers compromise their position, as Oswald felt that Bobby would influence the prisoners greatly. When Chairman Bobby clearly stated that only the prisoners could make their own decisions and that he would not compromise their stance nor their lives, he was then not allowed reentry into the prison yard to again reassure the prisoners of his return.

Between 6 and 6:30 P.M. Sunday, September 12, 1971, Chairman Bobby, then in Oakland, called Commissioner Oswald to explain that the prisoners had stated that "no guard would be killed or released", until he returned with further negotiative guidance for the prisoners. Returning to Buffalo, New York early Monday morning (at approximately 9:00 A.M. to try again to get into the prison, Bobby Seale, Chairman of the Black Panther Party, heard of the vicious attack upon the prison, over the car radio news station, while on his way to the prison. Oswald had carried out his instructions as follows: Oswald delivered an ultimatum to the prisoners early that Monday morning. The prisoners asked for time, time to receive negotiating guidance from the Black Panther Party. With the full knowledge that Bobby was coming to the prison, Oswald slyly "granted" only twenty minutes, at which point he lied and said that helicopters hovering over the prison saw the brothers inside slit the throats of eight guards. Oswald then carried out the conspiring murderous instructions, on orders from Rockefeller and Nixon, and gave the word to attack, assault and kill.

The Black Panther Party, one with the peoples of the World's Communities, calls for the people, and particularly in the U.S., to come forth and bring an indictment of First Degree Murder and Conspiracy to Commit Murder against Governor Nelson Rockefeller of New York and also against the U.S. President, Richard M. Nixon, for the same, of First Degree Murder and Conspiracy to Commit Murder of over 50 prisoners and guards at Attica State prison, New York, on September 13, 1971.

Some people are in jail who ought not to be, and some aren't who should be, but the moral is not that inmates should be dealt with in the same equal-to-equal way as, say, rebellious students should be treated by college administrators. Convicts are not free men, though they are men, which is often dismissed as sentimentality. That having been said, the case for storming the Attica State prison in New York last Monday by 1300 troopers, leaving 42 dead, is far from proved. Governor Rockefeller hopes it will be, for he believes there was no alternative to the order and no fault to be found with the manner in which it was carried out; one wonders why he thinks an investigation is necessary. It is necessary, of course, because the public has been shaken by the tragedy.

We do not need to wait for an investigation to discover why Rockefeller and the prison officials thought they had to do what they did. They told us in too great detail, to their later regret, within hours of the shootings: rebellious inmates had replied to an ultimatum by holding weapons to the throats of hostages; later, reporters were informed, five guards were found dead in their own blood, slashed by convicts; one convict was felled by a police marksman's sniper bullet an instant before he could slice a guard's throat; two guards were killed "the day before" the attack (rigor mortis had already set in and one of them had been castrated and stabbed again and again). "At that point, there was no other decision I could have made," said Corrections Commissioner Russell G. Oswald, who personally ordered the attack. The inmates had "forced a confrontation and carried out coldblooded killings," Governor Rockefeller said. To put it mildly, the last statement proved to be an exaggeration, but in the wild first moments, the authorities may not have known the truth. At any rate, the medical examiner who subsequently autopsied the dead hostages found that all the guards died from multiple gunshot wounds, not slashed throats, though there were signs of beatings. None was stabbed, although one suffered a slight knife wound on the back of his neck. (According to the coroner's office, however, four inmates did have their throats slashed.) The guards' death wounds were caused by "buckshot and high caliber missiles," and if the prisoners had guns, they couldn't have done that damage. No guard had been mutilated. Furthermore, although Oswald said that negotiations became hopeless when one of the guards died after inmates had ruthlessly shoved him from a second-story window, he could not explain how that was accomplished since all the prison windows had bars.

The Attica uprising is important not only because it is one of the largest prison rebellions, but because the state immediately granted, under duress, 28 of 30 prisoner demands and admitted that the reforms were overdue. Commissioner Oswald now says that he had had reforms in mind for some time, which does not raise the dead. Here is another instance where it is made to seem that to make reforms you have to make revolts.

Still, it was not this or that reform that basically concerned the officials. From the start, they viewed the rebellion in larger terms. "It threatened the security of the entire correctional facility of the state," even "the destruction of our free society," Oswald argued. In the very broadest sense, that is conceivable, though it is the sort of claim, as Walter Lippmann once wrote, "by which a bit of truth seems so marvelous that it is made to embrace the universe." Specifically, the inmates demanded such things as "less pork," "more fresh fruit," a minimum wage in the workshops, better recreational facilities and medical care, a more humane and tolerable life *in prison.* They appear to have asked for an end to censorship of reading materials, but made an exception of materials prison officials might consider threatening to "internal security." That some of the leaders were "revolutionaries" needs documentation. Certainly these demands we have mentioned were not revolutionary and were in fact granted. The sticking point was elsewhere.

What *was* nonnegotiable in the opinion of the authorities was the demand for amnesty from legal punishment for acts committed during the takeover. We do not see how that could ever have been granted, though from the prisoners' point of view, amnesty was the key. For of what value is more fresh fruit to a man who may later be condemned to death for acts during the uprising? Governor Rockefeller holds the opinion that he had no constitutional authority to grant amnesty, and that if he had had, he would not have used it. The first is a statement of law, the second a prudential judgment. On the whole, we think the governor's position on this matter is sensible, and for this reason: if you grant blanket amnesty you are saying that prison riots—whatever injury they inflict—cost nothing to those responsible. No prison can be run on that theory, and bad as they are and better as they should be, prisons cannot be done away with.

Has society the right ever to use force to put down a prison rebellion? It does have that right. But was it a right that had to be exercised at Attica, and if so, when and how? Whether the result would have been much different had state troops seized the prison two hours after the rebellion or two days later than they did, no one knows. Nor can anyone be sure whether the state could have regained control of the prison without bloodshed by extending the negotiations, but it might have and a personal appearance by Governor Rockefeller could have contributed to this end. By responding favorably to the plea of both inmates and hostages that he come to Attica, the least Mr. Rockefeller would have gained was time—and that is what the negotiators were fighting for.

Even if one accepts the judgment that no further talks would have produced a settlement respectful of the legitimate demands of the inmates and the legitimate authority of the state to run the prison and hold inmates accountable for crimes, it does not follow that what was done was best calculated to restore order and authority at minimum injury. What was to be lost by waiting out the rebels, starving them out if necessary. Nor is it only the pretended wisdom of hindsight that suggests that armed police and troops might have moved in quickly, but before firing, ordered the rebels to surrender. This is not the way it is done in a John Wayne movie, or in Vietnam, but should it not have been tried at Attica?

The official assumption throughout has been that Attica represented a symbolic confrontation between law and lawlessness, with implications for the future of prison discipline throughout America—and indeed, with impli-

resignation, or make the daily life of prison guards (none of whom at Attica is black) more secure? We doubt it.

All these questions will be with us for a long time, unresolved. Serious crime rose 176 percent from 1960 to 1970, and today there are more in jail than live in Ft. Worth, Texas—about 400,000. Most of them are young, more and more of them black and desperate. Jails are not for nice people who can be entrusted to make their own rules, *à la* participatory democracy. But neither are prisoners animals to be caged, and that is how they are thought of and handled in many places. It is almost as if penal institutions were designed to confirm *society's* inhumanity; and it did not take the explosion at Attica to tell us that neither society nor the convicts are the beneficiaries of that.

◼ WHY U. S. PRISONS ARE EXPLODING

U.S. News and World Report, September 27, 1971

What is producing the turmoil in prisons that reached such a bloody climax in Attica? A new kind of problem prisoner? Racism? Permissiveness? Or faults in the penal system itself?

A tragedy at Attica, N. Y., has jolted this nation into a realization that it faces a crisis in its prisons.

For years, violence has been increasing inside the walls of the country's 4,500 penal institutions that house some 400,000 prisoners. Officials have warned of a growing danger.

On September 13, that danger exploded into the bloodiest prison clash of this century.

More than 1,000 State troopers and police—backed by hundreds of National Guardsmen—stormed the Attica State Correctional Facility where 1,200 rebelling inmates had held 38 guards as hostages for four days. When the shooting ended, 10 guards and at least 30 prisoners were dead or fatally wounded.

Shock waves spread fast and far.

Trouble flared at other penal institutions in several cities, including Baltimore, Atlanta, Cleveland and Great Meadow, N. Y.

The Federal Bureau of Investigation sent out warnings to all prison officials to be alert for prisoner uprisings.

In Detroit, a search spurred by this warning turned up more than 150 weapons in the jail.

Outside, as well, tension grew. There were demonstrations—mostly by blacks—in support of the slain prisoners.

William Kunstler, attorney for some Attica inmates and Black Panthers, called for massive public demonstrations at the nation's prisons on October 2.

SEARCH FOR CAUSES

Nationwide, worried citizens and officials discussed two main questions:

What is causing the explosion in American prisons?
And what should be done about it?

Answers varied widely. But on one thing nearly all agreed: The Attica tragedy dramatized a widespread need for action to improve the penal system.

"The U. S. system of corrections is a total national disgrace," declared Representative William R. Anderson (Dem.), of Tennessee.

Prison conditions are "almost universally deplorable" and have a "dehumanizing" effect, said Senator Edward W. Brooke (Rep.), of Massachusetts.

Far more than prison conditions are seen as contributing to the current wave of trouble, however.

"A new kind of problem prisoner" is now being found in U. S. prisons, says New York's State Commissioner of Corrections, Russell G. Oswald.

In this statement, made weeks before he became personally involved in the Attica revolt, Mr. Oswald was referring to black militants. He described them as "the most awesome challenge" he has faced in his long career in criminology.

"They have the idea they are victims of a racist society," he said.

BLACK MAJORITY

When Attica erupted, officials estimated at least 65 per cent of the rebelling inmates and 90 per cent of the rebel leaders were black. Many others were Puerto Ricans.

William D. Leeke, director of the South Carolina department of corrections and president of the American Association of State Correctional Administrators, told "U. S. News & World Report":

"Prisons today are dealing with a different type of offender than they received in previous years. Many have drug problems. Then there are those who consider themselves political prisoners, not criminals."

Norman A. Carlson, Director of the U. S. Bureau of Prisons, said:

"The prisons are housing a particularly volatile group of offenders. The courts tend to put the mild offenders on probation. What we end up with are more aggressive, more assaultive people who are not easy to rehabilitate."

Today's trouble in prisons "reflects the new revolutionary tactics of

"ORGANIZED REVOLUTIONARIES"

New York Governor Nelson Rockefeller blamed the Attica uprising on "highly organized revolutionary tactics of militants," and said "outside forces" appeared to have played a role.

"We're reaping a harvest of the cult of permissiveness," said Fred T. Wilkinson, director of the Missouri State department of corrections.

Winston E. Moore, a Negro who is superintendent of Cook County jail in Chicago, blamed "racist" practices and poor administration and said white administrators all over the country now "have no choice" but to face the "racial tension inside their institutions."

Newark's black mayor, Kenneth Gibson, said, "When we look at prison conditions and the brutal use of force at Attica we see the same face of racism which caused and then put down with force civil disturbances in this country's ghettos."

Senator Edmund S. Muskie of Maine, a leading contender for the Democratic nomination for President, told the National Governors' Conference in San Juan, Puerto Rico, that "the Attica tragedy is more stark proof that something is terribly wrong in America" and demonstrates that "we have reached the point where men would rather die than live another day in America."

ATTICA'S "CLASSIC" PATTERN

In the Attica prison there existed several of what penologists describe as classic ingredients for trouble: Its population is mostly black or Puerto Rican. Its guards are white. As a "maximum security" institution, it had been sent many "problem prisoners."

It was not overcrowded, however, with about 2,250 inmates and a capacity of 2,370. It had been considered one of New York's better penal institutions. Prisoners had recently won some demands. And Commissioner Oswald—with a reputation as a reformer—was preparing further changes. He had spent two days at Attica a week before the riot explaining the changes to the prisoners, and had promised to consider grievances not included in his reforms.

Mr. Oswald, however, never got the chance to carry out his plans before trouble broke out.

A possible spark was the placing of a prisoner in solitary confinement.

"LIKE CLOCKWORK"

Next morning shortly after breakfast on September 9, about 1,200 inmates took over a large part of the prison.

"It went off like clockwork," said one prison official. "They knew exactly what they were going to do."

They seized more than 40 guards and prison employes as hostages and presented a list of 15 demands—which they later increased to 30.

Unless the demands were granted, the rebels threatened, the hostages would be killed.

Among the demands were: better food, porkless meals for Black Muslims, better education and recreational programs, "complete religious freedom," and improved medical treatment.

In four days of negotiation, Commissioner Oswald agreed to 28 of the 30 demands.

Two demands, however, were rejected as being beyond the power of prison officials or even the Governor to grant.

Those demands were for complete amnesty from criminal prosecution and transportation out of the U. S. to a "non-imperialistic country."

At the demand of the rebels, outsiders were brought in for negotiations. The outsiders included: Black Panther leader Bobby Seale, Black Panther attorney Kunstler, a Black Muslim minister, a State assemblyman, and several newsmen, both black and white. Governor Rockefeller declined to participate.

David Anderson, one of the black leaders brought in to negotiate with the rebels, said the talks deteriorated after the arrival of Mr. Kunstler because he raised the inmates' hopes of amnesty.

Governor Rockefeller criticized the roles played by both Mr. Kunstler and Mr. Seale. He said Mr. Seale "made a very impassioned speech to the prisoners that they should not agree, but hold out for amnesty."

As negotiations dragged on, the rebels made weapons, such as spears, knives and clubs, and fortified their position by digging trenches in the courtyard and erecting barricades in hallways.

To show they meant business, rebels displayed hostages with knives held at their throats. One hostage was beaten early in the outbreak and died of head injuries. Most of the hostages, however, were treated pretty well—given food, blankets and mattresses. Some injured hostages were set free.

One hostage, who escaped alive, credited Black Muslims with saving the guards' lives, saying Black Panthers "were the ones who were ready to kill us, right from the beginning, and die in what they called their 'holy war.' "

THE BREAKING POINT

Finally, on Monday morning, September 13, officials decided that possibilities of fruitful negotiation had been exhausted and that further delay in action would only increase the danger.

Governor Rockefeller sent in National Guardsmen to aid the State troopers, police and deputy sheriffs. A force of some 1,700 was assembled.

Helicopters dropped tear gas into the crowded courtyard.

Rebels, sensing the end, assigned an "executioner" to each hostage, holding a knife to his throat. A few hostages were put in a gasoline-filled

"I don't have the heart to do it," hostage Elmer Hughen said the executioner" whispered to him.

After the tear gassing, marksmen from prison walls opened fire, trying to pick off the "executioners." Troopers, meanwhile, were battering their way into the courtyard.

The gunfire lasted only a few minutes. The rebels were overwhelmed, the 28 surviving hostages rescued.

There were conflicting accounts of how the hostages died.

Prison authorities at first said most of them had their throats slit. Next day, a medical examiner said nine of the hostages died of gunshot wounds, the other of physical injuries.

Governor Rockefeller said that hostages apparently had been caught in the gas-shrouded crossfire of the would-be rescuers. Officials said the hostages had been dressed in prison garb by their captors. Some officials continued to insist, however, that there was evidence of throat slashings.

In addition to the 40 dead, at least 29 were wounded, a few seriously.

ASSESSING THE BLAME

Controversy developed over the way authorities handled the situation. Critics maintained that officials should have continued to negotiate instead of turning to force.

Governor Rockefeller defended the storming of the prison, saying: "There was no alternative but to go in."

A survey by "The New York Times" showed prison chiefs in at least eight States upheld the use of force. Some said the assault should have come sooner.

"The longer you wait, the more problems you face," "The Times" was told by Harold J. Cardwell, warden of the Ohio Penitentiary.

WHAT'S WRONG?

Broader questions were raised, however, by what happened at Attica: What's wrong with American prisons? And what should be done to improve them so as to help prevent any such tragedy in the future?

Penologists stress the need for better prison facilities. Of the 464 State prisons and reformatories in this country, 61 were built before 1900. Many are overcrowded and understaffed.

"Most prisons and jails are convict-run," George J. Beto, director, Texas department of corrections, said in an address to the Governors' Conference.

Most prisons also are regarded by penal experts as too large—often housing several thousand convicts.

"In my opinion, none should have more than 500 to 600 inmates," said E. Preston Sharp, general secretary of the American Correctional Association.

Better educational and job-training programs are urged by almost all concerned with prison problems. Failure of prisons to reform criminals is evidenced by statistics showing that about 80 per cent of all felonies are committed by "repeaters."

The Federal Government and many States have increased their spending on penal institutions. And Congress is showing a growing interest in prison problems. A Senate subcommittee recently held hearings on bills to finance model correctional facilities.

The chairman of the subcommittee, Senator Quentin N. Burdick (Dem.), N. D., said:

> My strongest hope is that the tragedy of Attica will furnish added impetus to the continuing efforts being made by corrections officials to enhance rehabilitation of offenders, to increase the effectiveness of prison security, and to find and correct the causes of prison rebellion.

■ EXPLOITING ATTICA

National Review, October 8, 1971

Long before the last shot was fired the events at Attica had begun to be processed as revolutionary myth. Trace, for example, the movement of attorney William Kunstler, all over the place at Attica, and moving like quicksilver ever since. First of all, Kunstler's relationship to the militant prisoners reeks of ambiguity. At one point, well on in the scenario, he informed the prisoners that representatives of "Third World Nations" were waiting for them across the street. The inescapable inference to be drawn was that the prisoners might hope for some kind of "political" asylum, though Kunstler himself must have known this to be impossible. Still, the connection with the "Third World" is integral to the myth, as is the idea that the prisoners' status was "political," and Kunstler was striking the correct notes. Then David Anderson, former executive director of the Rochester Urban League, a Negro who spent seventeen hours in the prison as a member of the negotiating committee, has charged that the effect of Kunstler's oratory at a crucial moment was to encourage the prisoners' intransigence, and lead them to believe that they could expect total amnesty. Yet Kunstler throughout presented himself as the prisoners' friend and advocate. In reality, they were the raw material with which he was working.

Appearing next at the funeral of Sam Melville in Manhattan, Kunstler again "spoke." "I was probably the last person to see Sam alive," he told the mourners. "I can't remember what I said, but I can remember him saying to tell everyone 'I'm at peace with the world.' I put my arms around him and embraced him. Everyone felt the time had come. I looked back as we were leaving the block and I could still pick out Sam's determined face between those two black men." Once again there is a sense of ambiguity. Yes, this was a funeral oration; but, last year, Sam Melville was convicted of

tively, assimilated Attica to the revolutionary underground and to last year's bombings, the bomber himself, meanwhile, metamorphosing into a "determined" revolutionist, "at peace with the world."

At his next stop, Kunstler assimilated Attica to Mayday[1] and to the Vietnam protest movement generally. Speaking at the Manhattan offices of the People's Coalition for Peace and Justice, Kunstler and Dave Dellinger[2] called for demonstrations over Attica in Albany and Washington. Kunstler, a lawyer, accused Governor Rockefeller and—by implication—President Nixon of "murder" and demanded that both be "punished." Antiwar demonstrators outside Rockefeller's office completed the equation. As the *Times* reported: "They denounced the Governor's role in the assault on the prison, and also President Nixon's failure to accept the Communists' proposals at the talks in Paris."

Like Kunstler, Tom Wicker, fresh from his eulogies of George Jackson, used Attica as an opportunity to display his own familiar set of equations. Attica was like Chicago in '68, like Kent State, like My Lai, like the handling of campus rebellions. In a vintage metaphor, he even ran the equation backward, speaking of "the lockstep education of the four-year university." Prison equals campus equals prison, all in "lockstep." His gravamen: American society is the Bastille. Wicker's hymns of rage were relentless, his metaphorical exploitation of Attica ecstatic. His book on Attica will no doubt appear, well, tomorrow, and we can hardly wait.

As might be expected, the reality at Attica does not exactly coincide with these mythologizations, and, while we still can do so, it is useful to keep hold of that reality. According to inmate testimony, for example, only some two hundred of the twelve hundred men involved in the events at Cellblock D actually supported the insurrection. "Two hundred men with pipes and things like that," one man said, "can control an awful lot of people when you're unarmed." The two hundred militants are more interesting—and useful—to the mythologizers than that reluctant majority. To the mythologizers, militants were paragons of gentleness and restraint. But what, then, are we to make of the three prisoners found stabbed to death, apparently in some sort of intramural fracas? (These bodies, all whites, seem to be the basis for the early throat-cutting reports.) The ready depiction of the authorities as monsters of arrogant brutality by Wicker, Kunstler, and the rest of the militants' constituency outside is contradicted by the problematical character of each crucial action. Who knows, really, whether Commissioner Oswald should have negotiated or not? Whether Rockefeller should have turned up? Whether the assault should have been sooner or later? Whether greater tactical restraint would have produced more dead or more live hostages? The problematical reality at each point fails to mesh with the revolutionary melodrama so useful to Wicker, Kunstler and the rest.

[1] Mayday is the occasion for international celebrations of the Communist Party and, more recently, for antiwar demonstrations.

[2] Dave Dellinger is a prominent activist who was an organizer of the 1968 Chicago demonstrations.

The myth also has potency inside the prison walls. Though we do not know what percentage of inmates now regard themselves as revolutionaries, the fact of politicization and the spread of revolutionary rhetoric is evident enough. Sam Melville, for example, was one contributor to a clandestine prison newsletter called "Eye of the Pig" which spread the message that "everyone here is a political prisoner, no matter how heinous the crime you were convicted of . . ." A stream of radical lawyers, many of them young and operating out of "legal collectives," proselytizes throughout the prison system. The revolutionary rationale, both justifying every crime and providing a sense of imaginative solidarity with the movement outside the walls, necessarily finds inmates receptive. The prisoners provide the movement with a new and malleable constituency. "Extreme radicalism is spreading," said New York City Correction Commissioner George McGrath, "and we have to expect more of it."

◼ POINTS TO CONSIDER

1. What determines the way in which a particular publication chooses to cover an event? What determines the picture which each publication in this section chooses to paint of the conflict at Attica? Do you know some newspapers or magazines whose coverage of particular events you can guess even before you read them?

2. Although the conflict at Attica Prison was not political in the usual sense, do you find evidences of political bias in some of the news coverage included in this section? In which pieces is the political bias especially strong? Can you find other subtler instances of political opinion influencing journalism? From reading the different accounts of the Attica conflict presented by the various publications in this section, can you make any educated guesses about the views held by each of these publications on other social or political issues?

3. In what ways are facts "slanted" in each of the articles? (See Duane Bradley, "What Is News?" page 95.) What discrepancies do you find in the reporting of the "facts" of the event? How do you account for these discrepancies?

4. Judging from the coverage included in this section, do you feel that the press did an adequate job in reporting this event? Do you feel that there are important gaps in the information provided or serious questions left unposed or unanswered? Explain.

5. What various journalistic approaches are represented in these selections, for example: eyewitness reporting, interviewing, quoting, analysis, projection? What various journalistic styles are represented in these selections, for example: businesslike, philosophical, intellectual, confrontative, sarcastic, emotive, detached, involved? How do these different approaches and styles contribute to your understanding of the event and its significance or to your own feelings about the event and its significance?

THIS WE REMEMBER/THE PICTURES THAT MAKE VIETNAM UNFORGETTABLE

John G. Morris   *Harper's Magazine*, September 1972

I remember clearly the night in early May, 1954, when I placed a call to Robert Capa in Tokyo from my home in Armonk, New York. *Life* magazine had asked him to pinch-hit for Howard Socharek covering the war in Indochina. As his editor-agent at Magnum Photos, it was up to me to make the deal. I had deep misgivings, recalling his many close calls of World War II, some of which we had shared.

"Don't think you *have* to go," I practically shouted across the Pacific. "It's not *our* war." But off he went. A fortnight later, while photographing a French army convoy making its way through the rice paddies southwest of Hanoi, he stepped on a land mine. He had called his last, self-assigned picture story, "Bitter Rice."

Robert Capa's death inspired obituary photo-essays in the world's picture magazines, his final pictures framed in the sprocket-holed margins of the film. We buried him in the old Quaker cemetery in Amawalk, New York. Few photographers know the spot, nor would Capa care, but when his huge French army coffin was placed in that hillside, it marked the unrecognized rebirth of one of the noblest, strangest—and perhaps most naive—crusades in the history of journalism: to end war by showing its true and terrible image.

Capa's last frame (Robert Capa/Magnum).

The crusade had begun in World War II with Edward Steichen, whose duty as a reconnaissance photographer in World War I had ended with revulsion—"How could men and nations have been so stupid?" After Pearl Harbor he became convinced that "if a real image of war could be photographed and presented to the world, it might make a contribution toward ending the specter of war."

Age sixty-seven, he volunteered for the U.S. Navy, formed the "Steichen group" of photographers, and finally took charge of all Navy combat photography. It may seem an odd enterprise for the man who also fathered "The Family of Man," but Steichen has never acknowledged any contradiction.

But World War II was a war in which one could somehow believe. *They* were the bad guys and *we* were the good guys and there was no sensation quite like that of riding the first jeep into a freshly liberated village and being showered with kisses, roses, and wine. The only guilt one felt, as a noncombatant photographer or reporter, was that others were doing your fighting for you. Or as Gerda Taro, the German photographer who was Capa's first love, said in Spain: "You get an absurd feeling that somehow it's unfair still to be alive." (Two days later she was dead, crushed by a tank.)

World War II was the still photographer's war. There were the twice-weekly newsreels, but the image of war that came into the home was carried by newspapers and magazines. It was the decade before television. News photographers captured the public's imagination. Only the syndicated columnists like Ernie Pyle, the radio commentators like Ed Murrow, and perhaps the guys from *Yank* and *Stars & Stripes*[1] (like Bill Mauldin) equaled them in prestige.

Yet the photographer in World War II, while scarcely realizing it, lived by the rules, written and implied. He cooperated fully with the censors. His pictures did not show unit designations, new weapons, camouflaged factories, or gun emplacements; if they did, they were retouched. The faces of the severely wounded and the dead were taboo, so the "next of kin" would not be offended. Finally, and this is crucial to an understanding of the formulation of public opinion at long range, the photographer did not show *his* side being ghastly. I recall the candor of the British censor through whom I attempted to pass some victims in Berlin. "Very interesting," he said. "You may have them after war."

The standard operating procedure established by WW II was to show *our* side fighting cleanly—bombs away in the brilliant sunshine of daring daylight raids. We could show a certain amount of suffering from *their* wanton attacks, but never so much as to lead to despair.

Photographically, their side lived by similar rules. You will never find a picture of Hitler inspecting the gas ovens of a concentration camp. And the Japanese were not shown pictures of the men they maimed at Pearl Harbor; they saw the spectacle of their victory from the air. Just as we gave our people the beautiful mushroom cloud over Hiroshima.

The result, intentional or not, glorified the war. The photographer's image was only selectively the true image, for his work, like the war itself, was largely intended to serve a higher purpose.

[1] *Yank* and *Stars & Stripes* were published by the United States Army.

Combat medical station (Larry Burrows/*Life*).

Capa had said he hoped "to become an unemployed war photographer," and he did, momentarily. Magnum Photos had been founded in the spring of 1947 as an international photographers' cooperative, with Capa its mainspring and Henri Cartier-Bresson of France, George Rodger of England, and David ("Chim") Seymour, a Polish-American, its principal cofounders. They decided to divvy up the world photographically. In this spirit, Capa went off to Russia with John Steinbeck, and he and other Magnum photographers undertook a worldwide assignment from the *Ladies' Home Journal* called, "People Are People the World Over." It made a deep impression on Edward Steichen and was to foreshadow the Family of Man exhibition.

But a new war—and a new kind of war—was booming. Korea, literally a cold war, marked the watershed among wars of this century. It ended not in victory but in truce its hero recalled from his command. It divided that country on an artificial boundary and by ideology; it divided the intellectual community and world opinion.

It also produced a change in the style and depth of combat photography. *Life* sent the old war horses: Carl Mydans, Margaret Bourke-White, and David Douglas Duncan (who had been a Marine photographer in World War II), along with the younger Hank Walker and John Dominis. They soon found themselves shooting a twofold tragedy: the story of American servicemen fighting a war they did not comprehend, and a people torn asunder, brother against brother.

Duncan maintains that Korea was a "good" war in that we were fighting side by side with Koreans in their defense against aggression. He recalls his picture of a wounded American being carried to safety by a Korean peasant. Carl Mydans likewise tells stories of blood brotherhood under fire between Korean and GI.

Saigon briefing (Philip Jones Griffiths/Magnum).

But the one-sided censorship of World War II broke down in Korea. European photographers tended not to see the war so ideologically. Magnum's great Swiss photographer, Werner Bischof, saw it as stark human tragedy. A team from England's *Picture Post* showed the brutality of South Korean troops so shockingly that *Picture Post*'s editor, Tom Hopkinson, was forced to resign (the British Establishment sided with the U.S.-U.N. effort). Margaret Bourke-White provided the war's summary statement in a *Life* essay on a divided Korean family that became one of the classics of photojournalism.

Duncan, asking *Life*'s editors to throw away the captions and let the pictures tell it, joined his Marine buddies in the frigid retreat from the 1950 Chinese offensive and pronounced, in "Christmas in Korea," a pictorial epitaph on the war.

Going on to Vietnam in 1953, Duncan was shocked to find an old-fashioned colonial war in progress—Foreign Legion, buglers, and all. "It was now nearly over. The cause was bankrupt from the start." His report in *Life* upset the State Department of John Foster Dulles, and Duncan was later personally chewed out by his big boss, Henry R. Luce. Whether or not Duncan's exposé had any influence on Washington's decisions *not* to rescue the French from disaster the following spring is not known. But his pictures, and those of Howard Sochurek, clearly revealed the moral bankruptcy of the French regime.

Neither Duncan nor Sochurek was at Dienbienphu when it fell on May 9, 1954. Robert Capa was not there either; he arrived in Hanoi a few days later.

As I came into my house on the night of May 25, 1954, the phone was ringing. The day had begun with dreadful news. I had been awakened in a little hotel where I was attending the University of Missouri's photographic workshop, to hear that Werner Bischof had been found dead on assignment in Peru. His station wagon had gone over a cliff. His wife, back in Zurich, was expecting a child at any moment. It was too much, and we decided to

Field interrogation (Sean Flynn/UPI).

try to suppress the news until she was safely delivered. I hurried back to New York by plane and then home.

The voice on the phone was that of a *Life* researcher, and she sounded distraught. She apologized, "I have to ask you some painful questions. . . ." So they knew. I said, "Yes, I've heard the news." And she began asking about Capa! I couldn't believe it. Capa! He was dead too! We were like brothers, the three of us.

"The diplomats at Geneva," reported *Life* in 1954, "signed a paper that forfeited almost everything the soldiers fought for." The U.S. did not sign, but pledged to support the Geneva accords—then promptly proceeded to sabotage them. For documentation see the Pentagon Papers. The press paid scant attention. During the remaining six years of the Eisenhower term there were no resident Western press photographers in Vietnam, North or South. The action was elsewhere: the Suez, Hungary, Algeria, Berlin, Cuba, the Congo.

The glamorous young Kennedy Administration further diverted the attention of press photographers, almost to the point of euphoria. It was the

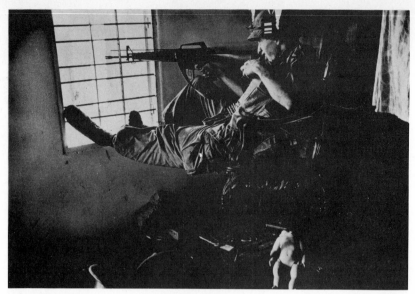

Tet offensive (Philip Jones Griffiths/Magnum).

slow-moving *National Geographic* that first caught a picture of an American soldier ready for combat, only to have the State Department talk the editors out of using it. The story, showing only the Vietnamese doing the fighting, was entitled, "Fighting the Red Tide." No war had been declared, but by late 1961 the first American serviceman, James T. Davis of Livingston, Tennessee, was killed—the first of 45,806 as this article goes to press. Unfortunately, there was no picture coverage.

Finally the situation was too big to be ignored, and the wire services beefed up their bureaus with first-rate men. Malcolm Browne came for Associated Press in November 1961, Neil Sheehan for United Press International in April 1962. On February 27, 1962, the AP transmitted its first Saigon news picture by radio. It showed an attack on Diem's Presidential palace during an abortive coup and was taken by Yuichi ("Jackson") Ishizaki, an AP stringer still working in Vietnam.

Then in June 1962 along came Horst Faas, the burly AP photographer who has put his stamp on press photography in Vietnam to this day, winning two Pulitzer Prizes and the grudging admiration of his colleagues. Born in troubled Berlin in 1933, Faas came to Saigon after covering the brutal civil wars in Algeria and the Congo. With odd detachment, he was able to photograph many scenes that would make many men turn away: a withered old woman clutching the body of a dead baby burned by napalm; a wounded Vietnamese ranger, blood trickling from his mouth, staring glassy-eyed. Faas looked war straight in the face.

While there was no censorship, the few correspondents who probed deeply were smeared as unpatriotic by the Administration and as downright enemies by the Vietnamese. François Sully of *Newsweek* was expelled for more than a year. President Kennedy tried to get the *New York Times* to recall David Halberstam.

Back home, editors were slow to realize the depth of feeling on all sides—and particularly the political complexity of the situation. When, in 1963, Malcolm Browne photographed a protesting Buddhist monk in the act of self-immolation in Saigon, it shocked many people. A great many newspapers, following the example of the *New York Times,* whose editors thought it "unfit for the breakfast table," suppressed the picture or played it down. "An editor who didn't run that picture wouldn't have run a story on the Crucifixion," frothed the late "Casey" Jones, editor of the Syracuse newspapers.

Many atrocity pictures revealing the brutal nature of the war were available in the early Sixties. Editors for the most part ignored them as "isolated incidents." Dickey Chapelle, the courageous ex-Quaker who became a gung-ho combat photographer (and later paid the price with her life), took a shocking picture of a Vietcong prisoner about to be executed by his captor, a South Vietnamese soldier standing over him with drawn gun. That was in early 1962. It was published only in an obscure little magazine.

Yet when Eddie Adams of AP, six years later, came up with his picture of the South Vietnamese national police chief shooting a prisoner on a Saigon street, it got front-page play, in New York and around the world. The *Times* had changed.

Meanwhile, a half-million U.S. troops had been committed to the unsavory war.

Street execution (Eddie Adams/AP).

Breakdown (Larry Burrows/*Life*).

Life bears a special responsibility, for better and for worse, in picture coverage of the Vietnam war. No other publication has tried so hard, going back to Capa's time. The roster of photographers who have covered it for them is remarkable: Duncan, Capa, Akihiko Okamura, Sochurek, Dominis, Burk Uzzle, Catherine Leroy, John Olson, Mark Godfrey, Co Rentmeeister, Vernon Merritt III, David Burnett. And Larry Burrows, who came to Vietnam in 1962—and will remain, somewhere, in Laos.

It was Thursday morning, June 8, 1944, in the London office of *Life* on Dean Street in Soho. Larry Burrows, a skinny, bespectacled darkroom boy of eighteen, had just finished fifty-two consecutive hours of work to get out the coverage of D-Day by Robert Capa and six other photographers. I persuaded him to come home with me, to the flat I shared with Frank Scherschel on Upper Wimpole Street, for a few hours' rest. Larry was in London on leave, since he had been drafted to work in the coal mines. ("Won't be much different from the darkroom," he had said when he got his notice, to conceal his disappointment at not being called to the Royal Navy.)

Scherschel was away, flying with the Air Force over Normandy. His big bed was empty. "You take it, Larry," I said.

"No, can't do that," Larry replied, and lay down on the floor.

With such humility, Larry Burrows was not going to tell *Life* what to say about the Vietnam war. He was content to show it. Who will ever forget his story of the Marine who broke down and cried, or of the little war cripple's return to his village, or of the Vietcong prisoners roped together, or of the grisly body count published in sickly color?

But, unfortunately, *Life* missed Burrows' point. After the Tonkin Gulf incident, *Life* carried a picture spread headed, "Heroes of the Gulf of Ton-

veterans."

It is so easy to side with the soldier. After all, *he* is not really responsible, exactly, and it's very difficult to be a photographer on his side and not side with his side.

This is the trap that I feel most war correspondents have fallen into, one time or another. Take Dave Duncan, who was recently in New York again with his exhibition and his books, including the two anti-Vietnam books, *I Protest!* and *War without Heroes.* Antiwar? They are and they aren't. Duncan has such compassion for the fighting man that his books, if one looks at and does not read them, satisfy the hawk as much as the dove.

Duncan's dilemma—and it is not unlike that of Eddie Adams and the late Henri Huet of AP, the late Kyoichi Sawada of UPI, John Olson of *Life,* and many other antiwar war photographers—was revealed when he attacked the Mylai massacre photographs taken by Ron Haeberle. They were technically poor photographs, and by themselves did not *prove* the atrocity (they show bodies in a ditch, but not the cause of death). But they corroborated the massacre, and as such they must rank with the most awful documents of this or any war.

FirstCav casualties (Henri Huet).

Refugees fording river. (Kyoichi Sawada/UPI).

Removing VC corpse (Kyoichi Sawada/UPI).

Duncan challenged Haeberle—in fact he tried to persuade the *Plain Dealer*[2] that night, since he happened to be in Cleveland and saw them running in the first edition—that the pictures were false. Duncan just could not believe this atrocity—of *any* U.S. servicemen. But finally, months later in a face-to-face confrontation with Haeberle at one of Cornell Capa's "Concerned Photographer" seminars at New York University, Duncan admitted that the pictures were real.

[2] The Cleveland *Plain Dealer*.

Mylai victims (R. L. Haeberle/*Life*).

Seymour Hersh, the reporter who won a Pulitzer by digging out the Mylai scandal, has said in the *Columbia Journalism Review* that in order to drive the story home, "television was needed—somehow just relying on newspapers to sear the conscience of America hadn't been working, or working too slowly."

But is television the answer? Hersh referred to the CBS interview with Paul Meadlo, in which Meadlo confessed to his part in the massacre. But the fact that Meadlo goes scot-free (albeit for good legal reasons), and that public sympathy seems to lie on the side of Lieutenant Calley, makes one wonder if the public's daily diet of televised war coverage has increased public understanding of the Vietnam war to any noticeable degree. Perhaps we have image fatigue?

A recent incident is enlightening. On June 8 a South Vietnamese plane accidentally dropped napalm on Vietnamese civilians near Anloc. Cameramen, both still and movie, were nearby. They caught the falling bombs and the screams of those burned as they fled the scene, including one little girl who tore her burning clothes off as she ran toward the cameras.

The resulting pictures were shown by the networks and ran on front pages of most newspapers. *Both* were effective. But it was the still picture that fixed the image, that called forth the editorials, that will stick in memories. In such moments it is the film that builds the emotional impression, but the still that remains forever. They complement and should not quarrel.

Accidental napalming (Nick UTT/AP).

"A military expert, to paraphrase, is one who carefully avoids all the small errors as he sweeps on to the grand fallacy." Thus wrote Laurence Stallings, not about Secretary of Defense McNamara but in his photographic history of *The First World War*.

Sadly, the same is true of the daily press—with exceptions. The daily lies should have been apparent. They were obfuscated in the net of Pentagon press agentry, cast so effectively over those young and naive photographers who thought of each day as a separate story. The outrageous paradoxes created by such immediate vision have been fully documented in a 1967 collection of photographs published under the title *And/or, Antonyms for Our Age.*

Thus it has remained to photographers who did *not* have to meet the deadlines of daily journalism to produce the strongest statements about the interminable war. Among them:

Akihiko Okamura, the Mainichi photographer whose book *This Is War in Vietnam* was the earliest (1966) full statement of the brutality of the war. Oddly, *Life* published his work as a color essay without fully realizing what it meant.

Philip Jones Griffiths, a Welshman whose *Vietnam, Inc.* is an all-out indictment of the American role in the war. Jones Griffiths is self-righteously strident in his condemnation of all things having to do with the U.S.—but while he may sometimes be sloppy in fact he is acute in principle.

Marc Riboud, a Magnum Frenchman (Magnum is almost above nationality) whose *Face of North Vietnam* subtly conveys the other side by understatement—the quiet dedication to nationalism (first) and socialism (second) that has somehow escaped American makers of policy.

Mark Jury, who went to Vietnam as just another GI and returned with a remarkable photographic diary, *Vietnam Photo Book,* showing Vietnam "like it is" to the soldier. Sample exchange: " 'Hello there, I'm Dr. Norman Vincent Peale from New York.' The trooper replied, 'Glad to meet you, sir, but I'm happy with the doctor I have now.' "

Don McCullin, a Londoner whose statement is not a book but a Scholastic filmstrip. McCullin kept asking himself *why* he was in Vietnam (after risking his life in Cyprus and Biafra). He repeatedly questions: "I've spoken to too many dead men. . . . Who needs fresh pictures? . . . Is anybody taking any notice?"

Who knows. The war goes on. A friend of Larry Burrows, learning of his death in Laos, said, "The tragedy is not that Larry died. The tragedy is that Larry died talking to the deaf."

Perhaps the world is deaf. Perhaps the world is also blind—to Burrows' pictures and to all the others. Conceivably, the crusade has been its own undoing. No matter how powerful the images of war these photographers have captured, our fascination tends to outweigh our horror. Photography provides insulation along with access. Pictures don't carry the odor. War stinks. There is nothing worse than the stench of the unburied dead. If that smell could only somehow accompany the images. . . .

Warscape, 1968 (Philip Jones Griffiths/Magnum).

POINTS TO CONSIDER

1. What is the crusade the author mentions? What role does photography have in it?

2. What differences does the article make apparent between the attitudes photographers had toward World War II and the Vietnam war? What differences between the two wars does the author describe with regard to censorship and the suppression of individual photographs?

3. What reasons do you think the author has for mentioning the deaths of so many war photographers?

4. What trap does the author believe that most combat photographers fall into?

5. What does the author have to say concerning the relative effectiveness of movies and still photographs in the crusade? What importance does he give to television?

6. In what way does the author feel the crusade might have been its own undoing? What is your feeling?

7. What does the author mean when he says, "Photography provides insulation along with access"? Do you agree? Is this also true for television?

8. What is the principal effect which each of the photos has upon you? How, in each case, does the photographer use some of the artistic means discussed in the Rissover article (page 319) to heighten the effect?

9. Do you think that the photos in this article make their "messages" sufficiently clear without captions or explanations?

■ PHOTOJOURNALISM

By permission of Richards Rosen Press.

Photograph by Ralph Crane. *Life* Magazine, © Time, Inc.

Photograph by James Foote. Photo Researchers, Inc.

Stanley J. Forman/*Boston Herald American*

Stanley J. Forman/*Boston Herald American*

Photograph by Leo L. Chabot.

Sports Illustrated photo by Herb Scharfman. © Time, Inc.

■ POINTS TO CONSIDER

1. What is the principal effect which each of the photos has upon you? Can you observe some examples of the photographers' having employed any of the artistic means discussed in the Rissover article (page 319) to heighten the effects?

2. Some people feel that good examples of photojournalism really require no captions. Do you think that the preceding photos make their "messages" sufficiently clear without captions or explanations?

3. What kinds of news items are best presented in photos, and what kinds are best presented in words? What can photos "say" that words cannot? What can words say that photos cannot?

4. Under what circumstances do you feel that film can present a news item better than a still photo can? When can a still photo be more effective than film?

YOU'LL LAUGH! YOU'LL CRY! YOU'LL WATCH THEM DIE!

Michael Arlen   *Playboy*, May 1972

Les Midgley, who is the executive producer of the *CBS Evening News* and therefore the man operably responsible for what 20,000,000 Americans watch as news each evening, six days a week, 52 weeks a year, is seated at the desk in his office, which is on the ground floor of the CBS News Building on West 57th Street in New York. The CBS News Building, one should say, is not much of a building as buildings go these days, certainly nothing like the CBS setup in Los Angeles nor the austere and meticulous, plant- and Brancusi-filled CBS Building that Frank Stanton[1] has erected on Sixth Avenue. From the outside, it is a nondescript three-story rectangle of red brick—a warehouse, perhaps, or an Eisenhower post office. Inside—well, it's clearly not a post office. Guards. Endless narrow corridors. Small offices. Large rooms full of teletypes, desks, typewriters, men in shirt sleeves. A room full of tape machines. Banks of tape machines. Television screens. The CBS News people take pleasure in that they are not in Mr. Stanton's building, in that they are over here on the wrong side of Ninth Avenue, in a warehouse of a building, in their shirt sleeves, putting out an electronic evening newspaper.

On the other side of the glass in Midgley's office is the newsroom where the Cronkite show is done—a real newsroom, real desks, real people working at the desks. "We don't use a studio like NBC," says one of the CBS people. The time is four o'clock in the afternoon. A November day; 1971. There are six desks in the room, ordinary gray metal desks, bunched together into three rows. In the far row, two men sit typing. The man in the red shirt is the chief national news writer. The man in the beard writes the foreign news. On the near side, one man, who seems to be in his early 20s, is holding a phone to his ear and typing at the same time. The man behind him is also typing. At the front desk in the middle row sits Walter Cronkite. He has a pile of copy in front of him. His lips move as he intones the copy in a low voice. He holds a stop watch in his hand. He pauses in his reading, scribbles corrections. Men in shirt sleeves pass in and out of the room. Girls with clipboards. Engineers. Inside Midgley's office, the Boston tape is over, although *Gomer Pyle* is still running silently on the top two screens.

"You can take out Henagan," says Midgley. "He doesn't make any sense."

Stan Gould, associate producer, is writing on his clipboard. "I can use the priest," he says.

"The priest doesn't make any sense, either," says Sandy Socolow, who is Midgley's assistant, a youngish, plump man in glasses and a suit.

"It may be understandable in Boston, but not here," says Midgley. "What do you have down for it?"

---

[1] Frank Stanton was, at the time this article was written, president of CBS.

A couple of minutes," says Gould.

A man runs into the office. "No audio from Atlanta."

A phone rings. Socolow picks it up. "Have you seen your film? Well, was it good, bad or indifferent?"

Midgley is listening in on the other phone. "Are you positive he was *there?*" he asks.

Socolow says, "OK, what kind of production problems are you going to give us? It's a self-contained run of track."

"No Shakne fore and aft," says Midgley.

"No Shakne," says Socolow.

Gould is on his way out of the office. "It's an R-three," says Socolow to Gould.

A girl in a black pants suit comes in, leaves the latest revised line-up for the evening: *1. Open; 2. Cronkite . . . live; 3. Ft. McPherson / Medina / Morton . . . VTR . . . 3.00 Atlanta; 4. Cronkite . . . live; 5. First commercial (Absorbine and Pontiac) . . . VTR 8 . . . 1.05; 6. Cronkite . . . live; 7. Washington / Living costs / Benton . . . Washington . . . 1.45—*

In the newsroom, some kind of flurry is going on. Cronkite is standing. The man in the red shirt and one of the other writers are standing at his desk. "Goddamn it, get on the phone and find out," Cronkite is saying.

Ron Vonn, another associate producer, steps into Midgley's office. Midgley is sipping a milk shake from a paper cup. He looks up. "I talked to Bruce Morton. He'll give us voice-over at the end of the trial." Vonn leaves.

Socolow says, "Threlkeld's on two-forty-six." Then, "Let me caution you, Mr. Midgley. Ron is going to run over."

Midgley picks up the phone. "Ron, is there anything that's going to raise a question of taste with us? Is there any problem with the mother or the children?" He nods and puts the phone down. "Two-thirty?" he says to Socolow.

"We have him down for three o'clock." says Socolow.

"OK, two-forty-five. We'll split the difference."

Vonn comes back in. "It doesn't look like the logistics are against us on jurors." Midgley reaches for a switch on his desk. The lower TV screen lights up.

Bruce Morton is leaning against a railing, looking at the ground. He looks up. "I'm ready whenever you are," he says with some impatience. "Well, what's the matter?" he says. "Bullshit," he says.

One of the writers comes in from the newsroom. "When are we going to hear from Kalb?" he asks.

"Kalb is supposed to call in by six," says Midgley. Out in the newsroom, Cronkite is standing talking, or apparently arguing, with Socolow.

Socolow comes back to Midgley. "It's the 'secret meeting' on Kalb's file. He says we have to have more on it or we ought to skip it until we do."

"I don't blame him," says Midgley. He picks up a phone "Try to get me Marvin Kalb in Washington," he says.

To get to the taping room, you walk out of Midgley's office, past the newsroom, down a corridor, through a door marked NO ADMITTANCE, past a secretary, past another NO ADMITTANCE door and into a large room filled with banks of machines. They are very much the new machines, our new 20th

Century machines—no rows of seamstresses and sewing machines, no looms, no great clanking wheels, iron, pistons, ugly things. These are trim, spare, rectilinear. Taller than a man. Gray and white. Now and then, a small red or green light. Dials. Oscilloscope screens. It is a large room, maybe 80′ × 80′. There are about 20 of these machines. In rows. At each of them, on a small swivel stool, sits an operator. Above his head, on the machine, a large roll of tape is unwinding. The dials read, COLOR HOLD . . . GREEN GAIN . . . BLUE GAIN . . . V HOLD . . . V SIZE . . . RED . . . PLAYBACK CONTROL . . . BLUE. The operator throws a switch. The tape roll moves in the opposite direction. On a TV screen in the machine, the face of F. Lee Bailey appears, talking into a microphone.

"More," says Vonn. Bailey is making a speech, although it's hard to hear his voice on the machine because of all the other machines. Behind Vonn, Gould is standing beside another machine, watching Henagan in Boston. "OK," says Vonn. The operator stops the tape. Bailey is still there on the screen in midsentence. Another man is beside him at the microphone. "I want to use the Morton audio bridge to get to where *this* guy starts to talk," Vonn says. "I want to take it from where Bailey goes over to this man and then cut to this close-up." The tape operator throws a switch, the tape spins backward, the voices making a kind of speeded-up Disney-cartoon sound. Then forward: Bailey walking to the microphone, speaking, arm extended. Stop, backward. Forward. Backward. Vonn stands behind the operator.

Somebody comes by. "Are we going with the San Francisco stuff?"

"I don't know," says Vonn. "We're going to see it at six."

A phone rings. Gould picks it up. Listens. Puts it down. "San Francisco won't be ready until six-fifteen," he says.

"What about Boston?" says Vonn.

"How do I know?" says Gould. "I don't see how they have time for it, but I'm going to get it ready until they tell me to dump it."

The operator at Vonn's machine has the tape positioned at the point where Bailey is extending his arm toward the man on the left. "There?"

Vonn looks. "Back it off twelve seconds and we'll lay video only for that."

Bailey's voice comes up: *"I've never gotten an acquittal for a nicer guy. . . ."*

"OK," Vonn says. "Now I want the cut to the head to come in right. OK?"

On Gould's machine, Boston school children are running down a street. On the machine next to him, Chinese soldiers are marching in a parade.

On another bank, Muhammad Ali is speaking at a press conference. "I've never felt better," he says against the sound of the Chinese military band.

"I don't *care* if we don't hear Bailey talking," says Vonn.

At six o'clock the face of Jim Jensen, the local CBS newsman, appears on the top screen; an NBC man appears on the second screen—both without audio. On the lower screen, Midgley and Socolow are watching Bob Shakne interview a convict recently released from Attica.

"What bothers me," says Socolow, "is the guy coming out so strong, saying he was in the uprising."

Vonn sticks his head in the door. "What about San Francisco?"

Midgley says to Socolow, "You're in great shape. Relax." To Vonn, "They're putting in the last San Francisco splices."

"Jesus," says Vonn.

Midgley says to Socolow, "Cammerbandge has the guy in his apartment, doesn't he? He says he has no doubt about his being in cell block D."

Gould comes into the office. "Is your piece ready?" asks Midgley.

"Attica? Or Boston?" says Gould.

"Boston."

Gould shrugs. "I was just given a good night on Boston."

A phone rings. Socolow says to Midgley, "San Francisco is coming on." A picture of a woman and two children appears on the lower screen. The voice of Dick Threlkeld of the San Francisco CBS station. The two kids are apparently victims of a mysterious killing disease. A third kid has already died. These two are now becoming sick. It's a sad story. The woman talks about her belief in God and about how she knows the kids won't die. Threlkeld's voice tells us there is no chance that they will live. Close.

"Two-twenty," says Socolow.

"Damn good piece," says Midgley.

"Any problems with San Francisco?" asks Vonn.

"None," says Midgley. "It's good. Two-twenty."

Outside in the newsroom, there is a good deal of activity. Two cameras are being wheeled in. One directly in front of Cronkite's desk, the other off to his right, just in front of Midgley's office. Cronkite is still working at his desk editing copy. The writers are still on the telephone or typing. A bank of lights is suddenly turned on overhead. The two writers in the far row of desks get up. A woman comes over and tidies up the surface of their desks. Another woman is taking the sheets of copy from in front of Cronkite and feeding them into the prompting machine, an ingenious device that has also been moved onto the floor, beside one of the cameras, and which consists of a TV camera that transmits each page of copy onto a TV screen attached to the large camera that's now facing Cronkite, where, by an arrangement of mirrors, is displayed the typewritten copy, complete with last-minute corrections, directly on the lens of the camera that Cronkite looks into. A third woman comes in with a tray of make-up which she puts down on the desk behind Cronkite, which has been entirely cleared of papers. Somebody calls, "Three minutes to air."

Cronkite gets up and goes into Midgley's office. "What about Kalb?" he says.

"Kalb is standing by," says Midgley.

"Let's forget Kalb," says Socolow.

Midgley looks at Cronkite. "Well, we don't need it," he says. "Let's dump it."

"Two minutes," someone calls. Cronkite goes back to his desk. He puts on his jacket, opens a drawer of his desk, takes out a pair of glasses, puts them on. The woman is dabbing his face slightly with make-up. The last two writers have gotten up and are standing out of the way. Cronkite is sitting down now. Socolow goes over, put a piece of paper on his desk. Cronkite is working on it. On Midgley's screen, there is the familiar clatter of the wire-services machines. A voice says, "And now, from our newsroom in New York, the *CBS Evening News* with Walter Cronkite." Cronkite is still working at his desk. On the screen, he appears behind the lettering, still working on something. Midgley gets up, closes the door to his office. Socolow sits in a chair by the telephone. A girl sits on the couch with a clipboard. The newsroom is bright with lights. On the screen, Cronkite looks up and, without missing a beat, moves into the opening rhythms of the evening news.

. . .

News. Right now in America, there are morning newspapers. There is news radio. Afternoon newspapers. Evening newspapers. *The 11 O'clock News. The Noon News. Eyewitness News. Action News.* Newsmagazines. Newsletters. Five minutes of news. Two minutes of news. Round-the-clock news. Cronkite. Brinkley. *The News of the Week in Review.* Harry Dalrymple wrapping things up at the news desk at station KPGT. "And so this was Wednesday, November third. . . ."

One thing is clear: Americans are getting an awful lot of news beamed at them, printed for them, yelled into their ears, tossed into the mailbox. Another thing also seems clear: Generally speaking, news is supposed to be a good thing. Television stations announce pridefully that they are expanding their 30-minute news show to a full hour. Networks take expensive ads in newspapers in order to proclaim their total number of news hours. People talk of hard news and soft news. Radio in many cases has expanded its news coverage to a full 24 hours: the all-news station. News is a meliorative word these days. A meliorative concept. Many print ads are now presented in the form of news reports. *Sports Illustrated* has been taking ads in newspapers to promote itself as the "third newsmagazine." Opposed to news, which is good, there is presumably opinion, which is biased and unreliable; and analysis, which is intellectual; and criticism, which is self-serving and unconstructive; or fiction, which is irrelevant.

If it's true, though, that Americans are on the receiving end of an unparalleled amount and velocity of news communication, then it must also be true that something is seriously wrong with our news-communication services, because, as a nation (and also as states, as townships, as individuals), we keep getting ourselves into such serious messes—messes that result in good part, anyway, from our having been told the wrong thing or from our having an evidently complex situation communicated to us in a simplistic way, which in effect amounted to our being told the wrong thing.

Consider the classic communication debacle: Vietnam. Today, of course, everybody has the message about Vietnam. It's a lousy war, right? We had no business going in there, right? Or, if we did, it certainly all went wrong and we should have pulled out. Right? But what, one asks, was the news in 1964? Or 1965? Or 1966? Or 1967? Or even much of 1968? That is a long, long time, and there was a lot of news. To be sure, one understands what happened. The Government said certain things were true that were not always true. Americans have generally been brought up to have faith in their Government. Besides, for a generation we have been exhorted to fight communism there, and there, and there . . . so why not *there?* One understands. Last year, I think, Cronkite declared in a magazine article that he had come round from being a moderate hawk on the war to wishing us out of it, to being a dove. Recantations over the Vietnam war somehow have a curious ring—as if the process of learning were more important than the thing learned, which is sometimes true and sometimes not. Walter Cronkite recants; Pete McCloskey recants; 203,000,000 Americans recant. But from what to what? And what is it they were told all those years by all that news?

Consider some of the other matters that have resulted in the country's experiencing the real and severe malaise that it is surely now experiencing—and will obviously have to live with and suffer with for some time to come. Consider the most important and troubling of all our problems: race. Black and white. Black versus white. Segregation. Integration. Whatever you call it. What was the news on that? Until Dr. King and James Meredith and Little Rock and the integration of the University of Georgia and Medgar Evers and Selma and all the other far-off, seemingly long-ago events, what was the news telling us? Joe Louis, the Brown Bomber? Race riots in Detroit? Harry Truman integrating the Armed Forces? When the news-absorbing public woke up one morning to find the National Guard rumbling into some village square, or Watts aflame, or some frightened school kids being turned away from, or thrust into, some school—where had all that news communication left us the night before? At what spot on the map? How good was the map?

Pollution. Ecology. Did nobody look at Lake Erie until 1967? I read in the paper that a large metals smelter on the West Coast had filed suit with the Government, protesting that, if forced to comply with a certain pollution ruling by a certain date, it would be driven perilously close to bankruptcy. The executives of the company doubtless have a point. So, doubtless, do the citizens of the nearby town who have been choking on smelter gases for the past—well—how many years? What did the news tell them about that? Where were *these* citizens on the map?

Do I seem to be saying that our news systems—our network news, our newspapers, etc.—have served us badly? In fact, I think that is only incidentally so. I think it is indeed true that, as in the case of Vietnam, a highly complex political situation was treated for many years by television news as a largely military operation—the dramatic battle for Hill 937, and so forth. Not only that, but the whole war was presented to us in isolated, disconnected bits of detail—a 30-second bombing raid here, a two-minute film clip of Khe Sanh there, another minute of President Johnson at the Manila Conference, 30 seconds of a helicopter assault—with the result that, even if we had been given the real information we needed to try to come to terms with the war, the way we were given it made it doubly difficult. I think it's true that television news is usually superficial. I think there are a lot of things wrong with all the news systems. Radio news is often nothing more than chopped-up wire-service copy (already chopped up) and then burbled onto the airwaves by a recommissioned disc jockey. Television news is also usually chopped up. And superficial. And tends to get its big ideas from newspapers. Newspapers, with a couple of exceptions, are often mind-blowingly parochial. Newsmagazines are less parochial, but only one 50th of the people in this country buy them and, even so, they mostly *follow* certified events, like everyone else.

Yet, having said all this, I'd like to say what I believe is more to the point: I think the people of this country, in a way, get better than they deserve from their news systems. Network news may be superficial, and it may have a slight Eastern bias, but—considering that it has to have some kind of businesslike relationship with its audience—the TV people put out a basically high level of afternoon newspaper. Better, anyway, than most afternoon newspapers. Morning newspapers vary hugely, and some are little more than paste-ups of the A.P. and the U.P.I. and a couple of syndicated columnists; but the A.P. and the U.P.I., despite their haste and superficiality, manage to move an awful lot of stuff in a given day, manage to tell this country more detail about itself than is true of most other countries.

The problem is, I think, that our concept of news is increasingly false, and *that* is what is serving us badly. This news, of which network X is going to give us 45 minutes more this year than last, may not be as useful a thing as we consider it to be. This news, which our newspapers take such pride in bringing us, and propose, in fact, to bring us more of, perhaps isn't as good a thing as we *say*, as we think it to be. Consider, for example, the thrust of change that has swept through virtually every aspect of modern life. Religion. Sex. Clothes. Consider the change that has swept through art forms. Look at the novel, which has always been a form of news, and observe its inner changes. How in the 18th Century it was a news of adventure, of the great migrations from the country to the city, the churning of urban and rural classes, *Clarissa,* Smollett, Defoe. How in the 19th Century it changed to provide the news of the new middle class, the manufacturing class, the new world of Dickens, George Eliot, Arnold Bennett, William Dean Howells. It told readers about the new people, how they lived, what they wore, how vicars had tea, what lawyers did at the office, all that *furniture.* And the 20th Century novel—while admittedly struggling with the furniture-describing heritage of the 19th, not quite sure where it's going, finding narrative shot away by movies and TV—still moves toward telling us what we intuitively need to know about our world, about the inside of people's heads (no longer furniture), about how men and women are in bed together, how they really are, how, at any rate, they think they are.

But news—newspapers, TV news, wire-service news—is still telling us of plane crashes. Hotel fires. The minister from such and such said this and that to so-and-so. A strike. A flood. "HUB MAN KILLS THREE." "SOCIALITE NABS BANDIT." And it does that because we seem to think we want that: fires, strikes, plane crashes, Hub man kills three. And the reason we think we want that, I think, is that we aren't nearly so serious about news as we allege. Or look at it this way: We say we're serious about news, so right away CBS and ABC and NBC and *The New York Times* and *Time* and *Newsweek* and all the rest of them rush to provide us with news—but time after time, it turns out to be the wrong news. It doesn't—apparently—much help us. It rarely tells us where we really are, because history is constantly appearing on our doorstep and telling us we're nowhere near where our map said we were. Admittedly, there is no news system one can conceive of that would provide us all with perfect maps; but our maps are *so* inaccurate, and require so much trouble, and tears, and often bloodshed to correct.

Clearly, the news we say we want is the old news. It somehow makes us feel good to read about a plane crash off Japan. It connects us to some ancient folk need, and maybe that is very strong, too strong, and maybe Armageddon will come mysteriously one afternoon, having been foretold by no less than four associate professors in Denver, a Swiss observatory and the *Berkeley Barb,* while the people of the most advanced nation in the world are still reading about a bus accident in Rangoon. Or Rome. Or Rochester, New York. It's perfectly likely—or so it seems to me—that we're never going to get a useful news system. In fact, in my darker moods, I can well imagine a situation developing in which the people of this country get so out of touch with what is actually going on beneath the surface that real trouble erupts, *real* trouble, and repression results, *real* repression (it certainly wouldn't be the first such cycle in history), and then, when the tanks are in place, and the guards are at their posts, and the trains are on time, and loudspeakers, or perhaps TV sets, are at the street corners—then we will have, or be given, a news system that finally will be properly attuned to the situation. Relevant.

But now, in the meantime, I think it might at least be worth while saying this much aloud: The news we congratulate ourselves on receiving, the news that our news systems congratulate themselves on transmitting, while allowing that in a more perfect world they would transmit *more* of it for us if only they could, if only they had a half hour instead of 15 minutes, 50 minutes instead of a half hour, a whole hour, a whole day, maybe, a whole week of—what? Folk entertainment. What? you say. Police-bribe scandal, rape, drowning—entertainment? I guess so. Two minutes of combat film from Vietnam—entertainment? I guess so—although maybe describing it as providing a kind of release, while giving the illusion of involvement, would be closer to it. The news we get, I think, is mostly this release, this kind of entertainment, no matter how grisly the subject, how much we even may weep at the result. We don't get it that way because *they* give it to us, nor because *they* are bad. We get it that way because we want it so. We call, they respond. Good luck, I say, to all of us.

. . .

The clock on Midgley's wall ticks toward seven. Seven is when the *CBS Evening News* goes on the air. Cronkite is still on the screen. He is winding up the taping. A commercial. During the commercial, Socolow steps into the newsroom, whispers something to Cronkite. Steps out again. The commercial is over. Cronkite is shuffling his papers. "And that's the way it is." he says. The familiar voice. The familiar inflection. "Wednesday, November third." End. People stream back into the newsroom. A writer sits back down at his desk. Cronkite walks into Midgley's office. Sits down in a chair. "I wish we could have done more with Kalb," he says.

"We couldn't reach Kalb in time," says Midgley. The Cronkite show is now on the air. Cronkite is on the third screen. Chancellor on the second. Reasoner on the top. Cronkite and Midgley watch the three screens. NBC comes on with something about China. Midgley turns up the NBC audio.

Cronkite says, "We're still one day ahead of them." The three networks carry the same report about Treasury Secretary Connally. Commercials. NBC and CBS have something on the dock strike. ABC is covering Lindsay.

Chancellor sits on his studio chair, detached, helpful. He runs through four quick items. Cronkite's face oncamera is backed by what seems to be a map of Vietnam. He tells us again about the DMZ. Then Dan Rather,

"No! I'll tell __you__ something, Walter! That's __not__ the way it is!"

Drawing by Chon Day; © 1974 The New Yorker Magazine, Inc.

Washington. The monetary crisis. Reasoner speaks about a copper crisis in Chile. Midgley sips another milk shake. Cronkite sits in his chair, swiveling it a bit from time to time. Then NBC comes on with its finale, a thing about the departure of the Washington Senators. Long. Weird. Arty camera shots of the empty stadium. "Jesus Christ," says Midgley. Then Cronkite is saying good night. Chancellor, Howard K. Smith. Good night, good night. The script girl closes her log sheet. The screens are dark. Midgley stands. He has a dinner to get to. Cronkite seems in no hurry to leave. He stretches his legs. His brow furrows. Midgley looks at him, on his way out. "I have to be uptown by seven-thirty," he says.

Cronkite looks at him. "You know," he says, "the thing that really breaks my heart is we never have enough time." Cronkite waves his hand. Midgley heads out the door.

■ **POINTS TO CONSIDER**

1. How is this article "reportage" in a way that the other articles in this chapter, aside from the Attica coverage, are not? In what ways does this approach add to or detract from what the author is trying to say?

2. Do the people the article describes working on the news seem to be disturbed or excited by the news events they are dealing with? What, according to the article, seems to be the one overriding concern with the tapes and copy that make up the television news program?

3. What criticisms does the author direct at television news in particular and at our news system in general? Do you think these criticisms are valid? Explain.

4. How does the author compare news to a road map? Do you feel this is a valid analogy? Explain.

5. Why does the author feel that news is basically a form of entertainment? When is news definitely not just entertainment?

6. What reasons does the author give for saying that we get the news we want? Do you agree? If not, what measures can we take to get better news?

7. Why, in a totalitarian police state, such as the author suggests could happen here, would the news system given us be at last "properly attuned to the situation"?

■ THE FUTURE OF ACCESS TO THE MEDIA

Jerome A. Barron   *Freedom of the Press for Whom?*, 1973

ROMANCE AND REALISM ABOUT FREEDOM OF THE PRESS

Freedom of the press is one of the more attractive phrases in American life, law, and myth. What does it mean? Why is it an important value in our society? Minimally it promises that newspapers cannot be restrained or intimidated by government for what they allow to be printed in their pages. The First Amendment to the U.S. Constitution states: "Congress shall make no law abridging freedom of speech or of the press." It says nothing about the actions of state legislatures. From 1791 until 1925 the First Amendment was thought to apply only to the federal government. In 1925, in a nearly forgotten case, the Supreme Court casually observed that "freedom of speech and of the press . . . are among the fundamental personal rights and 'liberties' protected by the due process clause of the Fourteenth Amendment from impairment by the States."*

Thus our present constitutional law of freedom of the press is only a little more than forty years old. Although the doctrine itself is far older, its usefulness as a practical safeguard is a twentieth-century phenomenon.

Changes in our approach to freedom of the press are bitterly resisted. Now an access-oriented approach is attacked as a violation of the concept because, it is urged, the Constitution speaks only to government and not to private power groups. But the law of freedom of the press was extended

*Notes will be found at the end of this reading.

from the national to the state governments in the past without constitutional amendment. The Supreme Court said the word "liberty" in the Fourteenth Amendment ("No state shall deprive any person of life, liberty, or property without due process of law") was a concept sufficiently broad to warrant the conclusion that it obligated the states to respect freedom of the press. I believe that the reference to freedom of the press in the First Amendment itself permits an interpretation today which will make the concept continuingly vital and meaningful. Such an interpretation would permit governmental action to provide for positive expression.

Our approach to freedom of the press has operated in the service of a romantic illusion: the illusion that the marketplace of ideas is freely accessible.

After the first World War, in a case involving a socialist who was prosecuted for distributing leaflets which were allegedly designed to "cripple or hinder the United States in the prosecution of the (first) World War," Justice Oliver Holmes wrote a memorable opinion:

> But when men have realized that time has upset many fighting faiths, they may come to believe even more than they believe the very foundations of their own conduct that the ultimate good desired is better reached by free trade in ideas—that the best test of truth is the power of the thought to get itself accepted in the competition of the market, and that truth is the only ground upon which their wishes can safely be carried out.[2]

A half a century later, Holmes' eloquent description of the free marketplace of ideas depicts an ideal, not a reality. There are enormous limitations on the "power of thought to get itself accepted in the competition of the market." In Holmes' concept of the marketplace of ideas the only limitation on the currency of ideas is an intellectual one. But there is no free trade in ideas. Ideas in a mass society are transmitted in the mass communications media of television, radio, and the press. Admission to them assures notoriety and public response. Denial assures obscurity and, apparently, frustration.

We assume that the only obstacles to debate and discussion are the penalties that the state may apply to unpopular debate and provocative discussion. Our law of freedom of expression, however, has done very little to insure opportunity for freedom of expression.

The traditional liberal position on ideas is essentially Darwinian. Ideas engage in a life of mortal combat and the fittest survive. In this struggle, the continuing menace has been seen to be government. That private power might so control the struggle of ideas as to predetermine the victor has not been considered. But, increasingly, private censorship serves to suppress ideas as thoroughly and as rigidly as the worst government censor.

Publishers are not the only private censors. Printers in a number of cases have refused to set in type copy submitted to them. Some printers have refused to work for underground papers. These papers have sometimes had to be printed far from the community in which they are distributed. The November 1970 issue of *Scanlan's Monthly* was rejected by fifty or sixty printing companies because of an article on guerilla warfare in the

U.S. The legal director of the American Civil Liberties Union, Melvin Wulf, was quoted in the *Wall Street Journal* as saying that repetitions of the Scanlan situation could destroy freedom of the press.[3]

But although the ACLU was very critical of private censorship in the Scanlan incident it has been ambivalent to the proposal for a right of access to the press. It held to the old liberal suspicion of government intervention and faith in the marketplace of ideas. The 1968 ACLU biennial conference in Ann Arbor, however, revealed deep disenchantment with the closed quality of the mass media. There was evidence of new sympathy for means of broadening public participation in the media, as in other powerful social institutions.

The ACLU Biennial Session recommended that the ACLU bring law suits to challenge the discriminatory refusal of advertisements and notices in publications. It was also suggested that the Communications Media Committee consider supporting media challenges when individuals and organizations are subjected to a pattern of derogatory treatment. In essence, this recommendation supported a right of reply. Finally, the establishment of a permanent citizens' advisory commission to audit and report on media performance on a national basis was recommended.

At a meeting after the Biennial Session, the Communications Media Committee offered a revised version of the recommendation to the National Board:

> That the ACLU bring selective lawsuits challenging the discriminatory refusal of non-commercial advertisements and notices in publications of general circulation on grounds of race, creed or color.

Neither the original nor the revision was approved.

Perhaps it was felt that commercial advertising has a lesser claim to First Amendment protection, but if the right is given only to noncommercial advertisements, the resulting public access to advertising would be fairly slender.

The ACLU proposal to include public notices about meetings as well as to permit advertisements is necessary. Many groups feel excluded from the daily press. Lack of publicity for their meetings and activities severely limit their opportunities to grow in status or influence in their communities.

Practically speaking, a right of reply is easy to implement because it is triggered by a newspaper attack. But suppose a newspaper does not attack but merely ignores? What then? Should the paper be compelled to provide so many pages to various groups in the community to do with what they choose? Commandeering of newspaper space would be a rather radical alternative. What the ACLU suggests is that, in view of the complete dependence of a community on its newspaper for notices of public events and meetings, at least there ought to be a way to compel their publication. It would be very similar to the legal notice advertising which most newspapers are now compelled to take under the law of most of the states.

The need for further development of cumulative remedies to provide access to the press is shown in recent cases where the black community was forced to pay for the most elementary kind of press recognition, while whites received it as a matter of course.

In the late 1960s, a protest was directed to the long-established refusal of the Lynchburg, Virginia, daily newspapers to publish the obituary notices of members of the Negro community. If a black man died, his family could tell the rest of the community about it only by purchasing a commercial advertisement.

Another situation arose in Montgomery, Alabama. The same company owns and publishes both the morning paper, the *Advertiser,* and the evening newspaper, the *Journal.* The company also publishes Montgomery's only Sunday newspaper, the *Advertiser-Journal.* That the same company owns the entire daily press in Montgomery is not surprising: the pattern is standard across the country. But the evils of monopoly are not usually so readily discernible. No Negro social announcements had ever graced the society pages of Montgomery newspapers: instead, the papers all had separate Negro social pages.

A group of Montgomery Negroes finally filed suit against the papers on June 15, 1971, in the federal district court. They said that the policy of the newspapers was an arbitrary denial, based solely on race. The argument was that refusal to publish Negro bridal announcements in the society section of daily newspapers violated the due process and equal protection clauses. They asked that private power groups be subjected to constitutional standards when they exercised "monopoly control in an area of vital public concern."

The court said it found this argument quite appealing, but it could not accept it.[4] Basically the case fell on the Achilles heel of the access to the press concept—the state action doctrine.[5]

Placing Negro social announcements on a separate Negro news page is an imitation in the media of the community social system. But segregation in public facilities has been found unconstitutional. The shibboleth that perpetuates a media-supported social system of racial discrimination is that newspaper action is private action and is therefore constitutionally immune. When voluntary continuation of a discriminatory policy by private newspapers is judicially enforced, then the discriminatory treatment should be considered state action. In Montgomery, an irrelevant confusion between freedom of the press and press absolutism has resulted in the federal court's continuing the now outmoded and romantic view that freedom for newspaper publishers is freedom of the press. This is an idea that dies hard. At that ACLU Biennial Session, some members were shocked by the suggestion that newspapers should be required to carry material and advertising opposing the basic editorial policy of the newspaper. This attachment to the rights of property is characteristic of the classic liberal position. What it ignores, however, is that as early as the late nineteenth century very conservative judges were persuaded to accept the idea that restricting the use of property was appropriate when the property owner had a monopoly in a business which clearly had a public interest.

No one thinks that the Board of Directors of AT&T approves of every conversation that goes along its telephone lines. The daily newspaper could never be treated as a common carrier to the same extent as the phone company, but community dependence on the daily press gives it something of a common carrier role, although the press has no reciprocal responsibilities to its readership.

But application of the law to the press is not forbidden. Although the press once vigorously argued to the contrary, it is now unmistakably clear that the antitrust laws, for example, apply to newspapers as well as to other businesses. In fact, one of the paradoxes in any discussion of press responsibility is that the press has not been slow to invite, in fact demand, government intervention where it is to the financial advantage of the press. Special mailing rates are provided by federal statute, for example. Some sections of the press have waged an energetic, insistent, and successful campaign for legislation to allow newspapers to share facilities in a given city.[6]

There is inequality in capacity to communicate ideas just as there is inequality in economic bargaining power. Indeed inequality of power to communicate is usually one aspect of inequality in general economic bargaining power. In the broadcast media, the VHF television outlets are almost completely in the hands of network affiliated stations, and possess the mass audience. The licenses of these stations are almost invariably renewed by the Federal Communications Commission at three-year intervals. The unregulated daily newspaper industry is equally unfriendly territory for new entrants and new voices. The cost of establishing a competitive daily newspaper is all but absolutely prohibitive.

Inequality in the ability to communicate ideas is so clear that few would dispute it. What is disputed is that the situation is a problem and that, as a constitutional matter, anything can be done about it.

ACCESS AND PROPAGANDA

In contemporary protest on both the Left and the Right, propaganda seems to be increasingly preferred over discussion and the approach of reason. When a federal court of appeals declared in 1971 that the FCC-supported ban on the sale of advertising time for controversial social or political purposes violated the First Amendment, *Broadcasting* said the ruling would prohibit broadcasters from rejecting "paid propaganda."[7]

Will then the rise of access to the media be finally a victory for propaganda? Jacques Ellul has written that there are two kinds of propaganda: agitation propaganda and integration propaganda.[8] Integration propaganda is aimed at adjustment. Agitation propaganda aims to turn resentment to rebellion. He thinks the United States offers the most important examples of the use of integration propaganda. Perhaps the primary problem in the United States is that protest is essentially agitation propaganda but the media has habituated the public to integration propaganda. Ellul's analysis helps us to appraise both the past consequences of lack of access to the media and to estimate the possible consequences of providing that access in the future.

Entry to the means of communication must necessarily, I think, take the edge off social anger. But, it is difficult to say whether the new access for paid ideological spots on broadcasting will be used for agitation or integration propaganda. The chief distributors of agitation propaganda in the United States today are unintentionally the broadcast media. By just providing news of the activities of those engaging in social rebellion, they spread agitation propaganda. Reporting and dramatizing protest feeds the protest movement.

At the present time, access to the media is obtained through applying external pressure rather than by obtaining formal permission.

A measure of the jaded standards of the media is that when protest leaves the level of reason, broadcast time and newspaper space become abundantly available. The "sit-in", the campus protest, the draft card burning, the flag burning, and the ghetto riot are all communications media in default. But not everything worth saying can be said in that way, or at least, not without grave risk of damage to the social order.

To confront the mass audience suddenly with agitation propaganda, when it is accustomed to a diet of integration propaganda, produces rage and disorientation. People see the electronic reality, but the truth makes them angry. They cannot believe in the reality of something that seems deliberately bizarre. They hope, and so partly believe, that the television portrayal of reality is staged and false. Surely, the youth posed with the clenched fist, the person spitting on the flag, would not exist if the television cameras were not turned on them.

For the protestor, media coverage enhances the credibility of his protest. Coverage reinforces the sense of outrage in sympathetic viewers by reassuring them that there are many like-minded spirits.

Some events are too massive, involve too many participants and too much violence, to have their authenticity doubted. An example was the 1968 racial disturbance which followed the death of Martin Luther King. Television coverage of the actual disturbances was actually muted in order not to incite others.

An important illustration of public skepticism about television was the popular reaction to television coverage of the Democratic National Convention in 1968. People refused to believe what they saw. They saw on their television screens police beating students and demonstrators on the head. They heard Senator Ribicoff speak out in indignation. They saw Mayor Daley shout back in anger at Ribicoff's charges. But the viewer reaction, measured by the letters received by the major networks, was overwhelmingly critical of television performance. Why? Because the barrage of agitation propaganda let loose on an unprepared public contradicted the world order which had been implanted in its mind through integration propaganda. People criticized the networks, claiming that the police response was shown but not the crowds' provocation. The integration propaganda, the myth, was that police do not punish political dissenters, only law-breakers. Since no law-breaking provocation had been shown, the assumption was made that the networks had conspiratorially refused to show the provocation in order to stimulate criticism of the Johnson Administration, Mayor Daley, and law and order in general.

We do not lack for examples in recent social history of unintentional media distribution of agitation propaganda. The student general strike of May 4–8, 1970, over the Cambodian incursion offered a challenge to the received myth of freedom of expression in the United States. The strike succeeded. The media reported the success and so became, as it often has in the recent past, the reluctant tutor and unwilling evangelist of protest.

The conflict is the product of confusion between television's sense of its duty to inform and its natural tendency and preference to entertain. Happily, some social upheavals permit the duty to inform and the preference to entertain to combine. The media then cheerfully use the technical proficiency at which they are masters and bring the upheaval to every home in the country.

Marshall McLuhan says the new electronic media have made the print-oriented conception of time irrelevant. The speed of information transmittal has increased to the point that rational decision-making is outmoded. For the frustrated and the impatient, the conventional decision-making process appears hopelessly slow. The consequence of the speed of information on television is "immediate involvement of the entire community." Thus, the student strike was announced on Saturday, May 2, 1970, by the President of the National Student Association. By the end of the week strikes had closed or crippled over four hundred colleges and universities across the country, in places with such tranquil reputations as the University of Idaho, the University of Kansas, and New Mexico State University.

What had happened to debate? The same thing that had happened to the political system itself. It did not respond. The President said that whether or not the war was popular he would continue it; the new left was encouraged to respond that whether or not a student strike (and they hoped a general strike) was popular, it had now become an indispensable and inevitable mode of protest.

In the long run broadcasters cannot shun controversy. Real controversy lives too close to violence and the entertainment potential of violence is too great to be ignored indefinitely by a profit-oriented, privately-controlled medium. But can routine and fair and extensive coverage and access for the conflicts and the contentions in the nation ever be a reality in the media?

Whether or not the usefulness of reply and debate on radio or television can be objectively demonstrated, the question remains, is broader access to the media necessary? Encouragement of access to the media responds to that which television itself has stimulated, the enormous need for all the components of our society to participate in it.

NOTES

1. *Gitlow v. New York,* 268 U.S. 652 (1925).
2. *Abrams v. United States,* 250 U.S. 616 (1919).
3. *Wall Street Journal,* December 10, 1970.
4. *Cook v. The Advertiser Company,* 323 F. Supp. 1212 (M.D. Ala. 1970).
5. *Chicago Joint Board, Amalgamated Clothing Workers v. Chicago Tribune,* 435 F. 2d 470 (2d Cir. 1970).
6. Newspaper Preservation Act of 1970, Public Law 91-353, 91st Cong. 2d Sess., S. 1520, July 24, 1970.
7. *Broadcasting,* August 9, 1971.
8. Ellul, *Propaganda* (1966).

1. On what Amendments to the Constitution are our current notions of freedom of the press based?

2. Does the author believe that there is today a free "marketplace of ideas"? What reasons and examples does he give?

3. Why are newspapers allowed under law to segregate their social pages while boards of education cannot constitutionally segregate their schools?

4. How, according to the author, are newspapers and the telephone system analogous? Does he feel that they should be subject, therefore, to the same legal restrictions?

5. What precedents does the author cite for compelling the media to give access to certain individuals who need it? Do you think that the government should force the media to make themselves more available to areas of our society that have been denied access to the media up to now? Explain.

6. What are agitation propaganda and integration propaganda? Give examples of each. What media are most likely to carry each?

7. What, according to the author, has been the principal source of agitation propaganda in the United States? Can you think of individuals and organizations who are aware of this phenomenon and make use of it?

8. What effects on the nature of protest does denial of access to the media create? What effects on society as a whole does the author suggest greater access to the media will have? Do you agree? Explain.

IDEAS FOR INVESTIGATION, DISCUSSION, AND WRITING

1. Using the appropriate journalistic approach, write an article of about three hundred words reporting some news event. The report should be as complete as possible including, if at all feasible, statements from the principal persons involved. Necessary background material should also be supplied as well as any other facts and details needed to give as complete and accurate an account of the event as possible. Supply the item with a headline and a subhead. Also indicate in what sort of newspaper this article would be likely to appear as well as where it would be likely to appear in the newspaper.

2. Write two news articles dealing with some controversial, contemporary event or issue. Slant the first article sharply toward one point of view, and slant the second article just as sharply toward the opposite point of view. Since slanting, to be effective, must not be obvious, it is advisable to confine yourself to the facts of the matter—or as will more likely be the case, some of the facts—as reported by newspapers and other media.

3. Cover a major news event such as a speech or demonstration which you are certain will be reported in the local newspaper or newspapers. Write an essay in which you compare your own recollections and impressions of the event with the version of the event presented by the newspaper. Using this comparison, come to some conclusion about the newspaper story. What aspects of the event were most emphasized. Why? What, if any, was the overall bias of the article? What "angle" did the article seem to be playing up? Was the article slanted? Did it make use of propaganda devices?

4. Write an essay analyzing and discussing as propaganda a portion of a political address. (You can find the texts of speeches in newspapers and in *Vital Speeches of the Day* in your library.) What propaganda devices can you find? What specific purpose is each device intended to serve? How effectively does it actually fulfill its purpose? Keeping in mind that the basic goal of propaganda is to focus attention on the emotions of an issue and not on the facts, evaluate the passage as a whole and give reasons for your conclusions.

5. Describe in an essay the editorial profile of a particular newspaper. How might you characterize the general editorial tendencies of the paper over the past ten years? What editorials or editorial campaigns can you cite as examples of this tendency? Are there exceptions or special cases? How are these explained? What are some of the paper's more specific editorial likes and dislikes? Can you cite examples of these particular idiosyncrasies? Do you feel that the editorial policy of the paper reflects, on the whole, the honest and consistent opinion of the editors and publisher, or can you see other pressures or interests at work?

6. Using evidence from the ads, covers, articles, fiction, cartoons, photographs, and other features of a particular mass magazine, analyze and discuss the magazine's image. As he reads the magazine, what sort of

person is the reader supposed to feel he becomes? What identity does the magazine give to those who are willing to suspend consciousness of their own identity while reading the magazine? How do the various features of the magazine help the reader slip into this temporary role? How does this image, e.g., the *Playboy* male or the *Cosmopolitan* female, compare with the sort of people who actually read the magazines? Is the disparity greater for some magazines than others? Is the disparity a source of potential harm? How?

7. Put together a small, one-issue newspaper, perhaps just the front page. The newspaper could be community or school oriented or could be of a satirical bent, a parody of a local daily or the official school paper. Ideally such a paper would include photographs, classified ads, commercial advertising, cartoons, comics, perhaps even an advice to the love-lorn column.

8. Using examples from newspaper articles and editorials, letters to the editor, pamphlets, posters, handbills, magazines, and public speeches, put together a compendium of propaganda illustrating all seven of the classic propaganda devices.

9. Follow up a story from a local paper. Choose a story which seems to you to have been inadequately handled or a story for which you might have access to information beyond what appeared in the original write-up. Provide background material, follow-up studies, and research into ancillary aspects of the situation. Write up the results of your investigation as a full-length news feature.

10. Make a study of the specialization of magazines and newspapers in this country. One approach to such a study could be the historical: What were the first magazines and newspapers like? What services did they perform? How did they change over the years? What commercial and technological forces led to today's vast proliferation of publications? Another tack might be the study of a few of these publications themselves. What are they? How are they financed? Who publishes them? Who reads them? Why? What services do they perform?

11. Investigate the changes that have taken place in newspaper or magazine publishing in the last ten years. What factors were responsible for the changes? What do they mean for the future of these media?

12. Write the editor of your local paper a letter of about 300 words concerning some controversial problem or issue. In this letter use at least four of the seven propaganda devices discussed in the essay "Elements of Persuasion and Techniques of Propaganda" (page 100).

13. Following much the same idea as the collection of articles dealing with the riots at Attica prison, make a scrapbook of news coverage of a single story, including first newsbreak, follow-ups, in-depth studies, editorial comment, political cartoons, and newsmagazine coverage from as many different sources and angles as possible. What observations can you make from this study about the development of a news story and the workings of the press?

14. Investigate the validity of McLuhan's assertion that if it weren't for classified ads, newspapers would be replaced completely by television.

15. Make a study of one or more of the newer journalistic phenomena such as the city magazines like *Seattle, New York,* or *Toronto Life;* the suburban newspapers, or the underground press. What needs do these publications attempt to fill? How well are they succeeding commercially? Why?

Part Three

Cartoons and Comic Strips: Previews and Viewpoints

I don't care a straw for your newspaper articles, my constituents don't know how to read; but they can't help seeing them damned pictures.

—William "Boss" Tweed
(1823–1878), a New York
political boss, about the
political cartoons of
Thomas Nast

[The comic strip] is spoken of as a new art form when, really, it's the oldest. The combination of text and pictures is the oldest and most classical art form.

—Al Capp
Quoted by Ed Wilks

[The "Peanuts" comic strip has] audiences in more than 1,000 newspapers in the United States and Canada, and more than 100 others in forty-one foreign countries. Charlie Brown and his friends speak in twelve languages around the world.

—John Tebbel

[Garry Trudeau, creator of "Doonesbury"] firmly turns away requests for interviews with the statement, "What I have to say of interest comes across in the strip."

—Allan Parachini

Cartoons and Comic Strips

HERBLOCK AND BILL MAULDIN: SIX EDITORIAL CARTOONS

"Remember the Good Old Days When We Only Worried About Russia Getting One?"
Copyright 1974 by Herblock in *The Washington Post.*

"Towering Inferno."
Copyright 1975 by Herblock in *The Washington Post.*

"Yes, Mr. and Mrs. America—This Is Your Life."
Copyright 1975 by Herblock in *The Washington Post*.

"WHY MESS UP A GOOD SYSTEM?"

HITCHHIKER

BOOKMARKS

Copyright © 1968 The Chicago Sun-Times and reproduced by courtesy of Wil-Jo Associates, Inc., and Bill Mauldin.

■ POINTS TO CONSIDER

1. On what cultural or political issue does each of the cartoons in this section comment? In what ways are the statements made by the cartoon more effective than other means of editorial expression, such as written or spoken opinion or a filmed documentary? What elements or expression does the editorial cartoon offer that these other media do not?

2. In what ways may the cartoon comments in this section be less effective than other means of expressing the same editorial opinions?

3. In what sense is almost every editorial cartoon an "argument by analogy"?

4. Do you find these cartoons funny? If so, why? Do you think humor is necessary for an effective editorial cartoon? Explain.

5. Why are most editorial cartoons critical rather than complimentary?

6. The cartoons in this section use only one frame or picture. What disadvantages does this limitation bring? (Compare "Doonesbury.") What advantages?

CARTOONISTS AROUND THE WORLD LOOK AT UNITED STATES INVOLVEMENT IN INDOCHINA, 1975

Atlas World Press Review, February, May, June, 1975

Isaac; reprinted in *Atlas World Press Review,* February 1975, from *El Sol de Mexico,* Mexico City.

Reprinted in *Atlas World Press Review,* May 1975, from ABC Madrid.

Reprinted in *Atlas World Press Review,* May 1975, from *Times of India*, Bombay, New Delhi.

Charmoz; reprinted in *Atlas World Press Review*, June 1975, from *Paris-Match*.

Reprinted in *Atlas World Press Review*, June 1975, from *Frankfurter Allgemeine,* Frankfurter.

Reprinted in *Atlas World Press Review,* June 1975, from *Dagens Nyheter.*

Trog—*Observer,* London (Rothco).

Henfil; reprinted in *Atlas World Press Review*, June 1975, from *O Pasquim*, Rio de Janeiro.

Reprinted in *Atlas World Press Review*, June 1975, from *Que Pasa*, Santiago.

"America welcomes the Vietnamese refugees."
Konk; reprinted in *Atlas World Press Review*, June 1975, from *Le Monde*, Paris.

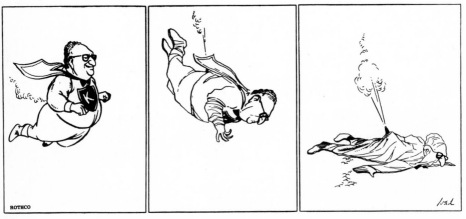

Vadillo—*Siempre*, Mexico (Rothco).

Reprinted in *Atlas World Press Review*, June 1975, from *Jugantar*, Calcutta.

" . . . and what was the War about?"

Vijayan; reprinted in *Atlas World Press Review*, June 1975, from *Hindu*, Madras.

1. What similarities and differences do you find between the cartoon techniques used in other countries and those of Herblock and Bill Mauldin? How do these cartoons employ a "language" that is international?

2. Do you find instances of the same symbol being used to make very different assertions? How, for instance, is Uncle Sam used to express different opinions?

3. The cartoons in this section show a wide variety of styles and techniques. How does the style of drawing affect the political message of each cartoon? How does it affect the subtler aspects of the cartoon such as emotional appeal and humor?

■ THE CARTOON IS AN OLD ART FORM

Ed Wilks   *St. Louis Post Dispatch,* May 4, 1972

"Blondie" is art. So, too, is "Hi and Lois." And "Steve Canyon" and "Juliet Jones" and "B.C." If accepting comic strips as art is a hangup, hang it up. That's what the Graham Gallery in New York has done.

Two floors of the Graham Gallery at 1014 Madison Avenue were hung with comic strips and cartoons in a recent showing of "Cartoon and Comic Strip Art."

"Blondie," "Hi and Lois," "Steve Canyon," "Juliet Jones" and "B.C." were among 145 catalogued hangings in the New York gallery which previously has opened its doors to paintings from the eighteenth to twentieth centuries, European decorative arts, old masters and contemporary artists. Missouri's Thomas Hart Benton, among others, has used it as a display room.

Robert Graham, gallery director, has been a prominent patron of comic strip art. Thus, Jerry Robinson, himself a cartoonist, is hardly to be considered an intruder in his role as consulting director for the show and author of an illustrated, 32-page catalogue who refers to cartoons and comic strips as a much-neglected art form.

Robinson's catalogue, in itself a collector's item (and redeemable as such for $2), pairs the comic strip with movies as the two most significant American art forms. Al Capp, the creator of "Li'l Abner," would disagree to a degree, however. But only as to scope.

The comic strip, said Capp from his Boston studio, "is spoken of as a new art form when, really, it's the oldest. The combination of text and pictures is the oldest and most classical art form. It's been found in Egyptian tombs and, not so long ago, somebody dug some things up in Central America that showed the Aztecs did it, too."

art, although most of the snub is directed to the strips. As suggested by Capp, who also was represented in the show, "Artists don't consider cartoonists artists because they also write, and writers don't consider cartoonists writers because they draw. So we're penalized for having one extra talent."

The Graham Gallery showing was a belated seventy-fifth anniversary celebration of the birth of the comic strip, as marked by the appearance of Richard Felton Outcault's "The Yellow Kid" in Joseph Pulitzer's *New York World* on February 16, 1896. There is some disagreement as to the true "first" in comic strips, but Outcault's offering would seem to be as good a starting place as any.

Robinson suggests that Bud Fisher's "Mr. A. Mutt Starts In To Play The Races," which first appeared in the San Francisco Chronicle as a horizontal strip in 1907 and soon became "Mutt and Jeff," was the first successful daily comic strip. A half-dozen years ago, David W. Kunzle, then tracing the history of comic strips under a federal grant, suggested that the first appearance was in 1492, when an anti-Semitic tract was published in Nuernberg as a propaganda device favoring the expulsion of Jews from that German city. Kunzle, however, nominates as America's first comic strip "The Katzenjammer Kids" of Rudolph Dirks, who developed a narrative sequence in his drawings for the New York American in 1897.

Capp and Kunzle agree that cartoonist art can be traced back to the sixteenth century works of such artists as Goya and Daumier.

It may be that the consideration of cartoons and comic strips as art depends on from what point in time they are viewed, as Capp suggests. "In their day," Capp said, "the string quartets of Mozart and Beethoven were considered to be the pleasure of the idle rich. It may not be until cartoonists have the decency to die that they'll be accepted."

"Comic strips are the size of a series of postage stamps," said Capp, "and so they are sloughed off as a trifle. But size has nothing to do with it. I've seen murals in Post Office buildings that didn't have one part of the art of an Alex Raymond or a Milton Caniff."

Raymond, who was killed 25 years ago in an automobile accident, drew "Flash Gordon" and "Rip Kirby." Caniff fathered "Steve Canyon" and, earlier, "Terry and the Pirates." To Capp, there isn't an illustrator anywhere to compare with Caniff—"He's certainly better than Sir John Tenniel, who illustrated 'Alice in Wonderland.' "

From Capp's point of view the comic strip "is the last stronghold of comprehensible art."

POINTS TO CONSIDER

1.   Do you agree with Al Capp that it is hard to consider drawings as small as cartoons and comic strips as "art"? (The Graham Gallery presumably hung large versions of the drawings.) Is there some justification for this attitude? Explain.

2. What, in your opinion, does one expect of "art"? Do comic strips live up to these expectations? Explain.

3. Do you feel that the question of whether or not comic strips are art is an important one? Why?

■ CARTOONISTS COMMENT ON THE MASS MEDIA AND POPULAR ARTS

DOONESBURY   by Garry Trudeau

Copyright, 1974, G. B. Trudeau/Distributed by Universal Press Syndicate.

Copyright, 1974, Universal Press Syndicate.

"I wonder what I did with that book I was halfway
through when the TV set konked out last fall?"

"The Better Half," by Barnes, reprinted courtesy The Register and Tribune Syndicate, Inc.

Beetle Bailey ® By Mort Walker

B.C. by permission of Johnny Hart and Field Enterprises, Inc.

GRIN AND BEAR IT   BY LICHTY

"I thought the way she kept her clothes on was
entirely unnecessary to the story!"

"Grin and Bear It" by George Lichty. Courtesy of Field Newspaper Syndicate.

ARCHIE—By Bob Montana

Copyright 1977 by Archie Comic Publications

TANK McNAMARA
by Jeff Millar & Bill Hinds

Copyright, 1975, Universal Press Syndicate.

THE WIZARD OF ID   by Brant parker and Johnny hart

"The Wizard of Id" by permission of Johnny Hart and Field Enterprises, Inc.

BLONDIE   By Dean Young and Jim Raymond

© King Features Syndicate, Inc., 1974.

CONCHY   James Childress

CONCHY by Jim Childress, courtesy of Field Newspaper Syndicate.

Hi and Lois   ®   By Mort Walker & Dik Browne

© King Features Syndicate, Inc., 1972.

■ **POINTS TO CONSIDER**

1. Each of the cartoons in this section can be considered a statement or assertion. How are these similar to the statements made on the same subjects by the articles in this book?

2. How are the "statements" made by the cartoons different from those made by articles? What does this suggest about the cartoon as a medium of expression?

3. What wide variety of media and art forms are commented upon by these cartoons? (See "An Introduction to Mass Media and Popular Arts," page 3.)

4. Studies have shown that many more people read the "funnies" in newspapers than read any other single section. Do you think that cartoons and comic strips, therefore, might be more influential than is usually thought? Explain.

5. When did you first start reading cartoons and comic strips? Are you presently a regular reader of cartoons and comic strips? Do you have some favorites? Why are they your favorites?

The monster speakers in the cluttered studio are woofing full blast with the sounds of the Rolling Stones. The cacophony hardly seems the ideal environment for the exacting rigors of sketching. But Garry Trudeau is not your average sketcher and the oppressively loud tunes are nothing less than the Muzak to which he toils—creating the characters of his satirical comic-strip success *Doonesbury.* As Mick Jagger wails about his lack of satisfaction, Trudeau is getting his—artfully inserting the stiletto, panel by panel, into yet another victim. Take that, John Mitchell. Take this, *Time.* The results, readers find, are either outrageously funny or just plain outrageous.

To Trudeau, the strip is simply his public voice, his vehicle to inveigh against social and political wrongdoing, and to cuff wrongdoers. That vehicle, marketed by Universal Press Syndicate (UPS), and now appearing in some 390 papers nationwide, makes Trudeau—at 26—an innovative force in a field traditionally dominated by the fatuous hijinks of the likes of Dagwood and Donald Duck. With an income estimated at $100,000 a year from the strip, and a growing following, *Doonesbury* has made Trudeau wealthy and famous.

The money is nice, of course. It has enabled him, among other things, to buy and renovate a brownstone in New Haven, Conn., that doubles as home and studio. The fame Trudeau can do without. In the past couple of years, he has shied from public contact and the insatiable demands journalists make on "celebrities." (This summer he hid in his bathroom for more than one hour to avoid a reporter from the Baltimore *Sun.*) He firmly turns away requests for interviews with the statement, "What I have to say of interest comes across in the strip." And so it does, with a force that has generated editorial controversy and raised policy questions for numerous editors.

The controversy stems from the loose, historical precedent established during the evolution of comic strips—that their principal goal was to entertain readers. From the time the Yellow Kid first cavorted across the pages of the New York *Sunday World* in February, 1896, down through the heyday of the Katzenjammer Kids, Gasoline Alley and Dick Tracy, comic strips were crafted to amuse without necessarily conveying a message of social significance. Tracy, at his best, did it by strip-mining the adventure lode—cannily cracking bizarre crimes. The Katzenjammer Kids drew laughs with their maddening pranks. Gasoline Alley elicited chuckles with gentle practical jokes and shopworn homilies. Putting it another way, most of the traditional strips have had what Trudeau once described as a "tranquilizing effect" on their readers.

There have been notable exceptions. In the 1950's, Al Capp created his legendary tyrant General Bullmoose, who bore a less than flattering resemblance to "Engine" Charley Wilson, the pompous head of General Motors and secretary of defense under Eisenhower. Wilson is most fondly remembered for his tactful statement that "what's good for General Motors is good

world. Joe McCarthy made appearances as an unshaven wildcat named Simple J. Malarkey, and Spiro Agnew blustered from panel to panel in the guise of an unprincipled and avaricious hyena. But such breaches of comic strip etiquette have been relatively few; the really heavy hitting was left to the editorial page cartoonists.

That is, it was left to the Herblocks and Oliphants until four years ago when John McMeel and Jim Andrews launched UPS by taking a flyer on Trudeau. He was then an undergraduate at Yale who was penning a strip for the Yale *Daily News,* entitled *Bull Tales.* The original idea was to cull a few laughs at the expense of then campus hero, quarterback Brian Dowling. But Trudeau occasionally took on the likes of Yale President Kingman Brewster. The strip caught the eyes and fancies of McMeel and Andrews, and, Andrews says now, "It was clear he was a comic genius."

The strip (with its new name) was launched in October, 1970, in 30 newspapers, including the Washington *Post.* Trudeau had changed the name at UPS's insistence. (They thought the title might offend readers.) Mike Doonesbury had been a *Bull Tales* original whose last name Trudeau concocted by combining a Yale slang term—doone—meaning a good natured fool, with the last syllable of the name of a college roommate named Pillsbury.

Trudeau promptly took out after bigger quarry than those available on the Yale campus. His bluntly direct approach—having prominent victims appear simply as themselves—was unique to comics and soon got him into trouble. Indianapolis Publisher Eugene C. Pulliam found the strip's editorializing too tough to swallow and canceled *Doonesbury* in his Indianapolis *Star,* Muncie *Press,* and Phoenix *Republic* just months after its debut. In May, 1972, Perry Morgan, then managing editor of the Akron *Beacon Journal* banned the strip because of what he termed its "political characteristics." The episode that proved to be the clincher for Morgan depicted Zonker Harris, the strip's irreverent freak, laying the blame for the Kent State killings squarely at the feet of former Attorney General John Mitchell. Reader response to the cancellation was immediate and outraged, and Morgan not only reinstated *Doonesbury,* but by way of apology dispatched a reporter to New Haven to buy Trudeau a lobster dinner.

The most celebrated incident of censorship came a year later when Trudeau had the strip's resident radical, Mark Slackmeyer, pronouncing Mitchell GUILTY, GUILTY, GUILTY, GUILTY of Watergate offenses. Ben Bradlee of the Washington *Post* was not the only editor who found that one offensive. The Los Angeles *Times* and Boston *Globe,* papers which along with the *Post* could hardly be considered Mitchell *aficionados,* chose not to run the episode. Bradlee attributes the decision to excise the episode to a desire "to be fair" to Mitchell. Bill Thomas, executive vice president and editor of the *Times,* gives what appears to be a more routine reason. The *Times,* he says, was merely following a policy of avoiding the imputation of guilt in a pending criminal trial. Editors at the *Post* and the *Globe* admitted to surprise at the volume of reader protest.

chanan agonizing in a bar over some contingency resignation speeches for Richard Nixon. That was enough for the Providence *Bulletin* to decide to move *Doonesbury* off the comic pages and onto the page directly opposite their editorial page. (The *Bulletin* has no op-ed page.) Considering the consistent reader outrage at periodic censorship, more papers may find that solution the palatable one.

More serious (at least to Trudeau and UPS) than the cancellations and periodic censorship was an incident that took place a couple of years ago when the strip was taking on self-styled Super Cop and hard-hat Mayor Frank Rizzo of Philadelphia. The Philadelphia *Bulletin* thought it prudent to change one word in one of the panels. "Foul," cried Trudeau, and UPS sent a strong letter of protest.

Jim Andrews, who acts as Trudeau's editor, admits that disputes occasionally arise between them, most frequently over the tone of *Doonesbury* dialogue. In one recent episode, Trudeau depicted Hunter Thompson, the controversial pop-journalist, uttering a reference to "big mothers." Andrews objected to the ribald inference and Trudeau changed the balloon to read "really big ones."

"Our relationship is such that it wouldn't come into open conflict," Andrews said. "It's not my style and it's not Garry's style. We have an editorial relationship and he responds to that. We talk about it whenever we disagree; sometimes he convinces me, sometimes the other way around."

Although the misdeeds of Watergate received the lion's share of time in *Doonesbury* over the past year, Trudeau has also belabored other institutions with telling and witty effect. Last March, he devoted a couple of weeks to a put-down of group journalism as practiced at *Time.* The gull was a remarkably inept correspondent by the name of Roland Burton Hedley, Jr., who blunders his way to hilariously erroneous conclusions while reporting a cover story on campus life in the 70's. The accuracy of the lampoon had many *Time* staff members in stitches but left others cold.

More recently, Trudeau has lifted stylus in tongue-in-cheek defense of women's liberation. The hero-person, one Joanie Caucus, fights the equality battle at Berkeley Law School with her black roommate, whom Trudeau shackles with a jive-talking, chauvinist dude boyfriend named Clyde. Joanie finds herself at Berkeley because when Trudeau drew her deciding what school to attend, real students at Berkeley put in an application for her.

What is it that has made *Doonesbury* such a runaway success? One simple reason is that it has attracted the kind of support from young readers exhibited by those at Berkeley's law school. They find the strip believable and identify with its characters. A recent reader survey conducted by the Chicago *Tribune* indicated that *Doonesbury* was gaining popularity most rapidly among strips run by the Trib. Assistant Sunday Editor Larry Townsend attributes that to tremendous appeal to readers in the 18–35 age category. Don Wright, Pulitzer Prize-winning editorial cartoonist for the Miami *News,* agrees. "His characters appeal to young people. He just pops them down in the middle of a mess or controversy and lets them flail away until the truth appears. He manages to do what I want to do—attack with a blood lust." Wright also has high praise for Trudeau's dialogue. "He's a damn good writer. His style is clean and uncluttered. (Trudeau writes the dialogue for the strip first—without the benefit of the Rolling Stones—then sketches in the characters.)

Nicholas Von Hoffman, who has collaborated with Trudeau on *The Fireside Watergate,* catalogues another Trudeau strength. "He has a golden ear. He pays attention to words and the way they're said, and captures the essence of what's there that most people don't hear." The power of the dialogue and Trudeau's use of a device perfected by Jules Feiffer—keeping the art in each panel reasonably static—increases the impact of the message.

Some critics, including gun-shy editors, find the message all too strong, the humor too harsh and brittle. They also question Trudeau's ability to sustain the strip's momentum in the less turbulent post-Watergate milieu. The growing number of *Doonesbury* advocates among newspaper readers tends to refute the criticism about excessive harshness. In fact, on subjects other than Watergate, Trudeau displays a droll, subtle sense of humor that works because it underwhelms rather than overpowers. Von Hoffman offers a rebuttal to those who question the strip's staying power. "First, I don't think he's going to have to worry about a lack of material in the future. But I also think he's shown that in other times his humor would take other forms." UPS obviously agrees. Trudeau's contract has two more years to run, and there is a six-year self-renewal option.

Trudeau has indicated that his interest in the strip will at least match the length of the contract. But he has also begun to immerse himself in other projects such as a book that attempts to offer a graphic record of Hitler's drive through Russia. For Trudeau, it is enough that *Doonesbury* "has gotten people involved, pro or con."

Most people would agree that Trudeau is indeed moving the comics in a direction they have rarely traveled.

POINTS TO CONSIDER

1.   What traditionally has been the principal goal of comic strips? How has "Doonesbury" departed from this tradition?

2.   What is "Doonesbury's" unique approach to comment on the political scene? What problems has this caused?

3.   How does "Doonesbury's" art increase the impact of its message? Can you think of other comic strips that use the same technique?

4.   Is "Doonesbury" generally alone in its stance of political protest, or can you find evidence of increasing political concern in other popular comic strips?

5. What, according to the article, is the reason for "Doonesbury's" success? Can you point out examples of these things in the "Doonesbury" strips included in this section?

6. Do you feel that "Doonesbury" has "gotten people involved, pro or con"? Explain.

THE MOVIEGOERS' ASSISTANCE PLAN

Garry Trudeau

DOONESBURY
by Garry Trudeau

DOONESBURY
by Garry Trudeau

DOONESBURY
by Garry Trudeau

POINTS TO CONSIDER

1. In what ways is the political comment of this series of comic strips similar to that of editorial cartoons? In what ways is it different?

2. Do you feel that this series of comic strips makes a "protest"? Explain.

3. What comments are these strips making about the functions of government and about people's attitudes toward their government? What comments are the strips making about movies and moviegoing? Do you agree with these comments? Why, or why not?

4. Do you find the characters in these strips believable? Why, or why not? How do these characters affect the nature of the intended political or social comments?

5. Do you find these comic strips funny? If so, why?

■ IDEAS FOR INVESTIGATION, DISCUSSION, AND WRITING

1. What does the drawing style contribute to the effect of a cartoon? Compare the drawing styles of several humorous cartoons—such as "Peanuts," "Beetle Bailey," "Andy Capp," and "The Wizard of Id"—with the drawing styles of several adventure or romance cartoons—such as "Juliet Jones," "Steve Canyon," "Dr. Kildare," and "Batman." How are the styles appropriate to the subjects?

2. Using some or all the published collections of "Peanuts" cartoons, write an essay discussing the changes in the comic strip over the years. How has the drawing style changed? How have the characters' personalities changed? How have their relationships to each other changed? Assuming that these changes were at least to some degree a popular demand, what conclusions can you make about what Americans find amusing? Do you find that these changes reflect changes in our whole society? How?

3. Compare similar comic strips from different countries. (For example, "Dagwood" versus "Andy Capp.") What differences are there in characters and their relationships to each other? To what extent do these differences reflect differences in the social attitudes and values of the two countries?

4. List and discuss the various character stereotypes used in cartoons. Psychiatrists, for instance, are usually pictured as middle-aged men with dark goatees and dark horn-rimmed glasses. Include examples from magazines and other sources. Do you think these conventions are really necessary? Why? Is there a way in which they could be considered harmful?

5. Write an essay comparing cartoons found in magazines such as *Playboy, Esquire,* or *True* with cartoons found in *Ladies Home Journal,* or *Redbook,* or *Good Housekeeping.* What differences are there? How do these differences reflect the appeals and attitudes of the respective magazines in which the cartoons appeared?

6. Using a number of sample cartoons, discuss the use of political cartoons as propaganda. What advantages does the cartoon offer the propagandist? In what ways is the cartoon less effective as a propaganda medium than the printed word, television, or radio?

7. Draw several propaganda cartoons dealing with unusual topics or topics concerning your school. Write an explanation of the propaganda devices you use in the various cartoons and the stylistic conventions you employ.

8. Draw several humorous cartoons. For each cartoon write a discussion which includes an explanation of any stylistic conventions used, an indication of what magazines the cartoon would be likely to appear in, and for what audiences the cartoon is intended.

9. Write an essay discussing the animated cartoon as an artistic medium. What peculiar advantages does the medium offer? Can you cite examples of cartoons which utilize these aspects of the medium? Why do you think most animated cartoon features are humorous in nature? What are some of the drawbacks to the animated cartoon as an artistic medium?

10. What supernatural features have we come to associate with still and animated cartoons—such as miraculous recoveries by characters that are beat up, blown up, shot up, or otherwise assaulted? What is the significance of these conventions? How can they be compared to dream images, or how can they be considered "poetic license"? How would you attempt to explain these conventions to someone who has never seen them?

11. Make a "pilot" for a comic strip. This pilot should include drawings and written character sketches of all the main characters as well as several three or four frame comic strip sequences.

12. Using a fairly large sampling, conduct a survey to determine who reads which comic strips and why. The survey should gather such significant information as occupation (or major), age, sex, frequency with which the comic section is read, or any other factor you would wish to attempt to relate to the reading of comics. The survey should be kept as brief as possible, however, to make it easy to administer. What conclusions can be made on the basis of your findings?

13. Analyze and discuss from an aesthetic, political, or sociocultural viewpoint the comics of the new culture: "The Fabulous Furry Freak Brothers," "Marvel Comics," or the comics of R. Crumb.

14. Investigate the relationship between comics, cartoons, and fine art. What distinguishes the work of artists like Daumier, Heinrich Kley, or David Levine from that of Jules Feiffer, Bill Mauldin, or MacPherson of the Toronto *Star?* What things do they have in common? When do line drawings cease to be comics or cartoons and become art?

15. Make a historical study of the political cartoon from its beginning to the present day. How have the styles of cartoons changed over the centuries to reflect the politics and times in which they appeared? What role have technological improvements played in the role of the political cartoon? How effective have cartoons been as political persuasion?

16. Using the same technique as the collection of cartoons on "United States Involvement in Indochina," assemble a folio of cartoons dealing with a single event or issue. How are the same techniques and symbols used to express different opinions on the same issue? How do individual drawing styles affect the cartoon's message?

Part Four

Popular Print: Previews and Viewpoints

It is simply something that journalists in the new form have gravitated toward. That rather elementary and joyous ambition to show the reader *real life*—"Come here! Look! This is the way people live these days! These are the things they do!"

—Tom Wolfe

The Playboy and Miss America represent The Boy and The Girl. They incorporate a vision of life. They function as religious phenomena and should be exorcised and exposed.

—Harvey Cox

. . . Many women today are shedding their age-old image as chaste bearers of virtue. They are coming to grips with their own sexual concerns and are talking about them with unprecedented candor.

—Diane K. Shah

Our influence is slow and subtle, and it is felt mainly by the young. They are hungry for myths which resonate with the mysteries of their own times.

We give them those myths.

We will become influential when those who have listened to our myths have become influential.

—Kurt Vonnegut, Jr.
speaking of and to
writers of fiction

Popular
Print

■ THE BEST-SELLER LIST

"The Talk of the Town"   *The New Yorker*, December 8, 1962

A recent *Times* best-seller list included a coloring book for adults, a journal kept by a child, a pamphlet of newspaper photographs with humorous captions, the autobiography of a baseball manager, the reminiscences of a lawyer who had appeared for the defense in a sensational Hollywood trial, a discussion of dieting, and a study of the sexual activities of unmarried women. These seven works, filling nearly half the slots in the nonfiction section of the list, had appeared there a combined total of a hundred and twenty-two weeks, and would presumably remain there until other books—of similar quality—were published to replace them. Fortunately, the list is meaningless; indeed, the only redeeming quality of best-seller charts in general is their inaccuracy. They are based on slim and unreliable evidence, they disagree among themselves, and as indicators of what is actually being bought and read they are almost worthless. Few bookstores are consulted, fewer report, and there is nothing to prevent the ones that do report from falsifying their records to suit their inventories. Moreover, the provincial storekeeper, like the rural citizen, has more than his share of the vote. A book that sells a hundred copies at the Brentano's on Fifth Avenue is given no greater weight in the surveys than one that sells nine copies at Scrantom's, in Rochester. The most popular books in any store are the ones that count; the margin and the region of their popularity are considered irrelevant. For the issue of November 25th, for example, the *Herald Tribune* survey was compiled on the basis of reports from only thirty-four stores; Vroman's, of Pasadena, was side by side with the Scribner Book Store, in New York. The *Times*, usually so scrupulous in supplying sources for its news articles, does not list the number, size, or location of reporting booksellers at all. An ambiguous paragraph in italics tells us that the *Times* survey is based on reports from "leading booksellers in 41 cities showing the sales rating of 16 leading fiction and general titles over the last 3 weeks." Which the 41 cities are, how many bookstores report in each, why the unlikely numbers of 41 and 16 were chosen (the *Tribune* has an equally inexplicable, though not nameless, 34 and 10), and what the meaning of the word "leading" is—these questions are unanswered. The reader is left with the list, to make of it what he will. Meanwhile, the inaccurate ratings perform a major disservice to serious writings, the sales of which are often damaged by omission from the list.

Even if the chart meant something, even if it were based on reliable records of national sales volume (records that publishers are particularly reluctant to issue), one wonders what value the best-seller list could have for the reading public. Most industries release such itemized sales figures only to trade journals, where the producer finds out what he may expect to sell—not the consumer what he ought to buy. The book chart, on the other hand, presumably tries to show the conformist how the literary herd is running—and encourages him to run away from literature with the herd. If manufacturers ordinarily refrain from publishing statistics to show what everyone else is wearing and eating, surely the literary journals need not insist on telling us what everyone else is reading—and telling it inaccurately be-sides. Since sales in the arts have never been an index to value ("Moby Dick" was not a best-seller in its time, nor were any of Henry James' novels after "The Portrait of a Lady"), it is hard to imagine what serious purpose the charts can have. If the list is intended merely as a helpful guide to the anxious semiliterate, the *Times* would perform a greater service by listing the exact stores and regions to which it applies. Most readers, after all, are not required to participate in literary discussions across the nation; each is ordinarily confined to his own geographical area, and a chart that showed which books were selling well at the *local* bookstore would save readers the embarrassment of being competent to discuss at a cocktail party in Pasa-dena only those books that were deemed best-sellers in Vermont.

POINTS TO CONSIDER

1. What are some of the reasons why the best-seller list is not an accurate indication of what books people are reading?
2. What does *The New Yorker* feel is the function of the best-seller list? What might be some of the beneficial functions of an accurate best-seller list? What are some of the detrimental effects of a best-seller list, accurate or not?

WHY THEY AREN'T WRITING THE GREAT AMERICAN NOVEL ANYMORE

Tom Wolfe   *Esquire,* December 1972

All of a sudden, in the mid-Sixties, here comes a bunch of slick-magazine and Sunday-supplement writers with no literary credentials whatsoever in most cases—only they're using all the techniques of the novelists, even the most sophisticated ones—and on top of that they're helping themselves to the insights of the men of letters while they're at it—and at the same time they're still doing their low-life legwork, their "digging," their hustling, their damnable Locker Room Genre reporting—they're taking on *all* of these roles at the same time—in other words, they're ignoring literary class lines that have been almost a century in the making.

The panic hit the men of letters first. If the lumpenproles[1] won their

---

[1] *Lumpenproles* are isolated or disenfranchised members of the proletariat: Accord-ing to the "literary class lines" Wolfe suggests, the journalists form the proletariat or lower classes.

point, if their new form achieved any sort of literary respectability, if it were somehow accepted as "creative," the men of letters stood to lose even their positions as the reigning practitioners of nonfiction. They would get bumped down to Lower Middle Class. This was already beginning to happen. The first indication I had came in an article in the June, 1966, *Atlantic* by Dan Wakefield, entitled "The Personal Voice and the Impersonal Eye." The gist of the piece was that this was the first period in anybody's memory when people in the literary world were beginning to talk about nonfiction as a serious artistic form. Norman Podhoretz had written a piece in *Harper's* in 1958 claiming a similar status for the "discursive prose" of the late Fifties, essays by people like James Baldwin and Isaac Rosenfeld. But the excitement Wakefield was talking about had nothing to do with essays or any other traditional nonfiction. Quite the contrary; Wakefield attributed the new prestige of nonfiction to two books of an entirely different sort: *In Cold Blood,* by Truman Capote, and a collection of magazine articles with a title in alliterative trochaic pentameter that I am sure would come to me if I dwelled upon it.[2]

Capote's story of the life and death of two drifters who blew the heads off a wealthy farm family in Kansas ran as a serial in *The New Yorker* in the Fall of 1965 and came out in book form in February of 1966. It was a sensation—and a terrible jolt to all who expected the accursed New Journalism or Parajournalism to spin itself out like a fad. Here, after all, was not some obscure journalist, some free-lance writer, but a novelist of long standing . . . whose career had been in the doldrums . . . and who suddenly, with this one stroke, with this turn to the damnable new form of journalism, not only resuscitated his reputation but elevated it higher than ever before . . . and became a celebrity of the most amazing magnitude in the bargain. People of all sorts read *In Cold Blood,* people at every level of taste. Everybody was absorbed in it. Capote himself didn't call it journalism; far from it; he said he had invented a new literary genre, "the nonfiction novel." Nevertheless, his success gave the New Journalism, as it would soon be called, an overwhelming momentum.

Capote had spent five years researching his story and interviewing the killers in prison, and so on, a very meticulous and impressive job. But in 1966 you started seeing feats of reporting that were extraordinary, spectacular. Here came a breed of journalists who somehow had the moxie to talk their way inside of any milieu, even closed societies, and hang on for dear life. A marvelous maniac named John Sack talked the Army into letting him join an infantry company at Fort Dix, M Company, 1st Advanced Infantry Training Brigade—not as a recruit but as a reporter—and go through training with them and then to Vietnam and into battle. The result was a book called *M* (appearing first in *Esquire*), a nonfiction *Catch-22* and, for my money, still the finest book in any genre published about the war. George Plimpton went into training with a professional football team, the Detroit Lions, in the role of reporter playing rookie quarterback, rooming with the players going through their workouts and finally playing quarterback for them in a preseason game—in order to write *Paper Lion.* Like Capote's book, *Paper Lion* was read by people at every level of taste and had per-

---

[2] Wolfe's own book, *Kandy-kolored, Tangerine-flake Streamlined Baby.*

haps the greatest literary impact of any writing about sports since Ring Lardner's short stories. But the all-time free-lance writer's Brass Stud Award went that year to an obscure California journalist named Hunter Thompson who "ran" with the Hell's Angels for eighteen months—as a reporter and not a member, which might have been safer—in order to write *Hell's Angels: The Strange and Terrible Saga of the Outlaw Motorcycle Gang.* The Angels wrote his last chapter for him by stomping him half to death in a roadhouse fifty miles from Santa Rosa. All through the book Thompson had been searching for the single psychological or sociological insight that would sum up all he had seen, the single golden *aperçu;* and as he lay sprawled there on the floor coughing up blood and teeth, the line he had been looking for came to him in a brilliant flash from out of the heart of darkness: "Exterminate all the brutes!"

At the same time, 1966 and 1967, Joan Didion was writing those strange Gothic articles of hers about California that were eventually collected in *Slouching Towards Bethlehem.* Rex Reed was writing his celebrity interviews—this was an old journalistic exercise, of course, but no one had ever quite so diligently addressed himself to the question of, "What is So-and-so *really* like?" (Simone Signoret, as I recall, turned out to have the neck, shoulders and upper back of a middle linebacker.) James Mills was pulling off some amazing reporting feats of his own for *Life* in pieces such as "The Panic in Needle Park," "The Detective," and "The Prosecutor." The writer-reporter team of Garry Wills and Ovid Demaris was doing a series of brilliant pieces for *Esquire,* culminating in "You All Know Me—I'm Jack Ruby!"

And then, early in 1968, another novelist turned to nonfiction, and with a success that in its own way was as spectacular as Capote's two years before. This was Norman Mailer writing a memoir about an antiwar demonstration he had become involved in, "The Steps of the Pentagon." The memoir, or autobiography (Appendix III), is an old genre of nonfiction, of course, but this piece was written soon enough after the event to have a journalistic impact. It took up an entire issue of *Harper's Magazine* and came out a few months later under the title of *The Armies Of The Night.* Unlike Capote's book, Mailer's was not a popular success; but within the literary community and among intellectuals generally it couldn't have been a more tremendous *succés d'estime.*[3] At the time Mailer's reputation had been deteriorating in the wake of two inept novels called *An American Dream* (1965) and *Why Are We In Vietnam?* (1967). He was being categorized somewhat condescendingly as a journalist, because his nonfiction, chiefly in *Esquire,* was obviously better work. *The Armies Of The Night* changed all that in a flash. Like Capote, Mailer had a dread of the tag that had been put on him—"journalist"—and had subtitled his book "The Novel as History; History as the Novel." But the lesson was one that nobody in the literary world could miss. Here was another novelist who had turned to some form of accursed journalism, no matter what name you gave it, and had not only revived his reputation but raised it to a point higher than it had ever been in his life.

[3] Success from critical respect and the recognition of colleagues rather than from popularity.

By 1969 no one in the literary world could simply dismiss this new journalism as an inferior genre. The situation was somewhat similar to the situation of the novel in England in the 1850's. It was yet to be canonized, sanctified and given a theology, but writers themselves could already feel the new Power flowing.

The similarity between the early days of the novel and the early days of the New Journalism is not merely coincidental. In both cases we are watching the same process. We are watching a group of writers coming along, working in a genre regarded as Lower Class (the novel before the 1850's, slick-magazine journalism before the 1960's), who discover the joys of detailed realism and its strange powers. Many of them seem to be in love with realism for its own sake; and never mind the "sacred callings" of literature. They seem to be saying: "Hey! Come here! This is the way people are living now—just the way I'm going to show you! It may astound you, disgust you, delight you or arouse your contempt or make you laugh. . . . Nevertheless, this is what it's like! It's *all* right here! You won't be bored! Take a look!"

If you follow the progress of the New Journalism closely through the 1960's, you see an interesting thing happening. You see journalists learning the techniques of realism—particularly of the sort found in Fielding, Smollett, Balzac, Dickens and Gogol—from scratch. By trial and error, by "instinct" rather than theory, journalists began to discover the devices that gave the realistic novel its unique power, variously known as its "immediacy," its "concrete reality," its "emotional involvement," its "gripping" or "absorbing" quality.

This extraordinary power was derived mainly from just four devices, they discovered. The basic one was scene-by-scene construction, telling the story by moving from scene to scene and resorting as little as possible to sheer historical narrative. Hence the sometimes extraordinary feats of reporting that the new journalists undertook: so that they could actually witness the scenes in other people's lives as they took place—and record the dialogue in full, which was device No. 2. Magazine writers, like the early novelists, learned by trial and error something that has since been demonstrated in academic studies: namely, that realistic dialogue involves the reader more completely than any other single device. It also establishes and defines character more quickly and effectively than any other single device. (Dickens has a way of fixing a character in your mind so that you have the feeling he has described every inch of his appearance—only to go back and discover that he actually took care of the physical description in two or three sentences; the rest he had accomplished with dialogue.) Journalists were working on dialogue of the fullest, most completely revealing sort in the very moment when novelists were cutting back, using dialogue in more and more cryptic, fey and curiously abstract ways.

The third device was the so-called "third-person point of view," the technique of presenting every scene to the reader through the eyes of a particular character, giving the reader the feeling of being inside the character's mind and experiencing the emotional reality of the scene as he experiences it. Journalists had often used the first-person point of view—"I was there"—just as autobiographers, memoirists and novelists had. This is very limiting for the journalist, however, since he can bring the reader inside the mind of only one character—himself—a point of view that often proves irrelevant to the story and irritating to the reader. Yet how could a journalist, writing nonfiction, accurately penetrate the thoughts of another person?

The answer proved to be marvelously simple: interview him about his thoughts and emotions, along with everything else. This was what Gay Talese did in order to write *Honor Thy Father.* In *M,* John Sack had gone a step further and used both third-person point of view and the interior monologue to a limited extent.

The fourth device has always been the least understood. This is the recording of everyday gestures, habits, manners, customs, styles of furniture, clothing, decoration, styles of traveling, eating, keeping house, modes of behaving toward children, servants, superiors, inferiors, peers, plus the various looks, glances, poses, styles of walking and other symbolic details that might exist within a scene. Symbolic of what? Symbolic, generally, of people's *status life,* using that term in the broad sense of the entire pattern of behavior and possessions through which people express their position in the world or what they think it is or what they hope it to be. The recording of such details is not mere embroidery in prose. It lies as close to the center of the power of realism as any other device in literature.

When we talk about the "rise" or "death" of literary genres, we are talking about status, mainly. The novel no longer has the supreme status it enjoyed for ninety years (1875–1965), but neither has the New Journalism won it for itself. The status of the New Journalism is not secure by any means. In some quarters the contempt for it is boundless . . . even breathtaking. . . . With any luck at all the new genre will never be sanctified, never be exalted, never given a theology. I probably shouldn't even go around talking it up the way I have in this piece. All I meant to say when I started out was that the New Journalism can no longer be ignored in an artistic sense. The rest I take back. . . . The hell with it. . . . Let chaos reign . . . louder music, more wine. . . . The hell with the standings. . . . The top rung is up for grabs. All the old traditions are exhausted, and no new one is yet established. All bets are off! the odds are canceled! it's anybody's ball game! . . . the horses are all drugged! the track is glass! . . . and out of such glorious chaos may come, from the most unexpected source, in the most unexpected form, some nice new fat Star Streamer Rockets that will light up the sky.

■| **POINTS TO CONSIDER**

1. What is the New Journalism? How is it similar to fiction? How is it different? How does it differ from traditional journalism? How is it similar?

2. How did the New Journalism develop? What gap does Wolfe believe it filled?

3. Can you think of some subjects or journalistic functions for which New Journalism might not be particularly well suited?

4. Describe the class conflict that Wolfe suggests exists in the literary world. What use does Wolfe make of this "class struggle" to present his ideas?

5. What are the four techniques of literary realism that New Journalism has borrowed? What particular power do these techniques give to New Journalism?

6. Why do you think that Wolfe says in his final paragraph, "Let chaos reign"? What does New Journalism owe to chaos and the breaking of old forms?

7. The selection from Joe McGinniss's *The Selling of the President, 1968,* which appears in the next part (page 287), is an example of New Journalism. When you read this selection, consider the ways in which the writer makes use of the New Journalism techniques discussed by Tom Wolfe. Do you find McGinniss's treatment of his subject effective?

■ ". . . BUT WORDS CAN NEVER HURT ME."

Kurt Vonnegut, Jr.   *Wampeters, Foma & Granfalloons,* 1974

Journalists and teachers are often bullied or fired in my country for saying this or that. But writers of novels and plays and short stories and poems have never been hurt or hampered much. They haven't even been noticed much by federal, state, or local governments, no matter how insolent or blasphemous or treasonous those writers may be. This has been going on now for nearly two hundred years.

If tyranny comes to my country, which is an old one now (and tyranny can come anywhere, anytime, as nearly as I can tell), I expect to go on writing whatever I please, without putting myself in danger, as long as what I write is fiction. The experience of American power structures with fiction since 1776 would appear to validate what is perhaps the first poem I ever learned by heart. A playmate must have taught it to me. It goes like this:

> *Sticks and stones*
> *May break my bones,*
> *But words can never hurt me.*

It is the feeling in several countries, I know, that fiction can hurt a social order a lot. And by fiction I mean any person's written report of what is going on in his head, as opposed to the daily news. Writers of such stuff, as Heinrick Böll[1] can tell us, have been jailed, put into lunatic asylums, exiled,

---

[1] Heinrich Böll is a prominent German novelist, winner of the Nobel Prize for literature in 1972.

or even killed sometimes—for putting certain words in a certain order. Politicians who do things like that to fiction writers should learn from the American experience that they are not merely being cruel. They are being preposterous, too. Fiction is harmless. Fiction is so much hot air.

The Vietnam war has proved this. Virtually every American fiction writer was against our participation in that civil war. We all raised hell about the war for years and years—with novels and poems and plays and short stories. We dropped on our complacent society the literary equivalent of a hydrogen bomb.

I will now report to you the power of such a bomb. It has the explosive force of a very large banana-cream pie—a pie two meters in diameter, twenty centimeters thick, and dropped from a height of ten meters or more.

My own feeling is that we should turn this awesome weapon over to the United Nations, or to some other international peacekeeping organization, such as the C.I.A.

What can tyrants, large and small, learn from my speech so far? That fiction writers are harmless. They may safely be allowed all the freedoms which birds have—to sing as they please, to hop about, to fly. Harsh authorities everywhere should learn this poem by heart, and recite it joyfully at the start of every day:

> *Sticks and stones*
> *May break my bones,*
> *But fiction can never hurt me.*

Thus ends the public part of my speech. I have a few additional words for you, my colleagues. Please don't repeat them outside this room. While it is true that we American fiction writers failed to modify the course of the war, we have reason to suspect that we have poisoned the minds of thousands or perhaps millions of American young people. Our hope is that the poison will make them worse than useless in unjust wars.

We shall see.

Unfortunately, that still leaves plenty of Americans who don't read or think much—who will still be extremely useful in unjust wars. We are sick about that. We did the best we could.

Most writers I know, all over the world, do the best they can. They must. They have no choice in the matter. All artists are specialized cells in a single, huge organism, mankind. Those cells have to behave as they do, just as the cells in our hearts or our fingertips have to behave as they do.

We here are some of those specialized cells. Our purpose is to make mankind aware of itself, in all its complexity, and to dream its dreams. We have no choice in the matter.

And there is more to our situation than that. In privacy here, I think we can acknowledge to one another that we don't really write what we write. We don't write the *best* of what we write, at any rate. The best of our stuff draws information and energy and wholeness from outside ourselves. Sculptors feel this more strongly than we do, incidentally. Every sculptor I ever knew felt that some spook had taken possession of his hands.

Where do these external signals come from? I think they come from all the other specialized cells in the organism. Those other cells contribute to us energy and little bits of information, in order that we may increase the organism's awareness of itself—and dream its dreams.

But if the entire organism thinks that what we do is important, why aren't we more influential than we are? I am persuaded that we are tremendously influential, even though most national leaders, my own included, probably never heard of most of us here. Our influence is slow and subtle, and it is felt mainly by the young. They are hungry for myths which resonate with the mysteries of their own times.

We give them those myths.

We will become influential when those who have listened to our myths have become influential. Those who rule us now are living in accordance with myths created for them by writers when *they* were young. It is perfectly clear that our rulers do not question those myths for even a minute during busy day after busy day. Let us pray that those terribly influential writers who created those myths for our leaders were humane.

Thank you.

POINTS TO CONSIDER

1. How has the Vietnam war "proved" that fiction has no effect on current political events? Do you think that this is really true? Explain.

2. Why are people who don't read or think much "extremely useful in unjust wars"?

3. What, according to Vonnegut, is the function of writers in a society?

4. What does Vonnegut mean by the term "myth"? Do you think that young people are particularly "hungry for myths"? If so, why? What does this suggest about leaders who no longer question the myths they absorbed years ago?

5. Does the fact that a novel by Vonnegut was burned by the board of education in a small town in North Dakota (see "Burning Vonnegut," page 437) disprove Vonnegut's point that "words can never hurt me"? Why, or why not?

■ FOR PAPERBACK HOUSES, THERE'S NO BUSINESS LIKE SHOW TIE-IN BUSINESS

Nancy Hardin   *Publishers Weekly,* February 17, 1975

Not so long ago the publishing rights for a movie tie-in book could be picked up for the cash equivalent of a song. That is, if the buyer was persistent enough to make his way past the indifference of whoever was handling the sale—usually someone in the publicity department of a film company who felt he had better things to do than shuffle papers for a slow grand or two.

That was then. In the past few years it's become a whole different ballgame. Film and publishing people have finally become aware of how much each can offer the other. And in this era of belt-tightening, film companies no longer turn up their noses at the income they can derive from even a small override on a successful tie-in.

Tie-ins come in several forms, with two common denominators whenever possible: a cover featuring the movie art or star photos, and a publication date timed to coincide with the national release of the film. The traditional type of tie-in consists of merely repackaging the edition which has already come out in softcover—or even hard, with a success like "The Exorcist," for example—to include a tie-in cover and, occasionally, an insert of stills from the film. The other garden-variety type of tie-in consists of a novelization of the screenplay, again with a coordinated cover and stills from the film occasionally included. Least likely to turn up on mass market racks is a third type of movie tie-in, the screenplay itself, containing dialogue and scene settings from the film, minus the more esoteric camera directions but almost always including stills. Some screenwriters feel that their work should only be published in the form in which it was written, and if their names carry enough weight—a William Goldman, say, or a Robert Towne or a Michael Crichton—and the film in question seems assured of success, a publisher may agree to go with the screenplay even though most readers apparently find the form difficult to read, and sales orders can be cut by about two-thirds, if even a highly successful film is published as a screenplay. Last, and least in number, since very few films are big enough to warrant such attention, are books written *about* a film—the making of it, its special effects, or whatever. Blockbusters like "Love Story," "The Godfather" and "The Great Gatsby" spawned such books; perhaps the most successful of the genre have been "The Making of 2001" and "William Peter Blatty on the Exorcist: From Novel to Film."

In the days when such deals didn't seem to count for much, an editor who had heard about a film that sounded promising would often have to scramble even to discover who owned the publication rights, much less where he could get hold of a copy of the script, or who was authorized to make a deal and draw up a contract. At best, there was a routine procedure. Someone from the merchandising or publicity department of the studio releasing the film in question would send around a blurry copy of the script, accompanied by what amounted to a form letter with information about the cast and a projected release date. After that, it was pretty much up to the editor to phone in a modest offer. As often as not, the editor in question had no particular expertise (beyond enjoying an occasional movie) in deciding which films to tie-in with; and even the big paperback houses had no one editor who was hired specifically to handle movie tie-ins, as nearly all of them have now (some even have a Los Angeles scout to boot).

At Avon Judy Weber notes that "one of the biggest changes in the past year or so is that there are more and more TV tie-ins and people are recognizing the importance of them." Even a one-shot television show with high ratings can sell large quantities of books. Ms. Weber cites "Go Ask Alice," a preexisting book which had 308,000 copies in print in softcover when the television show first aired in January, 1973, six months after its publication and then spiralled to an additional 1,709,000 in the 10 months following it. She also mentioned the after-the-fact novelization of "Sunshine," which came out, novelized by a distinguished writer, Norma Klein, with a first printing of 800,000 more than six months after the show was aired in November of 1973 and is now up to over 1,000,000 copies, a testament to the long-term sales effectiveness that a television special can have on a book tie-in. Bantam's "The Autobiography of Miss Jane Pittman" provides another case in point. Its first printing, in June of 1972, consisted of 160,000 copies; in January of 1973, when the Emmy-winning CBS television special was aired, there were still fewer than 200,000 copies out. But between January and November of 1974, 550,000 copies of the special tie-in edition were printed and shipped, 150,000 of them to coincide with the rerun aired on November 3.

Television has also boosted the book business in that bids from networks and TV producers have of late become competitive with those paid

GRIN AND BEAR IT   by Lichty & Wagner

3-27

"This court sentences you to five years and reserves the movie rights if you write a book."

"Grin and Bear It" by George Lichty and Fred Wagner. Courtesy of Field Newspaper Syndicate.

by film companies. And a new market is opening up for certain books that could not carry a feature film but work very well when adapted for television. Film director Ulu Grosbard points out that "it used to be that if a book was dead for films it was just dead. Now, thanks to TV, that's not so."

The tie-in boom is no surprise to Richard Fischoff at Warner Paperback Library. It is his view that people aren't essentially readers any more, that except for famous best-selling or category authors people don't buy by author, and that reading has become a time-killing activity rather than an avocation. This means that people who buy books are likely to be attracted by extra-literary factors such as eye-catching graphics, a photo of a star, a familiar logo—some recognition factor from a non-linear medium that makes the book stand out from the welter of other books on the stands. To Fischoff, tie-ins provide a way to get people back to enjoying reading. "Also prices for tie-ins are going up," he adds, "because of the competitive situation in the softcover industry. Whereas it used to be one or two houses bidding for a property, now half a dozen are going after the same thing. It's no longer a buyer's market. Agents, motion picture companies, publishers, writers, actors and producers—everyone seems to have realized there is pie now and they all want a piece of it." Or, as Patrick O'Connor, editor-in-chief of Popular Library, succinctly puts it, "In the old days, they wanted us . . . desperately. And now, we want them . . . desperately."

POINTS TO CONSIDER

1. What is a movie tie-in book? What are the several forms the tie-in book can take?

2. Why is a tie-in book least likely to take the form of a published screenplay?

3. What reasons does the article give for the success of tie-ins on the newsstand? Do you agree with the article's contention that reading has become a "time-killing activity rather than an avocation"—that is, something that's "fun"?

4. In what way does a tie-in book reinforce the effect of a movie as an "event" that Paulene Kael describes? (See page 355.)

■ THE PLAYBOY AND MISS AMERICA

Harvey Cox   *The Secular City,* 1966

Let us look at the spurious sexual models conjured up for our anxious society by the sorcerers of the mass media and the advertising guild.[1] Like all pagan deities, these come in pairs—the god and his consort. For our purposes they are best symbolized by The Playboy and Miss America, the Adonis and Aphrodite of a leisure-consumer society which still seems unready to venture into full postreligious maturity and freedom. The Playboy and Miss America represent The Boy and The Girl. They incorporate a vision of life. They function as religious phenomena and should be exorcised and exposed.

Let us begin with Miss America. In the first century B.C., Lucretius wrote this description of the pageant of Cybele:[2]

> *Adorned with emblem and crown . . . she is carried in awe-inspiring state. Tight-stretched tambourines and hollow cymbals thunder all round to the stroke of open hands, hollow pipes stir with Phrygian strain. . . . She rides in procession through great cities and mutely enriches mortals with a blessing not expressed in words. They straw all her path with brass and silver, presenting her with bounteous alms, and scatter over her a snow-shower of roses.*

Now compare this with the annual twentieth-century Miss America pageant in Atlantic City, New Jersey. Spotlights probe the dimness like votive tapers, banks of flowers exude their varied aromas, the orchestra blends feminine strings and regal trumpets. There is a hushed moment of tortured suspense, a drumroll, then the climax—a young woman with carefully prescribed anatomical proportions and exemplary "personality" parades serenely with scepter and crown to her throne. At TV sets across the nation throats tighten and eyes moisten. "There she goes, Miss America—" sings the crooner. "There she goes, your ideal." A new queen in America's emerging cult of The Girl has been crowned.

This young woman—though she is no doubt totally ignorant of the fact—symbolizes something beyond herself. She symbolizes The Girl, the primal image, the one behind the many. Just as the Virgin appears in many guises—as our Lady of Lourdes or of Fatima or of Guadalupe—but is always recognizably the Virgin, so with The Girl.

The Girl is also the omnipresent icon of consumer society.[3] Selling beer, she is folksy and jolly. Selling gems, she is chic and distant. But

---

[1] Spurious means counterfeit or false.

[2] Cybele was an ancient Roman goddess of nature worshipped in elaborate festivals.

[3] An omnipresent icon is a portrait, usually of a religious figure, present everywhere at once.

behind her various theophanies she remains recognizably The Girl.[4] In Miss America's glowingly healthy smile, her openly sexual but officially virginal figure, and in the name-brand gadgets around her, she personifies the stunted aspirations and ambivalent fears of her culture.[5] "There she goes, your ideal."

Miss America stands in a long line of queens going back to Isis, Ceres, and Aphrodite.[6] Everything from the elaborate sexual taboos surrounding her person to the symbolic gifts at her coronation hints at her ancient ancestry. But the real proof comes when we find that the function served by The Girl in our culture is just as much a "religious" one as that served by Cybele in hers. The functions are identical—to provide a secure personal "identity" for initiates and to sanctify a particular value structure.

Let us look first at the way in which The Girl confers a kind of identity on her initiates. Simone de Beauvoir says in *The Second Sex* that "no one is *born* a woman." One is merely born a female, and "*becomes* a woman" according to the models and meanings provided by the civilization. During the classical Christian centuries, it might be argued, the Virgin Mary served in part as this model. With the Reformation and especially with the Puritans, the place of Mary within the symbol system of the Protestant countries was reduced or eliminated. There are those who claim that this excision constituted an excess of zeal that greatly impoverished Western culture, an impoverishment from which it has never recovered. Some would even claim that the alleged failure of American novelists to produce a single great heroine (we have no Phaedra, no Anna Karenina) stems from this self-imposed lack of a central feminine ideal.

Without entering into this fascinating discussion, we can certainly be sure that, even within modern American Roman Catholicism, the Virgin Mary provides an identity image for few American girls. Where then do they look for the "model" Simone de Beauvoir convincingly contends they need? For most, the prototype of femininity seen in their mothers, their friends, and in the multitudinous images to which they are exposed on the mass media is what we have called The Girl.

To describe the mechanics of this complex psychological process by which the fledgling American girl participates in the life of The Girl and thus attains a woman's identity would require a thorough description of American adolescence. There is little doubt, however, that such an analysis would reveal certain striking parallels to the "savage" practices by which initiates in the mystery cults shared in the magical life of their god.

For those inured to the process, the tortuous nightly fetish by which the young American female pulls her hair into tight bunches secured by metal clips may bear little resemblance to the incisions made on their arms by certain African tribesmen to make them resemble their totem, the tiger. But to an anthropologist comparing two ways of attempting to resemble the holy one, the only difference might appear to be that with the Africans the

---

[4] Theophanies are visible forms of a god.

[5] To be ambivalent is to have conflicting feelings toward a person or thing.

[6] Isis, Ceres, and Aphrodite are all ancient goddesses. Isis was the Egyptian goddess of motherhood and fertility, Ceres the Roman goddess of vegetation (especially grain), and Aphrodite the Greek goddess of love and beauty.

torture is over after initiation, while with the American it has to be repeated every night, a luxury only a culture with abundant leisure can afford.

In turning now to an examination of the second function of The Girl—supporting and portraying a value system—a comparison with the role of the Virgin in the twelfth and thirteenth centuries may be helpful. Just as the Virgin exhibited and sustained the ideals of the age that fashioned Chartres Cathedral, as Henry Adams saw, so The Girl symbolizes the values and aspirations of a consumer society. (She is crowned not in the political capital, remember, but in Atlantic City or Miami Beach, centers associated with leisure and consumption.) And she is not entirely incapable of exploitation. If men sometimes sought to buy with gold the Virgin's blessings on their questionable causes, so The Girl now dispenses her charismatic favor on watches, refrigerators, and razor blades—for a price.[7] Though The Girl has built no cathedrals, without her the colossal edifice of mass persuasion would crumble. Her sharply stylized face and figure beckon us from every magazine and TV channel, luring us toward the beatific vision of a consumer's paradise.[8]

Besides sanctifying a set of phony values, The Girl compounds her noxiousness by maiming her victims in a Procrustean bed of uniformity.[9] This is the empty "identity" she panders.[10] Take the Miss America pageant, for example. Are these virtually indistinguishable specimens of white, middle-class postadolescence really the best we can do? Do they not mirror the ethos of a mass-production society, in which genuine individualism somehow mars the clean, precision-tooled effect?[11] Like their sisters, the finely calibrated Rockettes, these meticulously measured and pretested "beauties" lined up on the boardwalk bear an ominous similarity to the faceless retinues of goose-steppers and the interchangeable mass exercisers of explicitly totalitarian societies.[12] In short, *who* says this is beauty?

The caricature becomes complete in the Miss Universe contest, when Miss Rhodesia is a blonde, Miss South Africa is white, and Oriental girls with a totally different tradition of feminine beauty are forced to display their thighs and appear in spike heels and Catalina swim suits. Miss Universe is as universal as an American adman's stereotype of what beauty should be.

The truth is that The Girl can*not* bestow the identity she promises. She forces her initiates to torture themselves with starvation diets and beauty-parlor ordeals, but still cannot deliver the satisfactions she holds out. She is

---

[7] Charismatic means having great spiritual power or charm for appealing to people and gaining their support.

[8] Beatific means bringing bliss or joy.

[9] Noxiousness is harmfulness or injuriousness. A Procrustean bed is a rigid standard which everyone is supposed to fit (from the Greek legend of a highwayman who bound his victims to an iron bed and stretched them or lopped off part of their legs to make them fit it exactly).

[10] To pander is to act as an agent for something illicit or disreputable.

[11] An ethos is a set of values.

[12] The Rockettes are a chorus line of dancers who are featured in the elaborate musical shows at Radio City Music Hall in New York. They and the Miss America candidates are compared to well-trained rows of soldiers parading for a dictator or to the anonymous mass of workers in a state with rigid government controls.

young, but what happens when her followers, despite added hours in the boudoir, can no longer appear young? She is happy and smiling and loved. What happens when, despite all the potions and incantations, her disciples still feel the human pangs of rejection and loneliness? Or what about all the girls whose statistics, or "personality" (or color) do not match the authoritative "ideal"?

The Playboy, illustrated by the monthly magazine of that name, does for the boys what Miss America does for the girls. Despite accusations to the contrary, the immense popularity of this magazine is not solely attributable to pinup girls. For sheer nudity its pictorial art cannot compete with such would-be competitors as *Dude* and *Escapade. Playboy* appeals to a highly mobile, increasingly affluent group of young readers, mostly between eighteen and thirty, who want much more from their drugstore reading than bosoms and thighs. They need a total image of what it means to be a man. And Mr. Hefner's *Playboy* has no hesitation in telling them.

Why should such a need arise? David Riesman has argued that the responsibility for character formation in our society has shifted from the family to the peer group and to the mass-media peer-group surrogates.[13] Things are changing so rapidly that one who is equipped by his family with inflexible, highly internalized values becomes unable to deal with the accelerated pace of change and with the varying contexts in which he is called upon to function. This is especially true in the area of consumer values toward which the "other-directed person" is increasingly oriented.

Within the confusing plethora[14] of mass media signals and peer-group values, *Playboy* fills a special need. For the insecure young man with newly acquired free time and money who still feels uncertain about his consumer skills, *Playboy* supplies a comprehensive and authoritative guidebook to this forbidding new world to which he now has access. It tells him not only who to be; it tells him *how* to be, and even provides consolation outlets for those who secretly feel that they have not quite made it.

In supplying for the other-directed consumer of leisure both the normative identity image and the means of achieving it, *Playboy* relies on a careful integration of copy and advertising material. The comic book that appeals to a younger generation with an analogous problem skillfully intersperses illustrations of incredibly muscled men and excessively mammalian women with advertisements for body-building gimmicks and foam-rubber brassière supplements. Thus the thin-chested comic-book readers of both sexes are thoughtfully supplied with both the ends and the means for attaining a spurious brand of maturity. *Playboy* merely continues the comic-book tactic for the next age group. Since within every identity crisis, whether in teens or twenties, there is usually a sexual identity problem, *Playboy* speaks to those who desperately want to know what it means to be a man, and more specifically a *male,* in today's world.

Both the image of man and the means for its attainment exhibit a remarkable consistency in *Playboy.* The skilled consumer is cool and unruf-

---

[13] Mr. Riesman says that a young person's character is formed less by his family than by friends his own age and by the mass media which sometimes take the place of human friends.

[14] A plethora is an overabundance, an excess.

fled. He savors sports cars, liquor, high fidelity, and book-club selections with a casual, unhurried aplomb.[15] Though he must certainly *have* and *use* the latest consumption item, he must not permit himself to get too attached to it. The style will change and he must always be ready to adjust. His persistent anxiety that he may mix a drink incorrectly, enjoy a jazz group that is passé, or wear last year's necktie style is comforted by an authoritative tone in *Playboy* beside which papal encyclicals sound irresolute.[16]

"Don't hesitate," he is told, "this assertive, self-assured weskit is what every man of taste wants for the fall season." Lingering doubts about his masculinity are extirpated[17] by the firm assurance that "real men demand this ruggedly masculine smoke" (cigar ad). Though "the ladies will swoon for you, no matter what they promise, don't give them a puff. This cigar is for men only." A fur-lined canvas field jacket is described as "the most masculine thing since the cave man." What to be and how to be it are both made unambiguously clear.

Since being male necessitates some kind of relationship to females, *Playboy* fearlessly confronts this problem too, and solves it by the consistent application of the same formula. Sex becomes one of the items of leisure activity that the knowledgeable consumer of leisure handles with his characteristic skill and detachment. The girl becomes a desirable—indeed an indispensable—"Playboy accessory."

In a question-answer column entitled "The Playboy Adviser," queries about smoking equipment (how to break in a meerschaum pipe), cocktail preparation (how to mix a Yellow Fever), and whether or not to wear suspenders with a vest alternate with questions about what to do with girls who complicate the cardinal principle of casualness either by suggesting marriage or by some other impulsive gesture toward a permanent relationship. The infallible answer from the oracle never varies: sex must be contained, at all costs, within the entertainment-recreation area. Don't let her get "serious."

After all, the most famous feature of the magazine is its monthly foldout photo of a *play*mate. She is the symbol par excellence of recreational sex. When playtime is over, the playmate's function ceases, so she must be made to understand the rules of the game. As the crew-cut young man in a *Playboy* cartoon says to the rumpled and disarrayed girl he is passionately embracing, "Why speak of love at a time like this?"

The magazine's fiction purveys the same kind of severely departmentalized sex. Although the editors have recently improved the *Playboy* contents with contributions by Hemingway, Bemelmans, and even a Chekhov translation, many of the stories still rely on a repetitive and predictable formula. A successful young man, either single or somewhat less than ideally married—a figure with whom readers have no difficulty identifying—encounters a gorgeous and seductive woman who makes no demands on him except sex. She is the prose duplication of the cool-eyed but hot-blooded playmate of the foldout.

[15] Aplomb is assurance or poise.

[16] Papal encyclicals are letters of religious directive from the Pope to the bishops of the world.

[17] Extirpated means destroyed completely.

Drawing heavily on the fantasy life of all young Americans, the writers utilize for their stereotyped heroines the hero's schoolteacher, his secretary, an old girl friend, or the girl who brings her car into the garage where he works. The happy issue is always a casual but satisfying sexual experience with no entangling alliances whatever. Unlike the women he knows in real life, the *Playboy* reader's fictional girl friends know their place and ask for nothing more. They present no danger of permanent involvement. Like any good accessory, they are detachable and disposable.

Many of the advertisements reinforce the sex-accessory identification in another way—by attributing female characteristics to the items they sell. Thus a full-page ad for the MG assures us that this car is not only "the smoothest pleasure machine" on the road and that having one is a "love affair," but most important, "you drive it—it doesn't drive you." The ad ends with the equivocal question "Is it a date?"

Playboy insists that its message is one of liberation. Its gospel frees us from captivity to the puritanical "hatpin brigade." It solemnly crusades for "frankness" and publishes scores of letters congratulating it for its unblushing "candor." Yet the whole phenomenon of which *Playboy* is only a part vividly illustrates the awful fact of a new kind of tyranny.

Those liberated by technology and increased prosperity to new worlds of leisure now become the anxious slaves of dictatorial taste makers. Obsequiously[18] waiting for the latest signal on what is cool and what is awkward, they are paralyzed by the fear that they may hear pronounced on them that dread sentence occasionally intoned by "The Playboy Adviser": "You goofed!" Leisure is thus swallowed up in apprehensive competitiveness, its liberating potential transformed into a self-destructive compulsion to consume only what is *à la mode. Playboy* mediates the Word of the most high into one section of the consumer world, but it is a word of bondage, not of freedom.

Nor will *Playboy's* synthetic doctrine of man stand the test of scrutiny. Psychoanalysts constantly remind us how deep-seated sexuality is in the human being. But if they didn't remind us, we would soon discover it ourselves anyway. Much as the human male might like to terminate his relationship with a woman as he would snap off the stereo, or store her for special purposes like a camel's-hair jacket, it really can't be done. And anyone with a modicum of experience with women knows it can't be done. Perhaps this is the reason *Playboy's* readership drops off so sharply after the age of thirty.

Playboy really feeds on the existence of a repressed fear of involvement with women, which for various reasons is still present in many otherwise adult Americans. So *Playboy's* version of sexuality grows increasingly irrelevant as authentic sexual maturity is achieved.

Thus any theological critique of *Playboy* that focuses on its "lewdness" will misfire completely. *Playboy* and its less successful imitators are not "sex magazines" at all. They are basically antisexual. They dilute and dissipate authentic sexuality by reducing it to an accessory, by keeping it at a safe distance.

---

[18] Obsequiously means obediently or submissively.

Freedom for mature sexuality comes to man only when he is freed from the despotic powers[19] which crowd and cower him into fixed patterns of behavior. Both Miss America and The Playboy illustrate such powers. When they determine man's sexual life, they hold him in captivity. They prevent him from achieving maturity.

POINTS TO CONSIDER

1.   In what way does Miss America assume the proportions of a religious figure in current American culture?

2.   Describe the value system that Miss America represents in our culture. What dangers does the author point out that lie in trying to adopt this value system and in identifying with its symbol?

3.   Why do you think there have been no black Miss Americas?

4.   What is the *Playboy* "image"? How is this image similar to Miss America in its function and the value system it represents? How realistic is this image?

5.   What "needs" does *Playboy* fulfill for its readers? Do you feel as the author does that *Playboy* and Miss America tend to "crowd and cower" people "into fixed patterns of behavior"? Explain.

6.   In what sense is *Playboy* magazine, despite its photographs of attractive girls, basically an antisexual magazine?

SECRET URGES ON HER MIND

Diane K. Shah   *The National Observer,* June 7, 1975

You expected not to desire any other men after marriage. And you expected your husband not to desire any other women. Then the desires came and you were thrown into a panic of self-hatred. What an evil woman you were! How could you keep being infatuated with strange men? How could you study their bulging trousers like that? How could you sit at a meeting imagining how every man in the room would ____? How could you sit on a train ____ total strangers with your eyes? How could you do that to your husband? Did anyone ever tell you that maybe it had nothing to do with your husband?

[19] Despotic powers are tyrannical powers.

So muses Isadora Wing, poet protagonist of Erica Jong's runaway best-selling novel, *Fear of Flying.* Though the passage (quoted here with deletions), and indeed Isadora herself, may be offensive to some, the $6.95 book has sold more than 50,000 hardcover copies and, since November, 3 million in paperback. It's going into its 19th printing and sales have yet to fall off. Says Karen DeCrow, president of the National Organization for Women: "The book is an accurate statement about a generation of women growing up in the '50s. It shows how many of us are reflections and victims of the men we love."

All of which is nice for Jong, who is in Hollywood working on the screenplay for the forthcoming movie of *Fear of Flying* (possibly to star Barbra Streisand, Goldie Hawn, Brenda Vaccaro, or Madeline Kahn). But do real women, aside from Jong and DeCrow, actually *think* like that?

Says Jong: "I know people aren't buying it for the sex scenes. They are buying it, I suspect, because it portrays the conflicting feelings women have traditionally had about sex."

Many women, of course, would disagree. The young wife of a suburban Boston tax accountant exclaims: "I don't know any women like that, women who sit on trains looking at men like *that.*" And a prosperous Chicago woman in her 50s told her book group recently, "I think I can safely say that none of us in this room has ever had a sexual fantasy!"

Janet Stern, an instructor of literature at Northwestern University and leader of that book group, notes: "Many women are afraid to admit they have desired men other than their husbands. They think they're abnormal. But if you push them and prod them and reassure them enough, they finally admit they have." Indeed, one book-group member, to the visible discomfort of her colleagues, finally admitted she had once fantasized about Ronald Colman when making love to her husband.

In cities and towns across the land, many women are more openly exhibiting a new sexual frankness. Not that their sexual behavior or yearnings have necessarily changed. But now many women are increasingly admitting to themselves and others that they are indeed sexual creatures capable of desiring and enjoying the same activities and fantasies that have long been taken for granted in their menfolk. And they are becoming increasing vocal in their appreciation of masculine sex appeal.

"I wonder what kind of equipment he has on him?" the character Bea says of the real Robert Redford in the movie *Alice Doesn't Live Here Anymore.*

"Did you ever see his feet?" asks Alice.

"Feet?"

"I heard one time that's supposed to be an indication."

"Well," says Bea, "I did see a picture once. Wait. . . . They're huge! They're like . . . like *this!*"

Movie talk, to be sure. Yet the film, a box-office smash, has been called the first picture to portray women as they really are. Still for some real women, even pure guessing isn't enough. Witness the commercial success of Playgirl magazine—circulation 1.4 million—in which more stark-naked men can be found than in the Oakland A's locker room. And in competitor Viva—circulation 500,000—the most popular feature to date was on crotch-watching, a series of photographs showing the covered crotches of 19 well-endowed males.

THE GO-GOS ARE MALE

Though there is some suspicion that the magazines are being purchased by males, either homosexual or just curious about what excites women, Viva surveys show that 87 per cent of its circulation is paid for by women; Play-girl reports that of its 23 per cent male readership, 77 per cent are married.

Assuming these statistics are accurate, what appears to be happening, ladies and gentlemen, is that some ladies are beginning to behave more like some gentlemen. Blackjack dealers in Las Vegas report they are being hustled as never before by female tourists. The owner of Nevada's largest brothel reported "plenty of demand" for the two house studs his Mustang Bridge Ranch once offered, but says he canceled this service because women demanded more luxurious surroundings than regular clientele. An out-of-the-way go-go club in a Maryland suburb of Washington, D. C., is booked a month in advance. The attraction is—what else?—scantily clad male dancers. And the New England Telephone Co. employee in charge of tabulating obscene phone calls received three himself one week end from a deep-throated woman.

NEW SEXUAL FRANKNESS

But perhaps the most visible indicator of the new sexual frankness is that three mass-marketed, money-making magazines for women—Playgirl, Viva, and Cosmopolitan—are all unabashedly sex-oriented, while many other women's magazines regularly feature articles on sex. Indeed, Playgirl may have been the fastest-growing magazine in publishing history during its first 12 months. After only six issues its average monthly audience, according to a Target Group Index report, was 9.9 million—more than Cosmo's[1] 7.6 million and Penthouse's 9 million.

Says Playgirl editor Marin Scott Milam, 38: "We are the first generation of women to be taught that sex is to be enjoyed."

Perhaps. But some disagree strongly that commercial exploitation (generally by men) of women's interest in sex is the way to enjoy sex. Says NOW leader DeCrow: "That we would want to establish a playgirl culture to be equal to a playboy culture doesn't impress me greatly. I pity people who have to get their kicks out of looking at pictures, which I find very uninteresting, not to mention unsexy."

Though neither DeCrow nor feminist spokesperson Gloria Steinem equates such developments with female liberation, the raising of consciousness undoubtedly helped pave the way for acceptance of *Fear of*

---

[1] *Cosmopolitan* magazine.

Flying, Playgirl, Viva, and the movie *Alice.* Indeed, Jong, Milam, and Viva publisher Bob Guccione all agree that their literature could not have become commercial successes five—even three—years ago.

The sexual revolution of the '60s, made possible largely by the Pill, may have taken the worry out of sex—but it didn't remove the culturally instilled misgivings. Says Cosmo editor Helen Gurley Brown: "When I came to the magazine in 1965, we couldn't use the word 'orgasm' or refer to any anatomical parts of the body. It was not considered appropriate to be that frank."

Then along came a plethora[2] of sex literature: From Masters and Johnson,[3] reassurance that the female sexual appetite is as great as, if not greater than, the male's; from Helen Gurley Brown, the unblushing how-tos of satisfying that appetite. And finally, the powerful, pervasive effects of the women's movement. If equal pay, why not equal libido?

CANDOR WINS THE DAY

The result is that many women today are shedding their age-old image as chaste bearers of virtue. They are coming to grips with their own sexual concerns and are talking about them with unprecedented candor. The lead story in the March issue of Cosmo was on oral sex. In her record *Angels and Devils,* Dory Previn compares the love-making techniques of two of her boy friends, a truck driver and an artist. In *Jericho,* Joni Mitchell sings of "opening up" to a lover. And in a recent episode of *The Mary Tyler Moore Show,* Mary confesses that she is dating a ski instructor, with whom she has absolutely nothing in common, only because she finds him sexually attractive.

Says *MTM* producer Allen Burns: "We wanted to explore why it is that a woman always has to justify her boy friend by his intellect or his occupation. What's wrong with a woman being only sexually attracted to a man? Every relationship doesn't have to be important, does it?"

That TV heroine Moore is openly eschewing old double standards is but one more indication of the pervasiveness of the new sexual frankness. Authoress Jong says, "You wouldn't believe the letters I get from women that say 'Even though I'm 70 I can identify with your heroine.' "

NO SOCIOECONOMIC BARRIERS

Changing attitudes about sex seem to be spreading into all socioeconomic and age categories. If the majority of readers of Playgirl and Viva are college-educated women aged 18 to 34, the female clientele at Nick Simonetta's Hangar Club in Camp Springs, Md., defies demographic classi-

[2] A plethora is an overabundance, often an unhealthy overabundance.

[3] William H. Masters and Virginia E. Johnson, authors of *Human Sexual Response* and *Sexual Inadequacy.*

fication; they seem to represent every age, color, and income bracket. Bachelorette parties are not uncommon, nor are women wearing wedding bands who boast of leaving kids at home with daddy.

"You think my husband worries?" says one middle-aged woman. "Who ever heard of a woman raping a man?" Says another patron: "I think it's great to be able to come here and see something different than what I see at home. And here we can let it all hang out, which is nice when you have four kids to tend to."

Proprietor Simonetta, who seems flabbergasted by his club's overnight success, admits, "It's a sign of how much things have changed that we can exist in a suburban area without friction from the churches, the PTA, and the school board."

OOPS! THERE IT GOES AGAIN!

(True, but in nearby Baltimore County, where Nick sends some of his go-go guys to dance at the Merritt House, the Liquor Board ruled that men, like women must cover their nipples. This proved a problem: The adhesive strips the men used kept falling off when the dancers perspired.)

Taboos, of course, still abound. One of the most interesting concerns extramarital sex. Linda Wolfe, author of a soon-to-be-published book, *Playing Around: Women and Extramarital Sex,* interviewed 66 middle- to upperclass women who had had affairs. She found that not one had ever discussed her affair with anybody. Says Wolfe: "Women were always brought up to believe that once married they would never, never seek sex with another man. Then it happens—for whatever reason—and they think they are the only ones. They think, 'What's wrong with me? Why am I such a freak?' "

Little data exist on the prevalence of adultery among women. But a 1953 Kinsey study found that 26 per cent of those interviewed—median age 34—had been unfaithful to their husbands.

THE NEED FOR A PARTNER

Wolfe discovered that but for a few professional women who occasionally indulged in one-night stands—perhaps while on a business trip—most affairs lasted one to two years. At that point the women decided either to abandon the affairs or their husbands. Says Wolfe: "Although a few women sought lovers purely for sexual kicks, most wanted one primary partner, one person to love; if it wasn't the husband, then the lover. If the lover didn't work out, then they'd search for another one. Sometimes, after a brief affair, the woman decided, 'My husband is okay after all.' "

Public squeamishness over female adultery is such that when television's *Rhoda*—with her husband's approval—had dinner with a former boyfriend, the show was inundated with letters from outraged viewers, many of whom decided the date had not ended with dinner. Nevertheless, says producer Burns, "a few years ago we couldn't have even brought the subject up."

SELF-MADE TABOOS

Indeed, just what the public will accept is difficult to fathom. Says Burns: "We tend to make our own taboos. We have found that the public is much more open and willing to explore new areas than we realize. It's our own timidity that keeps them from getting explored." Though it has been implied that Mary, and Rhoda before she married, have had affairs with men, Burns says: "We don't feel we could show them in bed or coming out of a man's apartment. But who knows?"

Helen Gurley Brown admits to some taboos at Cosmo, mainly of her own making. "We've never done anything on wife-swapping," she says, "but then it's so *today*. And we've not written about anal sex. It . . . it's so *uncomfortable*, I just don't want to write about it. And we don't run male center folds any more, because who's going to get excited about a man hiding behind a bath towel? As for full frontal nudity, well, that's just not the kind of thing we do at Cosmo."

REQUESTS FOR MALE NUDITY

The subject of male nudity continues to be baffling as women ponder whether they like it or not. Playgirl editor Milam, who describes herself as "about as conventional as you can get" (indeed, she was late in returning a call because it was her husband's birthday, she said, and she had to bake the cake before she left for work), insists that center folds will one day replace college banners on a coed's bulletin board. "It's merely a process of getting used to it," she adds.

Viva, which surfaced in September 1973, didn't intend to introduce full frontal nudity for at least a year. "But we got so many letters from women accusing us of copping out," says publisher Guccione, "that we ran our first male nude in the fourth issue." And associate publisher and editor Kathy Keeton reports receiving two letters in one day from married women who complained, "Why do you give my husband more nudes in Penthouse than you give me in Viva?" Guccione publishes both magazines.

Still, there are indications that Viva may be backing off. For one thing, the picture that aroused the most fan mail was of New York Cosmos goalie Shep Messing's back. "We are finding," says Viva editor Patricia Bosworth, "there is no need to overemphasize male genitals in a woman's magazine." For another thing, Viva's per-issue advertising fell from 50 to 15 pages with the introduction of male nudes. It has yet to recover.

Though Playgirl manages a respectable 50 pages of advertising per issue, editor Milam ran into initial resistance from ad men. "At one agency a tremor went around the table when I produced a copy of the magazine. One man sighed, 'He looks so stupid, standing there like that.' Another admitted, 'I don't know how to react.' "

FOLLOWING MALE STEREOTYPES

Neither do many women. Guccione's Penthouse Pet for June, taking a break from a shooting session, flips through Viva and confides, "I don't much care for it."

Nor do many feminists. Social psychologist Nancy Russo of the American Psychological Association says, "Women are looking for new forms of sexual expression, and I think it's a shame they're following the male stereotypes."

Many feminist leaders, including Gloria Steinem, are opposed not so much to the concept of male nudes—"We were always interested in men's bodies," says Steinem, "we just lied about it"—as to the esthetic quality of the photographs. They contend there is nothing wrong with erotic pictures of men, or of women. "But," says Steinem, "these pictures show men in passive poses. There is nothing going on in them, nothing erotic, nothing sensuous." Guccione suspects the problem is that most photographers of nude men are men. "My success with Penthouse is that basically I am a horny photographer," he says. "What we need [to photograph nude men] is a horny female photographer. So far I haven't found one."

RISK OF REJECTION

The fine distinction between sensuousness and sexism may be one indicator that women will not lapse into traditional male stereotypes. And sociologist Ira Reis of the University of Minnesota finds that women still tend to be "person-centered" whereas men are far more capable of being "body-centered." Says he: "Sex with affection is still the preferred version for women." (Some men would argue they prefer sex that way too.) Nevertheless, most sociologists and psychologists agree that the new sexual candor is healthy. Some psychiatrists are recommending *Fear of Flying* to their patients. And some therapists are encouraging women to be more aggressive in their relationships with men—even at the risk of rejection.

It was perhaps, the risk of rejection that stopped Playgirl editor Milam from approaching one man recently. "I was driving to work and I saw this absolutely gorgeous man waiting for the bus. I really wanted to ask him to pose for the magazine. But somehow I just couldn't."

POINTS TO CONSIDER

1. What, according to the article, are the major causes of women's new openness about sex? Does the author feel that women's basic sexuality has changed? Explain.
2. Why does the author find the magazines *Viva, Playgirl*, and *Cosmo-*

politan particularly significant to her report on women's new sexual frankness?

3. The author makes no clear distinction between the kind of explicit "sexual fantasy" that the initial quotation from *Fear of Flying* describes and the vaguer "desiring" on the part of women for "men other than their husbands." Do you think this is an important distinction? Explain.

4. In what various mass media and popular art forms can you see indications of a new feminine frankness about sexual feelings? Why is this frankness less apparent in some media, such as television, than it is in others?

5. What objections are raised by feminists to male pin-ups? Do you find these objections valid? Explain.

◼ HOW *Ms.* MAGAZINE GOT STARTED

Editors of *Ms.*   *The First Ms. Reader,* ed. Francine Klagsbrun, 1973

First, there were some women writers and editors who began to ask questions. Why were the media, including women's magazines, so rarely or so superficially interested in the big changes happening to women? Why was our own work so unconnected to our lives? Why were we always playing the game by somebody else's (the publisher's, the advertiser's) rules?

Then there were questions from activists: women who were trying to raise money for an information service and self-help projects, particularly for poor or isolated women, and having very little luck. Mightn't a newsletter or magazine serve to link up women, provide a forum for new ideas, and generate income as well?

The two groups met several times early in 1971. Whether we were editors or potential readers, we all agreed that we wanted a new kind of publication, one that was both owned by and honest about women. Gradually, the idea of a full-fledged national magazine developed; a publication created and controlled by women that could be as serious, outrageous, satisfying, practical, sad, funky, intimate, global, compassionate, and full of change as women's lives really are.

We began to hold meetings—many meetings—and we made big plans. Then we spent many months making appointments, looking for backing from groups that invest in new ventures—and just as many months getting turned down. Flat. We usually heard one or several reasons like these from potential investors:

. . . all around us, magazines are failing; why spend money to buck the tide?

. . . Even though local "special interest" magazines are making money (curiously, anything directed at the female 53 percent of the population is regarded as "special interest"), they are bad investments compared to, say, apartment buildings, computer hardware, and the like;

. . . the more we insisted on retaining at least 51 percent of the stock, the more everyone told us that investors don't give money without getting control; who ever heard of a national magazine controlled by its staff?

. . . setting aside some of the profits (supposing there were any) to go back to the Women's Movement is so unbusinesslike as to be downright crazy—even publications made necessary by other reform or revolutionary movements haven't managed that;

. . . and finally, the investors said, there are probably only ten or twenty thousand women in the country interested in changing economic and social discrimination against women anyway; certainly not enough to support a nationwide magazine.

We got discouraged, but there was some support: friendly magazine people who thought we should try to find "public-spirited" money; women in advertising who were themselves trying to create ads that were a service to women instead of an embarrassment; and feminist speakers who had been traveling around the country and sensed that a mass audience was there. Most of all, there were the several women writers, editors, and many all-purpose feminist volunteers who were willing to contribute their talents in return for little except hope.

Then two concrete things happened. First, Katherine Graham, one of the few women publishers in the country, was willing to pretend that a few shares of stock in a nonexistent magazine were worth buying, a fiction that allowed us money for some of our out-of-pocket expenses. Second, Clay Felker, editor and publisher of *New York,* a weekly metropolitan magazine, suggested an unusual idea: *New York* would help us to produce a sample issue to prove that we could create a new kind of magazine, and that women would buy it. We would have the chance to win—or fail—in a nationwide test.

In more detail, *New York* offered to bear the full risk of the $125,000 necessary to pay printers, binders, engravers, paper mills, distributors, writers, artists, and all the other elements vital to turning out 300,000 copies of a Preview Issue. (Plus supplying the great asset of *New York's* production staff, without which the expenses would have been much higher.) In return, some of the *Ms.* articles and features would appear first as an insert in the year-end issue of *New York,* half of the newsstand profits (if any) of our own Preview Issue would go to *New York,* and so would all of the advertising proceeds. Though *Ms.* editors would be working without pay, we were assured of editorial control. The ads were to be *New York's* usual ones; otherwise, all the pages were ours.

It was an odd way to introduce a magazine, but a generous and unusual offer—the first time, as far as we knew, that one magazine had given birth to another without the "quid pro quo" of editorial control, or some permanent financial interest.

THE PREVIEW ISSUE

In a small office, with four people working full time and the rest of us helping when we could get away from our jobs, the Preview Issue was put together, start to finish, in two months.

The one-room office was crowded and sometimes heavy with concern that we would somehow deplete the strength of the Women's Movement by creating a test issue that did poorly, but it also had an atmosphere of camaraderie; of people doing what they cared about. Could there possibly be 100,000 women in the country who wanted this unconventional magazine? We had been listening to doomsayers for so long that we ourselves sometimes doubted it, but there was little time to worry and no way to turn back.

When the insert from our Preview Issue appeared as part of *New York* in December, 1971, the issue set a newsstand sales record; more than *New York* had ever sold before.

Of, course, said the doomsayers, women in a metropolitan area might be interested. But would we appeal to the women of Ohio or Arizona or Iowa?

The complete and autonomous Preview Issue of *Ms.*—dated "Spring 1972," because it was designed to remain on the newsstand for at least two months—was distributed nationally in January, 1972. It was a new entity on the newsstands and we wanted to make sure women knew about it. But when authors and editors visited various towns and cities to speak about the magazine, we were met with phone calls: "Where it is?" "We can't find a copy." "What newsstands are selling it?"

Worriedly, we called the distributor—and the truth finally dawned on us. The 300,000 copies supposed to last on the newsstands for at least eight weeks had virtually disappeared in eight days. *Ms.* had sold out.

Letters began to pour into our crowded office: more than 20,000 long, literate, rough, disparate, funny, tragic and very personal letters from women all over the country, including Ohio, Arizona and Iowa. They identified with the magazine, as with a friend, and had accepted it as their own.

Though inundated with mail, we still didn't realize how unusual its quantity and quality was until we asked the editor of another women's magazine—with a circulation of seven million, compared to our 300,000—how much editorial response each issue got. "About 2,000 letters," she said, "and a lot of them not very worthwhile. Four thousand letters of any kind is quite extraordinary."

Obviously, the need for an honest magazine by and about women was greater and deeper than we had thought. As much out of instinct as skill, we had connected with a great and deep cultural change. We were experiencing it ourselves—and we were not alone.

After the Preview Issue, we spent another three months looking for investors who believed in the need for such a magazine, and would therefore give us the backing we now knew we must have to get it going on a regular basis. We had one important condition: that the investor be willing to back us without taking financial and editorial control in return.

In spite of the endless appointments and months of looking, we can't take credit for finding Warner Communications. They found us. We are grateful to them for exploring many kinds of media. And we are especially impressed that they took the unusual position of becoming the major investor, but minority stockholder; thus providing all the money without demanding the decision vote in return. It was a step forward for women and for journalism.

Even with Warner's help, however, we had to reach the break-even point with a third of the money, and in a third of the time, that most national magazines have required. (The average seems to be $3 million and three years before a publication begins to show a profit.) And our hope is to be able to give a healthy percentage of our profits back to the Women's Movement; to programs and projects that can help change women's lives.

Six months after the Preview Issue, we had moved out of our one-room office to larger rooms in the same building; hired the people who had been working for so long, and new staff besides, and produced an issue dated July 1972—the first of our regular monthly productions. In it, we reported to our readers exactly what our financial and editorial status was, the mistakes we had made, and our plans for the next issues. It was a step toward open journalism, and one we have continued through periodic Personal Reports.

WHO ARE THE READERS OF *Ms.*?

We have found, from newsstand and subscription patterns, that the distribution of our readership pretty much follows that of the population, with the same relationship among urban, suburban, and rural: interest isn't confined to the East and West coasts, as people unfamiliar with the Women's Movement suppose. The only area with proportionately fewer readers is the South. Within each locale, the sales are greater wherever women gather: campuses, office buildings, supermarkets, and the like.

We are often asked about our readership among men, and also among black and other minority women. It's difficult to know real percentages and race can't be told from subscriber lists; men tend not to subscribe for themselves (they read their wives' or friends' copies, or buy single issues on the newsstand). But there are indicators. About 10 percent of our mail comes from men, for instance, and about 20 percent from women who identify themselves as black or other Third World women.

To find out more about ages, incomes, and life situations of our readers, we conducted a survey of our subscribers. Eighty-nine percent are between the ages of 18 and 49, and 71% are presently married. Only 15% belong to groups associated with the Women's Movement: we hope that means we are reaching out to new women, in addition to those who have access to feminist organizations and support.

Beyond the statistics, one thing stands out clearly: the intensity of interest our readers have in *Ms.* Not only do they write unprecedented numbers of letters in response to each article, poem, or story, but they take advertising pages almost as seriously as editorial pages. The ad letters we received in response to the Preview Issue concentrated on ads that didn't fit the editorial content; ads that seemed to say women spent all their money on make-up, clothes and the like. But since we've been able to go out after our own ads—ads that show women realistically and feature the full range of products women buy, not just feminine ones—we have had a predominately positive response. In either case, we pass all letters along to the companies concerned, and they do listen. Advertising practices are changing, and they will have to change much more—not because of this magazine's rather minor needs, but because advertising words and images are such a pervasive influence on our expectations and those of our children.

And there must be many readers with consciousness and a generous spirit. We have received hundreds of contributions, ranging from 50 cents to $100, to help pay for subscriptions for women who can't yet afford them. We matched some contributions with requests from women who have written to tell us that they need free subscriptions. Others are used to send subscriptions to women's prisons (about 30 so far), plus some individual female and male prisoners who have responded to the magazine, and rehabilitation centers for young people. Still others make subscriptions available to members of organizations such as the National Committee on Household Employment and the National Welfare Rights Organization.

BOOKS AND OTHER PROJECTS

This *Ms. Reader* is our second full-fledged book. Our first book, *Wonder Woman,* began as a story and cover in our July issue and grew into a big book of classic Wonder Woman stories that had been long out of print.

We also have a record, called "Free To Be . . . You and Me." It was put together by Marlo Thomas, who wanted to contribute to the Women's Movement, and to the childhood of a much-loved niece by volunteering her talents to a children's record. Marlo gradually gathered original songs and poems by such talented people as Carol Hall, Mary Rodgers, Bruce Hart, and Sheldon Harnick. Then she enlisted other performers: Carol Channing, Diana Ross, Mel Brooks, Robert Morse, Alan Alda, and Shirley Jones, among others. The result is a joyous and delightful record.

We always intended to establish a foundation that would allow a portion of eventual income created by this magazine to go back to the Women's Movement. (Since *Ms.* succeeded in breaking even in one year, we hope to be able to contribute soon.) The record album gave us the means to set up a foundation because Marlo and the other creative people involved wanted to contribute part of the money they would normally receive. So we have established the Ms. Foundation for Women, Inc. A variety of feminists will steer its course.

THE FUTURE

We continue to examine our actions and attitudes, assessing our gains, and analyzing our mistakes to see how we can best contribute to changing women's lives for the better and to exploring feminist goals. Perhaps the truth is, for us and for women everywhere, that none of us yet knows how to achieve all our feminist goals, and therefore ultimately humanist ones. Consciousness is not an absolute state, but a continual process of becoming. But we hope that *Ms.*—and the books and projects that grow from it—will continue to be a forum for exploration and a source of contribution to the ideals of the Women's Movement in the months and years to come.

After all, it's a very deep, basic, and long-term kind of change we are after. Eliminating the patriarchal and racist base of existing social systems requires a revolution, not a reform. But it's not a revolution we die for—it's one we live and work for. Every day.

■ POINTS TO CONSIDER

1. What kind of magazine is *Ms.*? What questions were raised which led to its founding?

2. What objections did the idea of a feminist magazine run by women meet with? How valid did these objections prove to be? Explain.

3. How did *Ms.* eventually get the backing it needed?

4. What makes the editors of *Ms.* feel that they have "connected with a great and deep cultural change"? Do you agree with this statement? Explain.

5. In what way might the editors' program for the women's movement be considered good business as well as a contribution to feminist reforms?

DOONESBURY   by Garry Trudeau

■ A BIBLE BUYER'S CATALOGUE

Time, December 20, 1975

With the recent rash of English translations, versions now available with both Testaments include:

King James Version (1611) A masterpiece whose cadenced phrasing is an indestructible part of Western culture. It is, in fact, something of a miracle that a church committee could produce a volume that three centuries later sells in the millions and can be found in perhaps two-thirds of America's homes.

Revised Standard Version (1952) A U.S. Protestant product that preserves the literary strength of the King James, with updated wording and changes based on more authentic texts. It is under continuing revision, with the next likely change to be elimination of "thee" and "thou" when addressing the Deity. Widely accepted (35 million in print) and available with Apocrypha for Catholics and Eastern Orthodox.

The Jerusalem Bible (1966) A majestic much-praised Catholic version, which is indebted to an earlier French translation but puts off some readers by rather self-consciously calling God "Yahweh." Historic because it broke with Jerome's ancient Latin text, and—in the preferable editions—offers modern critical notes.

New English Bible (1970) An elegant, churchly, yet readable British version under Anglican-Protestant auspices, drawn from ancient texts without depending on previous translations. Apocrypha available.

New American Bible (1970) A rigorously contemporary, sometimes spare, U.S. Catholic rendition. Also a translation from the original languages, it and the Jerusalem Bible are supplanting the Douay-Rheims Bible, a Catholic version contemporary with, but inferior to, the King James.

New American Standard Bible (1971) This stiffly worded revision of an earlier, neglected version has become a Fundamentalist favorite. Accused of slightly falsifying the text to make the Bible appear more accurate.

The Living Bible (1971) Scorned by purists for taking liberties with the text, this paraphrase by Evangelical Kenneth Taylor popularizes Holy Writ. It has sold nearly 19 million copies, many of them in supermarkets and dime stores.

Notable versions of one of the two Testaments:

The Holy Scriptures (1917) The authoritative Bible (*i.e.,* "Old" Testament) for Jews, based on older Bibles in English and with a 17th century sound to it. Scholars will complete an improved modern version in the 1980s.

New Testament in Modern English (1958) A graceful paraphrase, by English Parson J. B. Phillips, that makes the Gospels and letters come alive. The best choice for people who think they do not like the Bible.

Today's English Version (1966) A translation of the New Testament in basic, pared-down language; from the American Bible Society. Its distribution of 50 million copies surpasses Dr. Spock. Full Bible due in 1976.

New International Version (1973) The latest entry, a lucid, fresh rendering of the New Testament by an international panel of 108 Evangelical scholars who plan to publish a full Bible by 1978.

POINTS TO CONSIDER

1. In what ways can the Bible be considered "popular literature"?

2. What reasons are there for the existence of so many versions of what remains essentially the same book?

3. Do you own, or does your family own, a Bible? More than one? More than one version? Have you read more than one version? If so, what are your feelings about the differences between them?

IDEAS FOR INVESTIGATION, DISCUSSION, AND WRITING

1. Compare, in an essay, a representative sample or samples of contemporary popular fiction with popular fiction of the past. What similarities are there? What differences? Did the popular fiction of the past use basically the same appeals as that of our time? What are these techniques? (An example of an interesting comparison: The adventures of James Bond versus the Arthurian legends of The Knights of the Round Table.)

2. Write an essay comparing a popular novel with a more sophisticated literary treatment of the same topic. Examples might be a James Bond compared with Graham Greene's *Our Man in Havana* or with John Le Carré's *The Spy Who Came in From the Cold* or a detective novel compared with the detective stories of Poe or the Sherlock Holmes stories by Arthur Conan Doyle. What similarities can you find? Are they important? Why? What differences can you find in such things as character development, depth of ideas, complexity of plot? What would happen to the literary work if its author followed the same rules as the author of the popular work?

3. Analyze several examples of a particular type of popular fiction, such as science fiction, westerns, historical novels, or detective stories. What is the particular appeal of this kind of fiction? How does the novel achieve this particular appeal? Cite quotations and incidents from the books that illustrate your point. Does this type of fiction appeal to a certain specialized audience? How?

4. Using examples from several popular novels by different authors discuss the characteristics of the hero or heroine of popular fiction. What quality or qualities seem to be necessary to the protagonists of popular novels? How do different authors approach the problem of creating an acceptable protagonist? Why are these qualities important to the success of the book?

5. With reference to one or more appropriately sentimental popular novels, discuss James Baldwin's statement that "Sentimentality, the ostentatious parading of excessive and spurious emotion, is the mark of dishonesty, the inability to feel; the wet eyes of the sentimentalist betray his aversion to experience, his fear of life, his arid heart; and it is always, therefore, the signal of secret and violent inhumanity, the mask of cruelty."

6. Analyze a particular popular novel for narrative techniques. What tricks does the author use to keep you reading? What hints does he drop to tickle your interests? What tensions, questions, apprehensions does he manufacture so that you will keep turning the pages? What promise does he make? Does he disappoint you? If so, how?

7. In a comparative analysis of several popular novels or in an intensive analysis of a single popular novel, show how the author lets his protagonist—and thus the reader as well—have, in Edmund Wilson's words, "every possible kind of cake and manage to eat it too."

8. Compare a popular movie with its subsequent novelization. How does the nature of the printed medium affect the various elements of the movie, such as plot, character, theme? What is lost; what is gained? How do these

changes reflect the inherent superiorities or inferiorities of the novel as a popular medium?

9. Using figures from trade publications find out what books are the actual "best-sellers" both in terms of volumes sold and money income. Compare these figures with the "official" best-seller lists.

10. Make a before and after study which attempts to discover just what effect television has had on the reading habits of Americans. Are people reading more now? Less? Why? Is there any evidence that television has changed the quality of books themselves? What role has television had in the growing popularity of the "new journalism?"

11. Make a survey of who reads fiction and for what reasons. What kind of people read what kinds of fiction? What do they feel that they get out of it?

12. Find out if the novel is actually dead. Is the number of novels published actually declining? Are fewer novels sold per capita today than, say, ten years ago or twenty years ago?

13. Using evidence from the ads, covers, articles, fiction, cartoons, photographs, and other features of a particular mass magazine, analyze and discuss the magazine's image. As one reads, what sort of person is the reader supposed to feel he or she becomes? What identity does the magazine seem to offer those who care to identify with its image? How do the various features of the magazine help the reader slip into this role? How does this image, e.g., the *Playboy* male or the *Cosmopolitan* female, compare with the sort of people who actually read the magazines? Is this disparity a possible source of harm? Explain.

14. Put together a mock-up of a new magazine, including a cover, several ads, features, and perhaps a beginning paragraph for one or two articles. The magazine can be a parody, humorous (*Mad* magazine often presents new "magazines" of this sort), or of a more serious nature. With the magazine should be an introduction explaining the goals and editorial policy of the magazine, its intended audience, and why you think it will be an overwhelming success.

Part Five

Radio and Television: Previews and Viewpoints

It is a medium honestly endeavoring to reflect the tastes, standards, and interests of the many audiences—and the many publics—it reaches and serves. Still, there are those who are displeased and disturbed by television. . . .

There is, I fear, a distressing intolerance in the strident insistence of many that their own views—and only their views—should be seen or expressed on television. They feel that their standards and beliefs are the only ones fit for any audience to see.

—Thomas C. Swafford

Women are just not *human* in these [television] plays. They're not portrayed as thinking or feeling beings. They're shown as something between an animal and a human. The word "chick" best captures it.

—Shulamith Firestone
As quoted by Edith Efron

So stunning are the factors of size of [television] audience and speed of communication on the grand scale that the very rhythm of political life does seem revolutionized.

—Emmet John Hughes

This is an open society, and whether you like it or not, it does encourage cynicism. It makes demands on the maturity and judgment of the individual that are more severe than he ever had to meet when he had only the press to ponder.

—Alistair Cooke

Radio and Television

NO EXIT

Robert Lewis Shayon   *Saturday Review,* August 7, 1965

Life with the mass media in the privacy of home, where you can make choices, is difficult enough: the true test of character comes when one is confronted by the media in public. I flunked the test in recent weeks, in a plane over the Pacific, a restaurant in Philadelphia, a home in Boston, a taxi in New York, and a motel near the Canadian border. The last stop taught me a lesson and I pass it on to all fellow-sufferers in this sermon for a hot summer afternoon. Flying to Honolulu, there was a mix-up in my ticketing and I couldn't get dinner aboard the plane. I offered to pay the stewardess, but she said she couldn't sell me dinner, and I ruefully watched her throw the food away—but I got a free movie in color. I didn't want the movie: I wanted to do some work; but the lady in back of me cheerfully inquired if I would lower the back of my chair so she could see Frank Sinatra. The sound track was blissfully secreted in the plug-in earphones; but there loomed Sinatra on the rectangular screen ahead; and fuming, I finally quit and suffered the mob their taste. Back on the mainland a few weeks later, I dined at a small, pleasant restaurant in Philadelphia, enveloped by the *high-volume* signal of a local radio station. I knew it would be fruitless (and bad form) to ask the manager to switch off; but I couldn't resist asking him why he kept the station on.

The other diners would immediately complain, he said, if he tuned out. "People need it," he shrugged. "They really don't listen, but it makes a noise in the background and it permits them to talk. If there was silence, there wouldn't be any conversation. It would be dead in here."

The Boston experience came shortly after. I visited a home in the suburbs, where a woman was alone. She sat in a large room: the TV was on (it was early afternoon); but she was intent on a cross-word puzzle. Two rooms away, the radio was turned on, playing to nobody. In New York, another day, I got into a taxi at Penn Station. It was the evening rush hour; the hot city's garment center was clashing and raucous with west-side traffic: the cabbie had his dashboard radio belting above the din. I moaned inwardly but hid my frustration with another taxicab survey. "Do you have that radio on all the time?" I asked in a friendly fashion. "All the time. Never without it a minute," the driver answered.

"What do you usually listen to?" "Nothing," said the driver. "I don't hear a thing. No program. No commercial. I just have it on." "But why?" He turned the knob and shut off the radio. "See for yourself," he said. "I'd miss it. It's monotonous without it, driving all day." He turned the radio on again. "People get in the cab and start telling me their troubles. Like the guy who said he loved his wife but was going out with another dame. What should he do? he asks me. What do I care what he does? But I can't tell him that, so I turn up the radio real loud . . . like this . . . and they keep on jabbering away . . . and once in a while I throw them a yeah . . . yeah . . . yeah . . . but I don't hear a thing . . . not them . . . not the radio . . . nothing."

A few weeks after that, I was in Potsdam, New York, on a lecture engagement. I had breakfast at a motel's restaurant. The cheery waitress had her transistor radio atop the refrigerator the other side of the counter—and with my orange juice I had some bright and early upbeat country music. The local newspaper couldn't assuage my resentment. "Is there no surcease anywhere from this ubiquitous, tribal, electronic collectivism?" I grumbled to my All-Bran.

Suddenly I stopped in the middle of a grumble. The announcer had spoken a familiar name—mine. Along with other items of local news, he was mentioning the talk I was scheduled to give at a nearby college that morning. The music came on again; I went back to the newspaper; but I had been hit—dead on target. All that horrible noise which other people listened to—had instantaneously been transformed into something clear and significant when the right index clue had come up—my own specific involvement. I recalled the taxi-driver who had said: "The only time I listen is when they come on with traffic-bulletins. Then I tune in—with my mind." At all other times the medium of radio was without message: its sound, to him, was shelter from the job's monotony, escape from the unwanted signals of his passengers. To the lady in the Boston home, the unattended TV and radio sets were barriers against loneliness: to the diners in the Philadelphia restaurant the radio's chatter and music were curtains for privacy. The transistor atop the refrigerator in the Potsdam motel met some felt need of the waitress, probably without verbal content. The excommunication of boredom—or fear: this was the meaning of the color movie aboard the plane bound for Hawaii. There is no escape: the public media have interlocked us all. The only response is to learn tolerance—each to his own involvement.

■ **POINTS TO CONSIDER**

1. What services, other than providing news and entertainment, do radio and TV provide for the public? Give some examples from your own experience.

2. Why do restaurants, stores and shopping centers, doctors' and dentists' offices so often provide continuous background music?

3. What is the significance of Shayon's title? Do you ever feel that media over which you have no control—such as background music or someone else's radio or TV—is a nuisance? When? Can anything be done about it?

THE TOWN MEETING IS NOT DEAD—IT'S ALIVE AND WELL ON RADIO

Margaret McEachern   *Today's Health,* July 1970

"I've had it. I'm going to kill myself."

The voice on the telephone was cool and emotionless. The woman might have been saying she was going to wax the kitchen floor.

But she shocked not only the person she had called but thousands of others. For hers was a night call to a radio talk show.

Long John Nebel of WNBC, New York, recognized her voice. She had called him before and threatened suicide and, after his comforting words, had promised to call if she ever felt the urge again.

Nebel quickly wrote a note to his director to call the police to listen in, then kept her talking. She said she hadn't left the house for a year, that her son had joined the Navy, and that she was depressed and afraid to tell her husband that her physician had suggested psychiatric treatment.

She finally gave him her telephone number. Police promptly traced her address, raced there with a doctor, and arrived just as a neighbor, who also had recognized her voice, rushed in.

Such unscheduled melodrama could happen only on talk radio, a current happening that's fascinating millions of listeners around the country.

Topping radio popularity polls, these call-in programs are over-the-air telephone conversations between a moderator and listeners who remain anonymous. Some are aired around-the-clock; others are slated for late evening and early morning hours.

They're hosted by bright, fast-thinking, well-informed men who are prepared for—and take in stride—every type of personality and almost every imaginable question, from "How wide is the Panama Canal?" to "What's the best way to stop smoking?" They also have guest experts to answer callers, with a goodly number in medical and social work practice.

A kind of exciting town meeting of the air, the talk show both entertains and informs the public on a limitless number of subjects. There's no shortage of provocative topics: politics . . . crime in the street . . . the generation gap . . . the high cost of health care . . . drug addiction . . . air and water pollution . . . racial tensions . . . college demonstrations . . . The Pill . . . abortion . . . sex education in the schools.

Lighter topics range from wine-making, parking meters, and men's hair styles to skirt lengths, the joys of garlic, and how to train Fido to sit up and beg.

The men who preside over these shows have various titles: host, moderator, communicaster, talkmaster, talk jockey, ringmaster. They're an unusual breed, and they command salaries that top those in many other areas of radio. Essentially, they're entertainers. But they need more than show biz glibness and thick skins. They must be walking encyclopedias of information and have to be able to carry on constructive conversations on a broad range of subjects. They claim to spend about half their time in research and checking current publications.

Long John is one of the best-known hosts. His all-night show is about to enter its 15th year. It's estimated he's heard by some two million listeners in 35 states as well as in Canada. He receives some 100,000 pieces of mail yearly; some praise him, many are rough, and quite a few are simply obscene. In any case, the listeners react. Trade publications put Nebel's annual salary at more than $100,000.

Nebel is said to have devoted more time to medical and related health subjects than any other broadcaster in the business. He's received two medical citations—one from the Society of Internal Medicine, County of New York, "in recognition of distinguished services in enhancing understanding and rapport between the public and the internist," and one from the county's medical society "for improving the image of the practitioner of medicine."

Even the ladies are starting to talk-talk-talk as communicasters, though on a limited scale. WLOL in Minneapolis-St. Paul features on a part-time basis Mrs. Mary Kyle, editor of a weekly newspaper and member of President Nixon's Citizens Advisory Committee on the Status of Women.

The same station also has a recent university graduate and Viet Nam veteran to talk hard facts to young listeners. Dean Grauds can truthfully say to them, "I've been there, so don't try to kid me."

An adolescent boasting that he's experimenting with drugs gets little sympathy.

"Don't try to sell me on that garbage," Grauds will retort. "I know what marijuana is. I've tried it. And don't tell me it's 'groovy.' I've seen kids take the stuff, then cower under a table and bark like dogs. What's 'groovy' about that?"

The station's program director, Brad Johnson, says that talk radio in some ways is like listening to the couple next door who fight; you don't usually close your window but open it wider. And he feels it's a kind of voodoo doll for hate images.

Techniques vary, but usually a caller is put on "hold" on one of several incoming lines until the communicaster is ready to listen. Another staff member screens him quickly to make sure he isn't completely irresponsible. A seven-second delay of broadcast permits the host or his engineer to chop off "commercials," obscenities, or anything else objectionable.

Some stations don't go along with screening. They feel it's more exciting and spontaneous without it—a kind of Russian roulette. They think the audio delay is enough protection.

Anonymity helps eliminate the egocentrics and protects callers from being pestered by listeners who disagree with them. Also, many callers won't speak their minds if they have to identify themselves; they're subjected to too many economic, political, and social pressures. They're allowed to have their say as long as it's in good taste, within the prescribed time limit, and not redundant or annoying.

Because of the anonymity, persons who otherwise would suffer alone and in silence call in for help: homosexuals, drug addicts, alcoholics, ex-convicts, unmarried pregnant teen-agers, AWOL-ers, shoplifters.

Talk radio offers something for everyone. It's a handy shoulder to cry on . . . a punching bag for relief of tension . . . a friendly voice in a lonely room . . . a platform for exchange of facts and ideas . . . a helpful referral center which directs troubled callers to the appropriate community agency.

It attracts all kinds of callers in addition to "Mr. and Mrs. Average Citizen"—rabid sports fans, political "experts," gossipy women reporting on their neighbors' garbage cans or kids, jolly night-people, self-proclaimed philosophers, Bible thumpers, pontificators, professional Moms, and folks with "causes" ranging from breast feeding and prayer in space to vegetarianism, jogging, and the dropping of the big one on North Viet Nam. It lures hippies, pro-hippies, anti-hippies, and little old ladies who resent being associated with tennis shoes.

Two business executives in adjoining seats on a recent Pan American flight to Tokyo gleefully discovered they were regular callers to their local talk station. Each recognized the other's voice as soon as they had exchanged a few words.

Talk radio is a great remedy for loneliness, and there's a lot of that around. Such shows play an important role in the daily lives of specific groups: the elderly, at home or in nursing homes . . . the handicapped, unable to get around in public . . . housewives tied down with children and routine chores . . . the blind.

The programs bring the outside world to wheelchairs, beds, and kitchens. The listeners become part of a new "family," since many callers are "regulars," complete with such nicknames as Acid Annie, the Old Philosopher, Big John, and Zig-Zag. The listeners become concerned when one hasn't called in for several days.

"Is Bridget Baby out of town?" one will ask. Or, "Will Mr. X be on tomorrow to tell us more about how to stop drinking?"

The homebound women, especially the older ones, also become attached to the communicasters.

"How's your new baby?" one will ask. Or, "Did you get the cookies I sent?"

In turn, the young men at the microphones are patient listeners to the elderly, the perplexed, the worried, the pathetic, the frantic, and the harmless eccentrics.

Some callers are extremists with only one topic, and they unload their feelings week after week on the only person who will listen to them.

There's the man who lectures on the inequities of divorce settlements and rails against his former spouse. The communicaster may let him ramble on until his time is almost up, then cut him short with a gentle, "Wasn't there *anything* good about your wife in those 25 years?" Silence, then the caller may reply sheepishly, "Yeah, she baked a nice chocolate cake." The communicaster knows he'll be back the next day.

Or the man who bellows, "It's three A.M. and I've been hanging on for two hours to tell you you're a jerk!"

The host will laugh and ask, "Feel better now?"

Heavy breathing, then the caller will mutter, "Yeah. Now I'll go back to bed."

Or the hysterical woman: "The Greenies are coming! They're taking over the earth! Flee!"

The communicaster will reply soothingly, "There's a change of plans, dear. The head Greenie just called me on my private line; they're not coming."

A sigh from the woman. "Thank the Lord. Now I can relax and get my washing done."

Nobody's quite certain how talk radio got started, but it seems to have originated on the West Coast around 1963. Ben Hoberman, station manager at KABC in Los Angeles, is credited with having started the all-talk trend. He was the first to use the term "conversation radio" and the first to exploit the concept. He says that people always have been interested in voicing opinions. Letters to the editor are one outlet, but most folks prefer talking to writing.

The shows then gravitated East and soon were popular at such community-involved stations as WOR in New York, WEEI in Boston, and WCAU in Philadelphia.

In the upper Midwest, WCCO Radio in Minneapolis-St. Paul introduced part-time talk shows when the "man on the street" format began to fade in popularity. Jim Borman, director of news and special events, says that talk radio has some advantages: callers are willing contributors, whereas the man on the street who was buttonholed before a mike was often less willing and less well-prepared to express an opinion.

Talk radio plays a constructive role in extending health information to persons who otherwise might remain misinformed or uninformed or who might fall victim to fast-talking quacks. The stations bring in guests from universities, hospitals, medical societies, nursing homes, clinics, and practically every health and welfare agency in the nation.

The stations are extremely careful about these guests. They must be people with outstanding reputations in their specialties. Many are screened by local medical societies which, in increasing numbers, are seeing the value of these shows. And over and over, the communicasters emphasize, "See your doctor."

But an occasional quack may slip in—a nuts-and-fruit diet promoter or someone from a vaguely described "Friends of Cancer Victims Association." It usually takes only a question or two, however, before the communicaster sees the light and ushers them out . . . with apologies to the listeners.

There is no lack of topics: heart disorders, cancer, alcoholism, cerebral palsy, Medicare, Medicaid, epilepsy, schizophrenia, sterilization, abortion, birth control, drugs, muscular dystrophy, the common cold, mental health, insomnia, cyclamates, parent-child relationships. Name it and you'll learn more about it on talk radio. And you'll learn where to turn for advice and treatment.

POINTS TO CONSIDER

1. What various kinds of services do phone-in radio shows provide for their listener-participants? Why do people phone in to these shows?
2. Why does the author refer to the phone-in radio show as a "town meet-

ing"? What functions of a town meeting are currently performed by other media?

3. What abilities should the host of a good phone-in radio show have?

4. What precautions must a phone-in radio program take to protect its listeners?

5. Is there a locally produced phone-in radio show in your community? If so, what functions does it perform? Do you like to listen to it? Why, or why not? Have you ever phoned in? If so, why?

■ THE GOD-HUCKSTERS OF RADIO

William C. Martin   *The Atlantic,* June 1970

You have heard them, if only for a few seconds at a time. Perhaps you were driving cross-country late at night, fiddling with the radio dial in search of a signal to replace the one that finally grew too weak as you drew away from Syracuse, or Decatur, or Amarillo. You listened for a moment until you recognized what it was, then you dialed on, hoping to find *Monitor* or *Music Till Dawn.* Perhaps you wondered if, somewhere, people really listen to these programs. The answer is, they do, by the tens and hundreds of thousands. And they not only listen; they believe and respond. Each day, on local stations that cater to religious broadcasting and on the dozen or so "super-power" stations that can be picked up hundreds of miles away during the cool nighttime hours, an odd-lot assortment of radio evangelists proclaims its version of the gospel to the Great Church of the Airwaves.

Not all who produce religious broadcasts, of course, are acceptable to the scattered multitude for whom "gospel radio" is a major instrument of instruction and inspiration. Denominational programs and Billy Graham are regarded as too Establishment. Billy James Hargis and his Christian Anti-Communist Crusade are too political. Even faith healer Oral Roberts, once a favorite out there in radioland, has become suspect since he founded a university and joined the Methodist Church. For these believers, the true vessels of knowledge, grace, and power are people like Brother Al ("That's A-L, Brother Al"); the Reverend Frederick B. Eikerenkoetter II, better known to millions as "Reverend Ike"; C. W. Burpo ("Spelled 'B,' as in Bible . . ."); Kathryn Kuhlman ("Have . . . you . . . been . . . waiting . . . for . . . me?"); and the two giants of radio religion, healer A. A. Allen (of Miracle Valley, Arizona) and teacher Garner Ted Armstrong, who can be heard somewhere at this very moment Proclaiming The Plain Truth about The World Tomorrow.

The format of programs in this genre rarely makes severe intellectual demands on either pastor or flock. C. W. Burpo (Dr. Burpo accents the last syllable; local announcers invariably stress the first) and Garner Ted Armstrong usually give evidence of having thought about the broadcast ahead of time, though their presentations are largely extemporaneous. Some of the others seem simply to turn on the microphone and shout. Occasionally there is a hint of a sermon. J. Charles Jessup of Gulfport, Mississippi, may cite Herodias' directing her daughter to ask for the head of John the Baptist as illustrating how parents set a bad example for their children. David Terrell may, in support of a point on the doctrine of election, note that God chose Mary for his own good reasons, and not because she was the only virgin in Palestine—"There was plenty of virgins in the land. Plenty of 'em. Mucho virgins was in the land." Evangelist Bill Beeny of St. Louis, Missouri (Period. Beeny regards the Zip Code as a plot to confuse the nation), may point to the flea's ability to jump 200 times his own length as proof that God exists. Often, however, a program consists of nothing more than a canned introduction, a taped segment from an actual "healing and blessing" service (usually featuring testimonials to the wondrous powers of the evangelist), and a closing pitch for money.

The machinery for broadcasting these programs is a model of efficiency. A look at station XERF in Ciudad Acuña, Coahuila, Mexico, just across the border from Del Rio, Texas, illustrates the point. Freed from FCC regulations that restrict the power of American stations to 50,000 watts, XERF generates 250,000 watts, making it the most powerful station in the world. On a cold night, when high-frequency radio waves travel farthest, it can be heard from Argentina to Canada. Staff needs are minimal; less than a dozen employees handle all duties, from the front office to equipment maintenance. The entire fourteen hours of programming, from 6:00 P.M. to 8:00 A.M., are taped. Each week the evangelists send their tapes to the station, with a check for the air time they will use.

All announcing is done by Paul Kallinger, "Your Good Neighbor along the way." A pleasant, gregarious man, Kallinger has been with XERF since 1949. In the fifties, he performed his duties live. At present he operates a restaurant in Del Rio and tapes leads and commercials in a small studio in his home; he has not been to the station in years. A lone technician switches back and forth between the preachers and Kallinger from dusk till dawn. Kallinger recognizes the improbability of some of the claims made by the ministers and acknowledges that their motives may not be entirely altruistic. Still, he figures that, on balance, they do more good than harm, and he does his best to impress listeners with the fact that "these are faith broadcasts and need your tithes and love offerings if they are to remain on the air with this great message."

Who listens to these evangelists, and why? No single answer will suffice. Some, doubtless, listen to learn. Garner Ted Armstrong discusses current problems and events—narcotics, crime, conflict, space exploration, pollution—and asserts that biblical prophecy holds the key to understanding both present and future. C. W. Burpo offers a conservative mixture of religion, morals, and politics. Burpo is foursquare in favor of God, Nixon, and constitutional government, and adamantly opposed to sex education, which encourages the study of materials "revealing the basest part of human nature."

Others listen because the preachers promise immediate solutions to real, tangible problems. Although evidence is difficult to obtain, one gets the definite impression, from the crowds that attend the personal appearances of the evangelists, from the content and style of oral and written testimonials, from studies of storefront churches with similar appeals, and from station executives' analyses of their listening population, that the audience is heavily weighted with the poor, the uneducated, and others who for a variety of reasons stand on the margins of society. These are the people most susceptible to illness and infirmity, to crippling debts, and to what the evangelists refer to simply as "troubles." At the same time, they are the people least equipped to deal with these problems effectively. Some men in such circumstances turn to violence or radical political solutions. Others grind and are ground away, in the dim hope of a better future. Still others, like desperate men in many cultures, succumb to the appeal of magical solutions. For this group, what the preachers promise is, if hardly the Christian gospel, at least good news.

The "healers and blessers," who dominate the radio evangelism scene, address themselves to the whole range of human problems: physical, emotional, social, financial, and spiritual. Like their colleagues in the nonmiraculous healing arts, some evangelists develop areas of special competence, such as the cure of cancer or paralysis. Brother Al is something of a foot specialist—"God can take corns, bunions, and tired feet, and massage them with his holy love and make them well." A. A. Allen tells of disciples who have received silver fillings in their teeth during his meetings and asks, sensibly enough, "Why not let God be your dentist?" But most are general practitioners. On a single evening's set of programs, hope is extended to those suffering from alcoholism, arthritis, asthma, birth defects, blindness, blood pressure (high and low), bunions, calluses, cancer (breast, eye, lung, skin, stomach, and throat), corns, death, diabetes, dope, eye weakness, gallstones, heart disease, insomnia, kidney trouble, leukemia, mental retardation, mononucleosis, nervous breakdown, nervous itch, nicotine addiction, obesity, pain, paralysis, polio, pregnancy, respiratory problems, rheumatic fever, tuberculosis, tumors (brain, abdominal, and miscellaneous), ulcers, useless limbs, and water in the veins.

The continually fascinating aspect of the healing and blessing ministries is that they do produce results. Some of the reported healings are undoubtedly fraudulent. One station canceled a healer's program after obtaining an affidavit from individuals who admitted posing as cripples and being "healed" by the touch of the pastor's hand. Police officers have occasionally reported seeing familiar vagrants in the healing lines of traveling evangelists, apparently turning newly discovered disorders into wine. But these blatant frauds are probably rare, and a faith healer need not depend on them to sustain his reputation. He can rely much more safely on psychological, sociological, and psychotherapeutic mechanisms at work among his audience.

The testimonials that fill the broadcasts and publications of the healers point to two regularities in a large percentage—not all—of the reported cures. First, the believer had suffered from his condition for some time and had been unable to gain relief from medical or other sources. Long illness or disability can weaken emotional and mental resistance to sources of help that one would not consider in other circumstances. Second, most of the cures occur at actual healing services, when the deep desire to be made whole is transformed into eager expectation by a frenzied whirl of noise, anxiety, and promise, and the pervasive power of the gathered group of true believers.

In recent years, the miracle-workers have turned their attention to financial as well as physical needs. They promise better jobs, success in business, or, in lieu of these, simple windfalls. A. A. Allen urges listeners to send for his book *Riches and Wealth, the Gift of God.* Reverend Ike fills his publications and broadcasts with stories of financial blessings obtained through his efforts—"This Lady Blessed with New Cadillac," "How God Blessed and Prospered Mrs. Rena Blige" (he revealed to her a secret formula for making hair grow), "Sister Rag Muffin Now Wears Mink to Church," and "Blessed with New Buick in 45 Minutes." Forty-five minutes is not, apparently, unusually fast for Reverend Ike. He regularly assures his listeners, "The moment you get your offering [and] your prayer requests into the mail, start looking up to God for your blessing because it will be on the way."

These men of God realize, of course, that good health and a jackpot prize on the Big Slot Machine in the Sky are not all there is to life. They promise as well to rid the listener of bad habits, quiet his doubts and fears, soothe his broken heart, repair his crumbling marriage, reconcile his fussing kinfolk, and deliver him from witches and demons. No problem is too trivial, too difficult, or past redemption. Brother Al will help women "that wants a ugly mouth cleaned out of their husband." A. A. Allen claims to have rescued men from the electric chair. Glenn Thompson promises "that girl out there 'in trouble' who's trying to keep it from Dad and Mother" that if she will "believe and doubt not, God will perform a miracle."

The radio evangelists do not cast their bread upon the waters, however, without expecting something in return. Though rates vary widely, a fifteen-minute daily program on a local radio station costs, on the average, about $200 per week. On a superpower station like XERF the rate may run as high as $600. The evangelists pay this fee themselves, but they depend upon their radio audience to provide the funds. For this reason, some take advantage of God's Precious Air Time to hawk a bit of sacred merchandise. Much of it is rather ordinary—large-print Bibles, calendars, greeting cards, Bible-verse yo-yos, and ball-point pens with an inspirational message right there on the side. Other items are more unusual. Bill Beeny, who tends to see the darker side of current events, offers $25-contributors a Riot Pack containing a stove, five fuel cans, a rescue gun, a radio, and the marvelous Defender, a weapon that drives an attacker away and covers him with dye, making him an easy target for police. Ten dollars will buy a blue-steel, pearl-handled, tear-gas pistol, plus the informative and inspirational Truth-Pac #4. Or, for the same price, Evangelist Beeny will send his own album of eighteen songs about heaven, together with the Paralyzer, "made by the famous Mace Company." Presumably, it is safer to turn the other cheek if one has first paralyzed one's enemy.

The most common items offered for sale, however, are the evangelist's own books and records. Brother Al's current book is *The Second Touch*: "It's wrote in plain, down-to-earth language, and has big print that will heal any weak eyes that reads it." For a $5 offering C. W. Burpo will send his wonderful recording of "My America," plus a bonus bumper sticker advertising his program, The Bible Institute of the Air—"Be a moving billboard for God and Country." Don and Earl, "two young Christian singers from Fort Worth, Texas," offer for only $3 "plus a extra quarter to pay the postage back out to your house," albums of heart-touching songs and stories that include such old favorites as "Just One Rose Will Do," "A Tramp on the Streets," "Lord, Build Me a Cabin in Heaven," "Streamline to Glory," "Remember Mother's God," "A Soldier's Last Letter," "That Little Pair of Half-worn Shoes," "Just a Closer Walk with Thee" (featuring the gospel whistling of Don), and that great resurrection hymn, "There Ain't No Grave Gonna Keep My Body Down."

In keeping with St. Paul's dictum that "those who proclaim the gospel should get their living by the gospel," the radio ministers do not always offer merchandise in return for contributions. In fact, the books and records and magazines probably function primarily as a link that facilitates the more direct appeals for money almost sure to follow.

Brother Al, sounding like a pathetic Andy Devine, asks the faithful to send "God's Perfect Offering—$7.00. Not $6.00, not $8.00, but $7.00." An offering even more blessed is $77, God's two perfect numbers, although any multiple of seven is meritorious. "God told me to ask for this. You know I don't talk like this. It's got to be God. God told me he had a lot of bills to pay. Obey God—just put the cash inside the envelope." In addition to cash, Brother Al will also accept checks, money orders, and American Express— surely he means traveler's checks. Seven's perfection stems from its prominence in the Bible: the seven deadly sins, the seven churches of Asia, and so forth. Radio Pastor David Epley also believes God has a perfect number, but he has been reading about the apostles and the tribes of Israel. Quite understandably, he seeks a $12 offering, or the double portion offering of $24.

Brother Glenn Thompson, who also names God as his co-solicitor, claims that most of the world's ills, from crabgrass and garden bugs to Communism and the Bomb, can be traced to man's robbing God. "You've got God's money in your wallet. You old stingy Christian. No wonder we've got all these problems. You want to know how you can pay God what you owe? God is speaking through me. God said, 'Inasmuch as you do it unto one of these, you do it unto me.' God said, 'Give all you have for the gospel's sake.' My address is Brother Glenn, Paragould, Arkansas."

In sharp contrast, Garner Ted Armstrong makes it quite clear that all publications offered on his broadcasts are absolutely free. There is no gimmick. Those who request literature never receive any hint of an appeal for funds unless they specifically ask how they might contribute to the support of the program. Garner Ted's father, Herbert W. Armstrong, began the broadcast in 1937, as a vehicle for spreading a message that features a literalistic interpretation of biblical prophecy. The program has spawned a college with campuses in California, Texas, and London, and a church of more than 300,000 members. Characteristically, the ministers of the local churches, which meet in rented halls and do not advertise, even in the telephone book, will not call on prospective members without a direct invitation. This scrupulous approach has proved quite successful. *The World Tomorrow,* a half-hour program, is heard daily on more than four hundred stations throughout the world, and a television version is carried by sixty stations.

Several evangelists use their radio programs primarily to promote their personal appearance tours throughout the country, and may save the really high-powered huckstering for these occasions. A. A. Allen is both typical and the best example. An Allen Miracle Restoration Revival Service lasts from three to five hours and leaves even the inhibited participant observer quite spent. On a one-night stand in the Houston Music Hall, Allen and the Lord drew close to a thousand souls, in approximately equal portions of blacks, whites, and Mexican-Americans. As the young organist in a brown Nehru played gospel rock, hands shot into the air and an occasional tambourine clamored for joy. Then, without announcement, God's Man of Faith and Power came to pulpit center. Allen does not believe in wearing black; that's for funerals. On this night he wore a green suit with shiny green shoes.

For the better part of an hour, he touted his book that is turning the religious world upside down, *Witchcraft, Wizards, and Witches,* and a record, pressed on 100 percent pure vinyl, of his top two soul-winning sermons.

To prepare the audience for the main pitch, Allen went to great lengths to leave the impression that he was one of exceedingly few faithful men of God still on the scene. He lamented the defection from the ministry: "In the last few years, 30 percent of the preachers have stopped preaching; 70 percent fewer men are in training for the ministry. A cool 100 percent less preachers than just a few years ago." He chortled over the fate of rival evangelists who had run afoul of the law or justifiably irate husbands. At another service, he used this spot to describe the peril of opposing his ministry. He told of a student who tried to fool him by posing as a cripple; God struck him dead the same night. A man who believed in Allen's power, but withheld $100 God had told him to give the evangelist, suffered a stroke right after the meeting. And on and on.

When he finished, Brother Don Stewart, Allen's associate in the ministry of fund-raising, took the microphone to begin a remarkable hour of unalloyed gullery. At the end of his recitation, approximately 135 people pledged $100 apiece, and others emptied bills and coins into large plastic wastebaskets that were filled and replaced with astonishing regularity. And all the while Brother Don walked back and forth shouting to the point of pain, "Vow and pay, vow and pay, the scripture does say, vow and pay."

Despite the blatantly instrumental character of much radio religion, it would be a mistake to suppose that its only appeal lies in the promise of health and wealth, though these are powerful incentives. The fact is that if the world seems out of control, what could be more reassuring than to discover the road map of human destiny? This is part of the appeal of Garner Ted Armstrong, who declares to listeners, in a tone that does not encourage doubt, that a blueprint of the future of America, Germany, the British Commonwealth, and the Middle East, foolproof solutions for the problems of child-rearing, pollution, and crime in the streets, plus a definitive answer to the question, "Why Are You Here?" can all be theirs for the cost of a six-cent stamp. On a far less sophisticated level, James Bishop Carr, of Palmdale, California, does the same thing. Brother Carr believes that much of the world's ills can be traced to the use of "Roman time" (the Gregorian calendar) and observances of religious holidays such as Christmas. He has reckoned the day and hour of Christ's second coming, but is uncertain of the year. Each Night of Atonement, he awaits the Eschaton with his followers, the Little Flock of Mount Zion. Between disappointments, he constructs elaborate charts depicting the flow of history from Adam's Garden to Armageddon,[1] complete with battle plans for the latter event. Others deal in prophecy on more of an *ad hoc*[2] basis, but are no less confident of their accuracy. David Terrell, the Endtime Messenger, recently warned that "even today, the sword of the Lord is drawed" and that "coastal cities shall be inhabited by strange creatures from the sea, yea, and there shall be great sorrow in California. . . . God has never failed. Who shall deny when these things happen that a prophet was in your midst? Believest thou this and you shall be blessed."

To become a disciple of one of these prophet-preachers is, by the evangelists' own admission, to obtain a guide without peer to lead one over life's uneven pathway. Though few of them possess standard professional credentials, they take pains to assure their scattered flocks that they have divine recognition and approval. Some associate themselves with leading biblical personalities, as when A. A. Allen speaks of the way "God has worked through his great religious leaders, such as Moses and myself," or when C. W. Burpo intones, "God loves you and I love you." Several report appearances by heavenly visitors. According to David Terrell, Jesus came into his room on April 17, about eight-thirty at night and told him there was too much junk going around. "Bring the people unto me." Though some receive angels regularly, they do not regard their visits lightly. "If you don't think that it'll almost tax your nervous system to the breaking point," says the Reverend Billy Walker, Jr., "let an angel come to you." Other evangelists simply promise, as does Brother Al, "I can get through to God for you." In support of such claims, they point to the testimony of satisfied disciples and to their own personal success; the flamboyance in dress affected by some of the men obviously capitalizes on their followers' need for a hero who has himself achieved the success denied them.

In the fiercely competitive struggle for the listeners' attention and money, most of the evangelists have developed a novel twist or gimmick to distinguish them from their fellow clerics. C. W. Burpo does not simply pray; he goes into the "throne room" to talk to God. The door to the throne room can be heard opening and shutting. David Epley's trademark is the use of the gift of "discernment." He not only heals those who come to him, but "discerns" those in his audience who need a special gift of healing, in the manner of a pious Dunninger. A. A. Allen emphasizes witchcraft on most of his current broadcasts, blaming everything from asthma to poverty on hexes and demons. In other years he has talked of holy oil that flowed from the hands of those who were being healed, or crosses of blood that appeared on their foreheads. David Terrell frequently calls upon his gift of "tongues." Terrell breaks into ecstatic speech either at the peak of an emotional passage or at points where he appears to need what is otherwise known as "filler." Certain of his spirited words tend to recur repeatedly.

---

[1] Armageddon is the scene of a final battle between good and evil prophesied in the Bible (Revelation 16:16) to occur at the end of the world.

[2] *Ad hoc* is a Latin term meaning "for a particular time, situation, or purpose."

Rapha, nissi, and *honda bahayah* are three favorites. The first two may be derived from the Hebrew words for healing and victory. Unless the third is a Hebrew term having to do with motorcycles, its meaning is known only to those with the gift of interpretation. Terrell defends his "speaking in the Spirit" over the radio on the grounds that he is an apostle—"not a grown-up apostle like Peter or Paul; just a little boy apostle that's started out working for Jesus."

Once one has made contact with a radio evangelist, preferably by a letter containing a "love offering," one is usually bombarded with letters and publications telling of what God has recently wrought through his servant, asking for special contributions to meet a variety of emergencies, and urging followers to send for items personally blessed by the evangelist and virtually guaranteed to bring the desired results. One runs across holy oil, prosperity billfolds, and sacred willow twigs, but the perennial favorite of those with talismaniacal[3] urges is the prayer cloth.

Prayer cloths come in several colors and sizes, and are available in muslin, sackcloth, terrycloth, and, for a limited time only, revival-tent cloth. As an optional extra, they can be anointed with water, oil, or ashes. My own model is a small ($2\frac{1}{2} \times 3\frac{1}{2}$ inches) unanointed rectangle of pinked cloth. The instructions state that it represents the man of God who sent it, and that it can be laid upon those with an ailment, hidden in the house to bring peace and blessings, carried in the purse or pocketbook for financial success, and even taken to court to assure a favorable outcome. One woman told Reverend Ike that she had cut her cloth in two and placed a piece under the separate beds of a quarreling couple. She declared the experiment an unqualified success, to the delight of Reverend Ike—"You did that? You rascal, you! Let's all give God a great big hand!"

These scraps of paper and cloth serve to bind preacher and people together until the glorious day when a faithful listener can attend a live service at the civic auditorium or the coliseum, or under the big tent at the fairgrounds. It is here, in the company of like-minded believers, that a person loses and perhaps finds himself as he joins the shouting, clapping, dancing, hugging, weeping, rejoicing throng. At such a service, a large Negro lady pointed into the air and jiggled pleasantly. Beside her, a sad, pale little woman, in a huge skirt hitched up with a man's belt, hopped tentatively on one foot and looked for a moment as if she might have found something she had been missing. On cue from the song leader, all turned to embrace or shake hands with a neighbor and to assure each other that "Jesus is *all right!*" Old men jumped about like mechanical toys. Two teen-age boys "ran for Jesus." And in the aisles a trim, gray-haired woman in spike heels and a black nylon dress, danced sensuously all over the auditorium. She must have logged a mile and a half, maybe a mile and three quarters, before the night was over. I couldn't help wondering if her husband knew where she was. But I was sure she liked where she was better than where she had been.

If a radio evangelist can stimulate this kind of response, whether he is a charlatan (as some undoubtedly are) or sincerely believes he is a vessel

---

[3] Talismaniacal refers to talismans—objects which are supposed to confer supernatural power or protection on their owners.

of God (as some undoubtedly do) is secondary. If he can convince his listeners that he can deliver what he promises, the blend of genuine need, desperate belief, reinforcing group—and who knows what else?—can move in mysterious ways its wonder to perform. And, for a long time, that will likely be enough to keep those cards and letters coming in.

■ **POINTS TO CONSIDER**

1. What distinctions does the author make between "gospel radio" and other religious radio programs?

2. What are some of the reasons why "gospel radio" is popular with so many listeners? What needs does gospel radio serve for its audience?

3. What various approaches do the different radio preachers use to create personal identities and set themselves apart from the others?

4. What various kinds of mass media and popular arts, in addition to radio broadcasts, do radio preachers use to reach their "congregations"?

5. What examples of gospel radio are produced in your community? How do these local programs compare with the more widely broadcast programs which the author describes?

6. Why does the author refer to the radio gospel preachers as "God-hucksters"? Do you think this term is appropriate or not? Why?

■ # TELEVISION/WHAT PUBLIC? WHOSE INTEREST?

Thomas C. Swafford   *Cincinnati Horizons,* July 1974

As those who find themselves uncomfortable with television's new candor of the 1970's insist that all of society conform only to their own standards, they beseech an Omniscient[1] Someone to turn back the clock.

To suggest that rather than turn back the clock, they turn off their sets—or at least turn off the program that upsets them—is not enough. I recall one lady who wrote recently, saying: "Don't tell me to turn off my television, you have no right to bring this offensive material into my home!" I've learned the futility of pointing out that television only makes programs available; that she determines what comes into her home. But she went on, as do so many who write, saying: "You are licensed to serve the public. If you fail in that obligation, you should lose your license." She raises a point that demands exploration.

[1] Omniscient means knowing everything.

Broadcasting stations are licensed to serve the public interest, convenience, and necessity. "Interest," "convenience," and "necessity" may at times be somewhat vague and difficult to interpret precisely. Still I think they're more readily definable than "public." One might say that the public is everybody. And that's partly true. In which case, one would suppose that simply by making a list of everyone, everywhere in the country, we'd have the names of all the people who make up "The Public"—a task that would frustrate the most sophisticated computer. Even assuming it were possible to compile such a list, by the time it had been committed to memory banks, it would have changed. Some would have died; others would have been born. The public, in any finite sense, exists only for a fraction of a moment.

All this is rather abstract for anyone who's trying to run a station or a network to provide programs that will entertain and inform a public that is very vocal and demanding—and very fickle. For the broadcaster, the public can be categorized in terms of age, income and education. The buzz word for this compartmentalization is "demographics." Each compartment, every niche, delineates a different public, each with its own outlooks, interests, standards, and ideas of what is "convenient" or "necessary."

Television, this nation's only true mass medium, must endeavor to provide programming that is appealing to, and interesting for, each of those publics, which in total comprise The Public. There is, however, always the awareness that in the very act of appealing to one public, it's not only possible, but likely, we will disturb or alienate another public.

In responding to this kind of challenge, programming at CBS, for instance, ranges from the earthiness of *All in The Family,* through the topical, sometimes bawdy humor of *Maude,* and the occasionally risque *Mary Tyler Moore,* to the warmth and nostalgia of *The Waltons.* And, although infrequently, television has also offered drama which has brought distress to some, because of its stark reality. Both before and during each such dramatic program, we've cautioned that we're offering a drama, dealing with a mature theme in a mature manner, and we've suggested that parents and more sensitive viewers should exercise judgment and discretion. You could call it our own version of a PG (Parental Guidance) rating.

But, interestingly, all the films like *Virginia Woolf,* and the discussions of abortion on *Maude,* or of lesbianism on *Medical Center*—all of them together comprise a miniscule percentage of the total number of programs the CBS Television Network has presented in the past and current seasons. This fact seems to be totally lost in all the criticisms of television.

Just how candid have we been? Homosexuality has always been one of broadcasting's taboos, in spite of the fact that, according to reliable authorities, some ten percent of our population is, as they say, "gay." Early in the 1973-74 season, the CBS program *Medical Center* had an episode which dealt with the subject in a very frank manner.

Another forbidden subject in any entertainment context was abortion. Last season, on *Maude,* we broadcast a two-part episode discussing what happens when a 48-year-old woman finds herself with child. When that program was first aired, we received some 7,000 letters protesting most vehemently. When it was repeated last August, we at CBS felt enormous pressures from people who objected to the program. It was our feeling, however, that we had a deep commitment to re-broadcast the episodes.

Before and immediately after the repeats, we received 17,000 pieces of mail; all told, 24,000 letters protesting the two broadcasts. That is not an unimpressive outburst. But it becomes less impressive in the context of the 65 million people who saw one or more of the broadcasts.

All in the Family, of course, has made television history. At various times, it has dealt, in one way or another, with such subjects as menopause, impotence, menstruation, and Watergate. During the Christmas season just past, the program approached the topic of breast cancer, a subject important to every woman, and thus, to every man. Norman Lear is the Executive Producer of both *Maude* and *All In The Family,* and one of his many gifts is his ability to expose our blind spots. In a typical scene, a character will subtly, but certainly, shift his or her position, so that the liberal becomes conservative, and vice versa. He demonstrated this in a recent episode of *All In The Family* when Mike, the supporter of all liberal causes, found himself confronted by a subject in itself interesting: A woman's libido.[2]

All of the programs I've just mentioned are produced specifically for TV and the subjects and dialogue are controlled from start to finish. In dealing with material from another medium, where the material was originally intended for a theater audience rather than a home audience, we often take steps to protect the sensitivities of those in our audience who might find certain language offensive. For instance, in approaching the film version of Edward Albee's *Who's Afraid of Virginia Woolf?* we had a number of problems. First, we felt a duty to retain the dramatic integrity of a monumental motion picture as much as possible. But we also felt that some lines had to be minimized, particularly the "goddamns," all but one of which were deftly cut to "damns." We felt that, in some cases, the cumulative effect of all the "bastards" and "sonsofbitches" would deeply disturb many viewers. So with a scalpel, we edited some sixty-four seconds out of the picture. Apparently, our efforts were successful, because while thirty-three million viewers saw the film on February 2, 1973, only 1200 were sufficiently upset to write letters of complaint. However, one letter, which we treasured, was from Ernest Lehman who adapted the play and produced the film. He applauded us for the care and intelligence with which we had edited the picture.

Another Mike Nichols film, *The Graduate,* lent itself quite handily to minimal editing, and the elimination of some nudity, both obvious and subliminal. One scene in particular, however, during which Benjamin and Mrs. Robinson begin their affair, caused us concern. Again, we tried to edit the scene in question, but realized it made no sense. The scene was vital to the picture, because it said everything there was to say about Mrs. Robinson, Benjamin and their relationship.

Not so long ago, one of television's rules was that if you showed a man and woman in bed together, one of them had to have at least one foot on the floor. It's not clear what this proved, but, happily, this has changed. Thus, earlier this season when we broadcast a *Maude* episode which concerned itself with her husband's alcoholism, we were able to show Maude awakening in the morning to find her neighbor, Arthur, snoring at her side, having mistakenly stumbled into her bed after a drinking spree the night

---

[2] Libido refers to instinctual biological urges, especially those having to do with sexual desire.

before. The issue was alcoholism, and having Maude with one foot on the floor would not have added to the impact or the message of the program.

That's part of what television is all about, in The Year of Our Lord, 1974. It is a medium honestly endeavoring to reflect the tastes, standards, and interests of the many audiences—the many publics—it reaches and serves. Still, there are those who are displeased and disturbed by television. They are not just those who deplore a particular "moral tone." Other segments of our society make other demands of television, often with a disturbing shrillness.

There is, I fear, a distressing intolerance in the strident insistence of many that their own views—and only their views—should be seen or expressed on television. They feel that their standards and beliefs are the only ones fit for any audience to see. Increasingly, I find myself not just concerned, but actually shaken by the intolerance and invective that seems to be characterizing so much of our dialogue today.

I think, perhaps, we in television may be in a singular position to be aware of this diminishing tolerance of those who differ with us. Outrageous demands are made of television by hyphenated groups insisting that no one of their color or ethnic background ever be portrayed in anything other than a favorable light. Religious leaders are indignant if any program dares to present any theme or subject that runs counter to their own beliefs or dogma. A former FCC commissioner calls us in television "child molesters", and the phrase is immediately picked up by those who are determined to remake children's television in their own image. Incredibly, we hear the term "Nazi" tossed around casually in denouncing those who disagree with or question our own ideas.

A tide of fear and mistrust is rising around us as we are becoming an uneasy and uncertain people. As unyielding demands are made of television in the name of the public, there is in those demands an implicit distrust of that public, and consequently an inherent distrust of ourselves, and our beliefs. In the past several years, we've heard and seen great events thundering around us. We've felt great pressures, but we are displaying none of that quality of courage that Ernest Hemingway defined so eloquently. We are behaving with very little "grace under pressure."

We are becoming a graceless, petty people. Once lulled into self-satisfaction as we looked to our past, complacent as we contemplated our future, we now seem to find little reason, either for self-satisfaction or complacency. Once confident that God had, indeed, shed His grace on us, once certain that we had truly formed a more perfect Union, we now appear to be less certain, less confident. And emerging from this wavering confidence, I think I can see the symptoms of one of the most corrosive diseases: Self-Pity.

One of the first manifestations of self-pity is an eagerness to find some one or some thing to blame for our own shortcomings. As we looked into television's mirror and saw something less than perfect, I believe it was quite predictable that we would attack the mirror. When we look around us, we see crime and lust, and evidence of man's inhumanity to man, of his mortal failings, and his immoral acts. We behave as though we, and we alone, have been singled out by history to bear great burdens. We see man's weaknesses; we stare at society's scabs. We feel frustrations at our

"What does BLEEP mean?"

"Grin and Bear It" by George Lichty and Fred Wagner. Courtesy of Field Newspaper Syndicate.

own human frailties. But the fault is not in our sets; it is in ourselves. To change television will not change that fact. Although some seek proscriptions and prohibitions to inhibit television, something far greater is involved here. When broadcasting was born, back in 1920, it was free. Through the years, there have been erosions of that freedom, yet our system of broadcasting in this country still remains relatively free.

To inhibit that freedom further will be to betray not just ourselves, but all those who have struggled and worked and fought for that freedom. For posterity is also part of that constantly changing public, to whom not just those of us in broadcasting, but all of us, have a deep and continuing obligation.

POINTS TO CONSIDER

1. Why is it not enough simply to tell those who don't like certain programming to turn off their TV sets or to change channels?

2. What problems are there in defining the "public" of public interest? The author says that TV is honestly trying to reflect the tastes, standards, and interests of the many audiences—the many publics—it reaches and serves. Do you think this is possible? Explain.

3. Is television, as the author asserts, the only "true" mass medium? In what ways can this assertion be considered correct or incorrect?

4. What are some of the pressures that are brought to bear on the televi-

sion industry by special-interest groups? How does television deal with these pressures?

5. What examples of TV censorship does the author relate? What examples of "television's new candor" does he offer? Can you cite other examples? What important kind of de facto censorship does the author omit mentioning?

6. What reasons does the author give for the many attacks on the television industry? Do you agree with his reasons for them? Explain. Compared with other mass media, do you believe that TV generally offers more or less controversial material? Explain.

■ TV CHILDREN

Jerry Kosinski   *Comment*, N.B.C. Broadcast, September 3, 1972

With the advent of television, for the first time in history, all aspects of animal and human life and death, of societal and individual behavior have been condensed on the average to a 19 inch diagonal screen and a 30 minute time slot. Television, a unique medium, claiming to be neither a reality nor art, has become reality for many of us, particularly for our children who are growing up in front of it.

Imagine a child watching this little world within which Presidents and commoners walk; mice and lions, kissing lovers and dying soldiers, skyscrapers and dog houses, flowers and detergents, all are reduced to the same size, mixed together, given the same rank, and set in the same screen to be looked at. The child watches this crowded world as he or she pleases, while eating, yawning, playing. What is the outlook of such a child? What does it expect of the world? What can it expect?

It expects all things to be as equal as on television: neither bad nor good, neither pleasant nor painful, neither real nor unreal, merely more or less interesting, merely in better or worse color. It is a world without rank. To such a child, the world is to be looked upon; it is there to entertain its viewer. If it doesn't, one alters it by switching the channel.

In the little world of television, all is solved within its magic 30 minutes. In spite of the commercials, the wounded hero either rises or quickly dies, lovers marry or divorce, villains kill or are killed, addicts are cured, justice usually wins, and war ends. All problems are solved again this week, as they were last, and will be next week. Life on TV must be visual. This means single-faceted, revealed in a simple speech and through the obvious gesture. No matter how deep the mystery, the TV camera penetrates it.

Parents leave their children in front of the TV as baby sitter, because many feel it is infinitely safer to watch the Sesame world of television than to walk in the world outside of their home. But is it?

Unlike television, the child grows older. One day it walks out of the TV room. Against his expectations, he's finally put in a classroom full of other children. A child who has been trained to control the little world, by changing the channels when he didn't like it, and was accustomed to maintaining the same distance between himself and the world televised for his amusement, is naturally threatened by the presence of people he cannot control. Others push him around, make faces at him, encroach. There is nothing he can do to stop them. He begins to feel that this real world unjustly limits him; it offers no channels to turn to.

In this unpredictable world of real life, there are no neatly ordered thirty-minute private slots. Here, in life, the child brought up only as viewer must feel persecuted. Ironically, our industrial state offers few things that can be resolved in thirty minutes. But the teenager keeps expecting it; when it is not, he grows impatient, then adamant,[1] disillusioned, oscillating between the revolutionary scream, "Now," and a political cool "So what?" He is easily depressed and beaten down. In this world of hierarchy and brutish competition, he is challenged and outranked by others. Soon he believes he is defective; instead of coming of age, he's coming apart. This breeding of weak and vulnerable beings knows few exceptions. The kids of the upper classes counteract TV by being involved with real events—real horses, real forests, real mountains—all things they have seen, touched, experienced. They have been given an opportunity to exist outside the television room. However, many middle class children, and almost all from poor families are at the mercy of five or six hours of television a day.

My own attitude toward television is neutral. The medium is here to stay. The danger is in the use we make of it. I'm involved with TV the way I am with the motor car. The motor car has been with us for over 50 years, but it is only recently that we learned its exhaust pollutes our very environment.

In today's atomized,[2] disjointed technological society, with so little at-

---

[1] Adamant means unyielding or stubborn; oscillating means wavering steadily between ideas or courses of action.

[2] An atomized society is one which stresses individualism or the importance of smaller groups rather than institutions representing the whole of the society.

| Hi and Lois | ® | By Mort Walker & Dik Browne |

tention paid to the individual, man needs more than ever the inner strength to carry him through the daily pressures. This strength should come from early exposure to life at its most real—its sudden pleasures, joys and abandonment; but also its violence, its lack of justice, its pain, illness, and death. There is subtlety to man's fate which lies beyond the thirteen channels.

■ POINTS TO CONSIDER

1. To what extent do you agree with Kosinski that television "has become reality for many of us, particularly for our children"? Explain.

2. What are the characteristics of the TV world as the author describes it? How does the child relate to this world? How can he control it?

3. What does the author believe happens to the child upon leaving the TV room?

4. Do you believe, as the author asserts, that "almost all" children from poor families watch from five to six hours of television a day? Explain why you agree or disagree.

5. What analogy does the author imply between television and the motor car? Do you think the analogy is valid? If so, can you think of further points of similarity between the two?

6. Do you believe, as the author does, that TV insulates us from "life at its most real" and thereby breeds "weak and vulnerable beings"? Explain.

■ WHAT TV IS DOING TO AMERICA

Alistair Cooke   *U.S. News and World Report,* April 15, 1974

Q Mr. Cooke, what are the most striking effects on Americans of a quarter century of widespread television?

A The most striking thing to me is that television has produced a generation of children who have a declining grasp of the English language but also have a visual sophistication that was denied to their parents. They learn so much about the world that appeals immediately to their emotions, but I'm not sure it involves their intelligence, their judgment.

Q Are you suggesting that they have a great random knowledge but not an understanding of what it is they know?

A More or less. Things can come at you on television in a flash—in three seconds—which would take a fine teacher an hour or so to interpret. I noticed this every day of the two years that we were filming the "America" series.

Of course, I wrote as pithily as I could, as one must on television. Time and again I had to reduce an argument to two minutes, and then to a minute and 30 seconds, if I was in good form. Yet very often one sentence, and a picture and a chord of music, can give the essence of what you are trying to say.

Q **Of the influences that affect development of a child today, where would you place television?**

A I would say next to the mother and father—far ahead of school and church.

Q **What effect is television having on American society and the generation formed by this new experience?**

A It's awfully hard to tell. There's the problem that we are all getting more information now than we can cope with.

I think that's the reason for the sort of low-key hysteria—Thoreau's "quiet desperation"—that a lot of us live in. The images overwhelm our ability to make judgments or handle our government and our lives because we are so continuously aware of the disruption that's going on everywhere.

Q **Is our society more violent than it used to be because of television? Would the race riots and campus riots of the 1960s have happened without television being on hand to film the events?**

A I think the race riots would have happened anyway. Television quickened the general awareness of the blacks' chronic plight. That's the good side of it.

But television can also spark trouble, especially among sick people. It can trigger fashions—whether in "streaking" or in kidnaping. And I think sick or defeated—really insane—people have been given, through television, the imagination to plan or contemplate violent acts.

The most terrifying thing to me is the instant publicity that television can give to bad news, which can then be copied anywhere in the world. There's no way out of that. There is a behavioral scientist in Dallas who says the only way to cure the kidnaping plague is to deny kidnapers the media, both newspapers and television.

Q **How can television be regulated to minimize this extremely disruptive, almost revolutionary impact on a society?**

A Since the main commitment of television and any other news media is to get out the news, I don't see how they can fairly edit out terror.

Q **What is the impact of crime shows on television which portray a lot of violence, gun play and gore?**

A This is really the same question as: What is the effect of flagrant pornography? Does it stimulate bad behavior?

The tendency so far has been for the Establishment to say, "Yes, of course it does," and for the psychiatrists and sociologists to say, "No, of course it doesn't." They are both protecting prepared positions.

But we don't seem to have enough evidence to prove anything one way or the other. We all live by the one-case induction method—generalizing from some vivid personal example.

For instance, I knew a rich woman whose house was broken into one night by a white man and a white girl, a black man and a black girl.

They ransacked the house for jewelry and the like, bound her and her young daughter, found a maid downstairs and bound her. Then they said, "Well now, are you ready for the rape?" She said she wasn't ready to be raped. So they said, "All right, we'll have to rape the maid"—which they did. And when it was over, one of the men said: "It's 'Clockwork Orange,' baby! That's the name of the game." (They'd all been to see the movie, "A Clockwork Orange," which, as you know, was based on Anthony Burgess's futuristic novel about sadism and violence.)

I think it's most urgent that we should do exhaustive studies on children before we can give an answer to: Do people learn violence from television, or does it purge violence in them?

Q How do the networks know that there is a public demand for such things as violence?

A They just look at the rating system, which they accept as statistical gospel. But an awful lot of people use television as sort of audible wallpaper. That is, they argue, quarrel, sleep, play cards against it. The ratings say, "This is what people are looking at." But it's what they *would be looking at* if they cared to.

Q Who really runs television?

A Well, the people who bear the responsibility for the programs are the network presidents and the advertising agencies.

Q Do the television producers simply respond to a marketable demand for violent or superficial programs?

A There's no question that they respond to what will sell a product. We often forget that in our country the primary function of television is that of a merchant. But people forget that if gun play and neurotic families sell more detergents than classical drama and documentaries on saving our landscape, they'll get gun play and serials.

Q Is public television the alternative?

A In our society I think you have to have both public and private television. All the media should provide a service for the widest possible variety of people.

Q Does that mean the lowest common denominator?

A No. It should mean the *highest* common denominator. That's what television should aim at.

Q Would it be desirable or necessary in the U. S. eventually to follow somewhat the British pattern, where there is much tighter control over programing and commercials?

A It depends who has the control. A misunderstanding that's very current in the United States is that the alternative to television run by networks for sponsors is to have "government-owned" television.

Well, British television is not government-owned in any sense that the Spanish or the French is. It's a public corporation, maintained by the public's paying a license fee for owning a set. It's bound by the acts of Parliament, but it's never bound by the policies of the Government. In fact, most governments dread the BBC's independence to do as it pleases.

Some years ago, there was protest about the BBC monopoly, and eventually Parliament allowed another network. But the interesting thing to point out is the way the British run their commercial network.

On that network, it is not the advertisers—as in America—who bring you Alec Guinness or Julie Andrews. They buy time the way an advertiser for a newspaper buys space. They don't see a dry run of your editorial as a pilot before they buy. Advertisers on commercial television in Great Britain have no idea what they're buying, except that obviously a minute at noon costs less than a minute in prime time.

In other words, the advertiser is kept away from *production.* That's the important thing. The production companies put their shows on the commercial network and are just as free as the production teams employed by the BBC to do their own thing to the best of their ability. They are freed from outside, self-serving pressures.

Q What bothers you most about network shows?

A The thing that horrifies me most about commercials is the medical brainwashing that the family gets on television. It seems to me that it easily outweighs any lessons in chemistry or biology that the child picks up in school. When my own children were very small, I used to say, "I'll show you a book which tells you that that is not the way the stomach works at all—that you don't just take a tablet that goes 'pssssst,' and then feel great." We as a nation pride ourselves on being medically very literate. We love medical jargon: We prefer "lesions" to "swellings," and "clavicles" to "shoulder blades," and so on. Yet I truly believe that the body of our knowledge about medicine is fed to us from a very early age by commercials—and it's idiotic medicine. Mostly, it's either harmful or useless.

Q Has television changed the character of American government to the extent that a candidate who is not presentable on television can't become President?

A I really doubt that. I think we've put a premium on slickness—no question about it.

Q Are you saying that the television image of a candidate really is not very important to his success or failure?

A I think it is, but I think we tend to confuse handsomeness or gloss with character. The camera doesn't lie. It shows you the true man—and looking at some of the people we've elected, I'd say that we're as bad judges of human character as President Nixon seems to have been.

In other words, if there's an indictment, it's an indictment of the watcher, not the performer.

Q Basically, what is television's impact on politics?

A Oh, it's enormous. First of all, it has drastically simplified the convention game. Television has exposed the whole mechanism of politics. In the old days, we preserved our ideals and read only what we wanted to read. But today many, many more people know how cities are run, how conventions are run, how bills go through Congress, how they get shelved, how lobbies put the bite on legislators.

Q Does that have a healthy effect?

A I hope so—though ignorance was more blissful because you kept your ideals.

Q What positive things have you noted about TV's influence on U. S. society?

A Well, as I've implied, it gives people an enormously wider knowledge of the way our society is governed. Certainly, we have seen the face of injustice and of crime and of poverty in ways that unimaginative people would never have picked up from newspaper reports. In this way, the medium itself is a means of great reporting: You see a mother break down; you see a miner's miserable village. It forces you to take in more than you would ever care to read.

Q **Was that the case with the Vietnam war—that people began to get an immediate and vivid idea of war?**

A Yes. Vietnam was, to put it cold-bloodedly, the most interesting example of a general change in the attitude to war itself. I suggested earlier that maybe the change leads to very sloppy conclusions, such as that because war itself is hideous, all wars are useless. If we'd believed that 30 years ago, the States would now be run by *Gauleiters*.

Let's suppose you'd had television in 1916, and you had John Chancellor, Walter Cronkite and Howard K. Smith reporting the battles of the Somme: "Tonight the second battle of the Somme continues, and the British estimate their losses today at 60,000. The Germans' are estimated at 80,000. And now a message." Then on the next night they'd come on and say: "This is the third night of the battle of the Somme. Today's count of British casualties is 62,000." I believe there'd have been wholesale revolutions.

The point about Vietnam is that for the first time we had uncensored reporting from the field of battle. We didn't have much detail about the first World War when I was a little boy until the literature came out *after* the war. The reporting of Vietnam came out every day the war was on. We heard a great deal from men on our side who didn't know what they were fighting for and hated the war and were "agin" the Government. This is totally new in the human experience and, of course, from the military point of view, very corrosive of morale.

Q **Doesn't this fact handicap a free society in competing with totalitarian societies?**

A Absolutely. We never saw it better than in the reporting of Vietnam. We saw the agony and the waste and corruption. Every night we saw rickety children or wounded grandmothers and soldiers on litters—and men totally bored with the whole thing. The whole truth can be a very demoralizing thing.

The question is: Can we cope with the whole truth when we know that the Russians and the Chinese learn only what their Governments want them to know? In a way, this freedom is our pride, but it's also our agony. And television magnifies it enormously. Censorship controlled what we knew about the first World War and the second. Suppose we had seen a two-hour piece, filmed from helicopters and from the ground, on our destruction of Dresden. What would that have done to people?

Q **In that perspective, is this really a much more violent time than we've known in the past?**

A We've not had anything like 1919 [Chicago racial clashes] or the violence in Detroit in 1943, which was the only thing I've seen that could be really called a race riot. When the Southern whites moved up to Willow Run to work in defense production and the blacks started to move into the shabby neighborhoods that the whites occupied, that was murder for two days.

It's too simple to say that violence is worse than it's ever been. The point is that we *know* about it.

I once spent a week or so studying what happened in the spring of one year, 1926, that I had always looked back on nostalgically. I looked at what was happening all over Europe and the British Isles—anything that undoubtedly would have been featured in the evening news. It was a nightmare: famine in India, unemployment riots in Germany, Armenians starving, Britain paralyzed by a general strike, France fighting in Morocco, an army mutiny brewing in Spain.

You read about these things only if you wanted to. Now we see it all happen on television.

Q Does that give TV newsmen too much power?

A I think their power is inherent in the medium. There is no way out. The moment you put a man on the screen and he talks to you for 10 minutes, he has enormous power—as much power as his talent can command.

Q TV commentators are accused of lacking objectivity. Is that a just complaint?

A I don't think so. Of course, it should be the pride of a network to try to be totally objective, but one problem is that it's not very dramatic to be objective. Maybe your rating will go down. And the networks are just as interested in selling things through their news programs as they are on any other program.

Q Is it a bad idea to have three competing networks with competing news shows on *at the same time*?

A Yes, indeed, and this is where the networks should grow up. I was down in Florida a few weeks ago, where Walter Cronkite came on at 6:30 and John Chancellor came on at 7, instead of simultaneously as in New York. In that hour I got a much better feel for the whole news—and I would have liked also to be able to watch ABC. Then I could say the networks do a damn good job in their news shows.

In fact, I think the American networks do a better news job than any other system I know.

Q As you look down the road, what difference in American life will TV play in the future?

A Well, we know, for instance, that it's been an enormous help in closed-circuit teaching operations. A lot of teaching, I think, is going to be done by remote control—by good teachers instead of incompetent teachers. This may not be very good for the teaching profession, but in all the sciences, especially in medicine, it's a marvelous thing.

Q What do you see ahead in television's effect in other ways—in the way we talk, for instance?

A The thing that alarms me is that you can pick up bad habits quicker from television than anything else. I notice children really picking up the butchery of the English language from television, and especially from advertising prose. "Genteelisms" are absolutely riddling the language. I mean, people don't ever moisten their lips any more; they "moisturize." It doesn't rain in Chicago; we now have "precipitation activity in the Chicago area."

Between Madison Avenue and the Pentagon, nobody's ever going to be able to read the first chapter of Genesis. "Let there be light" will have absolutely no meaning. I heard a Defense Department official the other evening, and what he wanted to say was that we've got to be able to attack where we choose. But he didn't say that; he said he was going to "preserve our targeting options."

I hear children talking about "dentifrice." They don't know what toothpaste is.

Q Are Americans becoming more cynical as they view television and the extravagant promises it proclaims?

A Yes, yes, I think so. This is an open society, and whether you like it or not, it does encourage cynicism. It makes demands on the maturity and judgment of the individual that are more severe than any he ever had to meet when he had only the press to ponder.

Q Does this help make us a nation of spectators?

A Well, that brings us down to something no man can gauge—which is the general morale of the country. If we're a mature people, and we know what our freedom is about, and we remain aware that this great choice of opinion is a good thing, then we're free to make our own judgment without bitterness or hate.

But many people give up and slump into cynicism. And in the end, it comes down to our educational system, especially primary education. If the mass of the people are crudely, badly educated, they will soon give up their liberties for bread and circuses.

■ **POINTS TO CONSIDER**

1. What, according to Mr. Cooke, has been television's effect on children? On violence? On language?

2. What does Mr. Cooke say is television's primary function in America? How does this affect programming? How is British television different?

3. What does Mr. Cooke mean by TV's "medical brainwashing"?

4. What does he see as the most important difference between television news coverage and news that is read? How has this affected the individual's view of the world?

5. What effect does he feel television has had on politics in this country? On the Vietnam war? How does he explain these effects?

6. What improvements does he suggest might be made in television? Do you agree? Explain.

7. Does he feel that television makes Americans cynical? What remedy does he suggest? Do you agree? Explain.

■ YOUR SOAP-OPERA SITTER

McCalls, May 1974

"Dr. Laura Horton realizes when she goes out to dinner with Jim Phillips, who is temporarily handling Laura's missing husband Mickey's law practice, that Alice Horton, Mickey's mother. . . ."

If you can follow this tortuous[1] sentence, you must be a fan of NBC-TV's serial "Days of Our Lives." The excerpt comes from *Daytime Serial Newsletter,* a new monthly for soap-opera addicts who can't bear to leave their sets to go on vacation or cope with other interruptions in their TV-viewing schedules.

Keeping them up-to-date with summaries of the comings and goings and doings of their favorite soap characters is the job of publisher-writer Bryna Laub. A 28-year-old biologist, she gave up a teaching career to turn her soap-watching hobby into a profitable business. Her service now claims over 8,000 subscribers who pay $7.50 apiece for a one year's subscription.

■ POINTS TO CONSIDER

1. What is the *Daytime Serial Newsletter,* and what service does it offer?

2. How many people currently subscribe to the *Daytime Serial Newsletter?* What does this figure and the price of a subscription suggest as to the importance of daytime television serials in some people's lives?

3. Do you watch, or have you watched, daytime serials on TV? What do you think accounts for their appeal? If you have watched a particular daytime serial for a while and you resume watching it sometime later, do you feel that having missed a number of episodes greatly detracts from your enjoyment of the show? Why, or why not?

---

[1] A tortuous sentence is complex and full of strung-together details

■ IS TELEVISION MAKING A MOCKERY OF THE AMERICAN WOMAN?

Edith Efron   *TV Guide,* 1970

"You use our bodies to sell products! You blackmail us with fear of being unloved if we do not buy!"

The strident voice of a young feminist, Marian Delgado, broke through the orderly proceedings of a CBS stockholders' meeting in San Francisco, last April, to the consternation of CBS board chairman William S. Paley and CBS president Frank Stanton, while the latter was criticizing government authorities' "increasing pressures" on broadcasting. Neither of these gentlemen had anticipated the eruption of a new and strangely fierce pressure within their own citadel.

Miss Delgado, speaking for a group of about ten members of the Women's Liberation Front, continued her charge that CBS "abuses" women: the network, she declared, distorted and downgraded women's roles in its commercials and in its general programming. The disruption broke up the meeting—briefly—after which Mr. Paley insisted to the collected stockholders: "We do *not* dislike women." He pointed out that ten percent of CBS's administrative personnel is female. "Tokenism!" scoffed the feminists as they departed.

This little female assault on CBS was gleefully reported by broadcast journalists as an amusing aberration,[1] of no particular significance, by a handful of viragoes. But they were not quite accurate. The Delgado invasion was significant: it was a symptom of an agitation over TV's portrayal of women among a growing number of women of all classes, races and political persuasions, who are joining feminist groups from coast to coast or cheering them on silently.

TV, in fact, has become one of the prime targets of the feminists in their new and aggressive surge for equal rights for women.

In November 1969, 500 highly educated women from cities and campuses in Eastern United States—Baltimore, Boston, Bryn Mawr, Clark University, Cornell University, Penn State, Pittsburgh and elsewhere—met in New York to set up a congress to unite women. At this congress, one workshop concerned itself with women's "stereotyped . . . and derogatory . . . image most blatantly seen in the presentations of the mass media" and the "misrepresentation by the media of the movement for women's liberation. . . ." Among the results: the creation of an organization called Media Women, a newsletter on the subject, boycotts, and protests such as that led by Marian Delgado.

To discover exactly what the feminists object to in TV, we interviewed a group of them—most of them founders and leaders of feminist organizations, and some of them authors of serious books on women's problems.

---

[1] An aberration is an abnormality; viragoes are loud, domineering women.

Some hold very radical positions, some are more moderate. But all are united in an analysis of the damage TV is doing to women. Here's what they have to say:

Commercials, they say, offer a stereotyped and insulting picture of women. "It's disastrous!" says Susan Brownmiller, journalist, a member of Media Women and a TV news reporter for NBC and ABC for seven years. "The image of women in the commercials is that of *stupidity*. They're shown as stupid and helpless."

"They're blatant put-downs," says Anselma Del-Olio, actress and founder of the Feminist Repertory Theater in New York City. "They show the woman as a mindless boob and a masochistic slave—either a domestic servant or a sexy handmaiden."

"Commercials are legal pornography!" declares Ti-Grace Atkinson, member of the National Organization of Women and founder of the Feminists. "Women are shown exclusively as sex objects and reproducers, not as whole people."

And Shulamith Firestone, founder of the New York Radical Feminists, and author of *The Dialectic of Sex,* a book being brought out this fall by William Morrow, says, "The ads are creating really weird psychological effects. Women are being led to confuse their sexuality with individuality. What kind of sunglasses or bra they wear, whether they're blond or brunette, whether there's the right kind of wiggle in their walk, becomes absolutely crucial because their total worth as a human being becomes confused with a surface aspect. The ads are virtually generating erotomania[2] in women."

Similar charges are provoked by the portrayal of women in entertainment programming. Robin Morgan, writer, poet, member of several women's lib groups and mother of a year-old son, says: "The image of women in the plays is *dreadful*. At one pole there's the *I Love Lucy* stereotype, the brainless featherhead, and the sweet, dumb lovable blonde of *Petticoat Junction* and *Green Acres* who's helpless without men. In between, there's the maternal nurturing housewife, like Donna Reed or Julia—passive women who are defined in terms of their relationship to men—as wives or mothers or widows. At the other pole there's the male fantasy of the 'liberated' woman—the chic, hard, cold, sexy swinger with no ties, who obviously sleeps around and is not an economic drag on the man. And there's nothing else. It has almost no relationship with reality at all."

Shulamith Firestone says: "Women are just not *human* in these plays. They're not portrayed as thinking or feeling beings. They're shown as something between an animal and a human. The word 'chick' best captures it."

Is there any view of woman on TV that the feminists like? Yes, there is, but in our era it is unusually rare: it's the strong-minded, courageous heroine. Susan Brownmiller of Media Women says: "There's never been a heroic woman on TV, save for Emma Peel in *The Avengers*. That's the show I watch. I *love* that show! She's the only *strong* woman on television." And Shulamith Firestone says: "The best view of women you get is in movies of

[2] Erotomania is an abnormal or extreme sexual desire.

the thirties, where you got *strong* women. You can see Barbara Stanwyck portraying a woman who at least has *guts!*"

Commercials and series are not the only targets of the feminists' attack. News and talk shows, too, come in for their share of vitriolic[3] criticisms. Of general news coverage, Aileen Hernandez, the president of the National Organization of Women, says, "It is only relatively recently that women appear at all in news shows. You rarely see reports of women who have achieved anything of significance on these shows. Usually when you do see a woman she's involved in the same old claptrap about society or fashion." And Shulamith Firestone elaborates: "News departments don't consider women news. News equals the male government, the male war machine, the male world. There are fantastic women, women of great achievement in this country of whom people have never heard because the networks don't cover them."

Their protests against TV's coverage of Women's Lib itself are violent. They claim that it omits serious content and focuses on the lunatic fringe— a tiny fraction of hysterics with a professed desire to eliminate heterosexual relationships, childbearing, and generally to fold, spindle and mutilate the male of the species.

Anne Koedt, painter and member of the New York Radical Feminists, whose book on female sexuality is scheduled for publication this fall, says "On interviews they always ask you about two things—bra burning and violence! Bra burning is a nonexistent issue in the feminist movement. No one cares! Men just get a sexual kick out of talking about it.

"As for violence, what the male interviewers *really* mean is 'What will you do if we don't *let* you solve these problems?' It's *their* violence they're talking about!" And Anselma Del-Olio says: "The coverage of the feminist movement always contains an element of ridicule. There's all kinds of mocking editorializing, insinuations that we hate men. And on talk shows they surround you with put-down artists!

"But the editing of the film is where it's really at. They do a half-hour interview and take the most far-out thing that you've said—a conclusion which was a logical result of your whole exposition. But very conveniently they cut out all the *reasoning,* which means: they cut out *your* context."

Finally, news-department hiring policies, too, are attacked as "tokenism." Susan Brownmiller says: "I sat there for years and watched agents bring in *models* for news jobs. And I know for a fact that when a woman is considered, the networks are more concerned over her face than her abilities. Directors of news choose men simply in terms of performance, but they tend to lose their standards when it comes to women. And even when they've hired a few token women who are competent, they rarely give them a crack at important assignments."

These are by no means all the criticisms leveled at TV—but they are some of the essential ones. Is there any chance that the feminists—still a tiny minority of American women—will succeed in influencing TV if they keep up this barrage? Yes, there is.

Already one loud reverberation[4] has come from the advertising world

---

[3] Vitriolic means harsh and bitter.
[4] Reverberation is reechoing or resounding.

itself—unsurprisingly from an agency headed by a woman. Franchellie Cadwell, president of Cadwell Davis, Inc., made a speech before a body of professional colleagues recently in which she attacked "these horrendous commercials; created by men for women, that contemporary women find insulting beyond endurance." Under her leadership, Cadwell Davis has conducted a study showing that most American women loathe commercials portraying women as simpletons; and the company has announced a Women's Liberation campaign of its own. In the April 27 issue of the trade journal called *Advertising Age,* the agency published a manifesto, which read in part: "When over fifty-five percent of the women in the country are high school graduates and twenty-five percent have attended college, when women have achieved sexual freedom, aren't they beyond 'house-i-tosis'? At the very least women deserve recognition as being in full possession of their faculties. . . . We know the rumbles have sounded. The revolution is ready and one of women's first targets will be moronic, insulting advertising. . . . No force has demeaned women more than advertising."

Franchellie Cadwell is not the only powerful woman in the advertising world. Phyllis Robinson, vice president of Doyle Dane Bernbach Inc., and Shirley Polykoff of Foote, Cone & Belding, are just two of the women advertising potentates who take the same stand.

In addition, the entire communications world, which criticizes and influences TV content, is studded with feminist Trojan horses, as various top male editors—such as those of *Time, Newsweek* and *TV Guide*—have discovered. And the networks themselves are full of feminist borers-from-within.

Given this fifth column in advertising and communications, backed up by a slowly growing grass-roots feminist movement, it is more than likely that TV's portrayal of women will eventually be "humanized" in some degree. Certainly the men who run this medium are listening with at least one ear to this latest protest group, which includes some of their own wives, daughters and friends—women who have something on their minds besides how white their wash turns out.

POINTS TO CONSIDER

1.   What are the feminists' complaints about the images TV offers of women in its drama, news, and advertising? Do you feel that these complaints are justified? Explain.

2.   Do you think that the same or similar complaints could be made by men about their TV images, especially in advertising and situation comedies? Explain.

3.   How, according to the article, are women confused by their TV image? In your opinion, does television play a large part in shaping the behavior of those who watch it? Explain. (See Patricia O'Brien, "Housewife Image Tarnished on TV," page 66.)

4. How, according to the article, are women exploited on television? How are women treated in the news? What complaints do the feminists make about TV news coverage of their own movement?

5. What hope does the author hold out for the future of women's TV image?

■ THE IMPACT OF TV ON AMERICAN POLITICS

Emmet John Hughes   *The New York Times,* November 11, 1968

Has the power of television—now dramatized by the device of debate—really revolutionized the democratic process? Is the change more apparent than real? For better or for worse?

So stunning are the factors of size of audience and speed of communication on the grand scale that the very rhythm of political life does seem revolutionized. And a case can be at least plausibly argued that American political history has been decisively affected, these last eight years, by this revolution in technique.

Three witnesses—three of America's political giants—can be summoned to lend evidence to that case.

Richard M. Nixon in 1952 dramatically appeared on national television to explain to all the homes of America how he had financed his home, his career, his whole life—in a performance that made Checkers the nation's most famous dog since F. D. R.'s Fala. Hours, even minutes before that telecast, Mr. Nixon stood an excellent chance of making history as the first candidate on a national ticket ever to be stricken from the lists in mid-campaign as an insufferable embarrassment to his own party.

So nearly definite was this stern verdict of the party leaders that it is not enough to note that television remarkably served the man: it saved him. No other kind of apologia—nothing but television, with impact both massive and instantaneous could have spared Mr. Nixon swift retirement to the little town of Whittier, California, whose residents thronged the streets, just a few weeks ago, to hail the 1960 Presidential nominee.[1]

Dwight D. Eisenhower in 1956 spent an agonizing late spring in slow recovery from major surgery, following his earlier heart attack. His decision to run for re-election trembled in doubt for weeks; even the thought of it would have made a weaker man tremble. But it is hardly conceivable that

[1] The success of Richard Nixon's 1968 campaign for the presidency can be attributed largely to his skillful use of television. Nixon's TV campaign is well documented in Joe McGinniss's *The Selling of the President, 1968* (New York: Trident Press, 1969). An excerpt from the book, "Selling the President on TV," appears in this chapter, beginning on page 287. Since the Hughes article and the McGinniss book were written, television, as we know, has helped to return Mr. Nixon to his home in California.

even he would have elected to wage a national campaign were it not for the fabulous facilities of television to ease and simplify the ordeal.

John F. Kennedy in 1960 found his spring offensive for the Democratic nomination fatefully committed to the primary battle for West Virginia. His most ominous problem was the state's massive and pervasive hostility to a Catholic candidate. Only the most full and personal kind of campaign—directly reaching and affecting tens of thousands—could counter popular passions so diffuse, so widespread. And only television made such an effort conceivable.

Three different men, in three different years: for all of them, the road to this political moment took its crucial turning around the same extraordinary fact.

Towering personalities and dramatic incidents aside, the impact of television on American political life can be reckoned in a number of other ways. These are ways less crisply clear, yet perhaps more seriously historic and lasting.

First, TV makes political life itself more fluid and more volatile. Men can surge or stumble with astonishing speed—either triumphing over obscurity or tripping over a hasty or graceless public word or gesture. And issues can become as mercurial as individuals: A single performance before a sufficiently massive audience can virtually end an issue or precipitate one.

In the golden days of radio, the nightmare of performers in the studio was the mumbling of some indiscretion or vulgarity a moment before the microphone was dead. Now the politician almost lives before a live "mike" and camera. His world is tapped.

Second, TV forces much of the backstage machinery of political life to endure the same exposure. Conventions tend to become not national caucuses of politicians, but public spectacles, designed less for deliberation (or dealing) among the participants than the delight (or entertainment) of an audience. It is at least debatable whether this makes the event itself more sober or merely more contrived.

It is equally debatable whether the effect upon the audience is one of visual education, in a serious sense, or one of visual enjoyment just a notch or two above the level of the peepshow. What is not in doubt is the fact that the people *see* more.

Third, TV dramatically tends to nationalize political life. The citizen who can watch and hear Presidential candidates from his easy chair feels understandably less excitement than his father at the prospect of a "live" appearance in the local auditorium of a Congressman or even a Senator. Local political clubs—as centers of political life—tend to suffer and sag in appeal.

The firing of local partisan zeal, then, requires ever more prestigious names—as close to the top of the ticket as one dare demand. Ultimately, this could dictate, of course, greater dependence of all local tickets upon the national ticket.

Fourth, TV can strikingly shift political advantage toward those officeholders with easiest access to a national medium; these are national officeholders. It seems hardly an accident that 1960 has been notable for the fact that three of the four candidates on the national tickets come from the U. S. Senate—traditionally inferior to state governorships as sources of national candidates—while the fourth candidate, Henry Cabot Lodge, has enjoyed unique exposure on national television.

In the future of television, it would seem doubtful if the most distinguished governor, whatever his record or his personality, could come close to national candidacy without finding a way, first, to establish his identity as nationally as Washington leaders.

Fifth, accenting the person and the personal, TV both imposes new demands and offers new opportunity to the individual politician. This transcends the level of a Kennedy's concern with his hair or a Nixon's anxiety about his eyebrows (both appropriately adjusted for the current campaign). In the meeting—or the muffing—of issues, it puts new and heavy stress on the man himself.

Thus, for example, one astute political commentator, watching last spring's West Virginia primary, anticipated Senator Kennedy's massive victory on the basis of one response, discovered universally among all citizens queried a fortnight before election. This was the simple fact that all who had seen the Senator on television had reacted favorably, even if grudgingly. Enough television, then, logically would prevail. It did. But it underscored the fact that there could have been no effective substitute for this entirely personal attack on the political problem.

Sixth, TV obviously quickens the tendency of big politics to resemble big business. The cost of campaigning, of course, soars: the relatively easy political struggle of 1956 cost the G.O.P. some 2 million dollars for television and radio. The eager novice, in this televised political life, can afford to start unknown—but not unfinanced.

■ POINTS TO CONSIDER

1. What examples does Hughes give of the instances in which TV influenced national politics? What more current and even more dramatic instances can you cite?

2. According to Hughes, what are six important influences of TV upon American politics? Can you think of some examples to illustrate these influences? To what degree do you feel that each is a good or a bad influence?

3. What propaganda devices are commonly employed in TV political campaigning? (See Martin Quigley's "Elements of Persuasion and Techniques of Propaganda," page 100.) What instances can you recall in which a candidate's own campaign propaganda backfired and worked against him?

4. In what ways is it possible for TV to create political issues? (See Duane Bradley, "What Is News?" page 95, and Jerome A. Barron, "The Future of Access to the Media," page 167.) Explain, citing examples from recent years.

■ SELLING THE PRESIDENT ON TV

Joe McGinniss   *The Selling of the President, 1968,* 1969

One day Harry Treleaven[1] came into his office with two reels of movie film under his arm.

"Come on," he said. "I think you'd like to see this." We went into the big meeting room and he gave the film to a man in the projection booth.

The film was in black and white. There was a title: *A Face of War.* It had been made in Vietnam. It was the story of three months of fighting done by a single infantry platoon. There was no music or narration. Just the faces and sounds of jungle war.

Halfway through the first reel, Len Garment and Frank Shakespeare[2] came in. They were there for a one o'clock meeting. They took seats and began to watch the film. Neither spoke. They watched the men crawling single file through the jungle, heard the sound the leaves made as they brushed the faces of the men and heard the sound of rain and bullets and mortar shells in the night. The reel ended. The meeting was due to begin. Harry Treleaven turned to the projection booth. "Play the second reel," he said. Ruth Jones[3] came in for the meeting and watched the film for three minutes and left. "I can't sit through that," she said.

No one else spoke. There were only the men trying to kill and trying to avoid being killed in the jungle.

Twenty minutes later, with the film still running, Art Duram[4] said, "Don't you think we'd better start?" No one moved or gave any sign of having heard.

"It's half past one already."

Harry Treleaven sat up in his chair and looked at his watch. "All right, that's enough," he said to the man in the projection booth.

The lights came on in the room. No one spoke for a moment. Each man was still staring at where the film had been.

"That's the most powerful thing I've ever seen," Len Garment said.

"What is it?" Frank Shakespeare said.

Harry Treleaven stood and stepped toward the projection booth. "It's called *A Face of War,"* he said, "and it was made by the man I want to hire to do our spot commercials."

Originally, Treleaven had wanted David Douglas Duncan, the photogra-

---

[1] Harry Treleaven, a former advertising man, was creative director of advertising for the 1968 Nixon campaign.

[2] Len Garment, a partner in Nixon's New York law firm, was chief recruiter for the campaign. Frank Shakespeare was a former CBS executive who worked on the Nixon campaign team.

[3] Ruth Jones supervised the buying of radio and television time for the Nixon campaign.

[4] Art Durham was president of an advertising agency that produced Nixon campaign publicity.

pher, to make commercials. Duncan was a friend of Richard Nixon's but when Treleaven took him out to lunch he said no, he would be too busy. Then Duncan mentioned Eugene Jones.

Treleaven had wanted Duncan because he had decided to make still photography the basis of Richard Nixon's sixty-second television commercial campaign. He had learned a little about stills at J. Walter Thompson when he used them for some Pan American spots. Now he thought they were the perfect thing for Nixon because Nixon himself would not have to appear.

Treleaven could use Nixon's voice to accompany the stills but his face would not be on the screen. Instead there would be pictures, and hopefully, the pictures would prevent people from paying too much attention to the words.

The words would be the same ones Nixon always used—the words of the acceptance speech. But they would all seem fresh and lively because a series of still pictures would flash on the screen while Nixon spoke. If it were done right, it would permit Treleaven to create a Nixon image that was entirely independent of the words. Nixon would say his same old tiresome things but no one would have to listen. The words would become Muzak. Something pleasant and lulling in the background. The flashing pictures would be carefully selected to create the impression that somehow Nixon represented competence, respect for tradition, serenity, faith that the American people were better than people anywhere else, and that all these problems others shouted about meant nothing in a land blessed with the tallest buildings, strongest armies, biggest factories, cutest children, and rosiest sunsets in the world. Even better: through association with the pictures, Richard Nixon could *become* these very things.

Obviously, some technical skill would be required. David Douglas Duncan said Gene Jones was the man.

Treleaven met Jones and was impressed. "He's low-key," Treleaven said. "He doesn't come at you as a know-it-all."

Gene Jones, also in his middle forties, had been taking movies of wars half his life. He did it perhaps as well as any man ever has. Besides that, he had produced the Today show on NBC for eight years and had done a documentary series on famous people called *The World of . . .* Billy Graham, Sophia Loren, anyone who had been famous and was willing to be surrounded by Jones's cameras for a month.

Jones understood perfectly what Treleaven was after. A technique through which Richard Nixon would seem to be contemporary, imaginative, involved—without having to say anything of substance. Jones had never done commercial work before but for $110,000, from which he would pay salaries to a nine-man staff, he said he would do it for Nixon.

"A hundred and ten thousand dollars," Frank Shakespeare said after seeing *A Face of War.* "That's pretty steep."

"I wouldn't know," Treleaven said. "I have nothing to compare it to."

"It's pretty steep."

"He's pretty good."

"Yes, he is."

"What do you think?"

"Oh, I have no objection. That just hit me as a very high price."

I'd like approval to pay it right now. I want to hire him immediately.

"Fine," Frank Shakespeare said. "You've got it."

A day or two later Jones came down to Treleaven's office to discuss details such as where he should set up a studio and what areas the first set of spots should cover.

"This will not be a commercial sell," Jones said. "It will not have the feel of something a—pardon the expression—an agency would turn out. I see it as sort of a miniature *Project 20*. And I can't see anyone turning it off a television set, quite frankly."

That same day Jones rented two floors of the building at 303 East Fifty-third Street, one flight up from a nightclub called Chuck's Composite. Within three days, he had his staff at work. Buying pictures, taking pictures, taking motion pictures of still pictures that Jones himself had cropped and arranged in a sequence.

"I'm pretty excited about this," Jones said. "I think we can give it an artistic dimension."

Harry Treleaven did not get excited about anything but he was at least intrigued by this. "It will be interesting to see how he translates his approach into political usefulness," Treleaven said.

"Yes," Frank Shakespeare said, "if he can."

Gene Jones would start work at five o'clock in the morning. Laying coffee and doughnuts on his desk, he would spread a hundred or so pictures on the floor, taken from boxes into which his staff already had filed them. The boxes had labels like VIETNAM . . . DEMOCRATIC CONVENTION . . . POVERTY: HARLEM, CITY SLUMS, GHETTOS . . . FACES: HAPPY AMERICAN PEOPLE AT WORK AND LEISURE . . .

He would select a category to fit the first line of whatever script he happened to be working with that day. The script would contain the words of Richard Nixon. Often they would be exactly the words he had used in the acceptance speech, but re-recorded in a hotel room somewhere so the tone would be better suited to commercial use.

Jones would select the most appropriate of the pictures and then arrange and rearrange, as in a game of solitaire. When he had the effect he thought he wanted he would work with a stopwatch and red pencil, marking each picture on the back to indicate what sort of angle and distance the movie camera should shoot from and how long it should linger on each still.

"The secret is in juxtaposition," Jones said. "The relationships, the arrangement. After twenty-five years, the other things—the framing and the panning, are easy."

Everyone was excited about the technique and the way it could be used to make people feel that Richard Nixon belonged in the White House. The only person who was not impressed was Nixon. He was in a hotel room in San Francisco one day, recording the words for one of the early commercials. The machine was turned on before Nixon realized it and the end of his conversation was picked up.

"I'm not sure I like this kind of a . . . of a format, incidentally," Nixon said. "Ah . . . I've seen these kinds of things and I don't think they're very . . . very effective. . . ."

Still, Nixon read the words he had been told to read:

"In recent years crime in this country has grown nine times as fast as the population. At the current rate, the crimes of violence in America will double by nineteen seventy-two. We cannot accept that kind of future. We owe it to the decent and law-abiding citizens of America to take the offensive against the criminal forces that threaten their peace and security and to rebuild respect for law across this country. I pledge to you that the wave of crime is not going to be the wave of the future in America."

There was nothing new in these words. Harry Treleaven had simply paraphrased and condensed the standard law and order message Nixon had been preaching since New Hampshire. But when the words were coupled with quickly flashing colored pictures of criminals, of policemen patrolling deserted streets, of bars on storefront windows, of disorder on a college campus, of peace demonstrators being led bleeding into a police van, then the words became something more than what they actually were. It was the whole being greater than the sum of its parts.

In the afternoons, Treleaven, Garment and Shakespeare would go to Gene Jones' studio to look at the films on a little machine called a movieola. If they were approved, Jones would take them to a sound studio down the street to blend in music, but they never were approved right away. There was not one film that Garment or Shakespeare did not order changed for a "political" reason. Anything that might offend Strom Thurmond, that might annoy the Wallace voter whom Nixon was trying so hard for; any ethnic nuance that Jones, in his preoccupation with artistic viewpoint, might have missed: these came out.

"Gene is good," Treleaven explained, "but he needs a lot of political guidance. He doesn't always seem to be aware of the point we're trying to make."

Jones didn't like the changes. "I'm not an apprentice," he said. "I'm an experienced pro and never before in my career have I had anyone stand over my shoulder telling me to change this and change that. It might sound like bullshit, but when you pull out a shot or two it destroys the dynamism, the whole flow."

The first spot was called simply *Vietnam*. Gene Jones had been there for ninety days, under fire, watching men kill and die, and he had been wounded in the neck himself. Out of the experience had come *A Face of War*. And out of it now came E.S.J. [for Eugene S. Jones] #1, designed to help Richard Nixon become President. Created for no other purpose.

Video	Audio
1. OPENING NETWORK DISCLAIMER: "A POLITICAL ANNOUNCEMENT."	
2. FADEUP ON FAST PACED SCENES OF HELO ASSAULT IN VIETNAM.	SFX AND UNDER.

3. WOUNDED AMERICANS AND VIETNAMESE.	**R.N.** Never has so much military, economic, and diplomatic power been used as ineffectively as in Vietnam.
4. MONTAGE OF FACIAL CU's OF AMERICAN SERVICEMEN AND VIETNAMESE NATIVES WITH QUESTIONING, ANXIOUS, PERPLEXED ATTITUDE.	And if after all of this time and all of this sacrifice and all of this support there is still no end in sight, then I say the time has come for the American people to turn to new leadership—not tied to the policies and mistakes of the past.
5. PROUD FACES OF VIETNAMESE PEASANTS ENDING IN CU OF THE WORD "LOVE" SCRAWLED ON THE HELMET OF AMERICAN G.I. AND PULL BACK TO REVEAL HIS FACE.	I pledge to you: we will have an honorable end to the war in Vietnam. MUSIC UP AND OUT.

Harry Treleaven and Len Garment and Frank Shakespeare thought this commercial was splendid.

"Wow, that's powerful," Treleaven said.

Dead soldiers and empty words. The war was not bad because of insane suffering and death. The war was bad because it was *ineffective*.

So Richard Nixon, in his commercial, talked about new leadership for the war. New leadership like Ellsworth Bunker and Henry Cabot Lodge and U. Alexis Johnson.

Vietnam was shown across the country for the first time on September 18. Jack Gould[5] did not like this one any more than he had liked Connie Francis.

"The advertising agency working in behalf of Richard Nixon unveiled another unattractive campaign spot announcement," he wrote. "Scenes of wounded GIs were the visual complement for Mr. Nixon's view that he is better equipped to handle the agony of the Vietnamese war. Rudimentary good taste in politics apparently is automatically ruled out when Madison Avenue gets into the act."

The fallen soldiers bothered other people in other ways. There was on the Nixon staff an "ethnic specialist" named Kevin Phillips, whose job it was to determine what specific appeals would work with specific nationalities and in specific parts of the country. He watched *Vietnam* and sent a

---

[5] Jack Gould, a columnist for the New York *Times,* had written a negative opinion of an earlier Nixon TV campaign film which featured pop vocalist Connie Francis.

quick and alarmed memo to Len Garment: "This has a decidedly dovish impact as a result of the visual content and it does not seem suitable for use in the South and Southwest."

His reasoning was quite simple. A picture of a wounded soldier was a reminder that the people who fight wars get hurt. This, he felt, might cause resentment among those Americans who got such a big kick out of cheering for wars from their Legion halls and barrooms half a world away. So bury the dead in silence, Kevin Phillips said, before you blow North Carolina.

Another problem arose in the Midwest: annoyance over the word "Love" written on the soldier's helmet.

"It reminds them of hippies," Harry Treleaven said. "We've gotten several calls already from congressmen complaining. They don't think it's the sort of thing soldiers should be writing on their helmets."

Len Garment ordered the picture taken out of the commercial. Gene Jones inserted another at the end; this time a soldier whose helmet was plain.

This was the first big case of "political" guidance, and for a full week the more sensitive members of the Gene Jones staff mourned the loss of their picture.

"It was such a beautiful touch," one of them said. "And we thought, what an interesting young man it must be who would write 'Love' on his helmet even as he went into combat."

Then E.S.J. Productions received a letter from the mother of the soldier. She told what a thrill it had been to see her son's picture in one of Mr. Nixon's commercials, and she asked if there were some way that she might obtain a copy of the photograph.

The letter was signed: Mrs. William Love.

Almost all the commercials ran sixty seconds. But Jones did one, called E.S.J. #3: *Look at America,* that went more than four minutes.

Video	*Audio*
2. FADEUP ON FAST, DRAMATIC RIOT IN CITY, FLAMING BUILDINGS.	ELECTRONIC MUSIC UP FULL.
3. VIETNAM COMBAT.	ELECTRONIC MUSIC CONTINUES AND UNDER.
4. G.I. IN VIETNAM SLUMPS DEJECTEDLY.	R.N. America is in trouble today not because her people have failed, but because her leaders have failed. Let us look at America. Let us listen to America. We see Americans dying on distant battlefields abroad.

5. RIOTS & FIRES.	We see Americans hating each other; fighting each other; killing each other at home.
	We see cities enveloped in smoke and flame.
6. FIRE ENGINES.	We hear sirens in the night.
7. PERPLEXED FACES OF AMERICANS.	As we see and hear these things, millions of Americans cry out in anguish.
	Did we come all the way for this?
8. MONTAGE URBAN & RURAL DECAY—(hungry in Appalachia–poor in ghetto–ill-clothed on Indian reservations. Unemployment in cities and welfare in small towns).	MUSIC UP AND UNDER.
9. MONTAGE OF AMERICANS "CREATING AND CONTRIBUTING" MOTIVATES INTO CU's OF FACES. CONTINUING MONTAGE OF "CREATIVE & CONTRIBUTING FACES."	<u>R.N.</u> Let us listen now to another voice. It is the voice of the great majority of Americans—the non-shouters; the non-demonstrators.
	They are not racists or sick; they are not guilty of the crime that plagues the land.
	They are black and they are white —native born and foreign born —young and old.
	They work in America's factories.
	They run American business.
	They serve in government.
	They provide most of the soldiers who died to keep us free.
	They give drive to the spirit of America.
	They give lift to the American Dream.

They give steel to the backbone of America.

They are good people, decent people; they work, they save, they pay their taxes, they care. Like Theodore Roosevelt, they know that this country will not be a good place for any of us to live in unless it is a good place for all of us to live in.

This, I say, is the real voice of America. And in this year 1968, this is the message it will broadcast to America and to the world.

Let's never forget that despite her faults, America is a great nation.

| 10. STRENGTH AND CHARACTER OF AMERICANS—BUSY FACTORIES, FARMS, CROWDS & TRAFFIC, ETC. | R.N.
 America is great because her people are great. |

11. INTO MONTAGE OF SCENIC VALUES OF AMERICA FROM THE PACIFIC OCEAN TO DESERTS, TO SNOW-COVERED MOUNTAIN. BESIDE A STILL POND A MAN WAITS.

With Winston Churchill, we say: "We have not journeyed all this way across the centuries, across the oceans, across the mountains, across the prairies, because we are made of sugar candy."

12. DOLLY TOWARD SUNRISE. HOLD. FADEOUT.

America is in trouble today not because her people have failed, but because her leaders have failed.

What America needs are leaders to match the greatness of her people.

MUSIC UP AND OUT.

"Run it through again, would you please, Gene?" Len Garment said. 'There's something there that bothers me."

The film was rewound and played again.

"There, that's it," Garment said. "Yeah, that will have to be changed."

"What will have to be changed?" Jones said.

The film had been stopped just as Richard Nixon, reciting his litany to the "forgotten Americans," had said, "They provide most of the soldiers who died to keep us free." The picture that went with those words was a close-up of a young American soldier in Vietnam. A young Negro soldier.

Len Garment was shaking his head.

"We can't show a Negro just as RN's saying 'most of the soldiers who died to keep us free,'" he said. "That's been one of their big claims all along—that the draft is unfair to them—and this could be interpreted in a way that would make us appear to be taking their side."

"Hey, yes, good point, Len," Frank Shakespeare said. "That's a very good point."

Harry Treleaven was nodding.

Gene Jones said okay, he would put a white soldier there instead.

A couple of weeks later, when Treleaven told Gene Jones to shoot a commercial called *Black Capitalism,* he was surprised to hear that Negroes in Harlem were reluctant to pose for the pictures.

Jones had not been able to find any pictures that showed Negroes gainfully employed, so he decided to take his own. He hired his own photographer, a white man, and sent him to Harlem with instructions to take pictures of good Negroes, Negroes who worked and smiled and acted the way white folks thought they ought to. And to take these pictures in front of

GRIN AND BEAR IT   BY LICHTY

"Let's evaluate my campaign so far, Boys! . . . Has it been politically sound, historically impressive, and above all good television?"

"Grin and Bear It" by George Lichty. Courtesy of Field Newspaper Syndicate.

Negro-owned stores and factories to make the point that this is what honest labor can do for a race.

An hour after he started work, the photographer called Gene Jones and said when he had started lining Negroes up on the street to pose he had been asked by a few young men what he was doing. When he told them he was taking pictures for a Richard Nixon commercial, it was suggested to him that he remove himself and his camera from the vicinity. Fast.

Gene Jones explained to Harry Treleaven.

"Gee, isn't that strange," Treleaven said. "I can't understand an attitude like that."

■ POINTS TO CONSIDER

1. What was the main propaganda device used in the Nixon "commercials" described by the author? Can you find examples of other propaganda devices and advertising "tricks"? (See Martin Quigley, "Elements of Persuasion and Techniques of Propaganda," page 100, and Marjorie Burns, "The Advertiser's Bag of Tricks," page 18.)

2. Why do you think the ad agency had decided to use only Nixon's voice? What is your reaction to the statement that Nixon's TV campaign spots were designed to make him "seem to be contemporary, imaginative, involved— without having to say anything of substance"? What does this tell you about the nature of TV as a political campaign medium?

3. In what sense were the Eugene S. Jones film spots examples of "the whole being greater than the sum of its parts"? Can you give some illustrations of how this principle applies to other examples of popular art?

4. What conflicts does the author describe between the desire for artistic expression and the desire to sell a product?

5. What is the author's attitude toward Richard Nixon and the selling of Nixon? At what points in the piece does this attitude become clear?

6. What reasons does the author have for reporting the incident in Harlem? What contrasts does it point up between the people of Harlem and the ad men of Madison Avenue?

7. After reading this selection, would you agree or disagree with David Ogilvy's statement that "the use of advertising to sell statesmen is the ultimate vulgarity"? Explain. (See "Should Advertising Be Abolished?" page 79.)

Communication touches every fiber of our lives. The American communications mosaic includes a Defense Department hot line, a child tranquilized before a TV set, a ringing telephone, a politician campaigning by radio, a news service teletype, a fog-bound ship's radar, a hidden microphone in a business meeting, satellites, and computerized airline reservations.

When we speak of communications we often forget the social science implications of these technological achievements. How do they relate to all the other major characteristics and problems of our time (war, overpopulation, increased leisure, congested cities, mounting popular unrest)? How do they affect the creation and exercise of political power? How do they affect relations between family members—and nations? To understand where communications technology is taking us, we need more than the insights of economists and engineers. I think we need the vision of anthropologists, sociologists, psychologists, educators, political scientists, general semanticists[1] —and a poet or two.

I like to talk about trends rather than explosions or revolutions because they can be more easily seen, believed, and dealt with. Here are a couple of examples of what I mean. Before the transistor was invented it is unlikely that anyone, outside of a few scientists experimenting with the possibility, would have predicted it. Even then, however, one could detect a trend toward smaller and smaller vacuum tubes. Before the launch capability existed, few would have predicted the operation of space communications satellites. Now that the satellites are operational, however, it is easy to detect the trends toward greater satellite power, longer life, increased channel capacity, and precision of transmission beam. In short, I do not think it is useful for a layman to try to predict the wholly new transmission scheme that will be to the 1990's what the satellite has been to the 1960's. (How close could the communications system of 1969 have been predicted in 1938?) I do think it is useful to try to reflect upon the trends that are already visible.

The most significant trend in communications today is probably the trend toward instantaneous, ubiquitous,[2] no-cost access to all information. I do not for a moment suggest that we are going to reach that destination; I only suggest that what is happening today, and will likely continue for thirty years, can most easily be understood by navigating with that landmark on the far horizon. If we are 0.01 percent of the way there by 1970, we may be 15 percent of the way there by the year 2000—for we must also deal with a trend of acceleration in the rate of change. Now what do I mean by "instantaneous, ubiquitous, no-cost access to all information"?

---

[1] General semanticists are people who study words and symbols with the aim of clarifying and improving human communication and behavior. The study combines elements of both linguistics and psychology.

[2] Ubiquitous means being everywhere at the same time.

channels (in cables and satellites) are capable of moving increasingly more information, and thus more information per unit time. Computers process information faster than ever and are being coupled with communications networks. This is not a revolution, it is a trend that has existed throughout the history of man. It's going on now, and will continue. The only thing that is changing is the rate of acceleration in the speed of transmission. We will not reach literal instantaneity by the year 2000. There are many delays in the system, and the ultimate barrier of 186,000 miles per second shows no signs of crumbling. But that at least seems to be the direction of our journey.

By "ubiquitous" I simply mean that the number of points of access to a communications network are continuing to increase at an accelerated rate, even to the point of being personally mobile. You are never very far from a telephone instrument in the United States, and more are being installed every day. The ease of use of the system, even on a worldwide basis, and the increasing amount of information that can be obtained by telephone, is interacting with the increasing number of instruments to accelerate the trend. The Bell System's touch tone push-button sets, the direct distance dialing, and the relatively short period (approximately thirty seconds) that is needed to reach another phone produce increased telephone usage. The international telephone system is developing similar improvements. (These factors are also, of course, related to instantaneity.) More information can be accessed by telephone: library research desks, time and weather reports, stock market reports, and, of course, the data-phone interconnection of computers with the rapid increase in number, character and simplicity of terminal devices for home and office. Personally portable mobile communication devices are likewise increasing. Communication on ships and airplanes is common. There is an increasing number of mobile land vehicles with communications facilities, from earth moving equipment and fork lift trucks in warehouses to police cars and taxicabs. Mobile individuals are equipped with two-way radio equipment or paging devices on their person. Mobile teleprinters and computer access are just beginning what will probably be a trend that will include other terminal devices. The instruments of mass communication are undergoing the same trends. Television and radio sets are spreading throughout the world. The pocket transistor radio makes personally mobile mass communications possible everywhere, and the number of portable television sets is also increasing.

I do not predict a day of free communications. I do believe, however, that we can identify a trend of decreasing cost of communications that is likely to continue. This is, in part, the result of an accelerating and interlocked relationship between miniaturization, mass production and distribution, and reduced cost. Earthbound microwave relay towers can provide transmission facilities at about one percent of the cost of open wire circuits. Satellites are even cheaper for long haul traffic. The capacity of laser beams is reported to be so enormous that it is almost impossible even to compute the low cost of providing a circuit. Television and radio receiving sets continue to come down in price. Furthermore, it is important to distinguish between cost and price. Obviously, the sum total of prices paid for communications service must equal the sum total of the costs of providing that service plus a profit. But that does not tell you anything about either the costs to be allocated to a given service, or the pricing system that will be used to regain those costs. Example: the U.S. Congress has provided that the FCC may authorize free interconnection of the educational television stations in the United States. As we do that, it will not mean there will be no cost to the telephone company associated with providing this service; it will mean there is no *price* to the educational broadcasters. To the extent the service requires the telephone company to incur additional costs they will be absorbed by the prices charged for other services. Another example: local service and WATS (wide area telephone service). Within most local exchanges the costs of telephone service are assessed on a system-wide basis, and the prices charged are on a flat-fee-for-unlimited-use basis. WATS is a similar pricing scheme for "long distance" calls: for a flat fee a subscriber may make an unlimited number of calls within a defined area outside of his local exchange. Under such pricing schemes there is no additional cost to the user for using the service. He will make an economic judgment in deciding whether to get the service at all; once he gets it, however, he will use it without regard to economic judgments. Note that such pricing schemes have the same effect upon communications behavior as if they were technological innovations that made communications equipment and service available "free."

It is, of course, fanciful to suggest that by the year 2000—or any other year for that matter—we will have a world in which every human being will have access literally to "all" information. Like the other end points on our present trend lines, however, it seems a useful concept. Even today, anyone who can pay the subscription rates, or can use a major library, has access to—if not all information—at least considerably more information than he wants or can possibly use. The world's professional people are already at the point where they really have more desire for services that will edit, summarize, process, and retrieve relevant information than for services that merely give them access to more data. Yet that is really more an emotional judgment born of frustration than a rational preference. We need both. In any event, we have little choice—we are going to have access to more information with which to do our jobs whether we want it or not. The number of telephones that can be reached from any other telephone is increasing every year—a function of the increase in the absolute number of telephones and in the number of units that are interconnected. With an increase in research activity, publishing, leisure time, levels of education, and disposable income, the absolute amount of information, and the number of people who will want it, is multiplying rapidly. We have increased the number and sensitivity of apparatus for recording various phenomena. The computer continues to increase our capacity to receive, process and use this data. The international exchange of printed matter and films is today being augmented by television.

The program *One World* in 1967 was an immensely successful effort to interconnect television cameras around the world, via satellite, to TV stations which broadcast to an international audience made up of the largest number of viewers ever to watch simultaneously a single program or performance. The widespread coverage of the moon walk achieved similar ratings. I suspect we will share more such experiences. As computers take on the data retrieval tasks now done by laborious manual library searches, whole new worlds of information will be opened up to more widespread use. There is no reason video and audio tape libraries couldn't be made similarly accessible—and all of them from remote points if desired. (This is not to suggest the demise of pre-programmed "network" television offerings—there is the same desire for video information packaging as for print—only that the individual's *opportunities* for individual choice will expand.) So we are rapidly approaching the time—if we have not already passed it—when the principal impediments to "access to all information" will not be technological imperfections, the availability of circuits, or price, but the man-made inhibitions: copyright, proprietary business data, national security classifications, ignorance, inertia, and stubbornness.

Perhaps the single most important implication of "communications and the year 2000" is the extent to which it will be something which we have planned for, designed and built, rather than predicted. The space program will be found to have had its greatest impact, in my view, in philosophy and psychology—not new technology and scientific data. The greatest inhibitions to man's progress and happiness are those of his own making: "it's scientifically impossible," "we can't afford it," "but that would be socialistic," "it's illegal," "it's against our policy," "our church doesn't believe in that," "it's just not done that way." To remove these shackles from our minds required the preposterously expensive program necessary to get us to the moon. Now that we have done it we are beginning to change the way we talk about our opportunities: "if we can send a man to the moon we can certainly do . . ." has become the opening line of some very imaginative proposals. Political philosophy has become hopelessly confused and almost irrelevant in the frantic search for pragmatic solutions to common problems: the "socialist bureaucrats in Washington" are trying to sell their Post Office Department to the highest bidder in the marketplace; the "rugged individualists" of American business who cuss the "fuzzy-headed do-gooder liberals" are now profiting as government contractors in city building, job training and America's fifty-two-billion-dollar education industry, and are coming up with very humane proposals after sitting on commissions and task forces on civil disorders, employment, crime, and violence. Barry Goldwater's "conservative" economist, Dr. Milton Friedman, has proposed a guaranteed annual income ("negative income tax") as an alternative to welfare; it is a proposal that, in an earlier day, would have been rejected out of hand because of its "communist" origins ("from each according to his ability, to each according to his need").

Books like *Brave New World* and *1984* and much of our current writing have stressed the oppressive potential of "instantaneous, ubiquitous, no-cost access to all information." There was even substantial public protest when the telephone company in the United States wanted to take the "dehumanizing" step of abolishing the exchange names from the telephone numbers (that is, substituting 395-4321 for EXecutive 5-4321). Students at Berkeley have carried picket signs saying, "I am a person. Do not bend, fold, spindle or mutilate," as a protest to the faceless machines that require cards carrying such instructions. For every one person who sees advantage to a national data bank (for example, to more efficiently match job opportunity to available workers), there are a dozen who fear its power, and the impossibility of clearing error from one's record. The efficiency of automatic video tape recorders in filming auto accidents, and closed circuit television systems in doing the work of guards, must be balanced against the very understandable human protest at such "invasions of privacy." The wonders of powerful, miniaturized microphones and transmitters have already succeeded in severely limiting the places where one may confidently carry on a "private" conversation. Fears of wiretapping have substantially impeded the telephone system as a communications network.

We have moved from an age when political and economic power were measured in land, or capital, or labor, to an age in which power is measured largely by access to information and people. The man or institution which has the greatest political, military or economic power today is the one with access to the greatest amount of relevant information in the most usable form in the quickest time; and, in institutions or societies where popular understanding and support are relevant, the greatest access to the mass media. Thus, the problem in creating national or international satellite-direct-to-home radio and television is not technological; it is getting those who now control the mass media to agree on the individuals and procedures that will determine what is broadcast over that satellite channel. The problem in establishing cable television throughout the U.S. is not that of deciding where we will put all those wires; it is deciding who gets to hold the switch. The argument is being advanced that the mass media should be more like a common carrier; that the First Amendment guarantees of free speech must, today, extend to making the mass media available to those who want to use them. As cable television and laser beams replace an economy and technology of scarcity with one of abundance, that will be increasingly possible technologically. Whether it will be socially and politically possible remains to be seen.

I recall a conversation with representatives from fire and police departments in one of America's largest cities. Why, I asked, did they not establish mobile radio systems that would enable fire, police and national guardsmen at the scene of a particular incident to talk to each other? After some stumbling around the answer became quite clear: each wanted to retain power and control in his own organization. Within any paper-shuffling bureaucracy (corporate or government) power lies with he who controls the key to the filing cabinet. To make information that is now someone's personal domain easily accessible threatens his status and prestige—perhaps the justification for his job. Government agencies could very easily put their "public" information in computers that could be operated by any member of the public. They probably will not do so—but not because "it's scientifically impossible," or "it costs too much." The education establishment has been very slow to accept educational television—it has been viewed as a threat by many classroom teachers. They are unlikely to welcome with any greater enthusiasm programmed-instruction teaching machines in the home that any member of the family can use to study any subject of his choosing at his leisure. As former Secretary of Defense McNamara demonstrated at the Defense Department, the "management information system" lies at the heart of management's power over any large organization today. If access to that information is diffused, so is power. That is the reason—not economic or technical feasibility—it is unlikely there will be more than a handful of visual display terminals with access to management information data in any large organization.

We are witnessing on all sides today a revolution of "participatory democracy." The people want, as we say, a "piece of the action." Every candidate for President in 1968 advocated this concept in some form. It finds its philosophical counterpart in most of the civilized nations of the world today. It is, in my judgment, a function of increased communications, education and standard of living. Nation states grow obsolete, mass-appeal political leaders vanish, and the mass media in effect become government, as education is substituted for mass illiteracy, popular access to the mass media is substituted for dictatorial control over information by a single leader, identity and loyalty to one's institutional and professional affiliations are substituted for geographical relationships, and internationally understood professional languages are substituted for national languages and literature. I think those trends will accelerate before they slow down. No segment of the various movements of social protest has a very specific program at this point. But it is only a matter of time before they grasp the "information-is-power" concept even more fully.

We have already reached the point where the educational-social-economic-professional elites of Tokyo, London, Moscow, Washington, New York, and so forth, have much more in common with one another than they have in common with their own countrymen back in the rural villages. This is yet another trend. And the number being influenced by it is expanding geographically and economically. Trade, transportation and—especially—communication is the principal reason. The same music, television shows, and movies are seen and heard around the world. Every country loses a little of its individual character as it undergoes this process. Americans are concerned about the possible relation between violence in television shows and violence in our streets. But this is a matter of international concern as well, because these television shows are shown around the world. Finland, Spain and some other countries have taken action to prohibit the importation of some American television. But most countries have not, and the U.S. government makes no effort, so far as I know, to exert any control over the content, and possible impact, of our exported television product.

One of the principles to which America is dedicated, as an ideal, is that every individual should have the opportunity to attain the maximum growth and development of which he is capable. This is a revolutionary philosophy, impossible of complete attainment, and it has created considerable grief for our country, especially during the past few years. But we keep striving to come closer to this ideal each year, and we are as proud of our progress as we are determined to make up the remaining gap. It is why we must make available at no cost recreational facilities to develop the body, schools and libraries to develop the mind, and churches and national parks to develop the spirit.

Our progress toward "instantaneous, ubiquitous, no-cost access to all information" has important implications for our commitment to individual opportunity. President Johnson's last nomination to the FCC was Mr. H. Rex Lee, who, as a distinguished and imaginative Governor of Samoa, established an educational television system for the islands that has shown the world what our new communications techniques can mean in improving the quantity and quality of education while reducing its cost. At a time when the rate of illiteracy in the world is increasing rather than decreasing with every passing year it is obvious that some dramatic changes in educational techniques are called for. Governor Lee's electronic schoolhouse may suggest a way. And I would remind you once again in this context that we can make the informational resources of the world available "free" to the user if we choose to do so. We are not just playing with public-utility-rate-making metaphysics when we set telephone rates—we are affecting the individual opportunity of the world's people.

On signing the Public Broadcasting Corporation bill into law, President Johnson said, "Today our problem is not *making* miracles—but *managing* them." The space program has impressed upon us the realization that we have the human talent and economic resources to do anything worth doing if we are fully committed to its achievement. This realization substantially alters the task of the planner or forecaster. His task is no longer merely one of predicting technological and economic phenomena. He must call upon the resources of social scientists, philosophers and poets to assist him in his search for a set of values, or the goals that he seeks to achieve. For we are in the enviable if anomalous position of having capabilities that exceed our aspirations. Whether we know it or not we are making decisions today that will determine, irrevocably, the impact of communications upon our society and economy in the year 2000.

Each technological innovation in communications raises a number of questions. What will be its impact on our society? How can this new force most effectively be channeled to human good? Are unrestrained market forces or some form of government regulation most appropriate? Are new or amended laws or regulations necessary? What is the most economic and efficient way to achieve the ends sought? What are the forces regulating the development and rate of introduction of the new technology? Are they effective in serving interests beyond private economic gain? How can government be most effectively structured and administered to deal with the problem in question? What additional data, analysis, or other research is called for? Whether we make wise decisions, whether we mold our future intentionally, is up to us.

What will be the state of communications in the year 2000? Largely whatever we choose to make it. Of course, we must do more than simply utter the phrase, "The future is what we make of it." There is a limit to the capacity of human society to preplan its course of evolution, and even some question about the desirability of doing so. Our understanding here, and in those other countries with Commissions on the Year 2000, is motivated in part by our fascination with the advent of a new century. But we are also cognizant of the increasing desire on the part of post-industrial societies to prevent impersonal and unforeseen chance to force our society's evolution. At the same time we acknowledge that the natural forces in a market economy often have the capacity to achieve the goals that a society has set for itself. So what do we do? First, we should exert every effort to maintain and improve open societies, where conflicting information, interpretations and orthodoxies have an opportunity to be heard and tested. For we have an ultimate commitment to the ideal that a society must choose, through some form of the democratic process, what course it wants to follow. That choice is made more meaningful, especially in times of rapid change, when the alternatives are made clear and their implications have been fully enunciated. Secondly, we should endeavor to test all the change which is so surely to be part of the years ahead. I would hope that the next three decades would be known for our experimentation and pilot projects on a grand scale. And when we test, we will try to develop better standards for measuring the achievement of the human values so long cherished by all mankind.

■ | **POINTS TO CONSIDER**

1.   What does Nicholas Johnson see as some of the major trends in communications over the next quarter-century? What will be some of the benefits of the changes he observes? What may be some of the hazards?

2.   Do Johnson's observations about communications trends enlarge your recognition of the scope of mass communications media? What media does Johnson mention that you usually do not think about when you hear the term "mass media"?

3.   As people achieve increased opportunity for access to more information, what changes may have to be made to enable people to acquire and use this information in beneficial ways?

4.   How do you interpret the author's statement, "The space program will be found to have had its greatest impact . . . in philosophy and psychology—not new technical and scientific data"?

5.   What does the author see as the greatest problems in actualizing the creative expansion of mass communications which technology has made, and continues to make, possible?

6.   Do you agree with Johnson's judgment that "increased communications, education and standard of living" result in a situation in which "the mass media in effect become the government"? If you agree, do you welcome the situation?

7. How many examples can you think of to illustrate Johnson's observation that "information is power"?

8. What power, which we may not have seriously considered, may American television exert on other parts of the world?

9. What are some of the important needs which television could serve in the future beyond the needs it is currently serving in this country?

10. What significant social and philosophical questions are raised by the expansion of communications technology?

■ IDEAS FOR INVESTIGATION, DISCUSSION, AND WRITING

1. Interview a number of people of different ages and interests to discover if they listen to the radio, how much they listen, and what they like to hear. What groups listen to radio the most? What groups listen the least? What varied services does the radio perform for its different kinds of listeners?

2. Speak with some station managers and disc jockeys of local radio stations to learn how they arrange their programs, select their music, and schedule their advertising. What people or groups of people are the most influential in determining kinds and scheduling of programs, music, and advertising?

3. What functions can radio perform better than other mass media? How well do you feel it performs these functions? How could it improve its performance of these functions? What additional functions, if any, do you think it could or should perform?

4. What are some of the different services which TV provides its various viewers? Ask some people of different ages and interests for their opinions. To what extent do these services overlap those offered by other mass media? Which services does TV seem to be able to perform especially well?

5. Compare the kinds of weekday daytime TV shows to determine the audiences of each. How do the products or services advertised at these times and the styles of the commercials appeal to the audiences for which they are intended?

6. What effect has television had upon the education and upon the social activities of our society? How do you evaluate these effects?

7. In what ways does television news reporting differ from news reporting by other mass media? What advantages and limitations does TV news reporting have? How do you think it could be improved?

8. What are some of the different ways in which TV broadcasting can be financed? What are advantages and disadvantages of each? What services are currently offered by subscription television stations in this country?

9. Make a study of broadcasting and government. What effect has federal control had on radio and television? How are the other media different in this respect? How do federal licensing and censorship policies affect what is broadcast? What role has the government played in encouraging or stifling such new developments in broadcasting as pay television, cable TV, listener-sponsored radio, and educational television? In what ways could government policies be changed for the benefit of the public?

10. Investigate one or more examples of special interest radio stations, such as the right-wing gospel stations, the university stations, listener-sponsored and "underground" stations. What services do these stations perform? How are they funded? What, if any, is their political bias? Do you think these stations perform a genuine service to the public? Explain.

11. Make a study of available information on the psychological effects of TV and radio with a view to attacking or substantiating McLuhan's conten-

tion that TV is a "cool" medium, tending to lull and calm its viewers, while radio is a "hot" medium, tending to excite its listeners.

12. Do a study of educational television. When and where did it start? Where is it available? What programming is available? Is there any evidence of its effect on the educational level of those for whom it has been available? For example, how well does it compete with commercial programming as far as getting and holding viewer interest? What directions is educational TV taking? What recommendations could be made to improve educational television?

13. After making a number of personal interviews, do a study of the disc jockey. What is his training, his background? How well is he paid? What is his future? Why does he do what he does? What are his personal dreams? How does he account for his own popularity or for the popularity of other D.J.'s?

14. Investigate the organizational machinery existing in the television or radio industry for gathering and assessing consumer feedback. What provisions does the broadcast industry make for reading letters from listeners and viewers? Who reads these letters? How is their information compiled and presented? Does this service provide the listener and viewer with a real say in what he is to see and hear?

15. Investigate the possible effects television has had on the Vietnam war. Is there any evidence that TV coverage of the war has had any significant effect on public opinion about the war? Perhaps a survey could be made concerning people's reactions to the part of the war they have seen on television and whether they think this has influenced their thinking about the war.

16. Make an investigation into the business of making television commercials. How is a commercial conceived, written, and produced? Who makes it? How much does it cost? How is it determined whether a commercial is "successful" or not?

17. Make a study of cable television. What legal and technical problems has cable television encountered? With what results? What are the advantages of cable TV over broadcast television? What are its drawbacks? What effects could cable TV have on the entire television system? What conclusions can be made concerning the desirability of cable television?

18. Make a study of pay television dealing with the same main points as outlined for cable television above.

19. Write or outline a pilot for a new half-hour television series. Write character sketches for all the main characters. Explain the kinds of plots these characters will be involved in, what kinds of images they will project, and discuss as thoroughly as possible the appeal your series will make to viewers and why it will "sell."

20. Outline a pilot for an educational TV program (one half hour), perhaps using material expressed through the various media of film, cartooning, documentary reportage.

Part Six

Photography and Films: Previews and Viewpoints

The compelling clarity with which a photograph recorded the trivial suggested that the subject had never been properly seen, that it was in fact *not* trivial, but filled with undiscovered meaning.

—John Szarkowski

I think it safe to guess that 99.44 per cent of the movies made in the United States—and in the rest of the world, for that matter— . . . have communicated myths of one sort or another. They may have been gross myths, or they may have been myths that came so close to the romantic ideals, heroic concepts, and wishful thinking of the great middle-class that most of us were delighted and moved by them and regarded them as revelations of truth.

—Bosley Crowther

The classic Western has been described as a morality play. Talk about stereotypes! The guy in the white hat; the guy in the black hat; the guy who runs the saloon and probably the town, smokes expensive cigars, and is surrounded by a gang of red-eye-drinking gunmen; the good-natured dance-hall girl who will probably get shot saving the hero's life. Most of us were raised on such stereotypes.

—Thomas H. Middleton

As an art, movies have never been more fertile, various, or exciting, yet as an industry, it has never been more insecure or more self-destructive.

—David Elliott

The businessmen have always been in control of film production; now advertising puts them, finally, on top of public reaction as well. They can transcend the content and the quality of a film by advertising.

—Paulene Kael

Photog-
raphy and
Films

THE PHOTOGRAPHER'S EYE

John Szarkowski   *The Photographer's Eye,* 1966

The invention of photography provided a radically new picture-making process—a process based not on synthesis[1] but on selection. The difference
was a basic one. Paintings were *made*—constructed from a storehouse of
traditional schemes and skills and attitudes—but photographs, as the man
on the street put it, were *taken.*

The difference raised a creative issue of a new order: how could this
mechanical and mindless process be made to produce pictures meaningful
in human terms—pictures with clarity and coherence and a point of view? It
was soon demonstrated that an answer would not be found by those who
loved too much the old forms, for in large part the photographer was bereft
of the old artistic traditions. Speaking of photography Baudelaire said:
"This industry, by invading the territories of art, has become art's most
mortal enemy."[*] And in his own terms of reference Baudelaire was half
right; certainly the new medium could not satisfy old standards. The photographer must find new ways to make his meaning clear.

These new ways might be found by men who could abandon their alle-
giance to traditional pictorial standards—or by the artistically ignorant who
had no old allegiances to break. There have been many of the latter sort.
Since its earliest days, photography has been practiced by thousands who
shared no common tradition or training, who were disciplined and united by
no academy or guild, who considered their medium variously as a science,
an art, a trade, or an entertainment, and who were often unaware of each
other's work. Those who invented photography were scientists and painters, but its professional practitioners were a very different lot. Hawthorne's
daguerreotypist[2] hero Holgrave in *The House of the Seven Gables* was
perhaps not far from typical:

> *Though now but twenty-two years old, he had already been a country
> schoolmaster; salesman in a country store; and the political editor of a
> country newspaper. He had subsequently travelled as a peddler of co-
> logne water and other essences. He had studied and practiced dentist-
> ry. Still more recently he had been a public lecturer on mesmerism,[3] for
> which science he had very remarkable endowments. His present phase*

---

[1] Synthesis is the combining of elements to form a meaningful whole.

[*] Charles Baudelaire, "Salon de 1859," translated by Jonathan Mayne for *The Mirror
of Art, Critical Studies by Charles Baudelaire.* London: Phaidon Press, 1955. (Quoted
from *On Photography, A Source Book of Photo History in Facsimile,* edited by Beaumont Newhall. Watkins Glen, N.Y.: Century House, 1956, p. 106.

[2] The daguerrotype was an early photographic process in which an impression was
made on a silver-coated metallic plate and developed by mercury vapor.

[3] Mesmerism, derived from F. A. Mesmer's name, was a form of hypnotism practiced in the eighteenth and nineteenth centuries.

*as a daguerreotypist was of no more importance in his own view, nor likely to be more permanent, than any of the preceding ones.**

The enormous popularity of the new medium produced professionals by the thousands—converted silversmiths, tinkers, druggists, blacksmiths and printers. If photography was a new artistic problem, such men had the advantage of having nothing to unlearn. Among them they produced a flood of images. In 1853 the *New York Daily Tribune* estimated that three million daguerreotypes were being produced that year.† Some of these pictures were the product of knowledge and skill and sensibility and invention; many were the product of accident, improvisation, misunderstanding, and empirical experiment. But whether produced by art or by luck, each picture was part of a massive assault on our traditional habits of seeing.

By the latter decades of the nineteenth century the professionals and the serious amateurs were joined by an even larger host of casual snapshooters. By the early eighties the dry plate, which would be purchased ready-to-use, had replaced the refractory and messy wet plate process, which demanded that the plate be prepared just before exposure and processed before its emulsion had dried. The dry plate spawned the hand camera and the snapshot. Photography had become easy. In 1893 an English writer complained that the new situation had "created an army of photographers who run rampant over the globe, photographing objects of all sorts, sizes and shapes, under almost every condition, without ever pausing to ask themselves, is this or that artistic? . . . They spy a view, it seems to please, the camera is focused, the shot taken! There is no pause, why should there be? For art may err but nature cannot miss, says the poet, and they listen to the dictum. To them, composition, light, shade, form and texture are so many catch phrases. . . ."‡

These pictures, taken by the thousands by journeyman worker and Sunday hobbyist, were unlike any pictures before them. The variety of their imagery was prodigious. Each subtle variation in viewpoint or light, each passing moment, each change in the tonality of the print, created a new picture. The trained artist could draw a head or a hand from a dozen perspectives. The photographer discovered that the gestures of a hand were infinitely various, and that the wall of a building in the sun was never twice the same.

Most of this deluge of pictures seemed formless and accidental, but some achieved coherence, even in their strangeness. Some of the new images were memorable, and seemed significant beyond their limited intention. These remembered pictures enlarged one's sense of possibilities as he looked again at the real world. While they were remembered they survived, like organisms, to reproduce and evolve.

---

*Nathaniel Hawthorne, *The House of the Seven Gables*. New York: Signet Classics edition, 1961, pp. 156–7.

†A. C. Willers, "Poet and Photography," in *Picturescope,* Vol. XI, No. 4. New York: Picture Division, Special Libraries Association, 1963, p. 46.

‡E. E. Cohen, "Bad Form in Photography," in *The International Annual of Anthony's Photographic Bulletin*. New York and London: E. and H. T. Anthony, 1893, p. 18.

But it was not only the way that photography described things that was new; it was also the things it chose to describe. Photographers shot ". . . objects of all sorts, sizes and shapes . . . without ever pausing to ask themselves, is that or that artistic?" Painting was difficult, expensive, and precious, and it recorded what was known to be important. Photography was easy, cheap and ubiquitous,[4] and it recorded anything: shop windows and sod houses and family pets and steam engines and unimportant people. And once made objective and permanent, immortalized in a picture, these trivial things took on importance. By the end of the century, for the first time in history, even the poor man knew what his ancestors had looked like.

The photographer learned in two ways: first, from a worker's intimate understanding of his tools and materials (if his plate would not record the clouds, he could point his camera down and eliminate the sky); and second he learned from other photographs, which presented themselves in an unending stream. Whether his concern was commercial or artistic, his tradition was formed by all the photographs that had impressed themselves upon his consciousness. . . .

It should be possible to consider the history of the medium in terms of photographers' progressive awareness of characteristics and problems that have seemed inherent in the medium. Five such issues are considered below. These issues *do not* define discrete categories of work; on the contrary they should be regarded as interdependent aspects of a single problem—as section views through the body of photographic tradition. As such, it is hoped that they may contribute to the formulation of a vocabulary and a critical perspective more fully responsive to the unique phenomena of photography.

THE THING ITSELF

The first thing that the photographer learned was that photography dealt with the actual; he had not only to accept this fact, but to treasure it; unless he did, photography would defeat him. He learned that the world itself is an artist of incomparable inventiveness, and that to recognize its best works and moments, to anticipate them, to clarify them and make them permanent, requires intelligence both acute and supple.

But he learned also that the factuality of his pictures, no matter how convincing and unarguable, was a different thing than the reality itself. Much of the reality was filtered out in the static little black and white image, and some of it was exhibited with an unnatural clarity, an exaggerated importance. The subject and the picture were not the same thing, although they would afterwards seem so. It was the photographer's problem to see not simply the reality before him but the still invisible picture, and to make his choices in terms of the latter.

This was an artistic problem, not a scientific one, but the public believed that the photograph could not lie, and it was easier for the photographer if he believed it too, or pretended to. Thus he was likely to claim that

---

[4] Ubiquitous means being everywhere at the same time.

what our eyes saw was an illusion, and what the camera saw was the truth. Hawthorne's Holgrave, speaking of a difficult portrait subject said:

> "We give [heaven's broad and simple sunshine] credit only for de-
> picting the merest surface, but it actually brings out the secret charac-
> ter with a truth that no painter would ever venture upon, even could he
> detect it. . . . The remarkable point is that the original wears, to the
> world's eye . . . an exceedingly pleasant countenance, indicative of
> benevolence, openness of heart, sunny good humor, and other praise-
> worthy qualities of that cast. The sun, as you see, tells quite another
> story, and will not be coaxed out of it, after half a dozen patient at-
> tempts on my part. Here we have a man, sly, subtle, hard, imperious,
> and withal, cold as ice."*

In a sense Holgrave was right in giving more credence to the camera image than to his own eyes, for the image would survive the subject, and become the remembered reality. William M. Ivins, Jr. said, "at any given moment the accepted report of an event is of greater importance than the event, for what we think about and act upon is the symbolic report and not the concrete event itself."† He also said: "The nineteenth century began by believing that what was reasonable was true and it would end up by believing that what it saw a photograph of was true."‡

THE DETAIL

The photographer was tied to the facts of things, and it was his problem to force the facts to tell the truth. He could not, outside the studio, pose the truth; he could only record it as he found it, and it was found in nature in a fragmented and unexplained form—not as a story, but as scattered and suggestive clues. The photographer could not assemble these clues into a coherent narrative, he could only isolate the fragment, document it, and by so doing claim for it some special significance, a meaning which went be-yond simple description. The compelling clarity with which a photograph recorded the trivial suggested that the subject had never before been prop-erly seen, that it was in fact perhaps *not* trivial, but filled with undiscovered meaning. If photographs could not be read as stories, they could be read as symbols.

The decline of narrative painting in the past century has been ascribed in large part to the rise of photography, which "relieved" the painter of the necessity of story telling. This is curious, since photography has never been successful at narrative. It has in fact seldom attempted it. The elaborate nineteenth century montages of Robinson and Rejlander, laboriously pieced together from several posed negatives, attempted to tell stories, but

*Hawthorne, op. cit., p. 85.

†William M. Ivins, Jr., *Prints and Visual Communication.* Cambridge, Mass.: Harvard University Press, 1953, p. 180.

‡Ibid., p. 94.

these works were recognized in their own time as pretentious failures. In the early days of the picture magazines the attempt was made to achieve narrative through photographic sequences, but the superficial coherence of these stories was generally achieved at the expense of photographic discovery. The heroic documentation of the American Civil War by the Brady group, and the incomparably larger photographic record of the Second World War, have this in common: neither explained, without extensive captioning, what was happening. The function of these pictures was not to make the story clear, it was to make it *real*. The great war photographer Robert Capa expressed both the narrative poverty and the symbolic power of photography when he said, "If your pictures aren't good, you're not close enough."

THE FRAME

Since the photographer's picture was not conceived but selected, his subject was never truly discrete, never wholly self-contained. The edges of his film demarcated what he thought most important, but the subject he had shot was something else; it had extended in four directions. If the photographer's frame surrounded two figures, isolating them from the crowd in which they stood, it created a relationship between those two figures that had not existed before.

The central act of photography, the act of choosing and eliminating, forces a concentration on the picture edge—the line that separates in from out—and on the shapes that are created by it.

During the first half-century of photography's lifetime, photographs were printed the same size as the exposed plate. Since enlarging was generally impractical, the photographer could not change his mind in the darkroom, and decide to use only a fragment of his picture, without reducing its size accordingly. If he had purchased an eight by ten inch plate (or worse, prepared it), had carried it as part of his back-bending load, and had processed it, he was not likely to settle for a picture half that size. A sense of simple economy was enough to make the photographer try to fill the picture to its edges.

The edges of the picture were seldom neat. Parts of figures or buildings or features of landscape were truncated, leaving a shape belonging not to the subject, but (if the picture was a good one) to the balance, the propriety, of the image. The photographer looked at the world as though it was a scroll painting, unrolled from hand to hand, exhibiting an infinite number of croppings—of compositions—as the frame moved onwards.

The sense of the picture's edge as a cropping device is one of the qualities of form that most interested the inventive painters of the latter nineteenth century. To what degree this awareness came from photography, and to what degree from oriental art, is still open to study. However, it is possible that the prevalence of the photographic image helped prepare the ground for an appreciation of the Japanese print, and also that the compositional attitudes of these prints owed much to habits of seeing which stemmed from the scroll tradition.

TIME

There is in fact no such thing as an instantaneous photograph. All photographs are time exposures, of shorter or longer duration, and each describes a discrete parcel of time. This time is always the present. Uniquely in the history of pictures, a photograph describes only that period of time in which it was made. Photography alludes to the past and the future only in so far as they exist in the present, the past through its surviving relics, the future through prophecy visible in the present.

In the days of slow films and slow lenses, photographs described a time segment of several seconds or more. If the subject moved, images resulted that had never been seen before: dogs with two heads and a sheaf of tails, faces without features, transparent men, spreading their diluted substance half across the plate. The fact that these pictures were considered (at best) as partial failures is less interesting than the fact that they were produced in quantity; they were familiar to all photographers, and to all customers who had posed with squirming babies for family portraits.

It is surprising that the prevalence of these radical images has not been of interest to art historians. The time-lapse painting of Duchamp and Balla, done before the First World War, has been compared to work done by photographers such as Edgerton and Mili, who worked consciously with similar ideas a quarter-century later, but the accidental time-lapse photographs of the nineteenth century have been ignored—presumably *because* they were accidental.

As photographic materials were made more sensitive, and lenses and shutters faster, photography turned to the exploration of rapidly moving subjects. Just as the eye is incapable of registering the single frames of a motion picture projected on the screen at the rate of twenty-four per second, so it is incapable of following the positions of a rapidly moving subject in life. The galloping horse is the classic example. As lovingly drawn countless thousands of times by Greeks and Egyptians and Persians and Chinese, and down through all the battle scenes and sporting prints of Christendom, the horse ran with four feet extended, like a fugitive from a carousel. Not till Muybridge successfully photographed a galloping horse in 1878 was the convention broken. It was this way also with the flight of birds, the play of muscles on an athlete's back, the drape of a pedestrian's clothing, and the fugitive expressions of a human face.

Immobilizing these thin slices of time has been a source of continuing fascination for the photographer. And while pursuing this experiment he discovered something else: he discovered that there was a pleasure and a beauty in this fragmenting of time that had little to do with what was happening. It had to do rather with seeing the momentary patterning of lines and shapes that had been previously concealed within the flux of movement. The famous French photographer Henri Cartier-Bresson defined his commitment to this new beauty with the phrase *"the decisive moment,"* but the phrase has been misunderstood; the thing that happens at the decisive moment is not a dramatic climax but a visual one. The result is not a story but a picture.

VANTAGE POINT

Much has been said about the clarity of photography, but little has been said about its obscurity. And yet it is photography that has taught us to see from the unexpected vantage point, and has shown us pictures that give the sense of the scene, while withholding its narrative meaning. Photographers from necessity choose from the options available to them, and often this means pictures from the other side of the proscenium,[5] showing the actors' backs, pictures from the bird's view, or the worm's, or pictures in which the subject is distorted by extreme foreshortening, or by none, or by an unfamiliar pattern of light, or by a seeming ambiguity of action or gesture.

Ivins wrote with rare perception of the effect that such pictures had on nineteenth-century eyes:

> At first the public had talked a great deal about what it called photographic distortion. . . . [But] it was not long before men began to think photographically, and thus to see for themselves things that it had previously taken the photograph to reveal to their astonished and protesting eyes. Just as nature had once imitated art, so now it began to imitate the picture made by the camera.*

After a century and a quarter, photography's ability to challenge and reject our schematized notions of reality is still fresh. In his monograph on Francis Bacon, Lawrence Alloway speaks of the effect of photography on that painter: "The evasive nature of his imagery, which is shocking but obscure, like accident or atrocity photographs, is arrived at by using photography's huge repertory of visual images. . . . Uncaptioned news photographs, for instance, often appear as momentous and extraordinary. . . . Bacon used this property of photography to subvert the clarity of pose of figures in traditional painting."†

The influence of photography on modern painters (and on modern writers) has been great and inestimable. It is, strangely, easier to forget that photography has also influenced photographers. Not only great pictures by great photographers, but *photography*—the great undifferentiated, homogeneous[6] whole of it—has been teacher, library, and laboratory for those who have consciously used the camera as artists. An artist is a man who seeks new structures in which to order and simplify his sense of the reality of life. For the artist photographer, much of his sense of reality (where his picture starts) and much of his sense of craft or structure (where his picture is completed) are anonymous and untraceable gifts from photography itself.

[5] The proscenium is the arch which frames the front of a theater stage.

[6] Homogeneous means similar or uniform.

*Ibid., p. 138.

†Lawrence Alloway, *Francis Bacon.* New York: Solomon R. Guggenheim Foundation, 1963, p. 22.

The history of photography has been less a journey than a growth. Its movement has not been linear and consecutive, but centrifugal. Photography, and our understanding of it, has spread from a center; it has, by infusion, penetrated our consciousness. Like an organism, photography was born whole. It is in our progressive discovery of it that its history lies.

■ **POINTS TO CONSIDER**

1. What differences does the author point out between painting and photography in the nineteenth century? In your opinion, do these differences indicate that photography is less an "art" than painting? In what ways could photography actually be considered a more demanding medium for artistic expression than painting?

2. Why must a photographer "force the facts to tell the truth"? Is it possible for a photograph to lie? How?

3. Explain how the frame of a photograph "forces" a relationship on the objects within the frame. Might this be considered a kind of "lying?"

4. What does the author mean when he describes a picture as a "visual climax"? What things interact and contribute to this climax? Why is the result not a story?

5. Throughout the article, the author refers to the effect photography has had on the way not only photographers and artists, but all of us, see the world around us. Our notions of beauty in women might be one obvious example of the effects of this "massive assault on our traditional habits of seeing." Can you think of others?

BASIC VISUAL ELEMENTS OF THE PHOTOGRAPH AND THE MOTION PICTURE

Fredric Rissover

STILL PHOTOGRAPHY

Some people who admire drawing and painting used to argue that photography really is not an art form because it is not personal and creative—it simply reproduces its subject objectively. But few people hold this opinion any more. One reason may be that museums of fine art, like New York's Museum of Modern Art, have been displaying outstanding photographs in their galleries. Another reason may be that with the tremendous use of photography in journalism and advertising, the general quality level has risen as increasingly talented artists have come to work in the medium. As more good photography is produced and reproduced in great quantity, people who are exposed to it grow to admire and appreciate it. A third reason is that movies—photographs in motion—have called the attention of the public to the artistry of good photography.

All good photography demands that the photographer have a "good eye"; that is, he must be able to recognize the raw material which will provide good subjects for his photographs. An appealing photo often has an unusual or expressive or revealing subject. It may capture interesting forms or details. It may depict contrast or conflict in design or in action and emotion. Frequently, the photograph which attracts us most and lingers longest in our memories is one which presents vividly a specific subject or situation but which also suggests that the specific subject may be representative of the universal.

But spotting an appealing subject is just the beginning. When the photographer has found his subject, he must decide how to treat it. Like any other artist, he has a variety of ways that he can interpret his subject. The good photographer, consciously and instinctively, combines the elements of his art to achieve the effects he desires.

Perhaps the most immediately apparent element of the photographer's art is "framing": isolating a subject from its surroundings. In no other art form is the element of isolation so obvious and striking as it is in photography—in both still photos and movies. A commonplace and not particularly interesting object or detail is often called to our attention and becomes fascinating simply because the observant photographer has put a frame around it and isolated it for us on a piece of paper or a movie screen.

The element of framing in photography calls our attention to the composition of details, just as it does in painting. We notice the distribution of shapes and sizes, of textures, of lights and darks; and we notice the interplay of horizontal, vertical, diagonal, and curving lines. The element of framing also makes us aware of the ways in which similar or different objects exist near to or together with each other. This side-by-side relationship between the details within the frame is called "juxtaposition in space."

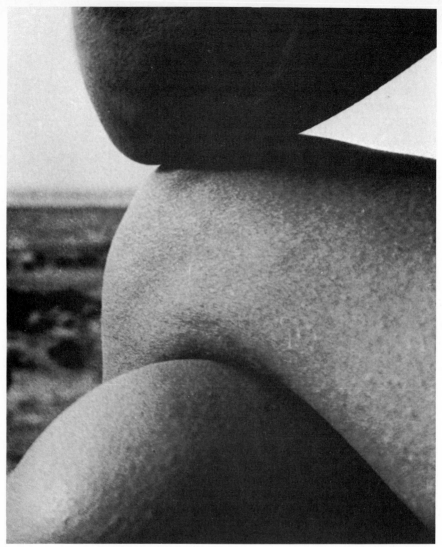

Photograph by Bill Brandt. Rapho Guillumette.

A good example of how photography can call our attention to the commonplace is seen in the picture just above. The subject is simply an elbow and two knees, but the special view of them which the photographer gives us transforms them into something new. The tight framing which detaches them from the rest of the body turns them into abstract shapes resembling a piece of modern sculpture. The lighting which provides striking highlights

Photograph by Wayne Miller. © Magnum Photos.

and shadows and which brings out a grainy quality in the skin suggests the solidity and roughness of carved stone.

Another example of effective framing can be seen in the photo above. In this picture of a mother nursing her baby, we see only the mother's bosom, the head of the baby, and the arm of the baby clinging to the mother. This limitation of subject forces us to concentrate on the idea of the mother's gift and the child's dependency rather than on the mother-and-child relationship in general. It also seems to blend the parts of both bodies into one harmonious pattern, as if to suggest that the mother and her child are, at this time, like a single being. Interesting juxtaposition in space is illustrated by the photo on page 322 in which a young boy on his way to school contrasts dramatically with the setting in which he walks—a bombed-out section of a city.

Closely related to the element of framing as an important component of the photographer's art is the element of "scale," or "relative size." The photographer can depict the relative importance of his details by comparing them to each other in size. Or he can greatly exaggerate or diminish the size of his subject or details to express his feelings about them.

Photograph by Otto Hagel. © Otto Hagel.

In the photo of the young pianist on page 323, the hands appear huge to suggest both the forcefulness of his playing and the importance of his hands and his music to his life. The two photos of mothers and their children, on pages 324 and 325, offer an interesting comparative study in relative size. In the picture to the left, the tall mother towers protectively over her two small children. The difference in size here is captured by the photographer but not created by him. In the picture to the right, however, the photographer places the little girl and the baby in the foreground and the

Photograph by Henry Crossman, ASMP.

mother behind them, making the mother look smaller by comparison and perhaps suggesting the all-absorbing importance of the two children to their mother who looks lovingly at them.

A third element of the photographer's art which greatly influences the effect of his picture is the "visual angle." Interesting visual angle is an important way of creating the illusion of depth. It also provides a way to present the subject in an unusual or provocative manner. Further, it can affect our interpretation of the subject just as the element of relative size

Photograph by Consuelo Kanaga.

Photograph by Wayne Miller. © Magnum Photos.

can. A low shooting angle in which we look up at the subject tends to make the subject look larger and more impressive; a high shooting angle in which we look down at the subject tends to make the subject look smaller and weaker.

Notice how in the photo of the man in the swamp, on page 326, the downward visual angle, combined with the relatively small size of the man and the framing of branches and leaves, makes the man appear to be a part of his surroundings and greatly influenced by them. By contrast, in the photo of the young man on page 327, the upward visual angle and the contrast of the bold face and fist against the plain background emphasize the forcefulness of the man and his attempt to stand out from or even dominate his surroundings.

Along with framing, relative size, and visual angle, there are several

Photograph by Ted Polumbaum. *Life* Magazine, © Time, Inc.

special optical effects which the photographer may employ. One of these is the regulation of the amount and quality of light in his pictures. With good use of light and dark obtained through natural or artificial lighting, filters, and various exposure times, the photographer can call attention to significant details and wash other details in obscuring glare or shadow. He can bring out textures and heighten or lessen the solidness, opaqueness, or sharpness of his details, thereby affecting the mood of the picture.

The photo of the sculptor at work on a portrait bust, on page 328, uses

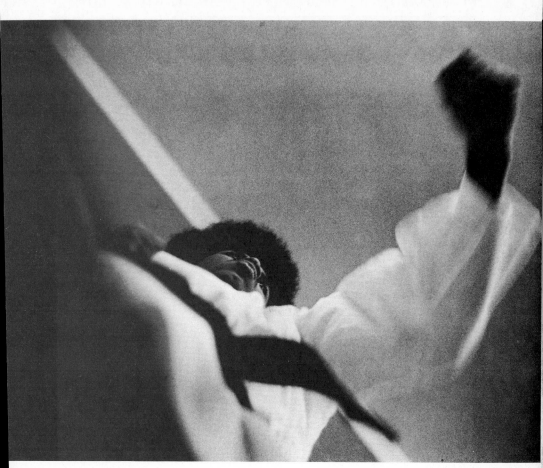

otograph by Howard Sochurek.

light and shadow effectively to contrast the softness of the curtains with the solidity of the sculpture and to create a similarity between the appearance of the artist and of his creation which suggests the close relationship of the two. The picture of a flock of sheep standing near the entrance of a cave, on page 329, combines effective framing with effective use of light. The framing creates the illusion that the sheep are emerging from the cave in a spiral pattern like the unwinding of the mainspring of a watch. If the picture had not been so closely framed, the illusion would have been lost as we saw the groups of sheep and individual sheep wandering in all directions farther from the cave. The lighting is bright enough to bring out the whiteness of the sheep, but not so intense as to wash out the textures of the sheep's wool and of the rocky hillside. The white sheep stand out just enough from the white and grey rock to appear different from it, but they blend in closely

Photograph by Stan Wayman. *Life* Magazine, © Time, Inc.

enough to suggest their harmony with it—their close relationship to their natural environment. The black shadows in the cave, around the legs of the sheep, and above and below the sheep contrast with the whiteness of the sheep, reinforce the spiral pattern of the sheep and the hillside, and provide a kind of natural frame within the picture.

By use of "sharp" or "soft focus" or by use of the two in contrast, the photographer affects the mood of his picture. Most pictures have sharp focus in which all the details are as clear as their size and the amount of light permit. But sometimes the photographer uses soft focus; that is, he chooses to blur the outlines and details of his picture to suggest an unreal, ideal, or dreamlike quality. Sometimes he uses both sharp and soft focus in the same picture to accentuate the illusion of depth, to call attention to a particular detail, or to contrast solid reality with the dreamlike.

In the portrait of the young man on page 327, a blurring of the arm and fist records his defiant gesture. The photograph at the top of page 330 creates a deliberate dreamlike quality with the use of soft focus while accentuating the crucial details with sharp focus.

"Multiple images" and "time exposures" form another group of optical effects which the photographer may use to advantage. Multiple images can depict imaginative or distracted states of mind by superimposing represen-

Photograph by George Krause.

Photograph by A. E. Woolley.

tations of mental images upon the images of solid reality, as in pictures illustrating visions or ghosts. The picture on page 331 was made by combining parts of several different negatives to create a multiple print with the vivid but unreal quality of a dream. Multiple and time exposures often translate time into space by blurring images to suggest motion or speed or by capturing in one picture a series of actions or a continuous action performed over a period of time.

A fourth optical device which the photographer may use to create expressive pictures is "deliberate distortion," which may be achieved with

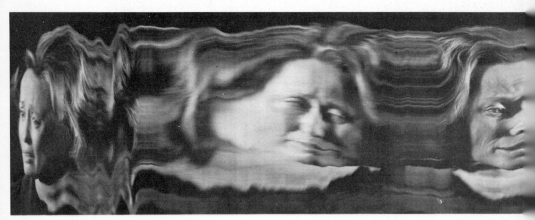

Photograph by Mottke Weissman.

Photograph by Jerry Velsmann.

lenses, prisms, mirrors, or filters when the picture is taken or by some chemical or mechanical means in the developing process. The photo at the bottom of page 330 illustrates the use of distorting mirrors and/or lenses to extend time and to intensify emotion. Distortion may suggest unreality or unusual mental states such as those created by mind-expanding drugs, it may create the macabre or the grotesque, or it may call our attention to the forms and patterns of common things by presenting them in an unusual way. Although deliberate distortion is not unusual in still photographs, it probably appears more frequently in movies.

MOTION PICTURES

Movies make use of all the elements of the art of still photography. The moviemaker is concerned with framing and juxtaposition in space, scale or relative size, visual angles, and special optical effects, such as amount and quality of light, sharp and soft focus, multiple and time exposure, and deliberate distortion.

Framing in motion pictures, as in still pictures, focuses the attention of the viewer on a limited subject and points up relationships between details. Sometimes in movies framing is used especially to prevent the viewer from seeing some details or some of the action. This may be done to build suspense, to prevent the viewer's seeing something particularly painful or ugly, or to force the viewer to imagine details for himself. Sometimes this can be used as a comic device if the viewer is led to imagine something one way and then is shown something quite different.

A special kind of framing which changes the normal dimensions of the screen picture is known as "masking." In masking, part of the picture is blocked out to make it appear tall and narrow, especially wide, or even circular. This is used to reinforce particular details such as knights in combat on a tall castle tower, a covered wagon caravan crossing a broad prairie, or an approaching pirate ship seen through a spyglass.

Relative size functions in movies as it does in still photos to suggest relative strength or importance; however, in movies the relative sizes change quickly with movement of subject or camera. The overall scale of the picture depends upon the distance of the camera from the subject and upon the lens used. The extents of view and the scales of size range from the long shot, which depicts a very restricted view on a large scale—a view of a distant-city skyline with buildings the size of sugar cubes—to detailed views of an eye or a trigger finger filling the whole screen. Special effects often are created with models or miniatures representing full-sized objects, such as ships in sea battle or towns attacked by monsters, or with images of people or objects of one size superimposed upon images of people or objects of another size to depict ghosts, midgets, or giants.

Visual angle is important in movies because it is so expressive and because it can change so rapidly to create a number of cumulatively effective impressions. Action viewed from a great height often suggests detachment while action viewed from below suggests victimization. Unusual camera angles can suggest odd or distressing circumstances or troubled states of mind. As with framing, visual angles can be employed to limit what the viewer can see or to create deliberate ambiguity. Often in movies the camera will adopt the point of view of a character for some part of the action.

The special optical effects used in still photography—controlling amounts and quality of light, sharp and soft focus, deliberate distortion, multiple and time exposures, and composite images—appear commonly in movies. In many cases, their use in movies is more complex and expressive than it is in still photos because the added elements of time and motion permit more variations and combinations.

In addition to the artistic elements shared with still photography, motion pictures make use of a number of other expressive visual elements related to movement within individual shots and to movement between and among shots. A movie "shot" is the action recorded on film during a single running of the camera—the action recorded between "roll 'em!" and "cut!" Shots range from a few seconds to a few minutes. Theoretically, a whole feature-length film could be made in one shot, but (except for a few experimental oddities) this is never done because to do so would rob the film of one of its most expressive techniques.

Movement within individual shots involves three basic components—movement of the subject, movement of the camera, and regulation of time. Movements of the subject can be horizontal, vertical, or diagonal, or some combination of these. In general, horizontal movement is less strong than vertical movement, and neither is as exciting as diagonal movement. Movement in toward the camera is usually more forceful and often suggests that action is about to occur, whereas movement away from the camera is less forceful and often suggests a suspension of action. Sometimes it signals the end of a scene or the end of the film. Movement in more than one direction, of course, tends to be more exciting than movement in a single direction, just as fast movement is more exciting than slow movement. All these generalizations, however, are open to exceptions.

Movements of the camera generally have the same emotional effects as movements of the subject. Horizontal motion is calmer, vertical action is stronger, and diagonal motion is more exciting, relatively speaking. Motion toward a subject is usually stronger than motion away from a subject. Movement in which the camera swings or pivots horizontally, vertically, or diagonally, is commonly known as "panning," while movement in which the camera focuses toward or away from the subject is called "zooming in" or "zooming out." Usually, the faster the panning and zooming are done, the more exciting they tend to be. Movement of the whole camera which concentrates upon and follows a particular subject, such as a moving car, is generally called "tracking."

Control of motion and time within individual movie shots helps to determine the dramatic effects of a film. If the film is shot at slower-than-normal speed and projected at normal speed, the motion will be faster than usual. Fast motion is used occasionally in comedies to exaggerate the awkwardness of some action or the hectic nature of a slapstick chase scene. If the film is shot at faster-than-normal speed and projected at normal speed, the motion will be slower than usual. Slow motion is sometimes used to give film action the quality of a dream or a memory. Often it is used to slow down the action of a natural process (like bird flight) or of a sports event (like a pole vault or a football play) to reveal all the details of motion. Another commonly used device is the "freeze frame." This involves reprinting one frame in succession so that the action is frozen in one moment of time, as in a still photograph. Many modern movies end with "freeze frames" which bring an abrupt halt to the action and leave the viewer to ponder the significance of a single image.

In general, the moviemaker regulates time for dramatic effect in the same way a playwright does. If details are important, they may be dwelt upon, whereas, if details are not important, they may be passed over quickly. This means that unimportant action lasting, say, an hour in reality may be represented on film in thirty seconds, while important action lasting five minutes in reality may take half an hour to present in all its dramatic significance on film. Very rarely does time in a film approximate time in reality.

In using the element of time for emphasis, however, the film maker has an advantage over the playwright. The film maker is not as restricted as the playwright to single physical points of view. He can employ, in addition to action within single shots, movement between and among shots. If for example, he wants to show a bit of action from a number of different angles or distances, he can splice together a number of different shots. Splicing together shots can move action instantly from one setting to another and suggest changes in time or circumstance. Movement from shot to shot can compress time if the movement is quick or involves many omissions. Or movement from shot to shot can make time seem to stand still or can extend time by repeating an action or parts of it in any of a number of effective variations. Brief shots may be used to underline increased activity or to build suspense, and these may be interspersed with longer shots to convey relative calm.

By splicing together shots, the film maker can achieve not only great mobility and emphasis through repetition and variation, but also effective comparisons and contrasts through juxtaposition in time. Whereas juxtaposition in space places details side by side for examination in a still photo or a single movie shot, juxtaposition in time suggests relationships between details in shots which occur near to each other in time. If, for example, we see a shot of a group of women gossiping and see immediately or shortly afterward a shot of hens in a farmyard, the comparison is clear. Or, if we see a shot of a murder being committed in a woods and then see shots of people picnicking nearby or of a quiet stream flowing past, the murder seems all the more brutal because of the peaceful contrasting shots. Juxtaposition in time can be used also to impart information by suggestion or to build suspense. If we see a shot of a young woman sitting on a park bench looking periodically at her watch, then see a shot of a young man hurrying through the park, and see finally a shot of two pigeons on a park path cooing to each other, we can infer that the man is hurrying to meet the woman in the park because they are in love. Or, if we see shots of a thief robbing a house intermixed with shots of a man walking toward the house, climbing the steps, and turning a key in the front door, the tension mounts because we anticipate a confrontation.

The process of selecting movie shots, determining their length, and assembling them is generally called "editing" and is performed by a film editor working with the movie director or by the director himself. The action of any film, therefore, is most strongly influenced by three sources: the screenwriter who suggests the action in his script, the director who controls the action as it is being filmed, and the editor (sometimes the director himself) who selects, cuts, and combines the shots after they are photographed.

In continental Europe, the term "montage" is used almost synonymously with editing, but in the United States montage refers to a more specific technique in which a sequence of short, rapid shots is used to represent a passage of time usually involving much activity. If, for example, in a film about prizefighting, a young boxer is working his way up to a championship fight over a period of three years, we may see many very brief shots of the boxer in training, the boxer pounding opponents, trains racing between cities, pages being torn off calendars, and newspaper headlines proclaiming greater and greater victories. Thus, in a minute or two, we are aware of three years' activity and progress. Montage can be used also to build excitement, as with a representation of a horse race in which we see many brief shots—featuring a variety of visual angles and relative scales of size—of horses' hooves biting the turf, jockeys urging on their mounts, graceful forms racing by a fence, and excited viewers screaming in the grandstand.

In editing or montage, the commonest transition between shots is made by splicing one shot directly to another so that we see one bit of detail or action replaced immediately by another. This instantaneous change is called a "cut." Other transitional methods besides the direct cut are sometimes used to achieve special effects. The "fade-out–fade-in," for instance, is the transition in which the picture dims out to black and the new picture grows gradually brighter out of the darkness. This technique is generally used to suggest a passage of time or a major change of place. The "mix," or "dissolve," is the transition in which the old and new pictures blend for a moment as the old picture disappears and the new picture takes its place. The dissolve can suggest a change in time or place and often suggests a movement into the past or into the not-immediate future, usually through memory or dreams. The variety of other transitional methods in films includes the "wipe," the "iris-out–iris-in," the "turnover," and the "blur-out–blur-in." In the wipe, an invisible line passes across the screen removing the old picture and replacing it with the new one. In an iris-out–iris-in, the old picture grows dark from the edges to the center, and the new picture appears from the darkness, growing brighter from the center to the edges. In a turnover, the whole picture seems to flip, and the new picture appears on the back of the old. These last three devices occur most often in comedies. The blur-out–blur-in is like the dissolve except that the picture grows wavy or slips out of focus during the transition. Like the dissolve, this often ushers in memories or dreams. With the growing sophistication of filmgoers over the years, the special transition method has steadily decreased and has been replaced by the direct cut. Today's film audiences are so used to flashbacks, flash forwards, and quick changes in time and space that they seldom require technical cues.

The ability to use movement effectively within shots and between and among shots characterizes the good film maker. He regulates time to dramatic advantage, utilizes imaginative movement of subject and camera within shots, and edits skillfully between and among shots—creating forceful juxtaposition in time and employing smooth transition—to achieve maximum expression through his art.

■ **POINTS TO CONSIDER**

Still Photography

1. In what ways is photography creative in the same sense that painting or poetry is creative? What is meant by a "good eye"? Why is this quality more essential to a photographer than to a painter?

2. What is framing? What are some of the effects that the use of framing can have on a picture? What is meant by the composition of a photograph? How is it related to framing? Why is a diagonal line more exciting than a vertical or horizontal line? What is meant by the term "juxtaposition in space"? How is it different from composition? How is it affected by framing?

3. How can the photographer alter the relative sizes of objects within a photograph? How can this help to express his feelings about the objects?

4. What is meant by the term "visual angle"? What effects can be achieved through the variations of its use? By a downward angle? By an upward angle?

5. What effects can be achieved through the use of special lighting techniques and variations in focus and exposure?

Motion Pictures

1. What dimension does the motion picture add to the photograph? How does this affect such considerations of still photography as framing, visual angle, relative size, and juxtaposition?

2. What are the three basic components of movement within an individual movie shot? What general effects are achieved through the use of horizontal motion? Vertical motion? Diagonal motion? What is panning? Zooming in? Zooming out? What effect is achieved by speeding up these techniques?

3. What effect is achieved through slow motion? Through fast motion? How does the moviemaker create slow motion and fast motion? What is a freeze frame? What effects can it achieve?

4. How can the moviemaker expand or compress time? What sort of events would most likely be compressed? Why? What sort of events would most likely be expanded? Why? Can you think of any examples of the use of these techniques in recent movies?

5. What is meant by the term "editing?" How can an editor build suspense? How can he convey a feeling of calm? What is montage? What is juxtaposition in time? How are these also a part of editing?

6. What is meant by the term "transition"? How does it relate to editing? What is the cut? the dissolve? the fade-out–fade-in? What effects do they achieve? What are some of the less common transitional devices, and what effects do they achieve?

MAGIC, MYTH, AND MONOTONY/A MEASURE OF THE ROLE OF MOVIES IN A FREE SOCIETY

Bosley Crowther   *Mass Media in a Free Society,* 1969

Use

Preachers and educators, social scientists and critics, have asked what are the movies doing to the people—or *for* the people. Are they helping to uplift and educate? Are they providing something more than entertainment? Are they providing *wholesome* entertainment? That is the word!

I bring up this point very early because I want to establish the fact that the movies are probably the most closely examined and frequently challenged medium we have. Although they are under no obligation by their cultural nature to communicate fact or truth, as presumably is the press, and they are certainly under no compulsion to perform the responsibilities of preachers and teachers in leading people in the paths of righteousness, they have been constantly called upon to perform these functions and assume these responsibilities. The movies have been candidly expected to be everything from a truant officer to an art.

Therefore, I put it to you that we must proceed with caution and care in defining our expectations of this medium, if we mean to be reasonable and fair. And we must also be sharply realistic in recognizing what movies actually are.

When movies were first exhibited to the public, they were magic, sheer magic—only that. They were an experience so novel and amazing that the thrill of looking at them—of seeing pictures actually moving before one's eyes, out of context from all experience of nature—was all anybody wished. Those were indeed the days when the medium—just the medium—was the message. That was enough. Thousands—even millions—of people were fascinated by the magic of random images moving on a screen.

But the novelty of mere movement didn't last long. Repetitions of railroad trains rushing at you or school girls skipping rope or factory workers coming out of factories soon became quite monotonous. Thus occurred the first indication of a phenomenon that has been persistent in the commerce of the screen: the pertinent peril of transition from magic to monotony.

How to use the magic medium to provide the public with something that would entice and maintain its interest was the problem of the inexperienced men who operated the funny little cameras. And, of course, they soon came up—quite by chance—with the telling of little stories that were essentially myths.

Folk stories they were—simple fictions right out of the cheap literature that was familiar, understood, and indeed demanded by the great majority of Americans. The magic movies became a mechanism for manufacturing and communicating myths—the myths of their fictitious contents and the myths of the heroes and heroines they evolved.

I think it safe to guess that 99.44 per cent of the movies made in the United States—and in the rest of the world, for that matter—since *The Great Train Robbery* have communicated myths of one sort or another. They may have been gross myths, or they may have been myths that came so close to the romantic ideals, heroic concepts, and wishful thinking of the great middle-class that most of us were delighted and moved by them and regarded them as revelations of truth. Or they may have been myths of such conspicuous and charming fantasy, such as the films of Charlie Chaplin or Walt Disney, that we found joy and reassurance in them.

There is no need to run a lengthy recount of the formulae of these myths—the convention that the good guys beat the bad guys in every crucial showdown of strength; that the good girl gets the good guy away from the bad girl, in the end; that every American soldier is basically a hero; that our country always wins its righteous wars. I challenge you to analyze any movie—any fictional movie, that is—with rare exceptions, and not find it a compound of a convenient and comforting middle-class myth.

Even those films which we have called documentaries, because they have appeared to organize and show us facts, and those obsolete items known as newsreels have been generally tinctured with myths because they have propagandized along lines of wishful thinking or they have mainly catalogued the happier aspects of our lives, such as beauty contests and horse races.

The screen has rarely been a conveyor of trenchant truth—of the real natures contained in men and the frequent injustices and ironies of society as they exist.

And even if there did come a film maker who wanted to manifest such things—who wanted to shock and disturb the preconceptions and the illusions of the middle class—we have had laws and regulations to restrict and control exposés. The mechanisms of statutory censorship by which the movies (and *only* the movies) were rigidly bound in this country after 1915—right down to within the past few years—kept the film makers from putting forth concepts that were really anything more than myths.

Indeed, I have often wondered, if we had had no statutory censorship—if anybody had been free to manufacture or merchandise any sort of film he wished—I have wondered if we would not still have had pretty much the same sorts of films—the same purveyance to a middle-class market, with its prejudices and tastes—as we did. For the Screen Production Code, which was adopted to regulate the output of Hollywood—to force it to accept moral strictures—was the consequence of reaction to the pressures and demands of citizen organizations that insisted upon their middle-class myths.

The defense of the code during its dominance was that it enforced some social values on films. But it did not do that. It simply forced a nervous adherence to the parochial[1] canons of its administrators' tastes. For instance, they thought divorce, abortion, or miscegenation[2] were not respectable. Therefore these things could not be shown as advantageous in a movie, and they could only be suggested in the most carefully guarded terms. There were dozens of other obfuscations[3] of reality supported by the code.

I am not saying that there weren't some good movies—some very good, entertaining ones—made under these restraints of middle-class taste and regulations. But for all their glints of realities—as in *The Grapes of Wrath,* for instance, or in the ironies of a *Citizen Kane*—they were pragmatically[4] designed to arrive at resolutions that perpetuated sentiments and myths.

So the first burst of sheer movie magic was followed by a long period of profitably merchandised myth, which only showed its mechanical obsolescence and its aesthetic monotony when radio came along. The magic and myths of silent movies were sufficient all through the First World War and into the 1920's. Then the sounds and voices that came out of that little radio provided the public with a new kind of magic, and the monotony of movies without voices crept in.

I don't suppose many of you know this, but the movies were in a calamitous state—virtually dying for lack of attendance—when they were miraculously saved by the magic of sound. The fortuitous injection of talking movies brought a new aesthetic[5] dimension and excitement to the screen. Attendance boomed, even though the Great Depression soon followed. The rotation from magic to myth occurred again. For even though many new subjects and devices of story-telling were allowed by dialogue and sound in movies, the contents continued to be myth. Poor Clark Gable married rich Claudette Colbert in *It Happened One Night.* Scarlett O'Hara regained Tara in *Gone With the Wind.*

I have dwelled on this historical rotation of magic, myth, and monotony because it does represent the basic pattern of the cultural and commercial progress of films. And its cyclical swing has been commanding right down to the present day.

What happened when a totally new magic called television came after the Second World War? It completely pre-empted the public's time, and quickly exposed the monotony of the conventional, repetitious theatrical films.

Most people assumed television was a new medium. It wasn't at all. It was and is motion picture projected in the home instead of in a theatre. True, the material projected by this means and the commercialized programming of it is somewhat different from the material and techniques of movies projected in theatres, and it is given the distinguishing name of Video Broadcasting. But it is movies, all the same, and its fascination lay at

---

[1] Parochial means restricted or within narrow limits. Canons are rules or codes.

[2] Miscegenation is a term, no longer in common use, for racial intermarriage.

[3] Obfuscations are confusions or obscurities.

[4] Pragmatically means "in a practical way."

[5] Aesthetic means artistic or appealing to a sense of beauty.

first in its magic—in the marvel of being able to sit at home drinking beer, eating pretzels, and watching movies for free.

As Alfred Hitchcock once said: "The invention of television was like the invention of inside plumbing. It did not essentially change the impulses of the individual. It simply made the accomplishment of the impulse more convenient and comfortable."

I assure you, good taste and critical judgment of the mass audience had nothing whatsoever to do with the encouragement given television. If good taste and critical judgment had ruled, the device would have died aborning.[6] It was simply the magic of the thing.

But again the theatrical movie lost its audience to an alarming degree, and again it was saved from disaster only by the chance uncovering of another magic of its own. That was the fascination of the giant, pseudo-three-dimensional screen, which allowed for the projection of images of a massive and thrilling size. This device quickly captured public enthusiasm, and its felicities were spread through several large-screen techniques of a nature that induced the making of mammoth spectacle films.

So again through mechanical magic the theatrical screen was miraculously saved from what was, by turn, becoming the monotony of TV. But it was notable that only an occasional movie—maybe one out of five—aroused public interest and enthusiasm to the point where it became a hit.

This new aspect in the rotation, this discovery that the incidence of theatrical hits—money-makers—was reduced by the contention of the also myth-projecting TV, caused dismay in the ranks of movie-makers and movie merchants, and they diligently sought to change or spice up the content of movies so as to pull the customers out of their homes.

One such attempt was the costly production of bigger and grander spectacle films—which, of course, were but further penetrations and projections of the platitudes of myth. Another was the exhibition of carefully picked, foreign films which had bold and uncommon dramatic content and were usually laced with surprising discoveries of sex. These brought on stern action by the censors, and this led film importers to bring court actions against statutory restraints. They were successful, and the barriers of censorship were progressively broken down.

In turn, American film makers injected their films with more elements of sex and compelled what we called a liberalization and now virtually an abandonment of their production code. Customers were attracted. A new series of myths about sex was launched. And the redundance of entertainments of this nature was headed toward another rotation of monotony.

As I say, I have dwelled upon this pattern—this cyclical flow of films—because I know this is a fact of movie commerce that no immediately foreseeable changes are likely to break. Right now we are seeing television competing with theatrical films by presenting home viewers with movies of comparatively recent vintage and quality. This is indeed an amazing and amusing irony: the Box making capital of the relics of its older and more eminent peer.

The already evident rejoinder of theatrical film makers is to come out with even bigger, more elaborate, more myth-pushing spectacle films, as,

[6] Died aborning means died during birth.

for instance, an extraordinary line-up of big musicals. Also evident is a move by producers to bring a new magic to the theatrical screen by adapting some of the multi-image techniques that were so sensational in film exhibits at Expo 67.

While in Hollywood recently I was given glimpses of two almost finished films that use uncommon and pictorially dazzling compositions and sequences of many images piled together at the same time within the panel of the large screen. The purpose is to compress information in these quick composites and multiply the intellectual and emotional effects. Other films using these techniques are being started. So perhaps here we go again.

What I wish to make clear by this insistence on the cyclical pattern in the history of films is the significant fact that mechanical innovation more than any essential improvement in dramatic content and social philosophy has accounted for the continuation and apparent progress of the commercial movie in our free society.

Caught between the fundamental cultural pressure of the mass audience for entertainment that is fashioned on myth and the constant demands of a galaxy of theatres for more and more product that they can merchandise, the never too intensely philosophical film makers have been prevented from exercising their skills on precisely true or bravely penetrating dramas. They have been pushed too often in the direction of mediocrity and thus eventual monotony.

This is the case with the great bulk of our movies—and it is this great bulk, of course, which has spread its coating of myth and deception over our willing society. The great majority of our American movies and many of those we have imported from abroad have done nothing more than assist our self-indulgence and support our eternal optimism and complacency.

If any one charge of malfeasance and culturally criminal negligence can be brought against the movies, it is that they have failed to present us and pervade us with realization of our true selves and of the world in which we live.

How much have movies really shown us and told us of the complex nature of the mind and the impulses of man? How much have they informed and enlightened us about the horror and futility of war? How fairly and comprehendingly have they hinted at—much less dramatized—the existence and the monstrous inequities of the race conflict in the United States?

As for the complex nature of the mind and the impulses of man, I would say and repeat that what the movies have given us has been largely a reflection of our comfortable middle-class myths. Man is often cruel and villainous, full of selfishness and greed. But that sort of man invariably gets his comeuppance. The good man—the man for all seasons, or maybe just for the football season—prevails.

I have often criticized too much sex in movies, when it was dragged in for mere sensation's sake. I have never criticized it when I felt the purpose and the achievement was to use it to comprehend and reveal the genuine appetites or hang-ups of characters, as was done in such films as the Swedish *Dear John* and the Anglo-Irish *Ulysses.*

As to the impact of showing sex in movies, or playing around with sex themes, I feel it is better when these things are treated frankly than when they are treated with sly suggestiveness and peek-in-the-bedroom leers. I think the way the affair of the young man and the older woman in *The Graduate* is handled is one of the more honest, mature, and moral details I've ever seen in an American film. Here we jolly well know what is happening, we are made to sense the physical sloppiness of it, and we are led to realize the boredom of the woman and the significant disgust of the young man. I have been greatly heartened by the way a myth is put forth and exposed in *The Graduate*.

My concern about too much sex in movies—too much phony, clumsy, leering sex, that is—is that it is simply artless and tasteless and as gauche[7] as someone using dirty words. It's like kids ogling nudie postcards, a juvenile pastime they have to outgrow. And I'm not too fearful the seeming excess of this in American and foreign films these days is likely to corrupt young people or encourage any further loosening of moral restraint. I suspect it is likely to generate an eventual mass monotony, not toward sex but toward these movies about sex. As Samuel Goldwyn once said, "Sex will outlive all of us."

I asked a moment ago how much our movies have informed us and enlightened us about war. How much have they made us sense war's horror, its degradation, dehumanization, and futility? Look at almost any American war film, from *The Big Parade* back in the silent films, to Frank Sinatra's *Van Ryan's Express,* or *The Dirty Dozen,* or John Wayne's *Green·Berets,* and you'll see a film that may show you the brutality and the gruesome discomfort of war, but you'll see the fellows you're made to root for as heroes, and you'll be led to have a vicarious[8] satisfaction in their triumphs or in their sacrifice, if they are killed.

Outside of a few films such as the French *La Grande Illusion* and Stanley Kubrick's *The Paths of Glory,* which grimly said that war is madness and the forcing of men into it is folly and injustice of the most inhuman sort, the run of war films is aimed at supporting the popular myth that war may be hell but it is one of those things that good fellows just have to do for their country every now and then.

Right now, of course, we are seeing a lot of war pictures on TV, actual news shots of fellows slogging, fighting, and dying in Vietnam. While this is valid information as to the nature and the anguish of that war, and most of it is presented to make us sense how dismal it is, I feel that the endless repetition of these pictures almost every night tends to numb the nerves and weary the emotions and put the constant viewer into a state of apathy.

What's more, the showing of such pictures right there in the Box, alongside cigarette commercials and serial dramas of the most banal sort, reduces them to the shock importance of, let us say, an automobile collision in *Peyton Place* or the heroic suffering and dying of men in *The Bridge on the River Kwai*. Somehow, I fear the illustration of war in Vietnam merges the reality of that sad conflict with the unreality we safely endure in our war-film myths, and we are not quite sure nor care, in some cases, whether we are seeing the fighting in Saigon or the blowing up of the bridge on the River Kwai.

[7] Gauche means awkward or clumsy and, usually, in poor taste.

[8] Vicarious means experienced through imaginative participation in the actions or feelings of others.

In short, our war films of the past have not prepared us for revulsion of the war in Vietnam, revulsion of the sort that many young people and many of us older ones have learned from other sources of enlightenment about war.

Neither have movies shown us, except in a few documentaries of late, and in one or two minor feature pictures, the immensity and the tragedy of the long drama of racial injustice that has been occurring in our midst. I can recall a half dozen or so movies that have forcefully dramatized some of the surface aspects of racial conflict and discrimination in the United States. There was *The Defiant Ones,* some years ago, with Tony Curtis and Sidney Poitier as two chain-gang convicts who have escaped and are shackled together so they have to cooperate, even though filled with mutual hate. There was *Intruder in the Dust,* a splendid picture about a white boy saving an elderly Negro from a threatened lynching in the South. There was *Nothing But a Man,* a moving drama of a young Negro husband who can't get a job.

There have been others, but not many, and certainly not enough to illuminate this most cruel and ironic situation in a free society. Nor enough to make us aware of the many natures and the many problems of Negroes, as we have presumably been made aware of whites.

In this connection, I might say that I am happy about the recognition and success that have come to Sidney Poitier as a fine performer, but I am worried about the stereotype of the strong, valiant, never-failing hero that he is being called upon to play. The man he is in *Guess Who's Coming to Dinner,* and even in *In the Heat of the Night,* is but an extension of the sentimental figure he was in *To Sir, With Love* and *A Patch of Blue.* This is again a calculated adjustment to the prevalence of middle-class myth. This is the standard ideal of the Good Negro. Next they'll have Mr. Poitier playing James Bond.

What this shows is the disposition of the average moviegoer to commit himself, to allow for self-improvement, with the attractive or the romantic type. Commitment to the unattractive, to the antisocial or even the psychotic type, is much more difficult and reluctantly extended by American audiences.

There has been no reluctance whatsoever by millions of people to let themselves become involved with the comical, sentimental, juvenile delinquencies of *Bonnie and Clyde.* Two rollicking, fun-loving youngsters who just happen to rob banks and kill people are allowed to be part of the current myth of liberated and just possibly misguided youth. And when these two people are gunned down by the nasty, sadistic police, it is accepted as a poignant demonstration that crime—no matter how unintended—doesn't pay. The taste for Bonnie and Clyde is one of the strangest manifestations of sentiment I have ever seen.

On the other hand, very few people will commit themselves, not even their minds, to the ugly pair of dark, inexplicable murderers that are represented so accurately and relentlessly in the film *In Cold Blood.* Here is a study and a drama that does show us something of the madness in our world, something of the kinds of dangerous people who are running loose, something of the terrifying weaknesses of our protective systems to prevent. This uncomfortable film shows too clearly the aberrant and animalistic nature of too many human beings. As from some of the films of Ingmar Bergman, people turn away from this one in disgust.

Mention of these two pictures brings up a matter that is startlingly conspicuous of great concern to many of us. That is the excess of violence that has been evident in films, the calculated displays of raw aggression, sadism, hurt, and shock.

Oddly enough, there is an artful minimum of actual graphic show of the committing of violence in *In Cold Blood.* The four mad murders are not literally shown, just the events leading up to their occurrence. Thus the imagination is that much more intensely fired.

But there is plenty of bloody, nauseous violence in the playful *Bonnie and Clyde,* and a hideous amount of gruesome sadism in *The Dirty Dozen,* culminating with a roomful of Nazi officers and their women being bathed in burning gasoline. There is torture in a film called *The Penthouse,* vicious cruelty and killing in one called *Point Blank,* terrorism and hurtful tormenting done by two hoodlums aboard a subway train in a little item called *The Incident,* and nice chunks of extra rare violence in any number of other films.

Why this sudden deluge hit us all of a heap some time ago, and is continuing, is not altogether clear to me. It may be because the film makers are always ready to follow a trend. The old motto in this creative business is, as it is in the dress industry, "If at first you do succeed, you keep on doing it until you fail.'" Well, it may be the trend-following film makers were very much impressed and inspired by the amounts of fantastic, grotesque violence there was in the successful James Bond films, and decided that this sort of stimulation was what the mass audience currently desired.

This is my only explanation for it. And this theory may be supported by other evidences that the public is committing and tolerating other violence in actuality and in myth. Anyhow, the deluge of it in movies, just at this critical time, has been exceedingly unfortunate, to my mind. It is a way of communicating and stimulating violent emotions that has not helped matters in the least.

To be sure, I am not able to prove this, as we never have been able to *prove* that movies alone, or what is in them, primarily inspire behavior patterns and essentially affect our ways of life.

I can only tell you, for instance, that at a showing of *Bonnie and Clyde* in a Broadway theatre, I saw and heard young fellows around me stomping their feet and squealing gleefully when the policemen were shot in the ambush scene and, at the end, when Bonnie and Clyde were mowed down.

Evidently there have been great changes in public values and tolerance of shock in the past few years, and maybe movies have been but reflecting such change. But I wonder whether this is an accurate estimation of the larger public sense of rightness and desirability. I ask whose ox is being gored.

This is a hasty, sketchy survey of what our movie communication is today—that is, in the major, dominant area of the theatrical commercial film. I have not made more than passing mention of minor kinds and uses of films—that is, in the line of documentaries, industrial and educational films.

In these areas, some exceptionally constructive and encouraging things are being done. The device of the motion picture is being employed to make films that shed light, agitate thought, study behavior, and generally educate.

An example of such picture-making is an excellent documentary called *A Time for Burning*. It is a literal, on-the-spot account of the confusions and reactions in the congregation of a Lutheran church in Omaha when the young minister tried to get his white parishioners to associate on a social and parochial[9] level with members of a Negro Lutheran congregation in the same city.

If you haven't seen this picture, you should see it. It is a startling, devastating, and sad revelation of middle-class behavior in the face of this burning issue of integration and humanity in these difficult times.

But I wouldn't be surprised if you haven't seen it, for its producers have had a difficult time getting distribution for it. It was shown briefly in a commercial theatre in New York, and it has been shown on educational television several times, I believe. It was also up for an Oscar, but it didn't win.

This is an example of the limitation of communication by movies of this sort in our free society.

What of the future? What progress or changes are likely for movies in the years ahead?

The most hopeful prospect for advancement, to my way of viewing it, lies in the expanding areas of interest and exhibition of films in the schools and colleges. The great phenomenon we have seen in the past decade of young people discovering cinema, not as we did when we were youngsters—in the front rows of our neighborhood theatres, watching Tom Mix or Humphrey Bogart—but in the theatres showing foreign films that offer kinds of entertainment and attitudes that are considerably different from those of Hollywood.

It is this growth of student interest, begun in the metropolitan universities and areas, and now spreading to colleges, universities, and high schools all over the United States, that has encouraged the opening of film societies and the distribution of special films—new imports, old imports, and American classics—on hundreds of campuses.

Thus a new appreciation of motion pictures and new values are being spread. Film making is being taught in university courses, and an expanding body of student-made films is now finding circulation on the college circuit. The ferment is intense.

My only concern about it is that it may encourage too many students who use cameras the way dilettantes[10] in the past used paint. In a sense, this surge of excitement about moviemaking by students may be but an extension of elementary school show-and-tell. Students may simply be demonstrating their precocity with movie cameras the way we kids used to demonstrate our precocity[11] with hand printing presses and saxophones.

But I guess that's all right. Out of this, some artful and skillful film

---

[9] Here, parochial means "within the parish of the church."

[10] Dilettantes are people who dabble in the arts but do not take them seriously.

[11] Precocity is premature or unusually early development.

makers may emerge. And certainly the appreciation of motion pictures that is being spread is splendid.

Some highly ambitious and esoteric[12] experiments in the usage of films for educating large masses of primitive peoples are being carried on by the National Film Board in Canada. In this sort of thing, and in the possibilities of computer-tape and long-line distribution of education films to school systems all over the country, there are prospects of progress with this medium.

I suspect, too, that the whole system of distributing commercial films in theatres may be radically changed with the ultimate perfection of a system of pay-TV. Feature films in the home—*without commercials* and with higher production qualities—could be the next big move of magic to shake up the inevitable slump into the next phase of monotony.

But this, of course, is likely to bring upon us the burden that has not been fully shed—that is, the burden of control of film content by some statutory agency. The present threat is what is called classification, the idea of judging and grading films as to their suitability for children. And this is but another way to impose the tastes of the middle-class preceptors and their censors on a free society.

I cannot be as brightly optimistic about the overall improvement of movie culture as some persons may be about the press. I know that the big periods of expanding energy in the content of films have come only after great and even calamitous crises in human affairs.

Perhaps we may have to undergo some terrible passage through a valley of social strife, some further upheaval, before we or our children witness an essential change in the culture of films.

And yet I continue to go to movies, to study and indeed enjoy them, even when I may be sitting there steaming at something in them that causes pain.

Perhaps I am like the husband of the lady my wife overheard talking to another lady in a beauty parlor one day. The other lady had asked her friend whether she had seen the film called *God Created Woman,* which was showing just at that time. *God Created Woman,* you may remember, was a sensational French film with Brigitte Bardot, and it was of such a nature that there wasn't any question that its principal character *was* a woman. "No, I haven't seen it," said the lady. "But my husband saw it the other day in New York. And he was shocked by it, absolutely shocked. Indeed, he was not only shocked the first time he saw it, but he was shocked the *second* time, too!"

Well, I'm sure we'll all keep on going to movies, and I daresay we'll keep on being shocked.

■ | **POINTS TO CONSIDER**

1.   What does the author mean by the term "myth"? How have myths (as

[12] Esoteric refers to knowledge that is restricted to a small group of people.

Mr. Crowther uses the word) played an important part in the history of our country? Of what use are such myths? Have we discarded any of our former American Myths in recent years? Why? Have we developed any new ones? What are they?

2. What is the pattern the author has observed in the development of American movies from the beginning to the present? What does he see as having been the chief source of change in this pattern? Do you think that the "movie as event" phenomenon described by Paulene Kael may be a part of this pattern? (See "Marketing the Movies," p. 355.)

3. What does the author say that the movies give us? What does he imply that they *should* give us?

4. What does the author see as the danger of film censorship laws? Do you agree?

5. What does the author think may be the result of "artless and tasteless" sex depicted in movies? Do you agree? What standards do you think should guide the depiction of sex in movies?

6. What important difference does the author point out with respect to violence as presented in *Bonnie and Clyde* and in *In Cold Blood?* What difference does he note in audience acceptance of the two films? What does he believe this comparison tells us about realism and the movie audience?

7. The author believes that sheer commercialism explains the large amount of violence in current movies. Do you agree, or do you think there may be other reasons? If so, what do you think they may be? (See Susan Sontag, "The Imagination of Disaster," p. 370.)

8. Do you agree with the author that television is not really a new medium but just movies reduced in size and shown in the home? Explain. (See Paulene Kael, "Movies on TV," page 390.)

9. From what sources does the author see the greatest hope for the "advancement" of the movies? Do you agree, or do you think change must come from other sources? Explain.

edeye ® **By Gordon Bess**

King Features Syndicate, Inc., 1975.

■ ON SHOOTING FIRST

Thomas H. Middleton   *Saturday Review,* September 25, 1973

A friend who had just read one of these columns was moved to tell me that she was fascinated by the whole spectrum of communication, not only verbal but non-verbal as well. That started one of those nice, rambling conversations that bounce and turn from one thought to another without ever really leaving the subject. We talked about gestures, words, facial expressions, body language, even smells, and we got around to symbols and how people react to them.

The most obvious symbols, we agreed, are flags. In recent years the American flag was thought by many of us to have been captured by the far Right. In fact, there was a film a few years ago called *The President's Analyst* (a very funny picture—the archfiend out to destroy the world turned out to be the telephone company) in which there was a line that went something like, "My neighbors are real Fascists. You know—fly the American flag. That kind of thing."

Lately, ringing reaffirmations by some of the Ervin committee senators of what I like to think of as American principles have made a beginning, in my mind at least, in restoring some of the glory to Old Glory.

The trouble with flags is that they seldon symbolize the highest human ideals of a nation. They take on their greatest emotional power when it's "us against them," especially in a war.

There was a group passing out free American flags to spectators going to the Rose Bowl game a couple years ago. There must have been thousands in that crowd who wouldn't accept them because at that time to wave a flag almost certainly would have been taken as an indication of support for our involvement in Southeast Asia.

Responses to symbols vary. One person might react to the stars on a general's shoulders with awe, another with vague distrust, and another with loathing. Few would react to the *man* without considering the stars. That, I suppose, is one of the reasons for the stars.

From symbols it's only half a shuffle to stereotypes.

It's difficult to escape stereotypes. We need abstractions in order to think effectively, and having abstracted, we often tend to stereotype. "What does the cop on the beat think about gun control?" Right away we're asking for trouble. We've implied that there is such an entity as "the cop on the beat." Having done that, we'll try to tell you what he thinks about gun control; and if we're not careful, we might try to tell you what he thinks about a lot of other things; and before you know it, we'll have gone from the abstract "cop on the beat" to a stereotype.

The important thing to have as a control element somewhere in your mind at all times is the awareness that though you may want to talk about "the cop on the beat," "the Black Panther," or "the military mind," there is no such thing. There are lots of different cops on lots of different beats, lots of different Black Panthers, lots of different military minds.

About a year ago, while I was making up a puzzle,[1] a television set was droning in the background, and a momentarily alert part of my ear picked up a line that brought me up short. I repeated it to myself incredulously and wrote it down on a slip of scratch paper. Wayne Morris evidently had said the line to Paul Fix. I went to the TV section of the paper and learned that the film was *Star of Texas* (1953). The line was, "You can't blame the rancher, Bill. He saw a man he thought looked dangerous, so he shot him."

Recently, while I was working on another puzzle and the Watergate hearings were on the same TV set, I happened across that scrap of paper in my desk drawer. Somehow the line is even more chilling this year than it was last.

The classic Western has been described as a morality play. Talk about stereotypes! The guy in the white hat; the guy in the black hat; the guy who runs the saloon and probably the town, smokes expensive cigars, and is surrounded by a gang of red-eye–drinking gunmen; the good-natured dance-hall girl who will probably get shot saving the hero's life. Most of us were raised on such stereotypes. I'll bet my boots and saddle that Wayne Morris in *Star of Texas* was a hero in the white-hat tradition. The man Wayne Morris's rancher couldn't be blamed for shooting might have looked dangerous because he was wearing a black hat. In the past seven or eight years the black hat has been replaced in real life by the "hippie" look, at least in the minds of many club- and gun- and power-wielding citizens. At the 1968 Democratic convention, you couldn't blame the Chicago police. They saw a lot of kids they thought looked dangerous; so they cracked their heads. At Kent State in 1970, some National Guardsmen saw some kids they thought looked dangerous; so they shot them.

It's a principle that's worked its God-awful mischief on an international scale, too, of course. Millions and millions of people have been killed because other people thought they looked dangerous, started building and displaying stereotypes, and came out waving their symbols and ultimately their weapons.

POINTS TO CONSIDER

1. What is a stereotype? Where does the word come from? What examples does the author cite? Can you think of others?

2. What connections does the author draw between stereotypes and abstractions? Do you agree that we need them to enable us to think about some things? If so, what kinds of things?

3. How are stereotypes different from symbols? What relationship does the author see between the two?

[1] Mr. Middleton makes up the Double-Crostic puzzles for *Saturday Review,* the magazine in which this column appeared.

4. What is the "control" the author talks about with relation to stereotypes? How does it work?

5. What danger does the author see in stereotypes? Do you agree, or do you feel that perhaps he overemphasizes the effects which some current stereotypes have upon people today?

■ TO FIND AN IMAGE/MOVIES AND LIFE AND BLACK PEOPLE

James Murray   *To Find an Image,* 1973

In June 1972 a crowd sat in a large, dark theater on 42nd Street between Seventh and Eighth avenues in New York City. It was three o'clock on a Wednesday afternoon and only about thirty of the four-hundred-odd seats were filled. The audience was mostly men sneaking away from work or the world or simply men with nothing to do. Some had apparently been bored to sleep.

This was movie watching, U.S.A.—a pastime, an escape from reality; ostensibly a way to be entertained. Sleepily or otherwise, all eyes were riveted on the huge screen down front.

About halfway back in the middle section of the main floor, a young mother—a black woman—sat with her two children. The boy, no older than five, squirmed in his seat by her side. She held the infant in her arms. Approximately an hour into a second-run movie called *Halls of Anger,* the baby started crying loudly. As if on cue, the son grabbed his distracted mother's arm and tried to gain her attention by conversing loudly.

Such scenes were not altogether rare at low-admission 42nd Street matinees; still, many in the audience were visibly annoyed and turned in their seats to stare silently and register their displeasure. Why had this black woman come all the way downtown (they assumed she was from Harlem) to a movie house in the middle of the week with her two children? How could she have expected the kids to sit quietly through a three-hour double feature?

Fundamentally, these questions reflect what most observers fail to realize—that movies have become the greatest sociological influence on black people other than their immediate environment. Not only is the search for entertainment a factor in their lives, but movies are also a way for black people to see themselves in relation to society as a whole.

Since the earliest days of motion pictures, Americans have responded enthusiastically to cinema. Never before had a medium—a mass medium—been able so effectively to take its audiences into past and future fantasies, exotic and forbidden locales, suspenseful and exciting intrigues. Generation after generation, spectators have been stumbling out of theaters weakened by incessant laughter, emptied by profuse weeping, inspired, gratified—even relieved—that the right people had once more triumphed over seemingly overwhelming obstacles.

And statistics indicated that black Americans have long enjoyed movies as a popular form of entertainment, spending proportionately more time in front of the big screen than their white counterparts. As could be exemplified by the young black mother, the reasons are numerous and significant.

The downtown theater itself was one stimulus. Away from the neighborhood with its trademarked ugliness and problems, the movie house presented elegant, more often garish and superficial, surroundings where even candy bore prestige prices, and stylish people came and mingled with anyone who could afford the price of admission.

Traditional stage plays, even with their closeness to live performers, were no substitute. Even as television came within reach of even welfare families, films remained a means of escape with more atmosphere for black audiences. They could leave their homes for a few hours and, at the movies, become involved more with the world outside their limited environment than they could anywhere else. The theater beckoned to them to come in and feel free to become involved with whoever starred in whatever story. With lush nightclubs, country clubs, and world excursions far beyond their means, where else could blacks see—if not experience—the American dream?

For years, black audiences identified with heroes in Hollywood films— heroes who were invariably white. Black children playing cowboy in front of tenement buildings wanted to be Alan Ladd, Gary Cooper, and John Wayne. Their fathers dreamed of relationships with Mae West, Marilyn Monroe, and Raquel Welch. Black women envisioned estates with luxurious mansions and scores of servants as the real and finest way to live. And of course there were blatant and obvious manifestations of this yearning to identify with whites. Processed hair styles, bleached blond hair, and the use of skin brighteners were attempts to copy the style, appearance, and mannerisms of screen heroes and heroines.

Possession of these superficial "keys" to a fantasy kingdom made the sight of the real world more jarring. The same old ugliness, inequity, and racism in society were still there, and the combination had a cumulative effect. As the black viewer felt compelled to return to the theater (often alone the second time) to see a particular film or performer, his dependence on film to escape society became even more significant.

From the beginning, filmmakers ignored black audiences as such. For although there were blacks in the earliest major films, they were not cast as heroes or heroines. They were not characters black audiences would relate to, much less identify with and emulate. They were often portrayed humorously, and while some blacks laughed, others were outraged.

A combination of forces brought a change. By the late 1960s, most blacks had given up hope that they would ever be absorbed into a color-blind society, and a phenomenon called "race consciousness" spawned the phrase, "I'm black and proud." The message was simple enough: only frustration resulted from blacks identifying with white heroes. Black America wanted (and was willing to pay for) its own heroes.

Astute businessmen that they were, leaders of the film industry translated some of their more popular (and financially successful) heroes and stories into "blackenized" versions that capitalized on carefully researched changing attitudes, and these also became popular (and financially successful).

The humble servants, happy domestics, and energetic singers and dancers of an earlier generation were no longer in vogue. Instead, proper gentlemen and professionals able to move about in their chosen fields and take care of business became more popular.

Because it proved more profitable, Hollywood allowed its black heroes to take on and (usually) to overwhelm white society. Black private eyes, policemen, cowboys, and even politicians were permitted to win; however, they still reflected a white view of black experience. This development was followed by a series of "relevant" films, supposedly reflecting the new black militancy. These soon merged into a collection of offensive images, with the emphasis on hustlers, charlatans, dope pushers, and numbers runners, whose token swipes at The Man and society did not minimize their crimes against the black people on the screen and those in theater audiences.

This type of movie did not satisfy the black community, and reports from Hollywood and around the country, from inside and outside the industry, indicated the need for an independent black-controlled cinema network. The concern and reaction were not new. Pioneers in the black community had begun to protest decades earlier, after realizing—as would their future counterparts—that if relevant, meaningful films were to be made, they would have to be made by independent black filmmakers.

Besides fulfilling the creative needs of black artists and the entertainment needs of black audiences, the films would be instrumental in reversing years of propaganda from an industry that had managed to exploit black performers and black audiences for fifty years. The proposed effort would also retrieve millions of misused box office dollars and place them at the disposal of talented black filmmakers.

THE FUTURE OF BLACK CINEMA

The first problem of black cinema is survival. When a new black women's magazine appeared several years ago, it was very distinctive due to the picture of a lovely black girl on the cover. The following month there were two other magazines on the stands with cover portraits of black women. By the time of its second issue the new magazine was being challenged.

Black filmmakers are being challenged by white producers and studios who see in the black film a source of easy revenue. The films that the studios employ blacks to produce and direct are no different from exploitation films made by whites. To say that the answer lies with black investors would be to oversimplify. People with enough money to produce a film must be found. These people must choose film investments rather than securities or futures or other proven financial ventures. After a film is produced it must be profitably distributed. Mishandling at any point can completely wipe out profits.

Film producers support distributors who support theater owners, and the process also works in reverse. Each element of the industry supports the others. Independent film producers are forced to buck the whole system. Books from independent black publishers have been refused by bookstores and ignored by critics. Black film producers face the same problem. The future of independent black film companies is therefore uncertain despite the success of Van Peebles or some of the early black filmmakers. Even now, as major black talents emerge, they are largely absorbed into white production companies. It is probable, then, that black films will be an influence and a force within the American cinema rather than a separate entity.

That is not to say there will be no independent black filmmakers. There have been black companies for over fifty years, and some undoubtedly will continue to flourish. But there are already indications that independent companies will not play the largest part in bringing black images to the screen. The companies springing up on both coasts have not yet shown the capacity for sustained productivity. Much of the impetus for these companies comes from the increased amount of trained black personnel.

Thanks to occasional help from the government and opportunities won for them by Belafonte, Poitier, Greaves, Van Peebles, Davis, and others, hundreds of young blacks have been trained in the scores of jobs required to make a feature film. Some are now working for the major studios. Others are supplying the needs of black producers and black production companies.

In other creative areas, there has been progress. John O. Killins, Ossie Davis, Lorraine Hansberry, William Branch, and Lonne Elder are among the blacks who have written feature films.

Blacks have also begun composing music for films. Three-time Academy Award nominee Quincey Jones scored forty films between 1966 and 1971. The music from *Shaft,* by Isaac Hayes, was a spectacular success and earned a gold record within weeks of its release. It sold as a single and as an album. The recorded sound track eventually earned platinum status, signifying two million dollars in sales. Hayes won several awards, including a Grammy and an Academy Award, for his first effort.

Film editor Hugh A. Robertson has made olympic strides. After winning an Academy Award nomination for his work with *Midnight Cowboy,* he moved on to *Shaft,* became a consultant on *Georgia, Georgia,* and then directed his first feature, *Hang Tough!* for M-G-M.

Greaves and Van Peebles are examples of the growing number of black filmmakers who have proved their cinematic ability and won prestigious film honors.

The black film itself has become the subject of serious study. Black film festivals were held at Knoxville College in 1970, at Spelman and Rutgers in 1971, and at the University of Pennsylvania in 1973. They offered the chance to study the old, compare the present, and talk about the future. With intellectual interest in black films, research and writing on the topic is increasing.

Organizations like the Hollywood chapter of the NAACP, and *Soul* are now giving film awards.

The creation of an image is one of the primary objectives of black filmmakers.

It may take five years. It may take longer, but there will come a day when a black man—any black man in the world—will walk into a theater, see himself in a movie, and learn something while being entertained. Something that will stimulate his emotions and increase his pride and self-respect. Something that will generate his concern for his fellow man. Something that will transform that concern into involvement. Something that will identify and communicate blackness, like an Aretha Franklin concert, a Malcolm X speech, a storefront church service, a Don Lee poem, or a young brother with billowing afro.

An image, a symbol, a style, a heritage. Something any black man will look at and about which he will say, "That's me . . . and it's good."

Black Cinema.

POINTS TO CONSIDER

1. What significant sociological influences have movies had upon black Americans? In what ways have these influences been positive and uplifting? In what ways have these influences been negative and degrading?

2. How were blacks usually portrayed in American movies made prior to 1960? Can you think of any exceptions? Cite some specific examples from movies you have seen (perhaps on TV).

3. What changes have occurred in the ways blacks are portrayed in American movies made since the early sixties? Cite some specific examples from movies you have seen. What forces have been responsible for some of these changes?

4. In what ways are some of the portrayals of black people in recent films just as false or negative as the ways they were often portrayed in earlier films? Have you heard the term "blaxploitation films"? What does it mean? Can you think of some recent films that do present positive or honest images of black American?

5. What other groups of Americans, besides blacks, have been portrayed in negative stereotyped ways in American movies? Give some examples from movies you have seen.

6. What black Americans can you name who have contributed to American movies in ways other than acting (as directors, writers, musicians, etc.)? If you can't think of many (or of any), why do you suppose that is?

7. What kinds of further changes must occur before American movies can present a consistently honest image of black Americans to the viewing public?

MARKETING THE MOVIES

Pauline Kael   *The New Yorker,* August 5, 1974

It's becoming tough for a movie that isn't a big media-created event to find
an audience, no matter how good it is. And if a movie has been turned into
an event, it doesn't have to be good; an event—such as "Papillon"—draws
an audience simply because it's an event. You don't expect Mount Rushmore to be a work of art, but if you're anywhere near it you have to go;
"Papillon" is a movie Mount Rushmore, though it features only two heads.
People no longer go to a picture just for itself, and ticket-buyers certainly
aren't looking for the movie equivalent of "a good read." They want to be
battered, to be knocked out—they want to get wrecked. They want what
"everybody's talking about," and even if they don't like the picture—and
some people didn't really care for "A Touch of Class," and some detested
"The Three Musketeers," and many don't like "Blazing Saddles," either—
they don't feel out of it. Increasingly, though, I've noticed that those who
don't enjoy a big event-film feel out of it in another way. They wonder if
there's something they're not getting—if the fault is theirs.

The public can't really be said to have rejected a film like "Payday,"
since the public never heard of it. If you don't know what a movie is and it
plays at a theatre near you, you barely register it. "Payday" may not come
at all; when the event strategy really works, as it has of late, the hits and the
routine action films and horror films are all that get to most towns. And if a
film turns up that hasn't had a big campaign, people assume it's a dog; you
risk associating yourself with failure if you go to see Jon Voight in "Con-
rack" or Blythe Danner in the messed-up but still affecting "Lovin' Molly."
When other values are rickety, the fact that something is selling gives it a
primacy, and its detractors seem like spoilsports. The person who holds out
against an event looks a loser: the minority is a fool. People are cynical
about advertising, of course, but their cynicism is so all-inclusive now that
they're indifferent, and so they're more susceptible to advertising than ever.
If nothing matters anyway, why not just go where the crowd goes? That's a
high in itself.

There are a few exceptions, but in general it can be said that the public
no longer discovers movies, the public no longer makes a picture a hit. If
the advertising for a movie doesn't build up an overwhelming desire to be
part of the event, people just don't go. They don't listen to their own instincts, they don't listen to the critics—they listen to the advertising. Or, to
put it more precisely, they do listen to their instincts, but their instincts are
now controlled by advertising. It seeps through everything—talk shows,
game shows, magazine and newspaper stories. Museums organize retro-
spectives of a movie director's work to coordinate with the opening of his
latest film, and publish monographs paid for by the movie companies. College editors travel at a movie company's expense to see its big new film and
to meet the director, and directors preview their new pictures at colleges.
The public-relations event becomes part of the national consciousness.
You don't hear anybody say, "I saw the most wonderful movie you never

heard of"; when you hear people talking, it's about the same blasted movie that everybody's going to—the one that's flooding the media. Yet even the worst cynics still like to think that "word of mouth" makes hits. And the executives who set up the machinery of manipulation love to believe that the public—the public that's sitting stone-dead in front of its TV sets— spontaneously discovered their wonderful movie. If it's a winner, they say it's the people's choice. But, in the TV age, when people say they're going to see "Walking Tall" because they've "heard" it's terrific, that rarely means a friend has told them; it means they've picked up signals from the atmosphere. It means "Walking Tall" has been plugged so much that every cell in a person's body tells him he's got to see it. Nobody ever says that it was the advertising that made him vote for a particular candidate, yet there is considerable evidence that in recent decades the Presidential candidates who spent the most money always won. They were the people's choice. Advertising is a form of psychological warfare that in popular culture, as in politics, is becoming harder to fight with aboveboard weapons. It's becoming damned near invincible.

The ludicrous "Mame" or the limp, benumbed "The Great Gatsby" may not make as much money as the producing companies hoped for, but these pictures don't fail abjectly, either. They're hits. If Hollywood executives still believe in word of mouth, it's because the words came out of their own mouths.

The businessmen have always been in control of film production; now advertising puts these, finally, on top of public reaction as well. They can transcend the content and the quality of a film by advertising. The new blatancy represents the triumph—for the moment, at least—of the businessmen's taste and the businessmen's ethic. Traditionally, movies were thought linked to dreams and illusions, and to pleasures that went way beyond satisfaction. Now the big ones are stridently illusionless, for a public determined not to be taken in. Audiences have become "realists" in the manner of businessmen who congratulate themselves for being realists: they believe only in what gives immediate gratification. It's got to be right there—tangible, direct, basic, in their laps. The movie executives were shaken for a few years; they didn't understand what made a film a counter-culture hit. They're happy to be back on firm ground with "The Sting." Harmless, inoffensive. Plenty of plot but no meanings. Not even any sex to worry about.

If the company men don't like a picture, or are nervous about its chances, or just resent the director's wanting to do something he cares about (instead of taking the big assignments they believe in), they do minimal advertising, tell him, "Let's wait for the reviews," or "We'll see how the reviewers like it," and then, even if the reviews are great, they say, "But the picture isn't doing business. Why should we throw away money on it?" And if he mentions the reviews, they say, "Listen, the critics have never meant anything. You know that. Why waste money? If people don't want to go, you can't force them to buy tickets."

A reviewer who pans a producer's picture is just one more person telling him he has no taste. When the reviewers praise movies that are allowed to die, the moneyman's brute instincts are confirmed, and the reviewers' impotence gives him joy. "Why must we sit back and allow the critics to determine if a film is acceptable as a consumer product?" Frank Yablans, the president of Paramount, asked this June. He was speaking to some two hundred people who work in television, explaining to them that word of mouth, which can defeat downbeat reviews, will be Paramount's target. A reviewer speaks out once, or maybe twice. The advertisers are an invisible force pounding at the public day after day. Unfavorable reviews are almost never powerful enough to undo the saturation publicity. Besides, curiosity about an event like "The Exorcist" is a big factor; as the woman quoted in *Variety* said, "I want to see what everybody is throwing up about."

■ POINTS TO CONSIDER

1. What does the author mean by a movie that is an "event"? How is the event created?

2. According to the author, why do people go to movies these days? Do you agree? Why did you go to the particular movie which you saw most recently?

3. Why, according to the author, are people more susceptible to advertising than ever? Do you agree? Explain.

4. Who, according to the author, controls film production? How does this control affect the kinds of movies we are given? Why?

5. What is the role of the movie critic in a movie's journey to success or oblivion? How can an unfavorable reveiw help a movie to become a hit?

6. Explain "word of mouth" advertising and reviewing. What importance does the author feel that word of mouth has these days on the success or failure of a particular movie? Judging from you own experience, would you agree or disagree? Why?

THE EXORCIST: REVIEWS AND OPINIONS

◼ THE EXORCIST

Stanley Kauffmann   *The New Republic,* February 9, 1974

I dragged my feet about going to *The Exorcist* because of the gimmicky subject, and the adverse reviews I saw made me purr at my prevision. But this film about the diabolic possession of a 12-year-old girl has become such a huge hit that I thought I ought to grit what's left of my teeth and investigate. I'm glad I did. In this case, anyway, *vox populi vox diaboli.*

This is the most scary picture I've seen in years—the *only* scary picture I've seen in years. (Though I admit I don't see many "horror" films. Too unhorrible.) I haven't been more scared by a film since Mary Philbin snatched the mask off Lon Chaney's face in *The Phantom of the Opera* in 1925. The reference to childhood is particularly apt because the point of *The Exorcist* is to cut through everything we've learned and cultivated, to get down to the talent for fright that we are virtually born with. I haven't felt so much like Robert Warshow's "man watching a movie," his *homme moyen,* since the same director, William Friedkin, did it the last time with his (quite different) *French Connection.*

Friedkin seems to have found his forte. He started serious *(The Birthday Party, The Boys in the Band),* but there he seemed strained, and obtrusive—like a tumbler in a ballet. Evidently what he needed was material where nothing mattered but the effects. *The French Connection* showed he had real gifts for gut punching; *The Exorcist* shows his gifts for chilling the spine. This new picture starts slowly: there's a lot of background material to be laid out and some of it is lingered on excessively; but when Friedkin centers on his main material—the possessed child in modern Washington, DC—he handles it with very exceptional skill. The cutting, the lighting, the sound track and, above all, the special effects have been ordered up carefully by the director and used precisely. Even the music is faultless—most of it by Krzysztof Penderecki, who at last is where he belongs. During most horror pictures that I see, I keep watching how it's done and waiting for it to be over. Here the directorial hand is quicker than the eye; and ear. Here I got frights and the pleasure of unmediated visceral response. Disbelief was canted, if not suspended, so that I could watch the story play out. And virtually all of this was Friedkin's doing.

William Peter Blatty wrote the screenplay, from his own best-seller, and produced the film. I haven't read the book and certainly won't now—I've *had* these jolts—but in the film script, anyway, there are some matters left unfinished. A prophecy that the possessed child makes about an astronaut: does it come true? What about the Washington detective (Lee J. Cobb)? Did he just quit investigating the case? The specific occasion for the satanic invasion is only vaguely hinted at, and then only at the end. It has something to do with a small silver religious medal that an archaeologist-priest dug up in Iraq; but how it got to this Georgetown house is never told us. If I'm putting this together right, then a point of irony was muffed: because one of the exorcising priests is himself the archaeologist who dug up that medal.

The theme of possession is an old reliable: it's the basis of a chief work in the Yiddish theater, Anski's *The Dybbuk*. The idea of the doom-haunted object has worked for dozens of minor writers, including Lord Dunsany and W. W. Jacobs. Blatty has blended the two elements in this story of a film actress (Ellen Burstyn) and her 12-year-old daughter (Linda Blair) living in a rented Georgetown house during the shooting of a picture in Washington. First, the house itself begins to act strangely—inexplicable noises, a shaking bed. Then the child begins to act strangely. Conventional medical procedures are explored; no help. Doctors themselves suggest exorcism. A psychiatrist priest is called (Jason Miller, the actor who is also the author of *That Championship Season*), and eventually an older priest who knows exorcism well (Max von Sydow). One reason I could go along with all this is that I know such things happen: a few years ago a rabbi told me he had recently been called on to perform an exorcism. Anyway, the ending of *this* exorcism is meant to provide a touch of Christian martyrdom, but this really doesn't carry much weight. The ending is a way out of the plot, that's all, and the plot is all that matters in this supernatural melodrama.

The moralistic critics—who invariably object when they happen not to like a current *instance* of horror or violence, although they may have been caroling the week before about Clint Eastwood or Hitchcock—bemoan the fact that a child is called upon to mouth some obscenities, pretty foul ones, and to perform an obscene-profane action (shoving a crucifix up herself). I don't see how the child's satanic possession could have been shown by having her exclaim "Darn!" and by breaking Mom's favorite vase. And in a world where 5-year-olds in TV commercials parrot stuff about detergents and cereals, with no point at all except selling goods, I'm not upset at Linda Blair's taking part in what she knew was a fiction. As for the horrors, the only time I had to avert my eyes was not for a demonic scene but for a "straight" scene in a hospital where doctors inserted long needles in the girl's neck in preparation for x-rays.

The Exorcist makes no sense. For instance, why couldn't the devil have done earlier what he does right at the end? It makes no more sense than a musical, has no more ambition toward sense than a musical. In both cases we accept the non-sense for the sake of entertainment. The theater where I saw *The Exorcist* was crowded with people being entertained by horror; they giggled after most of the possession scenes (*after,* not during), a sure sign that they had been shaken and had to right themselves. If you want to be shaken—and I found out, while the picture was going on, that that's what I wanted—then *The Exorcist* will scare the hell out of you.

POSTSCRIPT. To avoid spoiling the shock, I didn't mention that Linda Blair's voice was dubbed in the possessed scenes; I equivocated by saying that she "mouthed" obscenities. While the review was on press, publicity told us that Mercedes McCambridge was the voice of Satan. Devilish good, too.

FILMS

Robert Hatch

The Nation, February 2, 1974

I had planned to skip *The Exorcist,* since it seemed to me that a case of Satanic possession, alleged to have occurred recently in Washington's high-style Georgetown, raised a problem I could do without at this point in time. However, the film has become a national Yo-Yo craze: at the moment, it is showing in four of New York's first-run houses, with crowds two and three blocks long lining up patiently in the bitter weather; and people have been appearing on national TV news programs to boast that they fainted, vomited or otherwise disported themselves in the course of the devilish proceedings. It looks as though the very expensive picture ($10 million is the figure being bandied about) will be one of the industry's top grossers, and I decided I had better have a look.

The fact is that *The Exorcist,* made from William Peter Blatty's sub-literary bestseller of a few months ago (and now produced by him for the screen) is an exceedingly well-made bad picture. It invokes snobbish admiration of people rich enough to own a Mercedes and a butler, it denigrates medicine and psychiatry, it involves the Catholic Church in mumbo jumbo and, by grotesque make-up and camera trickery that is both slick and obvious, it turns a 12-year-old girl into a spectacle of loathsome ugliness for the sole purpose of mindless entertainment. It should be scorned, and when it opened every critic I read did indeed scorn it.

There remains the question of the audience. The film's thesis is that, when a person's body is invaded by the Devil, science is helpless to deal with the situation. Very likely. The person so seized is endowed with super-human powers, being able to speak in a multitude of voices and a variety of tongues; to read minds; to crack walls, hurl furniture and desecrate holy images by extra-physical means; to levitate and to rotate his or her head in a full circle (this last attribute, of which I'd read in the annals of demonology but never hoped to witness, does produce a stunning effect; it evoked by far the strongest audience response, far exceeding that produced by the Old One's disposition to regurgitate a viscous green plastic and recite the obscenities of the day). Meanwhile, the body of the victim becomes covered with sores, scabs and lacerations and her face is transformed into a mask of diabolical (naturally) hatred. However, if you examine her belly, you will find there a row of welts, pathetically spelling out the message, "Help me!"

In a situation like that what you want is a couple of intrepid priests who, armed with Bibles, vestments and holy water, will engage the Devil in mortal combat. For the Georgetown exorcism, the witch doctors chosen by the Church authorities are a stylish pair: one of them (Max von Sydow) is an elderly archaeologist with a bad heart who specializes in digging up the pre-Christian cities of the Near East, and who has found there disturbing evidence of ancient black magic; the other (Jason Miller) is a former prize fighter, whose faith in the Almighty has been unsettled by graduate study in psychiatry at "Harvard, Johns Hopkins and other places like that." These two selfless clerics lay down their lives to purge little Regan (Linda Blair) of her terrible intruder. The Devil takes lodgings in the younger priest, who instantly defenestrates.[1] Where the archfiend goes then is not stated, but I assume that, like Professor Moriarty, he will show up for the sequel.

If there had been movies 500 years ago, I can imagine that *The Exorcist* would have made an impression on the public that might have gratified Savonarola. But in some ways we do advance; very few people today believe in a fiery Hell down a hole halfway between Chicago and New Delhi, and the number who think that the Devil will jump down the throats of little girls would not crowd a closet, let alone a theatre. So why is the nation submitting itself to this exercise in unpleasant flummery? Seated behind me in the audience was a gaggle of high-school girls who began to scream the moment the lights went down and one or another of whom announced that she was about to faint at intervals thereafter. This, obviously, was the roller-coaster reaction—you can always find people, usually young and addicted to popcorn, who enjoy being scared out of their wits and are willing to pay for the privilege. But there have been other roller coasters on the screen recently and, though most of them have done well, they have not caused stampedes.

Part of the answer to the puzzle is that supernatural phenomena have been enjoying a vogue for the past ten years or so. We are the cheated descendants of the Enlightenment, susceptible to the suggestion that reason is a weak reed. ESP enjoys respectability, youthful messiahs from the Mysterious East do a brisk business in moral placebos and only a few weeks ago a fellow from Central Europe was astounding otherwise sober Londoners by his ability to bend keys, break jewelry and perform similar useful services by the power of thought alone. Science has taught us almost everything we need to know, except how to be virtuous and happy. Thus we are moved to hobnob with the supernatural again, and of course if you call upon God when you're in a tight fix, you must reckon with getting the Devil instead. Every gamble involves a risk.

Aside from that, we are surrounded today by wickedness of a miserably savorless kind. The decline in the standards of civic virtue (which is by no means an exclusively American trend) is both frightening and boring; your contemporary liar and cheat is devoid of both style and imagination. It may be a relief, then, to indulge in the fantasy that supreme evil—melodramatic, endlessly shocking, utterly without cause and subject to no natural defense—can be encountered in enviably luxurious surroundings. We may scream and faint to our heart's content, and are not called upon to do more, because the Devil is both invincible and nonexistent.

Finally, the new tolerance of explicit sexuality has given scope to a kind of perverse violence for which there seems to be a considerable appetite. It used to be said that, if the censors would let up on sex, sadism would fade from the screen. Instead, we have been getting ever larger doses of sadism, combined with overt or covert sex, which is what that game is really about.

There is no overt sex (bar the verbal clichés) in *The Exorcist,* but it is nevertheless a highly erotic film of a markedly degrading sort. Imagine that great hairy Devil right inside the body of that nice young girl, making her

---

[1] Defenestrates is a fancy way of saying the priest jumps out a window.

bed bounce, stimulating her to throw herself around in agonized frenzy, to kick a well-meaning psychiatrist in the groin, to bloody herself with a crucifix, to stick out her tongue in lubricious [2] contortions and utter all manner of unclean epithets in a rasping male voice. Sex, as anyone could have foretold, turns out to be a poor spectator sport (voyeurism is the most pathetic of manias) and the film makers must ring ever more extreme changes on it to keep the subject lively. So now we are given this twaddle about possession, and a predominantly youthful public flocks to the theatres to squeal and squirm. It takes more than an ounce of civet, these days, to sweeten the imagination.

[2] Lubricious means lewd. Epithet, as it is used here, means a term of abuse or contempt.

◼ "THE EXORCIST" AND ITS AUDIENCE

William S. Pechter   *Commentary*, March 1974

Though I saw *The Exorcist* before it opened, I saw it with an audience which filled a large theater, and I was aware while the film was being shown of sharing in a rare experience: the experience of seeing a film which has its audience reacting as one, completely in the palm of its hand. When the lights came up after the showing, I felt that the film I'd just seen was not only a film but an event, and that it was about to become one of the biggest popular successes in movie history (in fact, it is on its way to becoming *the* single largest grossing film of all time). The last time I had such a feeling was when I saw *The Godfather* (which also broke all previous commercial records), and indeed, it is tempting to describe *The Exorcist* as the *Godfather* of horror films: a work aspiring to be the ultimate creation in a given genre,[1] to surpass all others through its greater naturalism, and through its being more lavishly mounted and elaborately detailed. Actually, *The Exorcist* is much less good than *The Godfather*, without the earlier film's room for its actors or its narrative flair. But these faults, which would have crippled *The Godfather*, are much less detrimental to the essentially mechanistic character of the horror film, and in some ways (for instance, in the somewhat cryptic quality imparted to the film by its narrative lacunae and by its director's fragmented style) even contribute to *The Exorcist*'s effect.[2] For, much more than *The Godfather*, *The Exorcist* aims for a single, if perhaps not simple, effect: to frighten. Its "success" can be directly measured by its ability to induce fear.

Unlike *The Godfather*, *The Exorcist* has been getting a bad press, but I

[1] A genre is a class or category, usually used in connection with works of art.
[2] Cryptic means puzzling. Lacunae are gaps.

have yet to see a review in which it was indicated whether or not the film was actually found frightening by the writer. Rather, as in the case of the first critical coverage of porno movies, there is much worrying about the appeal to and effect on those others who constitute the film's audience, and a tone which remains oddly impersonal, whether hectoringly moralistic or nonchalantly flippant. My own opinion of *The Exorcist* happens to be somewhat higher than that of most other reviewers, though, were I to be asked how good it is, I could provide a fairly evenly balanced inventory of its virtues and defects. But if I were asked whether or not I found the film frightening, my answer would be: yes, extremely. My responses in this were no different from what I sensed to be the audience's. Like those other spectators, I sat there in an essentially defenseless state, and allowed myself to be worked on by the film; I watched *The Exorcist* and was gripped by fear. . . .

The Exorcist is about an exorcism which succeeds. But is it? To take it as this leaves too much out of account, most immediately the peculiarly muffled ("ambiguous" would be too high-flown a word) quality of its apparently triumphant ending. For if this is a victory over the devil, what kind of victory is it whose site is littered by the corpses of two priests, and whose beneficiary is an ordinary young girl at best unchanged by the experience she's been through? The "positive" reading of the film also fails to answer a question which might not be a legitimate one to ask of life (where criteria other than rationality may obtain), but is, I think, appropriately asked of *The Exorcist,* a work of art, or artifact, of someone's conscious devising. That question is "Why?"—why is this little girl the one possessed? Psychological indicators scarcely suffice—the girl's home, though broken by divorce and liberated in its language and mores, is hardly depicted as an example of *dolce-vita* decadence; indeed, the movie star is a loving and attentive mother. In any case, the film makes it unmistakably clear that the girl isn't just mentally disturbed, she *is* possessed.

I think that to ask the question, Why this girl?, in light of the film's muffled ending is to find the answer: the girl is a vessel, the devil's route to the priest, a priest wracked by guilt who at one point declares he's afraid he's losing his faith, and whose final attempt to take on the devil in individual combat might be seen as a surrender to pride as much as an instance of heroism. In seeing the film this way, a vital link is clearly provided by a dream the younger priest has before his involvement with the possessed girl, in which one of the diabolic artifacts unearthed at the archaeological excavation makes an otherwise inexplicable appearance.

Indeed, the very title of the work hints that it is one in which appearances will be deceiving, for it leads us to believe, from the way the older priest is introduced and reappears, that the titular exorcist will be he. But, in fact, the exorcist proves to be the younger priest. Given that, like the older priest, he dies, and, further, that he dies by suicide (at a time when he may already, for reasons of his own, be drawn to self-destruction), can one say that the film is about a possession which fails? For, whatever theological fine points may be involved, the destruction of the priests, and, above all, the act of suicide do seem to carry a kind of unequivocality. And here the film, which has been criticized for occasionally being softer than the novel (which I've since read), is harder: in the film, unlike the novel, the priest's life isn't prolonged so that he may be given the last rites of confession and absolution. He does remain alive long enough to press the hand of another priest who rushes to his battered body in an attempt to aid him. But since the dying priest may still be possessed (for surely the devil can't have been outrun by the mere speed of a leap from a window), this last fraternal gesture (toward a "worldly" priest, whom we've previously seen in the actress's social circle) is itself profoundly equivocal. Is the gesture of fraternity being extended by the dying priest, or by the devil?

Whether the film's audience consciously apprehends any of this in its experience of the work I don't know, but what that audience is nevertheless being given is, I think, a depiction of the rule of the devil, or of evil, or of chaos in this world, a celebration of the power of these things—by whatever name one calls them—to work their will. To say this is not to imply that the film's audiences are mere empty vessels into which such content is being poured, or celebrants at some sort of new Black Mass; it would be presumptuous in the extreme to assume that the film's image of the world is being granted those audiences' uncritical belief.

But in one particular, the film's image of the world *is* given an exceptionally striking credibility, and that is in the privacy and domesticity of its horrors: the sense of their existing, like skeletons in closets, unknown to anyone but a few principals behind the façades of pleasant houses on pleasant streets (not to say in the substantial Georgetown residences we associate with the pillars of society). And though it would be presumptuous to posit any too simple a relation between *The Exorcist* and its audience, it would be equally presumptuous to dismiss the film as no more than another horror film with a new gimmick, though, considered artistically, this is all it may be. After all, there have been films as sensationally horrific and as frightening as *The Exorcist* before. But a film doesn't achieve *The Exorcist's* phenomenal success without striking some responsive chord in its audience; and such success usually has less to do with shaping an audience's beliefs than with affirming what an audience believes already. And so this film, heading for its unique position among others, paints its picture of a world of hidden horrors, a malevolent world beyond our comprehension and control. One might err in making too much of *The Exorcist* just as in making too little of it, but nothing would be more presumptuous, I think, than to conclude that those people turning out in record numbers to see it are merely experiencing the thrills of a novel horror movie: to assume, because we cannot know exactly what they are feeling and believing, that they are feeling nothing, believing nothing.

A PSYCHOANALYST'S INDICTMENT OF "THE EXORCIST"

Ralph R. Greenson, M.D.　　　　　　　*Saturday Review*, June 15, 1974

The Exorcist is a menace, the most shocking major movie I have ever seen. Never before have I witnessed such a flagrant combination of perverse sex, brutal violence, and abused religion. In addition, the film degrades the medical profession and psychiatry. At the showing I went to, the unruly audience giggled, talked, and yelled throughout. As well they might: Although the picture is not X-rated, it is so pornographic that it makes *Last Tango in Paris* seem like a Strauss waltz.

Above all, I resent the way in which the movie depicts a twelve-year-old child who causes three deaths, inflicts untold suffering on everyone near and dear to her, and who, during seizures, shamelessly goes in for bloody masturbation with a crucifix—this, among other sexual perversities. Throughout, Regan, the afflicted child, is represented as being merely a poor innocent victim of demonic possession. The devil made me do it—that is the total explanation the film offers. Regan is not only quite innocent, says the movie, but also is burdened by no consequences of the experience—no memories, no scars, no inner conflict. It is significant that you never see or hear Regan struggle against the devil who possesses her.

The Exorcist is supposed to be based on a true instance of modern-day possession, but I wonder about that. Like most psychiatrists, I have seen patients with one or another of the hair-raising symptoms that plague Regan, but I have never encountered, or even heard of, any single patient bristling with all the bizarre, morbid symptoms the girl in the movie exhibits. It is my conviction that *The Exorcist* was contrived to appeal to a wide audience, to attract and scare the wits out of troubled and disoriented people—by appealing to their voyeuristic impulses, their sadism, and their masochism.[1] It also tries to titillate these unfortunates by making their panic-fears sexually exciting. Those in the audience who do *not* quake and shiver may well be experiencing a "counterphobic reaction"—a kind of chest-pounding pride in their ability to absorb all this shocking stuff without blinking an eye or turning a hair. And the women-haters among them will certainly applaud the film's shameless degradation of women's sexuality.

Am I putting the case too strongly? I think not. Just consider the movie's plot: Regan, a cheerful, healthy twelve-year-old girl, the only child of a divorced actress, gradually develops bizarre symptoms during sleep—symptoms alien to her character when she is awake. Strange knocking sounds fill her bedroom, her bed rises into the air, and she shouts profanities and blasphemies in a heavy masculine voice. As the illness progresses Regan develops coarse, masculine, waxy facial features, a black hairy tongue, and physical strength so prodigious that she has to be tied down in

---

[1] Voyeuristic pertains to pleasure derived from watching others secretly. Sadism is pleasure derived from causing pain; masochism is pleasure derived from being hurt or abused. All three of these terms are frequently applied to sexual practices.

bed. All medical and psychiatric attempts at diagnosis and treatment fail pitifully, and the frantic mother finally persuades a priest with psychiatric training to call in an old priest experienced in exorcism. The old man dies of a heart attack during the exorcism rite. In desperation, the younger priest takes over the exorcist's role, takes Regan's demon into himself, and kills both himself and the devil by plunging out the window of the girl's upper-story bedroom.

Now, all these improbable, hyperthyroid goings-on are dynamite at the box office, but I soon learned that the film's effect on some people is devastating. Several months ago I received a hysterical phone call from an intelligent, stable, young social worker whom I had known professionally for six years. She was in a state of utter panic and begged me to see her immediately. I saw her at my home, where she told me, shivering with fright, that her husband had persuaded her to see *The Exorcist* the evening before. Almost from the moment she left the theater, she had experienced a return of intense fears and phobias she could only dimly recall from her early childhood. She was afraid to be alone in a room even if her husband was elsewhere in the house, afraid to be in the dark, afraid to leave the house, and so on. It was easy for me to show her that the movie had remobilized her fears of God's punishment carried out by the Devil, with which her parents had threatened her in her early childhood. This insight was partially helpful, and after a few visits I arranged to send her to a colleague for further psychotherapy.

A week later, I received another emergency call, this one from a brilliant young university professor who had to see me "in order to let the devils inside me come out." He chose me because he felt I would not be killed by his devils. I had to see him three times in one day to allow him to rave, rant, cry, stamp his feet, bang his fists, until he became exhausted. At the end of the third visit, when he was relatively coherent, he told me that he had long felt he had an evil, psychotic core but that *The Exorcist* had convinced him that this core was the Devil himself. I also arranged for him to have further therapy. Both he and the young social worker, seemingly much improved, are still undergoing treatment.

Naturally, these closely related emergency cases caused alarm bells to ring in my mind. Asking around among colleagues of mine—men with impeccable institutional bona fides [2]—I found that all of them had also recently treated patients who had suffered disruption, "freaking out," or other psychotic episodes after seeing *The Exorcist*.

Inquiring further, I learned that acute neurotic and psychotic reactions to this picture were common right across the country. One survey reported an average of six men fainting and six women vomiting at every showing. An editorial in the *Journal of the American Medical Association* said, "*The Exorcist* is heady stuff. Men and women, having seen it or part of it, leave because they cannot tolerate it; they faint, they vomit, they are consulting physicians in the belief that they or their children are 'possessed.'"

This is not to say, of course, that *everyone* who sees the film will be harmed. People who are psychologically healthy will be untouched, disgusted, or even slightly amused by the lurid plot. But for people whose emotional equilibrium is unstable, the story may be quite different. The

---

[2] "Bona fides" in this case are professional qualifications.

young social worker mentioned above had, on seeing the picture, regressed back to childhood and was reliving fears she had experienced when she was four or five years old. In all, it is safe to say that the picture may well prove harmful to anyone whose emotional and mental balance is precarious.[3]

If there are devils outside us, they cannot be used to explain away our wrongdoings. We must come to realize that the fault is with our own *inner* devils: our passion for money and possessions, our frantic search for easy solutions, instant bliss, or oblivion, which pass for peace of mind. Add to this list our general apathy, which we disguise by giving out tokens of charity and kindness as long as they don't make us uncomfortable. These are some of the personal sources of our inner unease and discontent.

What all this means in practical terms is that we must set limits to permissiveness and to "social" explanations of personal misconduct. Further, we must all assume some responsibility for the horrors of our world today, from Bangladesh, Vietnam, Watergate, to the famine in India. We have to accept the fact that we are all part of the brotherhood of man, whether we like it or not. We can and must do more to help our fellow man. Otherwise, we will become not just a sick society, but worse—a morally corrupt one.

It is against this background that *The Exorcist* is a menace to the mental health of our community. It should be X-rated. (I have seen parents taking four- and five-year-old children to showings of the picture!) In these unstable times, when the President of the United States shows more concern for Lt. Calley than for the students murdered at Kent State, when we have peace with dishonor in Vietnam, and also Watergate, *The Exorcist* pours acid on our already corroded values and ideals. In the days when we all had more trust in our government, our friends, and ourselves, *The Exorcist* would have been a bad joke. Today it is a danger.

[3] Precarious means chancy or unstable.

■ IN ANSWER TO DR. GREENSON

Hollis Alpert   *Saturday Review*, June 15, 1974

The Exorcist, now in the sixth month of its phenomenal run, has been viewed by some fifteen million Americans, and will probably play for some fifteen million more before it heads for television (edited, naturally) and another seventy or eighty million viewers. Dr. Greenson's diatribe[1] and warning comes too late. The damage, if it is that, has been done and will go on. Early in the run there were, indeed, reports of fainting and vomiting in theaters, along with some hysterical reactions that came to the attention of

[1] A diatribe is a denunciation, a bitter criticism.

priests and psychiatrists, who were quick to inform the media of cases of so-called demonic possession. Curiously, though, the above reactions became rarer the more the popularity of the film widened.

Dr. Greenson perhaps came late to the movie, for he mentions that the audience he saw it with giggled, talked, even yelled during the performance. This has, of course, happened with a good many films besides *The Exorcist.* For instance, when I saw *The French Connection* the first time, the audience was merely quiet and appreciative. When I saw it again at a Manhattan neighborhood theater, there was a lot of yelling and encouragement to those being pursued by the cops.

There are a lot of factors that go into what the more peaceable among us may regard as excessive reactions to something fictional taking place on the screen. They might have to do with something going on in the body politic (though I doubt that anyone is responding to *The Exorcist* because of the Watergate affair, as Dr. Greenson indicates), but I'm afraid it would take a Ford Foundation grant and a team of researchers to come up with any authentic rationale. But one kind of excessive reaction is certainly that of Dr. Greenson, who built a couple of hysterical cases into a national attack of the jitters.

I have a few respected psychiatrists and psychoanalysts among my acquaintances, and, checking with them, I found none who reported any of his patients disturbed by *The Exorcist.* One did mention a patient who saw the movie and became nauseated. Warner Bros., the firm responsible for the film, has a policy of honesty with the media about the effects of the film on audiences. Yes, there were some cases of nausea in theaters during the first several weeks of the film's run. In fact, one Warners publicist reported to me with glee that during the film's first Hollywood preview, no fewer than three ladies fainted. That kind of thing, this publicist well knew, means big box office. But no one at Warners knows of any survey showing the extent of vomiting and fainting claimed by Dr. Greenson.

The theaters first chosen to show the film were what are known as prestige houses, and they attracted a relatively polite patronage. Then the film caught on with young people. It moved into areas where the patrons were working-class people and ghetto residents. With this audience-composition change, with the larger cross-section of film-goers (many of whom rarely attend films), audience reactions tended to be less polite. The owner of the Paris Theater, a nice little movie house next to the posh Plaza Hotel, was glad to see the long lines for *The Exorcist* constantly extending around the block, but he wasn't too happy about what was happening inside. "They're making a mess of the theater," he complained. But when he plays a sensitive foreign film, the lines are much shorter, the theater is less strewn with candy wrappers and cigarette butts, and there is less damage to the seats.

The thing is, *The Exorcist* became a sensation and a fad. A few of the more suggestible heard about the fainting and the vomiting (much played up by television talk shows) and promptly fainted and vomited. Whatever the excesses of the film itself may be, they are mild stuff compared with some of the horror-and-violence flicks that are current fare in thousands of our movie houses. Then, too, millions had already read *The Exorcist* in its hardcover and paperback versions; they were well prepared for what takes place on the screen. Not much danger to them, for they got what they had already expected.

But Dr. Greenson does make the charge that the film is pornographic. Apparently, he did not do some simple research, such as looking up the meaning of *pornography* in the dictionary. Few of the censorial-minded do, I've found. My dictionary defines *pornography* as follows: "(1) originally, a description of prostitutes and their trade: hence, (2) writing, pictures, etc., intended to arouse sexual desire." I saw no prostitutes in the film, and I know of no one whose sexual desires were aroused by it. Sorry, but it doesn't qualify as pornography.

However, if you do watch carefully, you might be able to infer that poor little Regan is going in for some bloody masturbation with a crucifix. The same scene was in the book, so book readers knew what was happening, and, as has already been mentioned, millions of others already knew in advance of seeing the picture. The film, by the way, was made with the advice, counsel, and cooperation of some members of the Jesuit priesthood, and little objection to the scene has come from that quarter. The Catholic Film Office rated the picture "A-4," which means suitable for adults with reservations. They didn't specify the reservations, and that rating probably also helps account for the lack of an "X" for the picture. If the Catholics, who are inclined to disfavor films with erotic implications, saw no eroticism in the film, then there couldn't have been very much of it. But why blood on the crucifix? Well, William Friedkin, the director, a stickler for detail, realized Regan had to be a virgin. Ergo, the blood. Maybe he should have fudged it. Dr. Greenson mentions "other sexual perversities." I guess he means when Regan. . . . But that particular implication slid right by a number of viewers I questioned.

But where Dr. Greenson goes utterly wrong is when he takes the film to be a story about a girl who develops bizarre *symptoms,* an *illness.* Not at all. It's a story about a devil, a demon, of pre-Christian origins (that prologue in Iraq was not there for local color) who uses a lovely child for his malevolent work. It's not about a *neurotic* or a *psychotic* child. She's not a suitable case for treatment! That's the whole point, and it was utterly lost on Dr. Greenson.

Like it or not, the film was devilishly well done. True, no one consulted Dr. Freud. But a good many specialists *were* consulted, with the aim of making the fantastic story as believable, as involving to audiences, as possible. In that, the film-makers quite obviously succeeded. They made a

JTS ®

By Charles M. Schulz

shocker. But no one is being handcuffed and led into a theater to see it. *Caveat emptor.*[2] I have some friends, a few cases here and there, who I feel were harmed, not helped, by psychiatric treatment. But should I therefore go crying, for all to hear, that psychiatrists are dangerous?

POINTS TO CONSIDER

1. What makes *The Exorcist* a particularly important movie from a reviewer's standpoint?

2. What objections do the reviewers make to *The Exorcist?* What aspects of the movie do the reviewers praise?

3. On what points do the reviewers seem to agree? What are some of the major points of disagreement?

4. Describe briefly your overall impression of the movie created by the reviews and if you saw *The Exorcist,* contrast it with your impression of the movie itself.

5. How does each of the reviewers attempt to account for the film's tremendous audience appeal? What is your opinion of why the film was so popular? What do you think that people get from a movie like *The Exorcist?* If you saw it, what did you get from it?

6. Do you believe, as Dr. Greenson suggests in his article, that a movie can actually be a "menace"? If so, how?

THE IMAGINATION OF DISASTER

Susan Sontag   *Against Interpretation,* 1965

Ours is indeed an age of extremity. For we live under continual threat of two equally fearful, but seemingly opposed, destinies: unremitting banality and inconceivable terror. It is fantasy, served out in large rations by the popular arts, which allows most people to cope with these twin specters. For one job that fantasy can do is to lift us out of the unbearably humdrum and to distract us from terrors, real or anticipated—by an escape into exotic dangerous situations which have last-minute happy endings. But another one of the things that fantasy can do is to normalize what is psychologically unbearable, thereby inuring us to it. In the one case, fantasy beautifies the world. In the other, it neutralizes it.

[2] *Caveat emptor* is a Latin phrase meaning "Let the buyer beware."

The fantasy to be discovered in science fiction films does both jobs. These films reflect world-wide anxieties, and they serve to allay them. They inculcate a strange apathy concerning the processes of radiation, contamination, and destruction that I for one find haunting and depressing. The naïve level of the films neatly tempers the sense of otherness, of alien-ness, with the grossly familiar. In particular, the dialogue of most science fiction films, which is generally of a monumental but often touching banality, makes them wonderfully, unintentionally funny. Lines like: "Come quickly, there's a monster in my bathtub"; "We must do something about this"; "Wait, Professor. There's someone on the telephone"; "But that's incredible"; and the old American stand-by (accompanied by brow-wiping), "I hope it works!"—are hilarious in the context of picturesque and deafening holocaust. Yet the films also contain something which is painful and in deadly earnest.

Science fiction films are one of the most accomplished of the popular art forms, and can give a great deal of pleasure to sophisticated film addicts. Part of the pleasure, indeed, comes from the sense in which these movies are in complicity with the abhorrent. It is no more, perhaps, than the way all art draws its audience into a circle of complicity with the thing represented. But in science fiction films we have to do with things which are (quite literally) unthinkable. Here, "thinking about the unthinkable"—not in the way of Herman Kahn, as a subject for calculation, but as a subject for fantasy—becomes, however inadvertently, itself a somewhat questionable act from a moral point of view. The films perpetuate clichés about identity, volition, power, knowledge, happiness, social consensus, guilt, responsibility which are, to say the least, not serviceable in our present extremity. But collective nightmares cannot be banished by demonstrating that they are, intellectually and morally, fallacious. This nightmare—the one reflected in various registers in the science fiction films—is too close to our reality.

A typical science fiction film has a form as predictable as a Western, and is made up of elements which are as classic as the saloon brawl, the blonde schoolteacher from the East, and the gun duel on the deserted main street.

One model scenario proceeds through five phases:

1. The arrival of the thing. (Emergence of the monsters, landing of the alien space-ship, etc.) This is usually witnessed, or suspected, by just one person, who is a young scientist on a field trip. Nobody, neither his neighbors nor his colleagues, will believe him for some time. The hero is not married, but has a sympathetic though also incredulous girlfriend.
2. Confirmation of the hero's report by a host of witnesses to a great act of destruction. (If the invaders are beings from another planet, a fruitless attempt to parley with them and get them to leave peacefully.) The local police are summoned to deal with the situation and massacred.
3. In the capital of the country, conferences between scientists and the military take place, with the hero lecturing before a chart, map, or blackboard. A national emergency is declared. Reports of further atrocities. Authorities from other countries arrive in black limousines. All international tensions are suspended in view of the planetary emergency. This stage often includes a rapid montage of news broadcasts in various languages, a

meeting at the UN, and more conferences between the military and the scientists. Plans are made for destroying the enemy.

4. Further atrocities. At some point the hero's girlfriend is in grave danger. Massive counterattacks by international forces, with brilliant displays of rocketry, rays, and other advanced weapons, are all unsuccessful. Enormous military casualties, usually by incineration. Cities are destroyed and/ or evacuated. There is an obligatory scene here of panicked crowds stampeding along a highway or a big bridge, being waved on by numerous policemen who, if the film is Japanese, are immaculately white-gloved, preternaturally calm, and call out in dubbed English, "Keep moving. There is no need to be alarmed."

5. More conferences, whose motif is: "They must be vulnerable to something." Throughout, the hero has been experimenting in his lab on this. The final strategy, upon which all hopes depend, is drawn up; the ultimate weapon—often a super-powerful, as yet untested, nuclear device—is mounted. Countdown. Final repulse of the monster or invaders. Mutual congratulations, while the hero and girlfriend embrace cheek to cheek and scan the skies sturdily. "But have we seen the last of them?"

The film I have just described should be in Technicolor and on a wide screen. Another typical scenario is simpler and suited to black-and-white films with a lower budget. It has four phases:

1. The hero (usually, but not always, a scientist) and his girlfriend, or his wife and children, are disporting themselves in some innocent ultra-normal middle-class house in a small town, or on vacation (camping, boating). Suddenly, someone starts behaving strangely or some innocent form of vegetation becomes monstrously enlarged and ambulatory. If a character is pictured driving an automobile, something gruesome looms up in the middle of the road. If it is night, strange lights hurtle across the sky.

2. After following the thing's tracks, or determining that It is radioactive, or poking around a huge crater—in short, conducting some sort of crude investigation—the hero tries to warn the local authorities, without effect; nobody believes anything is amiss. The hero knows better. If the thing is tangible, the house is elaborately barricaded. If the invading alien is an invisible parasite, a doctor or friend is called in, who is himself rather quickly killed or "taken possession of" by the thing.

3. The advice of anyone else who is consulted proves useless. Meanwhile, It continues to claim other victims in the town, which remains implausibly isolated from the rest of the world. General helplessness.

4. One of two possibilities. Either the hero prepares to do battle alone, accidentally discovers the thing's one vulnerable point, and destroys it. Or, he somehow manages to get out of town and succeeds in laying his case before competent authorities. They, along the lines of the first script but abridged, deploy a complex technology which (after initial setbacks) finally prevails against the invaders.

Another version of the second script opens with the scientist-hero in his laboratory, which is located in the basement or on the grounds of his tasteful, prosperous house. Through his experiments, he unwittingly causes a frightful metamorphosis in some class of plants or animals, which turn carnivorous and go on a rampage. Or else, his experiments have caused him to be injured (sometimes irrevocably) or "invaded" himself. Perhaps he has been experimenting with radiation, or has built a machine to communicate with beings from other planets or to transport him to other places or times.

Another version of the first script involves the discovery of some fundamental alteration in the conditions of existence of our planet, brought about by nuclear testing, which will lead to the extinction in a few months of all human life. For example: the temperature of the earth is becoming too high or too low to support life, or the earth is cracking in two, or it is gradually being blanketed by lethal fallout.

A third script, somewhat but not altogether different from the first two, concerns a journey through space—to the moon, or some other planet. What the space-voyagers commonly discover is that the alien terrain is in a state of dire emergency, itself threatened by extra-planetary invaders or nearing extinction through the practice of nuclear warfare. The terminal dramas of the first and second scripts are played out there, to which is added a final problem of getting away from the doomed and/or hostile planet and back to Earth.

I am aware, of course, that there are thousands of science fiction novels (their heyday was in the late 1940's), not to mention the transcriptions of science fiction themes which, more and more, provide the principal subject matter of comic books. But I propose to discuss science fiction films (the present period began in 1950 and continues, considerably abated, to this day) as an independent sub-genre, without reference to the novels from which, in many cases, they were adapted. For while novel and film may share the same plot, the fundamental difference between the resources of the novel and the film makes them quite dissimilar. Anyway, the best science fiction movies are on a far higher level, as examples of the art of the film, than the science fiction books are, as examples of the art of the novel or romance. That the films might be better than the books is an old story. Good novels rarely make good films, but excellent films are often made from poor or trivial novels.

Certainly, compared with the science fiction novels, their film counterparts have unique strengths, one of which is the immediate representation of the extraordinary: physical deformity and mutation, missile and rocket combat, toppling skyscrapers. The movies are, naturally, weak just where the science fiction novels (some of them), are strong—on science. But in place of an intellectual workout, they can supply something the novels can never provide—sensuous elaboration. In the films it is by means of images and sounds, not words that have to be translated by the imagination, that one can participate in the fantasy of living through one's own death and more, the death of cities, the destruction of humanity itself.

Science fiction films are not about science. They are about disaster, which is one of the oldest subjects of art. In science fiction films, disaster is rarely viewed intensively; it is always extensive. It is a matter of quantity and ingenuity. If you will, it is a question of scale. But the scale, particularly in the wide-screen Technicolor films (of which the one by the Japanese director, Inoshiro Honda, and the American director, George Pal, are technically the most brilliant and convincing, and visually the most exciting), does raise the matter to another level.

Thus, the science fiction film (like a very different contemporary genre, the Happening) is concerned with the aesthetics of destruction, with the peculiar beauties to be found in wreaking havoc, making a mess. And it is in the imagery of destruction that the core of a good science fiction film lies. This is the disadvantage of the cheap film—in which the monster appears or the rocket lands in a small dull-looking town. (Hollywood budget needs usually dictate that the town be in the Arizona or California desert. In *The Thing from Another World* [1951], the rather sleazy and confined set is supposed to be an encampment near the North Pole.) Still, good black-and-white science fiction films have been made. But a bigger budget, which usually means Technicolor, allows a much greater play back and forth among several model environments. There is the populous city. There is the lavish but ascetic interior of the space ship—either the invaders' or ours—replete with streamlined chromium fixtures and dials, and machines whose complexity is indicated by the number of colored lights they flash and strange noises they emit. There is the laboratory crowded with formidable machines and scientific apparatus. There is a comparatively old-fashioned looking conference room, where the scientist brings charts to explain the desperate state of things to the military. And each of the standard locales or backgrounds is subject to two modalities—intact and destroyed. We may, if we are lucky, be treated to a panorama of melting tanks, flying bodies, crashing walls, awesome craters and fissures in the earth, plummeting spacecraft, colorful deadly rays; and to a symphony of screams, weird electronic signals, the noisiest military hardware going, and the leaden tones of the laconic denizens of alien planets and their subjugated earthlings.

Certain of the primitive gratifications of science fiction films—for instance, the depiction of urban disaster on a colossally magnified scale—are shared with other types of films. Visually there is little difference between mass havoc as represented in the old horror and monster films and what we find in science fiction films, except (again) scale. In the old monster films, the monster always headed for the great city where he had to do a fair bit of rampaging, hurling buses off bridges, crumpling trains in his bare hands, toppling buildings, and so forth. The archetype is King Kong, in Schoedsach's great film of 1933, running amok, first in the African village (trampling babies, a bit of footage excised from most prints), then in New York. This is really not any different from Inoshiro Honda's *Rodan* (1957), where two giant reptiles—with a wingspan of five-hundred feet and supersonic speeds—by flapping their wings whip up a cyclone that blows most of Tokyo to smithereens. Or, the tremendous scenes of rampage by the gigantic robot who destroys half of Japan with the great incinerating ray which shoots forth from his eyes, at the beginning of Honda's *The Mysterians* (1959). Or, the destruction, by the rays from a fleet of flying saucers, of New York, Paris and Tokyo, in *Battle in Outer Space* (1960). Or, the inundation of New York in *When Worlds Collide* (1951). Or, the end of London in 1968 depicted in George Pal's *The Time Machine* (1960). Neither do these sequences differ in aesthetic intention from the destruction scenes in the big sword, sandal, and orgy color spectaculars set in Biblical and Roman times—the end of Sodom in Aldrich's *Sodom and Gomorrah,* of Gaza in de Mille's *Samson and Delilah,* of Rhodes in *The Colossus of Rhodes,* and of Rome in a dozen Nero movies. D. W. Griffith began it with the Babylon sequence in *Intolerance,* and to this day there is nothing like the thrill of watching all those expensive sets come tumbling down.

In other respects as well, the science fiction films of the 1950's take up familiar themes. The famous movie serials and comics of the 1930's of the adventures of Flash Gordon and Buck Rogers, as well as the more recent spate of comic book super-heroes with extraterrestrial origins (the most famous is Superman, a foundling from the planet, Krypton, currently described as having been exploded by a nuclear blast) share motifs with more recent science fiction movies. But there is an important difference. The old science fiction films, and most of the comics, still have an essentially innocent relation to disaster. Mainly they offer new versions of the oldest romance of all—of the strong invulnerable hero with the mysterious lineage come to do battle on behalf of good and against evil. Recent science fiction films have a decided grimness, bolstered by their much greater degree of visual credibility, which contrasts strongly with the older films. Modern historical reality has greatly enlarged the imagination of disaster, and the protagonists—perhaps by the very nature of what is visited upon them—no longer seem wholly innocent.

The lure of such generalized disaster as a fantasy is that it releases one from normal obligations. The trump card of the end-of-the-world movies— like *The Day the Earth Caught Fire* (1962)—is that great scene with New York or London or Tokyo discovered empty, its entire population annihilated. Or, as in *The World, the Flesh, and the Devil* (1959), the whole movie can be devoted to the fantasy of occupying the deserted city and starting all over again—Robinson Crusoe on a world-wide scale.

Another kind of satisfaction these films supply is extreme moral simplification—that is to say, a morally acceptable fantasy where one can give outlet to cruel or at least amoral feelings. In this respect, science fiction films partly overlap with horror films. This is the undeniable pleasure we derive from looking at freaks, at beings excluded from the category of the human. The sense of superiority over the freak conjoined in varying proportions with the titillation of fear and aversion makes it possible for moral scruples to be lifted, for cruelty to be enjoyed. The same thing happens in science fiction films. In the figure of the monster from outer space, the freakish, the ugly, and the predatory all converge—and provide a fantasy target for righteous bellicosity to discharge itself, and for the aesthetic enjoyment of suffering and disaster. Science fiction films are one of the purest forms of spectacle; that is, we are rarely inside anyone's feelings. [An exception to this is Jack Arnold's *The Incredible Shrinking Man* (1957).] We are merely spectators; we watch.

But in science fiction films, unlike horror films, there is not much horror. Suspense, shocks, surprises are mostly abjured in favor of a steady inexorable plot. Science fiction films invite a dispassionate, aesthetic view of destruction and violence—a *technological* view. Things, objects, machinery play a major role in these films. A greater range of ethical values is embodied in the décor of these films than in the people. Things, rather than the helpless humans, are the locus of values because we experience them, rather than people, as the sources of power. According to science fiction films, man is naked without his artifacts. *They* stand for different values, they are potent, they are what gets destroyed, and they are the indispensable tools for the repulse of the alien invaders or the repair of the damaged environment.

The science fiction films are strongly moralistic. The standard message is the one about the proper, or humane, uses of science, versus the mad, obsessional use of science. This message the science fiction films share in common with the classic horror films of the 1930's, like *Frankenstein, The Mummy, The Island of Doctor Moreau, Dr. Jekyll and Mr. Hyde.* (Georges Franju's brilliant *Les Yeux Sans Visage* [1959], called here *The Horror Chamber of Doctor Faustus,* is a more recent example.) In the horror films, we have the mad or obsessed or misguided scientist who pursues his experiments against good advice to the contrary, creates a monster or monsters, and is himself destroyed—often recognizing his folly himself, and dying in the successful effort to destroy his own creation. One science fiction equivalent of this is the scientist, usually a member of a team, who defects to the planetary invaders because "their" science is more advanced than "ours."

This is the case in *The Mysterians,* and, true to form, the renegade sees his error in the end, and from within the Mysterian space ship destroys it and himself. In *This Island Earth* (1955), the inhabitants of the beleaguered planet Metaluna propose to conquer Earth, but their project is foiled by a Metalunan scientist named Exeter who, having lived on Earth a while and learned to love Mozart, cannot abide such viciousness. Exeter plunges his space ship into the ocean after returning a glamorous pair (male and female) of American physicists to Earth. Metaluna dies. In *The Fly* (1958), the hero, engrossed in his basement-laboratory experiments on a matter-transmitting machine, uses himself as a subject, accidentally exchanges head and one arm with a housefly which had gotten into the machine, becomes a monster, and with his last shred of human will destroys his laboratory and orders his wife to kill him. His discovery, for the good of mankind, is lost.

Being a clearly labeled species of intellectual, the scientists in science fiction films are always liable to crack up or go off the deep end. In *Conquest of Space* (1955), the scientist-commander of an international expedition to Mars suddenly acquires scruples about the blasphemy involved in the undertaking, and begins reading the Bible mid-journey instead of attending to his duties. The commander's son, who is his junior officer and always addresses his father as "General," is forced to kill the old man when he tries to prevent the ship from landing on Mars. In this film, both sides of the ambivalence toward scientists are given voice. Generally, for a scientific enterprise to be treated entirely sympathetically in these films, it needs the certificate of utility. Science, viewed without ambivalence, means an efficacious response to danger. Disinterested intellectual curiosity rarely appears in any form other than caricature, as a maniacal dementia that cuts one off from normal human relations. But this suspicion is usually directed at the scientist rather than his work. The creative scientist may become a martyr to his own discovery, through an accident or by pushing things too far. The implication remains that other men, less imaginative—in short, technicians—would administer the same scientific discovery better and more safely. The most ingrained contemporary mistrust of the intellect is visited, in these movies, upon the scientist-as-intellectual.

The message that the scientist is one who releases forces which, if not controlled for good, could destroy man himself seems innocuous enough. One of the oldest images of the scientist is Shakespeare's Prospero, the over-detached scholar forcibly retired from society to a desert island, only partly in control of the magic forces in which he dabbles. Equally classic is the figure of the scientist as satanist (*Dr. Faustus,* stories of Poe and Hawthorne). Science is magic, and man has always known that there is black magic as well as white. But it is not enough to remark that contemporary attitudes—as reflected in science fiction films—remain ambivalent, that the scientist is treated both as satanist and savior. The proportions have changed, because of the new context in which the old admiration and fear of the scientist is located. For his sphere of influence is no longer local, himself or his immediate community. It is planetary, cosmic.

One gets the feeling, particularly in the Japanese films, but not only there, that mass trauma exists over the use of nuclear weapons and the possibility of future nuclear wars. Most of the science fiction films bear witness to this trauma, and in a way, attempt to exorcise it.

The accidental awakening of the super-destructive monster who has slept in the earth since prehistory is, often, an obvious metaphor for the Bomb. But there are many explicit references as well. In *The Mysterians,* a probe ship from the planet Mysteroid has landed on earth, near Tokyo. Nuclear warfare having been practiced on Mysteroid for centuries (their civilization is "more advanced than ours"), 90 per cent of those now born on the planet have to be destroyed at birth, because of defects caused by the huge amounts of Strontium 90 in their diet. The Mysterians have come to earth to marry earth women and possibly to take over our relatively uncontaminated planet. . . . In *The Incredible Shrinking Man,* the John Doe hero is the victim of a gust of radiation which blows over the water, while he is out boating with his wife; the radiation causes him to grow smaller and smaller, until at the end of the movie he steps through the fine mesh of a window screen to become "the infinitely small. . . ." In *Rodan,* a horde of monstrous carnivorous prehistoric insects, and finally a pair of giant flying reptiles (the prehistoric Archeopteryx), are hatched from dormant eggs in the depths of a mine shaft by the impact of nuclear test explosions, and go on to destroy a good part of the world before they are felled by the molten lava of a volcanic eruption. . . . In the English film, *The Day the Earth Caught Fire,* two simultaneous hydrogen bomb tests by the U.S. and Russia change by eleven degrees the tilt of the earth on its axis and alter the earth's orbit so that it begins to approach the sun.

Radiation casualties—ultimately, the conception of the whole world as a casualty of nuclear testing and nuclear warfare—is the most ominous of all the notions with which science fiction films deal. Universes become expendable. Worlds become contaminated, burnt out, exhausted, obsolete. In *Rocketship X-M* (1950), explorers from Earth land on Mars, where they learn that atomic warfare has destroyed Martian civilization. In George Pal's *The War of the Worlds* (1953), reddish spindly alligator-skinned creatures from Mars invade Earth because their planet is becoming too cold to be habitable. In *This Island Earth,* also American, the planet Metaluna, whose population has long been driven underground by warfare, is dying under the missile attacks of an enemy planet. Stocks of uranium, which power the force-shield shielding Metaluna, have been used up; and an unsuccessful expedition is sent to Earth to enlist earth scientists to devise new sources of nuclear power.

There is a vast amount of wishful thinking in science fiction films, some of it touching, some of it depressing. Again and again, one detects the hunger for a "good war," which poses no moral problems, admits of no moral qualifications. The imagery of science fiction films will satisfy the most bellicose addict of war films, for a lot of the satisfactions of war films pass, untransformed, into science fiction films. Examples: the dogfights between earth "fighter rockets" and alien spacecraft in the *Battle of Outer Space* (1959); the escalating firepower in the successive assaults upon the invaders in *The Mysterians,* which Dan Talbot correctly described as a nonstop holocaust; the spectacular bombardment of the underground fortress in *This Island Earth.*

Yet at the same time the bellicosity of science fiction films is neatly channeled into the yearning for peace, or for at least peaceful coexistence. Some scientist generally takes sententious note of the fact that it took the planetary invasion or cosmic disaster to make the warring nations of the earth come to their senses, and suspend their own conflicts. One of the main themes of many science fiction films—the color ones usually, because they have the budget and resources to develop the military spectacle—is this UN fantasy, a fantasy of united warfare. [The same wishful UN theme cropped up in a recent spectacular which is not science fiction, *Fifty-Five Days at Peking* (1963).] There, topically enough, the Chinese, the Boxers, play the role of Martian invaders who unite the earthmen, in this case the United States, Russia, England, France, Germany, Italy, and Japan.) A great enough disaster cancels all enmities, and calls upon the utmost concentration of the earth's resources.

Science—technology—is conceived of as the great unifier. Thus the science fiction films also project a utopian fantasy. In the classic models of utopian thinking—Plato's Republic, Campanella's City of the Sun, More's Utopia, Swift's land of the Houyhnhnms, Voltaire's Eldorado—society had worked out a perfect consensus. In these societies reasonableness had achieved an unbreakable supremacy over the emotions. Since no disagreement or social conflict was intellectually plausible, none was possible. As in Melville's *Typee,* "they all think the same." The universal rule of reason meant universal agreement. It is interesting, too, that societies in which reason was pictured as totally ascendant were also traditionally pictured as having an ascetic and/or materially frugal and economically simple mode of life. But in the utopian world community projected by science fiction films, totally pacified and ruled by scientific consensus, the demand for simplicity of material existence would be absurd.

But alongside the hopeful fantasy of moral simplification and international unity embodied in the science fiction films, lurk the deepest anxieties about contemporary existence. I don't mean only the very real trauma of the Bomb—that it has been used, that there are enough now to kill everyone on earth many times over, that those new bombs may very well be used. Besides these new anxieties about physical disaster, the prospect of universal mutilation and even annihilation, the science fiction films reflect powerful anxieties about the condition of the individual psyche.

For science fiction films may also be described as a popular mythology for the contemporary *negative* imagination about the impersonal. The other-world creatures which seek to take "us" over, are an "it," not a "they." The planetary invaders are usually zombie-like. Their movements are either cool, mechanical, or lumbering, blobby. But it amounts to the same thing. If they are nonhuman in form, they proceed with an absolutely regular, unalterable movement (unalterable save by destruction). If they are human in form—dressed in space suits, etc.—then they obey the most rigid military discipline, and display no personal characteristics whatsoever. And it is this regime of emotionlessness, of impersonality, of regimentation, which they will impose on the earth if they are successful. "No more love, no more beauty, no more pain," boasts a converted earthling in *The Invasion of the Body Snatchers* (1956). The half earthling–half alien children in *The Children of the Damned* (1960) are absolutely emotionless, move as a group and understand each other's thoughts, and are all prodigious intellects. They are the wave of the future, man in his next stage of development.

These alien invaders practice a crime which is worse than murder. They do not simply kill the person. They obliterate him. In *The War of the Worlds*, the ray which issues from the rocket ship disintegrates all persons and objects in its path, leaving no trace of them but a light ash. In Honda's *The H-Men* (1959), the creeping blob melts all flesh with which it comes in contact. If the blob, which looks like a huge hunk of red jello, and can crawl across floors and up and down walls, so much as touches your bare boot, all that is left of you is a heap of clothes on the floor. (A more articulated, size-multiplying blob is the villain in the English film *The Creeping Unknown* [1956].) In another version of this fantasy, the body is preserved but the person is entirely reconstituted as the automatized servant or agent of the alien powers. This is, of course, the vampire fantasy in new dress. The person is really dead, but he doesn't know it. He's "undead," he has become an "unperson." It happens to a whole California town in *The Invasion of the Body Snatchers,* to several earth scientists in *This Island Earth,* and to assorted innocents in *It Came from Outer Space, Attack of the Puppet People* (1961), and *The Brain Eaters* (1961). As the victim always backs away from the vampire's horrifying embrace, so in science fiction films the person always fights being "taken over"; he wants to retain his humanity. But once the deed has been done, the victim is eminently satisfied with his condition. He has not been converted from human amiability to monstrous "animal" blood-lust (a metaphoric exaggeration of sexual desire), as in the old vampire fantasy. No, he has simply become far more efficient—the very model of technocratic man, purged of emotions, volitionless, tranquil, obedient to all orders. The dark secret behind human nature used to be the upsurge of the animal—as in *King Kong.* The threat to man, his availability to dehumanization, lay in his own animality. Now the danger is understood as residing in man's ability to be turned into a machine.

The rule, of course, is that this horrible and irremediable form of murder can strike anyone in the film except the hero. The hero and his family, while grossly menaced, always escape this fact and by the end of the film the invaders have been repulsed or destroyed. I know of only one exception, *The Day That Mars Invaded Earth* (1963), in which, after all the standard struggles, the scientist-hero, his wife, and their two children are "taken over" by the alien invaders—and that's that. (The last minutes of the film show them being incinerated by the Martians' rays and their ash silhouettes flushed down their empty swimming pool, while their simulacra drive off in the family car.) Another variant but upbeat switch on the rule occurs in *The Creation of the Humanoids* (1964), where the hero discovers at the end of the film that he, too, has been turned into a metal robot, complete with highly efficient and virtually indestructible mechanical insides, although he didn't know it and detected no difference in himself. He learns, however, that he will shortly be upgraded into a "humanoid" having all the properties of a real man.

Of all the standard motifs of science fiction films, this theme of dehumanization is perhaps the most fascinating. For, as I have indicated, it is scarcely a black-and-white situation, as in the vampire films. The attitude of the science fiction films toward depersonalization is mixed. On the one hand, they deplore it as the ultimate horror. On the other hand, certain characteristics of the dehumanized invaders, modulated and disguised— such as the ascendancy of reason over feelings, the idealization of teamwork and the consensus-creating activities of science, a marked degree of moral simplification—are precisely traits of the savior-scientists. For it is interesting that when the scientist in these films is treated negatively, it is usually done through the portrayal of an individual scientist who holes up in his laboratory and neglects his fiancée or his loving wife and children, obsessed by his daring and dangerous experiments. The scientist as a loyal member of a team, and therefore considerably less individualized, is treated quite respectfully.

There is absolutely no social criticism, of even the most implicit kind, in science fiction films. No criticism, for example, of the conditions of our society which create the impersonality and dehumanization which science fiction fantasies displace onto the influence of an alien It. Also, the notion of science as a social activity, interlocking with social and political interests, is unacknowledged. Science is simply either adventure (for good or evil) or a technical response to danger. And, typically, when the fear of science is paramount—when science is conceived of as black magic rather than white—the evil has no attribution beyond that of the perverse will of an individual scientist. In science fiction films, the antithesis of black magic and white is drawn as a split between technology, which is beneficent, and the errant individual will of a lone intellectual.

Thus, science fiction films can be looked at as thematically central allegory, replete with standard modern attitudes. The theme of depersonalization (being "taken over") which I have been talking about is a new allegory reflecting the age-old awareness of man that, sane, he is always perilously close to insanity and unreason. But there is something more here than just a recent, popular image which expresses man's perennial, but largely unconscious, anxiety about his sanity. The image derives most of its power from a supplementary and historical anxiety, also not experienced *consciously* by most people, about the depersonalizing conditions of modern urban society. Similarly, it is not enough to note that science fiction allegories are one of the new myths about—that is, ways of accommodating to and negating—the perennial human anxiety about death. (Myths of heaven and hell, and of ghosts, had the same function.) Again, there is a historically specifiable twist which intensifies the anxiety, or better, the trauma suffered by everyone in the middle of the 20th century when it became clear that from now on to the end of human history, every person would spend his individual life not only under the threat of individual death, which is certain, but of something almost unsupportable psychologically—collective incineration and extinction which could come any time, virtually without warning.

From a psychological point of view, the imagination of disaster does not greatly differ from one period in history to another. But from a political and moral point of view, it does. The expectation of the apocalypse may be the occasion for a radical disaffiliation from society, as when thousands of Eastern European Jews in the 17th century gave up their homes and businesses and began to trek to Palestine upon hearing that Shabbethai Zevi had been proclaimed Messiah and that the end of the world was imminent. But peoples learn the news of their own end in diverse ways. It is reported that in 1945 the populace of Berlin received without great agitation the news that Hitler had decided to kill them all, before the Allies arrived, because they had not been worthy enough to win the war. We are, alas, more in the position of the Berliners than of the Jews of 17th-century Eastern Europe; and our response is closer to theirs, too. What I am suggesting is that the imagery of disaster in science fiction films is above all the emblem of an *inadequate response.* I do not mean to bear down on the films for this. They themselves are only a sampling, stripped of sophistication, of the inadequacy of most people's response to the unassimilable terrors that infect their consciousness. The interest of the films, aside from their considerable amount of cinematic charm, consists in this intersection between a naïvely and largely debased commercial art product and the most profound dilemmas of the contemporary situation.

POINTS TO CONSIDER

1.   Susan Sontag says that fantasy both "beautifies" and "neutralizes" our lives. How does her observation relate to the mass media function of "compensation" discussed in the introductory essay to this book (p. 3)?

2.   Ms. Sontag also says that "all art draws its audience into a circle of complicity with the things represented." To what extent does this observation relate to the function of "socialization" discussed in the introductory essay?

3.   "Science fiction films," says Ms. Sontag, "are not about science. They are about disaster." What kinds of "disaster films" other than science fic-

tion have been popular in the past five to ten years? Name some. Could *Dr. Strangelove* be considered a "disaster film"? Could *The Exorcist?* Could *Jaws?*

4. Why do you think that disaster films have been so popular in the past five to ten years? In what ways do these films reflect an aspect of social reality? Do you agree with Ms. Sontag that "modern historical reality has greatly enlarged the imagination of disaster"? In what ways?

5. What does Ms. Sontag see as the moral implications of most science fiction disaster films? In what ways are we, the audience, morally distanced from rather than morally involved with these disasters? Are we more or less morally involved with other kinds of recently popular disaster films such as *The Poseidon Adventure* and *Earthquake?*

6. Could the popularity of disaster films reflect a general desire of the public to be less involved morally with the real disasters, actual and potential, which surround us today? What do you think?

■ VIOLENT MOVIES CREATE VIOLENT KIDS

David Shaw   *Today's Health,* October 1974

The experiment seemed reasonably simple:

Psychologist Richard Walters, Ph.D., would show one group of men a filmed knife fight. He would show another group of men a film of nonviolent drama. Then he would bring the two groups together to watch a third group performing several work tasks under his direction.

Every time someone in the third group made a mistake, the members of the first two groups were to push buttons that would give the worker an electric shock. The intensity of the shock could be varied at will.

The result: The men who had seen the knife fight jolted their victims far more frequently—and far more severely—than those who had seen the nonviolent drama. The filmed violence, Dr. Walters concluded, "aroused aggressive tendencies" which were "readily translated into harsh, aggressive action."

Dr. Walters died in 1967, three years after he conducted his experiments at the University of Waterloo, in Ontario, Canada. His studies have since been repeated elsewhere, often using children, and his conclusions substantiated.

And yet, the Motion Picture Association of America (MPAA), the agency responsible for rating the acceptability of movies, has made virtually no effort to restrict the accessibility of violent movies to children. Countless movies have been given an MPAA "X" rating ("forbidden to anyone under 18") because of explicit sex, but only one—*I Drink Your Blood*—was so rated solely because of violence . . . and even that rating was changed to "R" ("children under 18 admitted only when accompanied by parent or

_____) when a few scenes were cut. The MPAA message is clear: Making love is supposed to be, somehow, corrupting; making death, however, is just fine.

This is not a plea for censorship. I have long argued that there should be no laws prohibiting adults from seeing or reading anything they want—no matter how grisly or pornographic. But with so much scientific evidence demonstrating the adverse effects that filmed violence has on some children, there certainly ought to be—at the very least—more stringent guidelines available to parents who do not want their children exposed to mayhem, murder, and massacre on the motion-picture screen.

There are, of course, those who maintain that film violence is cathartic, even purgative—that it provides a harmless outlet for normal tensions and aggressions. That may, indeed, be true—with most well-balanced adults and with many well-balanced children. But the testimony of experts is overwhelming on what happens to the emotionally troubled child when he is exposed to film violence:

"For some children, the impact of violence so graphically portrayed and so available may be deeply disturbing. A child who is already struggling with his own aggressive feelings may be unable to cope with the open aggression so portrayed"—Josette Frank, former director of children's books and mass media for the Child Study Association of America;

"Children with borderline psychopathic tendencies may be pushed to overt delinquent behavior by violent entertainment"—Isidore Ziferstein, M. D., a psychiatrist at the Southern California Psychoanalytic Institute, in Los Angeles;

"Any normal, emotionally stable person will view grisly acts portrayed on the screen with abhorrence and never give a thought to emulating the brutality. But consider the possible reaction of the emotionally unstable who are teetering on the brink of abnormal behavior. Often, a scene of explicit cruelty can contribute to pushing them over the edge"—George Seaton, two-time Academy-Award-winning director and former president of the Motion Picture Academy of Arts and Sciences.

Even the healthy child, whose mind is, nevertheless, in its formative, impressionable stages, may suffer from exposure to film violence. Three years ago, the U.S. Surgeon General's Advisory Committee on Television and Social Behavior warned that violent entertainment "may be contributing, in some measure, to the aggressive behavior of many normal children."

The harmful impact of film violence is at least threefold:

It subconsciously makes the child more restive, more aggressive, more hostile.

It provides the child with specific behavioral models to emulate.

It teaches the child that violence is an acceptable, indeed a preferred means of resolving any problem.

There are many more specific examples where children, consciously or unconsciously, acted out the film violence they've seen. Cleveland police arrested a gang of teenagers who—saying they had styled themselves after the "Untouchables"—buried a man under a hail of bricks. The same thing happened in Chicago. Experiments at the University of Washington showed that nursery-school children exposed to an aggressive cartoon film displayed more aggressive responses with a toy immediately afterward than a control group shown a less aggressive film. A similar experiment, at Stanford University, showed that preschool children who witnessed the actions of an aggressive adult in a motion picture and then were subjected to mild frustration tended to imitate the kind of hostile behavior they had seen. (Even adults have manifested violent, antisocial behavior after having seen violent movies. In 1960, a 20-year-old lab technician killed three Los Angeles women after seeing Alfred Hitchcock's *Psycho;* more recently, in 1972, Arthur Bremer, a 21-year-old former busboy and school janitor, shot down Alabama's Governor George Wallace after seeing *A Clockwork Orange.*)

About 10 years ago, most of the concern over violent entertainment and children centered on television. Now that concern has shifted to the neighborhood movie theater—a change triggered, in part, by the new trend in movie violence ushered in by Sam Peckinpah's 1969 study in blood lust, *The Wild Bunch.*

Movie violence has been with us since the pistol-whipping scene in *The Great Train Robbery,* filmed in 1903, but Peckinpah seems to have taken violence to new depths. In most pre-Peckinpah movies, when someone was shot, all the viewer saw was a gradually spreading crimson stain on the victim's shirt. In *The Wild Bunch,* blood spurted all over the screen. In one especially gruesome (and gratuitous) scene, a man's throat was slit—the knife slashing across the wide screen in agonizing verisimilitude, the blood cascading forth as from an exploding ketchup bottle. Those viewers who didn't jerk their heads away and close their eyes sat drinking it all in, proud of the machismo[1] that enabled them to watch the gore, unblinking. Neither condition—nauseated aversion or sadistic bravado—is a particularly healthy one. And Peckinpah's next film, *Straw Dogs,* was even more violent—more violent, more graphic, more bloody.

But neither *The Wild Bunch* nor *Straw Dogs* carried an "X" rating.

The same is true of last year's biggest box office success, *The Exorcist.* Yet, so grotesque and frightening was that movie that viewers vomited and fainted and ran away in terror. Ralph R. Greenson, M.D., clinical professor of psychiatry at the University of California at Los Angeles Medical School, says *The Exorcist* is "a menace, the most shocking major movie I have ever seen," and he tells of two friends—a social worker and a university professor—who became panicky and paranoid after having seen the film.[2] If two stable, intelligent adults suffered that reaction, what fears and insecurities might *The Exorcist* have aroused in the millions of young children who rushed to see it?

The Exorcist, after all, revolves around the grotesque transformation of a 12-year-old girl into a demon-possessed, sexually perverse murderess. She is responsible for three deaths, masturbates frantically with a crucifix, and plunges everyone around her into emotional hell. If one of the functions

---

[1] Machismo is a code of exaggerated masculine behavior that includes showing how tough one is. The term comes from a Spanish word for a young bull.

[2] See "A Psychoanalyst's Indictment of *The Exorcist,*" p. 365.

of movie-as-escapism is to induce the viewer to identify with the characters on screen, one can only imagine the nightmares, aggressions, and unspeakable fantasies that children in *The Exorcist* audience have subsequently envisioned for themselves.

Most sociologists see the new movie violence as an industry response to the violence of everyday life. The moviemakers must provide more and "better" violence, the theory goes, merely to compete with the violent realities of presidential assassination, My Lai, muggings, Charles Manson, the SLA, the Zodiac, Sirhan Sirhan. But violence only begets violence, and today's children may be growing up psychologically habituated to violence. We may be raising a generation of aggressors—and movies are partially responsible.

It must be admitted, of course, that there are different kinds of violence, and that not all are potentially harmful to children. This Halloween, for example, children who go to midnight horror shows may be able to choose from such macabre "G" ("for general audiences") and "PG" ("parental guidance urged") classics as *Cauldron of Blood, Crucible of Horror, Flesh Feast,* and *Face of the Screaming Werewolf.*

Superficially, the very titles of these films would seem to raise questions about their suitability for children. But studies have shown that unrealistic violence of the sort displayed in monster movies and oldtime Westerns and gangster movies rarely is harmful. Even the children perceive this violence as fantasy.

"They see it as belonging to a story, not to reality," says Seymour Feshbach, Ph.D., professor of psychology at the University of California at Los Angeles. "They realize that isn't the way you ought to behave. But the more realistic the violence, the more detail and blood you show, the more the movie becomes a teaching mechanism."

Dr. Feshbach drew his conclusions from a series of studies he conducted with children. In one such study, he found that the same film footage described to one group as fictional and to another group as actual newsreel coverage drew more violent responses from those told it was news coverage.

"Conventional violence . . . is not really violent at all, but only make-believe, after which the dead will rise again and toddle off to the commissary for burritos and beer," says Charles Champlin, the *Los Angeles Times* entertainment editor. "But there is also the impaling of a man's arm by a thrown pitchfork and . . . the execution of a kind old man who is bound hand and foot and then shot again and again at close range."

For Champlin, "the slaughter of the defenseless is the hardest kind of violence to see, the most personally threatening and nightmarish." For psychologists and psychiatrists, it is precisely that kind of violence—the new movie violence, violence as obscenity, violence as realistic as it is shocking—that children should be shielded from.

It is absolutely preposterous for the motion picture industry to take a relatively hard-line position on sex in the movies, when there isn't a single study demonstrating a causal relationship between screen sex and sex crimes; instead, the industry must concentrate its energy on violent movies where there is evidence aplenty of just such a link. The MPAA must enact a more stringent code on violent movies. Ratings must give parents a far better idea of what to expect in blood and gore when they send their children off to the neighborhood movie theater. If the industry does not act, parents will have to act for themselves by establishing local film review boards to publish ratings and guidelines on violent movies. It is the least they can do for their children.

POINTS TO CONSIDER

1. Describe the experiments the author cites which show connections between filmed violence and real-life violence. What three effects does the author point out that filmed violence can have on children?

2. What examples does the author cite of film violence connected with real-life violence? Can you think of others?

3. What differences does the article point out between the "realistic" violence of Sam Peckinpah and that of most monster movies and old-time Westerns?

4. What reasons does the article give for the current popularity of movie violence? Do you agree with this explanation? Explain.

5. What is the MPAA? What role has it played in regulating movie violence? What recommendations does the article make to the MPAA? Can you add recommendations of your own?

6. Judging from your own experience, do you feel that watching violent movies tends to make people more violent? Explain. How do violent movies affect you?

WHAT HAS HAPPENED TO MOVIE AUDIENCES?

David Elliott   *Chicago Daily News*, 1971

Among all the devil theories of what's wrong with films today, the most important of all may be the movie audience, and whatever happened to it.

This question has been pushing itself forward since the introduction of mass television in the late 1940s. Television has been among us in strength for 20 years, but only recently has the United States film industry faced up to the question of what happened to the mass audience.

Only recently has it recognized that all of its short-haul salvations are not going to provide an answer. New films, I believe, drove the facts home.

The first was "Blow-Up" in 1967, which made so much money so unexpectedly that it made all of the rules look foolish. Although assisted by a bit of controversial nudity, it was a slow, stylized and richly enigmatic[1] film by an esoteric Italian director. Yet it made a fortune in both art houses and popcorn palaces.

The lessons of "Blow-Up" were heavily underlined in 1969 by "Easy Rider," so heavily that the industry went on a binge of imitations. "Easy Rider" had a little sex, some drugs, but again, and above all, that enigmatic lyricism, as undefined as the audience that made it successful.

Hollywood, which had always depended on pegging each film to an established market, could not bear to leave the audience undefined, of course. That is why in 1968 Jack Valenti, president of the Motion Picture Association, ordered a survey of public movie tastes by the firm of Daniel Yankelovich, Inc.

The results were provocative. The survey showed that 50 per cent of all Americans over 16 never, or almost never, go to the movies. And 50 per cent of those who do go are between 16 and 24. Further, and most distressing, it was found that although most people like nothing better on television than movies, and prefer movies in theaters to those on TV, they still don't frequent their local theater.

The usual explanations are offered. Television and high movie-going costs are the main ones. But the bruising fact remains: Since the postwar movie boom, the weekly film audience has fallen from 75,000,000 people to about 15,000,000, from almost 50 per cent of the population to 7 per cent.

Hollywood could still get by very well, if that 7 per cent were a really dependable audience. But it is not, and except for the emerging new black film audience, there are no safe markets for any movie today. And that is why Hollywood is frightened, confused and stripping down for survival.

Those who drew the easy, obvious conclusions from "Easy Rider" were quickly confounded by their own wisdom. The "Easy Rider" generation films, with few exceptions, died miserably at the box office. Although this was less expensive than the flop of the big multimillion dollar musicals following "The Sound of Music," it was even more alarming because the "Easy Rider" specials were pitched to the industry's future.

In the 1930s, a cycle like the Andy Hardy films could be counted on to last long enough for the producers to make their money and churn out a new cycle before the jaded public retreated to the radio. But the "Easy Rider" boom died while the ink was still cooling on the press releases.

The kids went for "Five Easy Pieces" in 1969, but not "Zabriskie Point" in 1970, for "Woodstock" in 1970 but not "Mad Dogs and Englishmen" in 1971. They failed to groupie around Mick Jagger in "Performance" or James Taylor in "Two-Lane Blacktop," but they did see both Joe Dallesandro in "Trash" and Goldie Hawn in "Cactus Flower." They paid to see Costa-Gavras's "Z" in 1970, but ignored his less flashy, and politically voguish, "The Confession," in 1971.

Even more revealingly, the kids provided much of the mass audience for "Love Story" and "The Love Bug," "Patton" and "Airport," and "Beyond the Valley of the Dolls" as well as "Butch Cassidy."

[1] Enigmatic means puzzling; esoteric refers to knowledge that is restricted to a small group of people.

In her review of the British youth revolution film "If . . ." Pauline Kael wrote that "Many people are beginning to treat 'youth' as the ultimate judge—as a collective Tolstoyan[2] clean old peasant. They want to be on the side of youth; they're afraid of youth."

More concretely, they want to sell youth to itself. And yet most of the great suckering operations have fallen dismally short of their hopes. The reason, clear by now, is that youth is not a monolithic audience, straining after the carrot of relevancy, but is instead an audience both divided among itself and but a fraction—though a big one—of the total film public.

What we need is a more inclusive and slightly more cynical typology of the film audience today.

The following four-part sketch is an attempt at providing one:

(1) The drop-outs, or the Saturday matinee irregulars. These are the masses once dear to the movie mogul's heart, mostly over 30 and once the majority of the moviegoers, who now have lost the movie habit. When they do go today, it is a special occasion, and one usually prompted by a good word-of-mouth from their friends.

(2) The kids. Probably the biggest movie audience today, these are the sons and daughters of the drop-outs. They see movies on dates, on weekends, enjoy drive-ins and helped to make a success not only of "Love Story" but of vampire and motorcycle movies as well.

While more sympathetic than their parents to such "far-out" films as "M-A-S-H" and "Brewster McLoud," they have avoided and thereby killed most of the "radical" youth films. They like John Wayne and Robert Mitchum, Jane Fonda and Dustin Hoffman, and I suspect they attend films for the same reason their parents once did: It's a good way to get out of the house, to date a girl, to pass the time. Surveys show that most of them stop attending films regularly after marriage or, even more fatal, the birth of children.

(3) The fans. Serious but not obsessed, open to films both as art and as entertainment, the fans include both young people and many older ones as well. But they seem to be increasingly fickle, and such fine movies as "The Conformist" and "Adalen 31" perished without their support. Somehow, they have allowed the art film boom of the early 1960s to fizzle away.

(4) The buffs. Mostly young, devoutly partisan, really concerned about film-as-art (and film-as-polemic[3]), this audience can make or break the small art film in New York, but in the rest of the country they cluster around the universities with little commercial impact.

We could add others, such as children, ethnic viewers and the underground clique. But these are the four principal audiences today.

Although they at times overlap, they don't actually share the same ground. As each group gets smaller, their patronage of films gets larger, and their tastes more difficult to satisfy.

The result is that the whole film medium is caught in a bind. While the mass audience is fond of movies, it is becoming increasingly less familiar

[2] Tolstoyan refers to the famous Russian writer, Leo Tolstoi (1828–1910), author of *War and Peace* and other fiction, who spent his later years living like a peasant on his own estate and writing essays on nonviolent social reform.

[3] A polemic is a controversial statement, usually in opposition to a commonly accepted opinion or tradition.

with them. While the more select, taste-forming audience is familiar, it is both fickle and too small to support a large industry.

Ideally, this will change as the audience is educated to higher levels of taste. But, alas, college film training today often pushes the prospective fan, curious and open-minded, into the less tolerant camps of buffoonery, where cultural overachievers thrive, and taste buds glisten like knives.

Television usually mutilates our film heritage or abandons if for the synthetic slick of made-for-TV movies. Color is also a discriminating factor. That is why we are much more likely to see the wretched 1966 version of "Stagecoach," directed by Gordon Douglas, than the great but black and white John Ford original.

The fractured audience is here to stay. The present situation will not change until Hollywood fully accepts it. Stability will come, not by the audience changing and coming to the film medium, but by the industry changing itself.

Marginal theaters will, of course, be driven out of business. Those that remain will have to streamline their operations to a new level of efficiency.

Another hopeful, but less likely possibility is the growth of a cine-club movement in which film enthusiasts underwrite, through subscriptions, either the distribution or actual production of films. A flourishing phenomenon in Europe for many years (Jean Renoir's "La Marseillaise" was financed by French trade unions), the cine-club has never caught on in this country. But people are now giving it serious thought.

As an art, movies have never been more fertile, various or exciting, yet as an industry it has never been more insecure, or more self-destructive.

At the heart of the problem lies this crisis of the audience. But once it has been resolved, our hopes for film will bear no limit.

POINTS TO CONSIDER

1. Does the author believe that the movie industry understands the nature of the current movie audience? What evidence does he cite to support his belief? What measures does the industry seem to be taking to deal with the problem? (See Paulene Kael, "Marketing the Movies," page 355.)

2. Why do you think that understanding the movie audience is so much more important to the movie industry today than it was twenty-five years ago?

3. According to the survey cited in the article, what percentage of Americans attend movies? Of these, what age group forms the highest single group? What percentage of the population attends movies each week?

4. What is the "fractured audience"? What are its elements? Do you feel that the author's analysis could be particularly helpful to movie-makers?

5. What are cine-clubs? Waht hope do they offer the film industry?

■ MOVIES ON TV

Pauline Kael   *The New Yorker,* August 5, 1974

Movies could easily go the way of the theatre—and faster, since the moneymen have no aesthetic[1] commitment whatever. And probably there'd be less lamentation for movies than for live theatre. Because, of course, there's television. But it's not the same medium. And though if you don't read a book when it comes out you can read it a year later, if you don't see a movie when it comes out, and wait to see it a year later on television, you're not seeing what you could have seen in the theatre. (Nor do you see that movie if you wait to see it in a college, or at a film society in a cheap, grainy 16-mm. reduction.) What's lost on television is the visual beauty, the spatial sense, the fusion of image and sound—everything that makes movies an art form. And movies made directly for television almost never have these qualities; one talks of TV movies in terms of pace and impact and tension, and occasionally—with the prestige ones—subject and performances, but who talks of television movies in terms of beauty? Movies made for TV, or movies made for a big screen and shown on TV, are reduced to just what the businessmen believe in—the bare bones of entertainment. There is something spurious about the very term "a movie made for TV," because what you make for TV is a TV program.

Television as we have it isn't an art form—it's a piece of furniture that is good for a few things. There's a problem of dimensions: no matter what people say, the screen is too small, and that's why the thing TV does best is a closeup of a person being asked a direct question—because both you and that person knew that it operates like a lie detector. For perhaps most Americans, TV is an appliance, not to be used selectively but to be turned on—there's always something to watch. If a hundred million people see a movie in two showings on TV, that doesn't mean what it would if a hundred million people saw it in theatres. Sure, forty-two million people saw "The Autobiography of Miss Jane Pittman," but they saw it sandwiched between two other shows. TV stars with audiences larger than the world has ever before known are eager to appear in a real movie—which, even if a hit, will be seen by only a handful, relatively speaking (until it, too, winds up on TV)—because they know that on TV they're part of the furniture. On TV they're mundane, they're reduced to the routinely, boringly tolerable. There's an aesthetic element in the phrase "larger than life," and the artists working in the movie medium instinctively take that into consideration. What is on the big screen has an aesthetic clarity denied to the box; when you're watching a movie in a theatre, you don't need a voice telling you what you have just seen.

There have been some few subjects filmed for TV which nobody would finance for theatres, because it's generally understood that people won't pay to see a film on a subject like that of "I Heard The Owl Call My Name" or "Jane Pittman" or "The Execution of Private Slovik." But a few TV shows

---

[1] Aesthetic means artistic or appealing to a sense of beauty.

with social themes shouldn't become the occasion for big headlines in the press about how television "has been growing bolder." Bold is just what these shows aren't; even when they're made as well as possible, they're mincingly careful. And they're not a key to new opportunities on TV so much as a key to the constriction of opportunities for moviemakers: moviemakers can't get backing for pictures with social themes—or with any real themes at all. Probably it's true that people wouldn't pay to see the films on social themes which they'll watch on television, but that's because those subjects are treated in the sober, limited TV manner. We have no way of knowing how the public might respond if a hugely talented filmmaker with adequate resources and a campaign to back him took on a large social theme. Nobody has had the chance in decades.

Television represents what happens to a medium when the artists have no power and the businessmen are in full, unquestioned control. People's TV expectations are so low and so routinized that "Brian's Song" can pass for an event, and a pitifully predictable problem play like "Tell Me Where It Hurts," in which Maureen Stapleton plays a middle-aged housewife who joins a women's-lib group and has her consciousness raised, is received by the press as if it marked a significant advance. And what sort of opportunities does *normal* television offer for the development of talent? Here are the words of Brandon Stoddard, A.B.C.'s vice-president in charge of motion pictures for television:

> I am interested in emotional jeopardy, not physical jeopardy. I want the viewer to really care about the people and to feel something when it is over. . . . I have nothing against exploitative material if it is done right, and the way to do it right is to translate it into human drama rather than gimmicks. I don't want to know about the two Vampires in the casino in Las Vegas. I want to know about the man they are attacking and how it will affect his life. . . . We are looking everywhere for story ideas and even calling colleges to get some new blood into this.

Movies as an art form won't die and go to the heaven of television. If they die, they'll be truly dead. Even if the shift in the audience toward the crude and insensitive is only a temporary derangement,[2] it could be sufficient to destroy movies.

POINTS TO CONSIDER

1. What differences does the author point out between a movie shown on television and a movie shown in a theater?
2. What does the author mean when she says that TV is an "appliance" and not an "art form"? Why do TV stars want to make movies? What does

[2] Derangement is insanity.

the author mean when she says, "When you're watching a movie in a theater, you don't need a voice telling you what you've just seen"? Do you agree with the author's assessment of TV's artistic possibilities? Explain.

3. What is the author's opinion of TV's new "boldness"? Why does she feel that movies with "social themes" appear on television and not in movie theaters?

4. Who are the "moneymen"? How does the author describe their influence on television? What influence do they have on movies as art? What does she see as their attitude toward art in movies and television? What possible future effect does she suggest they might have on movies?

WRITING

1. Why do some people believe that photography is not as "artistic" a form of expression as painting? To what extent do you agree? What limitations does photography have in comparison to painting? What can photography do that painting cannot?

2. To what extent do you feel that photography is as "artistic" a form of expression as painting? What evidence can you cite that others feel as you do? Who are some of our country's best-known photographers? Can you use some examples of their work to help you prove your point?

3. How does news photography differ from "the more artistic kinds" of photography? To what extent do they overlap? Can you find some examples of "artistic" news photography to prove this point? What well-known news photographers are admired for the artistic qualities of their work?

4. To what extent has photography changed the way in which we learn about or understand the world about us? Compare photography to print as a way of learning. To what extent has photography taken some of the glamor out of our lives?

5. To what extent do current films portray life as you believe it really is, and to what extent do you think they portray life as we would like it to be or as we prefer to think it is? How is the view of reality in the movies affected by the prejudices and taboos of society? Do you believe the films have changed much in the ways that they portray reality over the past fifty or so years?

6. How great an effect do you feel that the film—as both "artistic" and "informative" medium—has upon the attitudes and behavior of our society? Why does it not have a greater effect?

7. What effects—in terms of both content and techniques—has the great popularity of television had upon the kinds of films being produced today? To what degree do you think the effects have been favorable? To what degree do you think they have been unfavorable?

8. Compare the technical devices used for achieving effects in early movies with the technical devices used for achieving effects in current movies. Which of the early film techniques do we still use frequently and which have we largely abandoned? Why? Which recently introduced film techniques seem particularly effective in terms of contemporary interests and tastes? Why?

9. Some film critics have felt that color and sound detracted from rather than enhanced the artistic qualities of movies. Why? To what extent do you agree or disagree? Why?

10. Read a best seller that has been made into a film, and then see the film. What additions, deletions, and changes in emphasis have been made in the film version? To what extent is the film version more complex or less complex than the book version? What explanations can you offer for these changes? To what extent are the changes essential because of the change in medium, and to what extent were the changes made for other reasons?

would be different if you had not read the book?

11. Try to write a scenario or a shooting script for a silent film based upon a story you have read or upon an original idea. How will you communicate the ideas and emotions in purely visual terms? How will time serve as an important consideration in helping you to achieve your effects? Assuming you will actually make the film, how will your limitations of time, money, and technical equipment affect your movie? Why do you think that film-making has become such a popular hobby of late?

12. How does the experience of watching a movie in a theatre differ from the experience of watching live theatre or of watching television? What do these other media offer that film cannot?

13. Studying many photographs by a number of photographers pursue the idea of a personal style in a photographer's work. What makes the work of a particular photographer uniquely "his"? What effects, techniques, subjects does he favor? Is it possible for a photographer's style to be as easily recognized as that of a painter? Why?

14. Investigate the effects the photograph and photographic processes have had on publishing. What new kinds of publications has the photograph helped create? (the Time-Life books, "coffee table" books, etc.) How have other photographic processes affected the printing industry and, indirectly, what is printed?

15. By examining the fine art of the last thirty or forty years, attempt to determine what effect the photograph has had upon art and the artist. Has the photograph put the artist "out of business?" or has it freed him for investigation of things other than representation?

16. Make a short, silent film. Best results would probably be obtained by first writing a scenario and shooting script and then sticking as close to the script as possible. If making an actual film is not possible, a shooting script, using all the proper terms (pan, zoom, close-up, and so forth), can prove almost as enlightening a project.

17. Investigate the star system in films. How did it begin? Was the star system inevitable? Is it actually on the wane as some people contend? Why? What advantages does the star system have for the production and marketing of films? What disadvantages?

18. Investigate McLuhan's contention that because viewers have been massively exposed to fifteen-, thirty-, and sixty-second commercials on television, movies can now use far greater freedom in dealing with a narrative plot line. Is plot actually as near obsolescence as he would have us believe?

19. Study the techniques and processes of film special effects. What role do they play in films? How are the individual effects achieved?

20. Make a study of Hollywood as it is treated in literature. Such books as Nathaniel West's *Day of the Locust,* F. Scott Fitzgerald's *The Last Tycoon,* Budd Schulberg's *What Makes Sammy Run?* and Evelyn Waugh's *The Loved One* all offer insights into Hollywood as a place and as a cultural phenomenon.

21. As a companion study to the above or as a separate analysis, examine the image of Hollywood as presented by the movie magazines. What sort of place would these magazines have you believe Hollywood is? According to them, what sort of people are the movie stars? What aspects of the stars' lives do the magazines emphasize particularly? Why?

Part Seven

Popular Music: Previews and Viewpoints

The whole body of American folk and pop music is such a thickly woven mesh that certain styles are continually crossing and recrossing other styles.

—Robert Shelton

Where soul is really at today is pop music. It emanates from the rumble of gospel chords and the plaintive cry of the blues. It is compounded of raw emotion, pulsing rhythm, and spare, earthy lyrics—all suffused with the sensual, somewhat melancholy vibrations of the Negro idiom.

—*Time*

Maybe we should say that folk music is not so much any particular group of songs and singers, but rather it is a process, an age-old process of ordinary people making their own music, shaping old traditions to fit new situations.

—Pete Seeger

Indeed, everything about the music industry of the '70s is reminiscent of Hollywood in the '30s and '40s: moguls, superstars and promoters operating in a world charged with sex and power and conspiring to sell slick, tuneful packages to a voracious public.

—*Time*

Give me the making of the songs of a nation, and I care not who makes its laws.

—Andrew Fletcher (1703)
As quoted by John Culkin

Popular
Music

■ ROCK: THE UNSPEAKABLE MIX

W. T. Lhamon, Jr.   *The New Republic,* March 2, 1974

The pop performer back in the '30s, Nathanael West said, was a hooked trout writhing on the audience's line. Think, then, of rock groups shuddering today on an electrically amplified bass beat and screaming treble. There is a line between rock performer and rock audience, but it is less a fishing than a mainline.[1] And the present rush[2] is total: nothing short of epilepsy and electroshock, simultaneously induced. Nor is it therapeutic: Janis Joplin, Jim Morrison, Jimi Hendrix and the Stones' own Brian Jones have been among the most notable casualties of that high voltage power line. The Beatles fell apart on it. It has helped create the alternating currents of even Bob Dylan's mercurial style. Dylan once said that he accepted chaos, but he wasn't sure it accepted him. The Rolling Stones also accept chaos, but in song after song chaos surely accepts them. Only the Stones have been able to conduct the present electricity, flirt with its death-wish, and diffuse it back toward the audience. And only they have stayed the same while they grew. Thus they have added to rock music while never abandoning—instead revealing—its essential power.

Their relation to their audience has been less prophetic than seismographic.[3] From the moments of their best early songs, like "The Last Time" and "Satisfaction," they have been catching the signals in the noise and amplifying them. If most of the signals suggest that cultural noise is increasing, then the suggestion constitutes just one of the many paradoxes in their genius. "That man comes on the radio. And he's tellin' me more and more about some useless information, supposed to fire my imagination: I can't get no . . . Oh no no no . . . no Satisfaction": these lines from "Satisfaction" are perhaps the only universally recognized classics in rock music. But the words are submerged in the anarchy of the rock sounds. The lyrics whang in the same noise about which the Stones complain, yet the music continues to celebrate noise by revealing it as positive anarchy—a spicy soup. There's truth in the pejorative saw that rock audiences mostly don't listen to words. Rock audiences listen instead to a different authority. It's not the pure Word they are after, but the unspeakable Mix.[4]

The words on Stones cuts are only good therefore, when heard within the contexture of the band and within the multiple layers of nuance that their singer, Mick Jagger, juices from seemingly banal phonemes. Also Jagger himself has reiterated that the words are unimportant, so much so that he intentionally mumbles the bad lines when they come up, mumbles them back into the music. For them, the mix is more important—a fact which

[1] Mainlining refers to the practice of injecting drugs directly into the veins.

[2] Rush here refers to the sudden, often violent, initial effect of a drug on the drug user.

[3] A seismograph is an instrument for measuring the violence of earthquakes.

[4] The author here alludes to the mixer, which is an electronic device for balancing, blending, and mixing signals from the individual instruments of a rock group into what emerges from the amplifiers as the group's final sound.

even sympathetic auditors like Dylan have fought against. For example Dylan reputedly told the Stones he could have written "Satisfaction," but that they could never have written "Tambourine Man." Jagger's response was to admit that likely truth but to wonder, could Dylan *sing* "Satisfaction"?

Most of the great Stones songs, from "The Last Time" and even "Play with Fire" through "Sympathy for the Devil" and "Gimme Shelter" and on to "Winter" are about the end of this world, the coming apocalypse and the beyond. What's beyond is moot. In "Gimme Shelter," storm and floods are threatening the singer's "very life today"; war, rape, murder are all "just a shot away"; so if he doesn't get shelter, he'll "just fade away." But into what? Into love: "Love, sister, it's just a kiss away." And so uncertainty boogies on because "kiss away" may mean either that love is close, or that love is a mere something to kiss goodbye. And in "Winter," the singer announces a "cold, cold winter" in which "a lotta love is all burned out," but he goes on to hope for, and act out, a "long, hot summer," during which "a lotta love will be burnin' bright." In fact the song seems to be poised upon the actual moment of breakdown: "I wish I been out in California when the lights on all the Christmas trees went out. But I been burnin' my bell, book and candle, and the restoration plays has all gone 'round." Then, as in other songs on this album, there are the doubts; will the singer be able to give anyone else shelter after the darkness arrives?: "I wanna wrap my coat around ya . . . I wanna but I can't afford ya."

These songs approaching and exploring the interface and environs of cultural death have played every jukebox in the land, come over every airwave into every cruising AM radio, pumped into every back-brain of the Western world's counterculture, and hopped up its every dancing foot. Apocalypse, the guitars and the highhat proclaim, is good times. Moving toward noise and let-loose energy is good times. It's good, rock audiences feel, more than think, to move toward entropy, toward random energy, toward "useless information," toward a total promiscuity where all modes, all styles, each diction, every voice and note are mixed into an overcooked stew where all discrete systems are broke, broken, broken down, running into—not merely juxtaposed with—one another. Yes! The title of this last album, "Goat's Head Soup," is not an accident.

The goat in the soup, as the full-color picture included in the album suggests, is the threatening fertility, demon sway and black magic marinating in the soup of the age. The other pictures, on the cover, are David Bailey shots of each band member, veiled in distorting gauze, seeming to be submerging with a smile in the same soup. These images capture the enduring image of the band: a group welcoming and creating the chance to explore the volts beyond discreteness (they've always been past discretion), beyond the styles they and their times grew up with, beyond the customary orders of the day. A few bars in one of the best "Soup" songs, "Coming Down Again," says it well: "Slipped my tongue in someone else's pie, tasting better all the time . . . Being hungry, it ain't no crime."

Tongue? Someone else's pie? Rock music has always caught itself between moaning and meaning, between pimples and posterity. So the first thing to admit is that the Stones are often outrageously obscene and very nasty. But there's more, for they are promiscuous in the root sense of being *pro-mix*. The visual signature on their latest album labels is a red hanging-out tongue; they call their touring plane the Tongue, perhaps because it slips them into different lands with different languages all over the world. And their recorded voices are anything but their native London tongues. They sing put-ons, put-downs, Appalachian lays, delta blues, urban blues, Texas blues, Nashville country, blackface-vaudeville, hard rock, psych rock, demon rock. And they mix them, running through several styles in one song, even merging more than one in a single line. More than any other group, rock or jazz, gospel or pop, they sing in tongues. Singing or talking tongues is an energy trip, a passing over into another state on the total mix of all sound, with all discrete meanings merged in a rush, a rush which approximates a mode ineffably beyond this world of linear, un-tongued discourse.

The Rolling Stones have hung together longer than any other rock group (except, I suppose, for the Beach Boys and The Band, now touring again with Dylan). Perhaps because the events of the decade since their first single in June 1963 impinge on their consciousness, history has preoccupied the Stones—noticeably since "Sympathy for the Devil," but more strikingly in this album than in any of their others. "Dancing with Mr D.," "100 Years Ago," "Coming Down Again," "Silver Train" and "Winter"—in short, most of the prominent tunes on the album—directly address the problem of living within history and the opportunity to plunge out. From this angle, the other songs are hints about how the Stones are living until the Last Time arrives. "Hiding away," for example, will be neither easy nor for everyone. But the song speaks very much to the present by bespeaking, as Dylan's resurfacing does, a refocused, hard-edged music which is as important in its sphere as the newest poetry, fiction and films are in theirs. Not incidentally, too, the spheres are really no longer that separate. Anyone listening to this album while reading Burroughs, Thompson, Pynchon, Wurlitzer, or watching Bertolucci, Godard, Altman, Siegel and others will not only catch cross references but also enrich the separate pleasures.

The sliding style of Stones songs—as if they were bending whole forms, not just a single blue note—is the best feature of the kind of rock that the Stones savor, for it distinguishes them from blues on the one hand and jazz on the other. Blues is a round form by definition; it takes up an experience—lost lover, loneliness, feeling hung, aimless trucking—feels it poignantly, expresses a coping attitude which accepts the irreversibility of the experience, and fades out with the mood better understood but still there, essentially there. Fine jazz, like Coltrane's, like Miles Davis', often offers an alternative, transcendent, expanded consciousness for the aural grabbing. The form of blues copes but doesn't transcend, while jazz transcends but doesn't cope—leaving, therefore, a gap. Rock—rock like the Stones play—transports between the two. The best examples of this style that I'm trying to locate are those groups or musicians who are at home with the different individual modes—the first Butterfield Blues Band doing "East/West," or John McLaughlin (who has played with Miles Davis) teaming with Carlos Santana to play "Let Us Go into the House of the Lord." Each of these examples is of a music that moves an audience on a hallucinogenic journey from one place and style through others, wrapped exhaustingly in what the Stones have called "the silk sheet of time" ("I Got the Blues"), into zones of magnificently released energy.

"Goat's Head Soup" shows the Stones have realized that the singer is just a voice, a tongue, and the song carries the tongue, submerging it in the soup when occasions demand. It's the song not the singer. And the Stones are now doing more with the song than is any other rock group.

Although no band has had a larger crush on America or has so totally lavished itself on every example of American funk from T-shirts through Slim Harpo and Buddy Holly to Los Angeles, they are the one band that America will never—can never—assimilate. America loved the Beatles, gorged on them and ended by mushing them in muzak. Other groups sing Dylan songs, as they did the Beatles'. But nobody ever recuts a Stones number. The Stones are to popular music what Nathanael West has been to the American novel, only darker, deadlier, more the satanic majesties they claim to be: more a torch than West's thorn in the side. Play with the Stones and you play with a tongue of fire.

■ POINTS TO CONSIDER

1. How does the author describe the relationship between the rock performer and his audience? What effect does this have on the performer? From your own experience, would you say that this is a valid description of the rock phenomenon? Explain.

2. What is the "mix"? How is it essential to what is usually understood as "rock"? How does the author relate it to promiscuity? To talking in tongues? Explain why you feel these comparisons are or are not valid.

3. How does the author differentiate between the Stones' rock and jazz on the one hand and blues on the other?

4. Why can America never assimilate the Stones?

■ SOUL: SINGING IT LIKE IT IS

Time, June 28, 1968

Has it got soul? Man, that's the question of the hour. If it has soul, then it's tough, beautiful, out of sight. It passes the test of with-itness. It has the authenticity of collard greens boiling on the stove, the sassy style of the boogaloo in a hip discotheque, the solidarity signified by "Soul Brother" scrawled on a ghetto storefront.

But what *is* soul? "It's like electricity—we don't really know what it is," says Singer Ray Charles. "But it's a force that can light a room." The force radiates from a sense of selfhood, a sense of knowing where you've been and what it means. Soul is a way of life—but it is always the hard way. Its essence is ingrained in those who suffer and endure to laugh about it later. Soul is happening everywhere, in esthetics and anthropology, history and dietetics, haberdashery and politics—although Hubert Humphrey's recent declaration to college students that he was a "soul brother" was all wrong. Soul is letting *others* say you're a soul brother. Soul is not needing others to say it.

Where soul is really at today is pop music. It emanates from the rumble of gospel chords and the plaintive cry of the blues. It is compounded of raw emotion, pulsing rhythm and spare, earthy lyrics—all suffused with the sensual, somewhat melancholy vibrations of the Negro idiom. Always the Negro idiom. LeRoi Jones, the militant Negro playwright, says: "Soul music is music coming out of the black spirit." For decades it only reverberated around the edges of white pop music, injecting its native accent here and there, now it has penetrated to the core, and its tone and beat are triumphant.

No Moon in June. Soul music is sincerity, a homely distillation of everybody's daily portion of pain and joy. "It pulls the cover off," explains Jim Stewart, a former banker and country fiddler who heads Memphis' soul-oriented Stax Records. "It's not the moon in June. It's life. Sometimes it's violence and sex. That's the way it is in this world. Sometimes there's animal in it; but let's face it, we've got a lot of animal in us." The difference between Tin Pan Alley and Soul is not hard to define. A conventional tune-smith might write: "You're still near, my darling, though we're apart/I'll hold you always in my heart." The soul singer might put it: "Baby, since you split the scene the rent's come due./Without you or your money it's hard, yeah, hard to be true." . . .

Hollers & Blues. Negroes have been sifting their sorrows in songs for centuries. It started, says Mahalia Jackson, who is now 56, with "the groans and moans of the people in the cotton fields. Before it got the name of soul, men were sellin' watermelons and vegetables on a wagon drawn by a mule, hollerin' *'watermellllon'* with a cry in their voices. And the men on the railroad track layin' crossties—every time they hit the hammer it was with a sad feelin', but with a beat. And the Baptist preacher—he the one who had the soul—he give out the meter, a long and short meter, and the old mothers of the church would reply. This musical thing has been here since America been here. This is trial-and-tribulation music."

Out of the matrix of these Negro work songs, field hollers and spirituals of the 19th century sprang the first crude country blues. It was spread by bardic singers with guitars or harmonicas—beggars, itinerant farm laborers, members of jug bands and medicine or minstrel shows. Then, with the Negro migrations to Northern cities in the early decades of the 20th century, the blues gathered a more elaborate accompaniment around itself (sometimes a jazz group) and moved into theaters, dance halls and recording studios. This was the era of Bessie Smith's classic records. By the 1930s a new style was forged around tenements, speakeasies and rent parties—a harsher, more nervous brand of blues that reflected the stress and tempo of urban living. This style mingled with the blaring jazz and blues that swept out of the Southwest during the swing era (Andy Kirk, Count Basie), and so the stage was set for the emergence, after World War II, of rhythm & blues.

Proxy Performances. Even more slashing and frenetic than urban blues, R & B introduced amplified guitars, honking saxophones and gyrating singers in lamé costumes. Popularized and commercialized as it was, it still retained the fundamental quality of the blues. Such was the force of R & B, in fact, that white singers of the 1950s quickly saw the potential for lifting it out of the limited Negro market and filtering it into the far more lucrative pop field. Much if not most of what the white public knew as rock 'n' roll during this period consisted of proxy performances of Negro R & B music by people like Elvis Presley and Bill Haley. The success of the white performers produced a caustic resentment among the Negro musicians, many of whom still bridle at the irony of it all—they produced the music, but the white men cashed in on it. In those days, the only way for Negroes to really make it in the white world was to do precisely and painfully what the Nat King Coles and Lena Hornes did: forsake their own music and sing white pop.

All this began to change with such English rock 'n' roll groups as the Beatles, the Rolling Stones and the Animals, who made a point of crediting their sources—not only R & B figures such as Chuck Berry and Bo Diddley, but also country and urban bluesmen such as John Lee Hooker, Muddy Waters, T-Bone Walker and B. B. King. "Until the Beatles exposed the origins," says Waters, "the white kids didn't know anything about the music. But now they've learned that it was in their backyard all the time."

Jubilation Shouts. Meanwhile, the rhythm-&-blues strain was picking up new momentum, while post-Beatle rock charged off on its own creative path. The man who gave R & B its fresh thrust was a blind, Georgia-born bard named Ray Charles, one of the most hauntingly effective and versatile Negro singers in the history of pop music.

Negroes had always rigorously maintained a distinction between gospel and blues—the sacred and profane—despite the affinity of their sounds. But Charles boldly brought them together, blending foot-stamping orgiastic jubilation shouts with the abrasive, existentialist irony of "devil songs." He even carried over the original gospel tunes and changed the words to fit the emotion. "Lord" became "you," or "baby," and it didn't matter if the bulk of the prayerful text remained the same. Thus Clara Ward's rousing old gospel song, *This Little Light of Mine,* became Charles's *This Little Girl of Mine.* (A wonderful identification!) Oldtimers who had once been forced to choose between the two genres were offended. "I know that's wrong," said Bluesman and former Preacher Big Bill Broonzy. "He should be singing in a church."

But Charles's innovation brought waves of gospel talent into the blues field and at the same time offered blues performers a chance to employ the climactic cadences and mythic ritual of black evangelism. Some of his more ardent followers adopted stage mannerisms in which they appeared to be seized by God: they tore off their clothes, called for witnesses, collapsed and rose up again. The bespangled James Brown's whirling, convulsive performances have even been analyzed as enactments of the Crucifixion.

Most important, once Charles broke the barrier between gospel and blues, the way was open for a whole cluster of ingredients to converge around an R & B core and form the potent musical mix now known as soul—among them in Critic Albert Goldman's words, "a racial ragbag of Delta blues, hillbilly strumming, gutbucket jazz, boogie-woogie piano, pop lyricism and store-front shouting."

Chitlin Circuit. It was not long before the soul sound began to move directly into the white market of pop music, and its purveyors started outstripping their white imitators. Charles was the first to reach a mass white public, starting as far back as 1955 with his hit record, *I Got a Woman.* In more recent years, a string of others have come along behind him. Lou Rawls, for example, is a former gospel trouper who spices his blues songs with reminiscences of his boyhood in Chicago's South Side slums. He used to work only in the Negro nightclub "chitlin circuit." As for radio, Rawls says, "I never got played on the top 40 stations because they said I was too, uh—well, not too limited, but too . . ." Black? "Yeah." Now Rawls's albums sell upwards of 200,000 copies from coast to coast and are played throughout the radio band. He has filled Manhattan's Carnegie Hall three times in concert appearances.

Before this started happening, soul music was recorded mostly by small independent companies and shipped straight to the South's black belt and the North's big-city ghettos. Now the upsurge of nationwide soul-oriented firms is so strong that it has jostled the balance of power in the pop record industry. Manhattan-based Atlantic, with such singers as Aretha Franklin, Wilson Pickett, and Sam & Dave, can now sell more records in a week (1,300,000) than it did in six months in 1950; now it ranks with the top singles producers in the business. Detroit's Motown Records, formed eight years ago by Berry Gordy, Jr. with a $700 loan, last year grossed a soulful $30 million. Gordy's slick, carefully controlled "Motown sound" (noted for its rhythmic accent on all four beats of the bar instead of the usual R & B emphasis on alternating beats) has launched, among others, Diana Ross and the Supremes, Marvin Gaye, Smokey Robinson and the Miracles, Stevie Wonder, and Martha and the Vandellas.

Badge of Identity. By all the commercial yardsticks used in the trade, soul has arrived—and it has arrived in the hit parade as well as the "race market," in the suburbs as well as the ghettos, in the Midwestern campuses as well as Harlem's Apollo Theater.

By yardsticks used outside the trade, soul's arrival is even more significant. Since its tortuous evolution is so intertwined with Negro history and so expressive of Negro culture, Negroes naturally tend to value it as a sort of badge of black identity. "The abiding moods expressed in our most vital popular art form are not simply a matter of entertainment," says Negro Novelist Ralph Ellison. "They also tell us who and where we are."

Militant young Negroes put a more defiant slant on it. Explains Charles Keil, a white ethnomusicologist and the author of *Urban Blues:* "For a Negro to say 'B. B. King is my main man' is to say 'I take pride in who I am.' With this self-acceptance, a measure of unity is gained, and a demand is made upon white America. 'Accept us on our own terms.' "

Yet when soul solidarity is founded on a fellowship of suffering, it may involve not a demand for white acceptance but an outright exclusion of whites, as Godfrey Cambridge makes clear. "Soul is getting kicked in the ass until you don't know what it's for," he says. "It's being broke and down and out, and people telling you you're no good. It's the language of the subculture, but you can't learn it, because no one can give you black lessons."

Used in this way, the soul concept becomes a mystique, a glorification of Negritude in all its manifestations. The soul brother makes a point of emphasizing Negro inflections such as "yo" for "your," of abandoning slang words and phrases as soon as they reach universal currency, of eating foods such as chitlins, pig's feet and black-eyed peas, in mastering a loose, cocky way of walking down the street—in doing all the things that are closed off or alien to Whitey.

Blue-Eyed Soul. Does this mean that white musicians by definition don't have soul? A very few Negroes will concede that such white singers as Frank Sinatra and Peggy Lee have it, and Aretha also nominates Frenchman Charles Aznavour. A few more will accept such blues-oriented whites as the Righteous Brothers, Paul Butterfield, and England's Stevie Winwood—largely because their sound is almost indistinguishable from Negro performers. But for the most part, Negroes leave it up to whites to defend the idea of "blue-eyed soul," whether by the criterion of talent, experience or temperament. Janis Joplin argues it this way: "There's no patent on it. It's just feeling things. A housewife in Nebraska has soul, but she represses it, makes it conform to a lot of rules like marriage, or sugarcoats it."

If the earnest racial jockeying can be suspended, the question of who has soul actually becomes intriguing, if rather fanciful fun. The very elusiveness of the soul concept invites a freewheeling, parlour-game approach. Not long ago, in an eleven-page feature on the soul mystique, *Esquire* half seriously argued that there are only two kinds of people in the world: the haves and the have-nots—soul-wise. Others have taken up the sport, which promotes the engaging notion that important personalities of history and legend can be classed in these terms.

As for those to whom soul is anything but a parlour game, one thing is certain: the closer a Negro gets to a "white" sound nowadays, the less soulful he is considered to be, and the more he is regarded as having betrayed his heritage. Dionne Warwick singing *Alfie?* Impure! Diana Ross and the Supremes recording an album of Rodgers and Hart songs? Unacceptable! Yet many "deviations" may be solid professionalism, a matter of adapting to changing audiences. As Lou Rawls says, "Show business is so vast—why should I limit myself to any one aspect if I have the capabilities to do more?"

On the other hand, some soul singers are so deeply imbued with the enduring streams of blues and gospel, so consumed by those primal currents of racial experience and emotion, that they could never be anything but soulful.

POINTS TO CONSIDER

1. What seem to be some of the hard-to-pin-down characteristics of soul music? What seem to be some common elements in the music and the lyrics of soul music you have heard?

2. Why do you think it is so difficult to arrive at a clear-cut definition of the term "soul"?

3. What are the historic roots of soul music? What various kinds of music have influenced or contributed to today's soul music?

4. How did soul music become known to, and popular with, white audiences? What factors have accounted for its ever-increasing popularity?

5. What was Ray Charles' important contribution to contemporary soul music?

6. In what ways does soul music serve as "a sort of badge of black identity"? With what other elements of black American culture has the term "soul" become identified?

7. Do you think that any white musicians (or other whites, for that matter) can be said to have "soul"? Why, or why not?

THE BIG SOUND FROM THE COUNTRY

David Gahr and Robert Shelton   *The Face of Folk Music,* 1968

Where does folk music end and commercial country music take over? We pose the question, but can offer no simple answer.

The whole body of American folk and pop music is such a thickly woven mesh that certain styles are continually crossing and recrossing other styles. Nowhere is this interweave more evident than in the music generally associated with Nashville, the music loosely called "Country and Western."

A good many performers in the forty-year history of Country and Western music began as "folk performers." Some never left the precincts of folk music, while others are continually walking both sides of the musical street, changing their choice of performing style for a given song or instrumental.

Contemporary Country and Western music has changed so much, has become so sophisticated, that it is difficult to recall that nearly all of it was born in folk-oriented style. Many white folk performers later "crossed over" into the patently more commercial style of Country and Western. Yet the majority of Bluegrass performers to be discussed here remained solidly in the center of the bridge that connects folk tradition with present-day Nashville music.

There has been an unfortunate tug-of-war between those folk fans who regard Country and Western music as an area for their study and enjoyment and those who make minute distinctions between what is pure folk and what is "corrupted" or commercial.

It is this sort of élitist approach[1] toward folk music and its peripheral expressions that has retarded the folk movement's ability to stay in touch with greater parts of the population. Ethnic snobs[2] and traditional determinists think, with much persuasive argumentation on their side, that "their" music is superior. At the same time, they are denying themselves the vast excitements and stimulations of kindred and tangential musics, which, while not "pure" have much else to commend themselves.

All this by way of introduction to the lively world of Nashville music. Nashville is the capital of an international music industry. It has become the vortex of a recording, publishing, broadcasting, and personal-appearance network that spreads around the world. Nashville is known by many nicknames: Music City, U.S.A.; Tin Pan Valley; the Capital of Country Music. Nashville is not only the world center of what has become a $100,000,000-a-year country music industry, but it is also a recording center for a lot of other pop musics, a center now rivaling the supremacy of New York and Hollywood in range of activity and number of musicians and recordings involved.

As to country music, the size of its international audience is almost impossible to calculate. If we say that there are some 35,000,000 country fans in the United States and Canada, what total can be supplied when we add Britain, Ireland, Australia, Scandinavia, Germany, South Africa and Japan? To be conservative about it, let's say fifty million deep-dyed fans of country music, many of whom would be folk fans if some of the folk leaders didn't persist in keeping their music "élite" and of such arid delimitations as to allow no mass appeal.

At any rate, out of Nashville spin some 15,000 live performances annually. There are about five hundred song-writers living in the Nashville-Davidson County district, and the more than two dozen recording studios there are kept busy, often on a round-the-clock basis.

How did the industry happen to center itself in Nashville? The answer can be given in three little words: "Grand Ole Opry." This unbelievably indestructible American radio show and institution, born November 28, 1925, was to provide the nucleus for the entire country music industry. With ever-traveling performers making the rounds, it was only their return to Nashville to appear on station WSM's "Opry" that made them available for recording.

The announcer-host of the WSM "Barn Dance," the show that was to evolve into "Grand Ole Opry," was a former newspaper man named George D. Hay, who had earlier helped station WLS in Chicago start its "Barn Dance." The performers on that first WSM show were an eighty-year-old bearded fiddler named Uncle Jimmy Thompson and his niece, Eva Thompson Jones, who played piano and sang. Uncle Jimmy scraped out an hour's worth of old jigs, reels, and sentimental parlor and country songs. After only

[1] The élitist sees himself in a special limited group of people who are more knowledgeable.

[2] Ethnic snobs insist upon "cultural purity."

a few minutes, requests began to pour into the station from listeners by wire and telephone. The new show was a hit.

Just two years later, George Hay, known widely by his nickname, "The Solemn Old Judge," renamed the show "Grand Ole Opry," and it has since become the grand old dinosaur of American radio. Having missed airtime only during a few of President Franklin D. Roosevelt's "Fireside Chats," the "Opry" is believed to be the oldest continuous broadcast in radio. Either directly on its clearchannel station or through subsidiary syndicated shows, the country music on the "Opry" reaches some 10,000,000 persons each week.

When the "Opry" started, country music was also in its early phases. Mostly, it was just a rural folk music, put onto early radio to fill the vacuum for entertainment for regional audiences. Folk-country music was beginning to score with the simultaneous growth of electric recording. (The first country recording *of consequence* was Fiddling John Carson's Atlanta sessions of 1923.) As ironic as it may seem, it was two electronic media, recording and radio, that were to transform a regional folk music into an international industry.

The content of a four-hour "Opry" broadcast today or the infinite variety of music recorded in Nashville reflect how comprehensive the term "country music" has become. It includes ballads, heart songs, Bluegrass, Western songs, train songs, breakdowns, fiddle and guitar tunes, hoedowns, and a lot more. Country music embraces a wide range of styles, from the strictly traditional folk-oriented to bright, urbane love ballads or novelty or sacred tunes that have a distinctly modern flavor. As in jazz and pop music, there are such a variety of styles and approaches to Country and Western music that each have their strong adherents.

As I wrote in *The Country Music Story* (Bobbs-Merrill), the soundtrack of a documentary on country music would carry a symphony of varied sounds:

"It would be the clang of an electric guitar, the subtle fretting of Merle Travis's unamplified guitar; the piercing, stirring "Gloryland March" of Wilma Lee and Stoney Cooper; the yodeling of Kenny Roberts; the devilish banjo tricks of Don Reno; the clunk of Stringbean's old banjo; Pappy McMichen's bow sliding across his 1723 Italian violin, which he has to call a fiddle; Johnny Cash pointing his guitar at an audience as if he were going to hold them up; a screaming "Howdy" from beneath Cousin Minnie Pearl's straw hat; Jimmy Wakely singing to his horse; Zeke Clements explaining how to skin a cat to make a banjo; Archie Campbell telling a racy story one minute and singing a gospel song the next; Ralph Peer telling rustic auditioners to relax and sing out in a Southern hotel room; Ernest Tubb speaking like a benign Lincoln in a ten-gallon hat; Hank Williams crying his lonesome words into a microphone; Jimmie Rodgers hearing a whistle in the night. It is a rare and exciting sound."

It would be next to impossible to compress my history of Country and Western music into one essay. . . . All that can be hinted at, for the urban folk fan, is that there is a tremendous amount of musical quality lying over the hills to Nashville. There is also a lot of junk, pap, commercial garbage. The student or fan of Country and Western music, therefore, has a greater job of selectivity to tread between the dross and the ore. But it is worth the effort, if only to catch one of the heartfelt gospel songs of Roy Acuff, the "king of country music"; to marvel at the guitar virtuosity of Chet Atkins; to sense the beautiful part-singing of The Blue Sky Boys; to watch Cousin Emmy's dynamic manner on stage; to roar at the unhusked corn of Homer and Jethro or Grandpa Jones.

Too many thousands of performers make up the vast Breughelesque[3] canvas of America's "other popular music," Country and Western, to be touched on here. We can only urge that you try to give Country and Western another listen—to find out why Buck Owens and George Jones and their hard-driving "honky-tonk" style of singing is so popular; to sense Roger Miller's place in a continuum that places his "King of the Road" in a direct line of descent from the hobo songs of Cliff Carlisle, to see how Hank Snow and Ernest Tubb are latter-day twigs off the sturdy branch that produced Jimmy Rodgers, "the singing brakeman" and "the father of country music," way back in the mid-1920's.

One area where the folk fan seems most closely in touch with country music is that large overlapping zone called Bluegrass. Thanks to the popularizing of such city stalwarts as Mike Seeger and Ralph Rinzler, Bluegrass is widely known to nearly every folk fan. Here is a style of rural ensemble musicmaking, vocal and instrumental, that is almost an equivalent of rural string-band jazz, and an equally compelling cousin of the varied instrumental bands of European and Latin-American villages.

To tell it in its simplest outlines, Bluegrass evolved from the string bands who were active in the 1910's and 1920's. These string bands, such as Gid Tanner and The Skillet Lickers, had, in turn, evolved from earlier banjo-fiddle combinations of the nineteenth century. Even that trend can be found to have been an American variant of Irish and Scottish pipe and flute ensembles. Whatever this circuitous line of descent, Bluegrass style as we know it today, was largely set in the late 1940's by a series of seminal bands led by the great Kentucky singer and mandolin player, Bill Monroe.

Monroe's bands were to be the seed-bed of Bluegrass. Through its various formations passed nearly every major Bluegrass stylist of our time. The leading offshoot of Monroe's Bluegrass Boys were Lester Flatt and Earl Scruggs, whose own band, The Foggy Mountain Boys, have in their own time become the nation's leading "glamour" Bluegrass band. Scruggs's virtuosity on the five-string banjo is, of course, legendary and actual at the same time. He gave the instrument a fluidity and lyricism that was almost unknown before, and his style of picking has been widely imitated.

During the height of the urban folk revival, there were to be nearly as many excellent city-based Bluegrass bands as there were in the country. As with country bands, the urban pickers generally kept the same instrumentation of guitar, banjo, mandolin, Dobro (a steel guitar fretted in the Hawaiian manner), and bass. The voices were to be as athletic and free as were the instruments, with the overall sound adding up to a kind of whirlwind magic. Among the best of the city bands are The Greenbriar Boys and The Charles River Valley Boys, New Yorkers and Bostonians respectively, who added

[3] Breughelesque refers to the style of Pieter Breughel (1520–1569), a Flemish painter known for his canvases active with scenes of peasant life.

country-born members and went on to become important style-setters in the folk revival.

Of course, to single out just a few country and city Bluegrass bands scarcely does justice to the breadth of this important subdivision of American folk and country music. But for the person seeking an introduction to one of the more exciting musical styles of our era, the recordings of these groups would speak volumes.

The debate about whether to consider all of Country and Western music as part of the folk stream will not end overnight. What is clear is that a growing catholicity of taste[4] is happily spreading through the folk movement, beginning to embrace neighboring musical styles that have esthetic validity, if not purity. It is in this spirit that the work of the John Edwards Memorial Foundation at the University of California at Los Angeles is to be praised.

Here is a study and research center devoted generally to American folk music, but specifically to the Country and Western field. It is the hope of many of us who regard Country and Western as a viable field for study, that the Edwards Foundation will prosper and grow. It appears to be the reigning philosophy of many at the foundation that Hank Williams is as worthy of study as is The Texas Drifter, Goebel Reeves; that Johnny Cash is at least as important as some unknown folk minstrel who never made a cent commercially, but who stuck stubbornly to his own native tradition. It is such approaches as this that make one feel that the folk movement in the United States is really coming of age, beginning to understand that there are popular musics of value even though they do not measure up to the rigorous standards of a purely traditional esthetic.[5]

But while appreciating this, one must also have respect for the tireless proponents of the older music. In this regard, one can have nothing but praise for such groups as The Friends of Old-Time Music, a small and definitely non-profit organization that brought to New York and many other cities of the Northeast the very best in obscure country musicians. Working independently at first, and later cooperating with the Newport Folk Foundation, the Friends of Old-Time Music were trying to say that the folk musicians who had been passed over by Nashville had as much to say, in human and musical terms, as any star turned out by Country and Western music.

The musical-revival trio The New Lost City Ramblers was also trying to spread the wonder and magic of string-band music of the 1920's and 1930's with its own playing. Soon, The New Lost City Ramblers were themselves losing work to the musicians they had helped rediscover from the past. The success of The Ramblers ironically worked to make the music and musicians they studied come to the fore while the group that had done this so painstakingly was actually receding quietly into oblivion. This selfless form of activity represents perhaps one of the glowing, little-known aspects of the folk revival that gave it beauty and ethics and honor.

In the face of those for whom the folk revival was either just a vehicle to peddle their own wares, their own dogma, or their own egos, the work of

---

[4] Catholicity of taste is liberality with a broad range of interest and understanding.

[5] An esthetic here is a set of artistic values.

The Friends of Old-Time Music and The New Lost City Ramblers will help remind everyone of what the best impulses were among the city youngsters who helped produce the folk revival of yesterday, today, and tomorrow.

POINTS TO CONSIDER

1. How are the mass media responsible for turning a regional art form with a limited audience into a popular art form with millions of fans?

2. How did Nashville happen to become the country music capital of the world?

3. What different kinds of music are included in the general term "country music"? Who are some of the best-known country music performers?

4. Are there any differences between "folk music" and "country music"? If so, what are they? Can you give some examples? What is "bluegrass," and how does it overlap the two? Who are some well-known "bluegrass" musicians?

5. What groups are trying to spread the popularity and encourage the serious consideration of country and western music? What other popular art forms do you know of that have recently become subjects for "serious consideration"?

THE FOLK PROCESS

Pete Seeger   *The Incompleat Folk Singer,* 1972

The folk songs we love are masterpieces of composition. We can say this even though we know that no one person composed them. In some cases we are able to name the authors of the lyrics, but remember: these authors started on a firm basis of tradition, which guided them at every turn, in choice of words, meter, rhyme and image.

The tunes, harmonies and rhythms may never have been played exactly alike but are the products of centuries of traditions from England, Ireland, Africa, etc., brought to this continent and more or less amalgamated by thousands of singers over a period of several hundred years.

Maybe we should say that folk music is not so much any particular group of songs or singers, but rather it is a process, an age-old process of ordinary people making their own music, reshaping old traditions to fit new situations. Some songs have more of this process; others have less. But even old ballads like "Barbara Allen" were probably influenced at some time in their long history by individuals in the music professions. And even the pop song on the radio has been influenced in some way by folk music.

Think of folk music as a process; then the history of any folk song will show continual change, contradictions, action and interaction of opposing influences. Now, this might be called, in the term of my mother-in-law (a wonderful woman), diabolical materialism. But we have support here from scientists, such as the late Alfred North Whitehead, mathematician and philosopher. He said: *"The process is the actuality."*

In other words, if you want to understand any phenomenon, study it in motion. If you could suddenly solidify all the water in a brook, and measure it, would that be the brook? An engineer wishing to throw a bridge across it must study it in motion, its origins and destinations, its fluctuations. He tests its qualities at many places and times. He must study the stream as a process. A pail of its water dipped up would no longer even be part of the brook.

Likewise, a song is ever moving and changing. A folk song in a book is like a picture of a bird in mid-flight printed in a bird book. The bird was moving before the picture was taken, and continued flying afterward. It is valuable for a scientific record to know when and where the picture was taken, but no one is so foolish as to think that the picture *is* the bird.

Thus also, the folk song in the book was changing for many generations before it was collected, and will keep on changing for many generations more, we trust. It is valuable for a scientific record to know when and where it was collected, but the picture of the song is not the song itself.

If you think of folk music as a process, you know that words and melodies may not be so important as the way they are sung, or listened to. The process includes not only the song, but the singer and the listeners, and their situation. In this sense, a mountaineer singing a pop song to some neighbors in his cabin might have more of folk music in it than a concert artist singing to a Carnegie Hall audience an ancient British ballad he learned out of a book.

After defining folk music (as a process, rather than any set repertoire of songs) to a class at the Idyllwild Music School in California, I was still asked by a student: "Just how do you define a folk song, then?" I tried to dodge the issue.

"It's like two geographers arguing the exact boundaries of the Rocky Mountains. One says they run all the way from Mexico to Canada and beyond. The other says no, they are just a few big peaks in Colorado. Perhaps it is necessary for the geographers to be able to draw a line on their maps some place, but for you and me, does the exact name matter that much? We climb a mountain for the view. Likewise, we can sing a song because it is a good song, not because of its classification."

"Not me," says the student. "I am a classroom teacher. My music supervisor says I can teach folk songs to the students, but not pop songs. I have to know."

Ah ha! Here is the source of the trouble, is it not? A phony value judgment: "Folk songs are good. Pop songs are bad."

Isn't this similar to the trouble that racists have in defining the difference between colored and white races? "White is good; colored is bad." Now, maybe it is important for an anthropologist to analyze physical and cultural differences of peoples. But for you and me the important thing is to accept a man or woman on their individual worth. Only by ignoring phony value judgments based on such trivial aspects as skin coloring and eye slanting can we see our way to a peaceful world.

So can't we agree that there are good and bad folk songs, good and bad pop songs?

"Yes," says the student, "but I still have to be able to define a folk song. My supervisor insists."

All right, let's define our process, and see if we can put it to work. It's an age-old process, of learning and singing mostly by ear, of formally untrained musicians, singing for fun, not for pay, to friends and neighbors, and from time to time changing or creating verses or melodies as events move them to.

"That lets me out," says the student. "I'm a trained music teacher, teaching songs from a book for pay. And my supervisor would chop my head off if he found me changing any of the songs."

Hm.

Hmmmmmm.

I do believe the only solution is to confound the enemy. If he asks, "Is it a folk song?" tell him "Frankly, no. None of the songs you have ever taught in the schools are strictly folk songs." Back up your claim with copious reference to the experts. You can do it. Be so damn particular in your definition of folk music that even the supervisor will beat a retreat. Show him that a lot of what he has been calling folk music is not really authentic folk music. When he finally throws up his hands and says, "Well, it may not be folk music, but it's good music to teach the children," then you've got him licked. For if he can say it, you can too.

Sometimes a method of arguing like this is the only way. It's like when a Unitarian friend of mine, a minister, was asked by a fundamentalist, "Do you believe, or not, that Jesus Christ was the son of God?"

"Of course he was," says my friend, looking the other straight in the eye, "and so are we all."

A few years ago Dr. Duncan Emrich, then in charge of the Archive of American Folk Song, in the Library of Congress, expressed with heavy finality to me: "In a few years there will be no more folk singers in America." And in the sense in which he was speaking, I had to agree with him. There are only a few of the genuine old country-ballad singers left, who have not been influenced by radio, TV, and book learning. And if a sophisticated urbanite tries to consciously reject these influences, he usually ends up looking and sounding more precious and affected than if he'd gone ahead and been normally jazzy.

But what Emrich didn't figure was that new traditions of folk music will emerge, even though the old ones will have faded. All definitions change with the centuries. What is called a "play" nowadays is far different from what was called a "play" in Shakespeare's time. The definitions of folk songs and folk singers are liable to change also.

Folks will insist on it.

In the 60s there was a flood of good new American songs written by young people who are singers and guitar pickers, who try out their new songs every week on small, informal audiences. They know right away how their song is being received, and if it needs amending.

Are these songs folk songs? They might fit one definition, but certainly would not fit another. The important thing is: are they good songs? Do they sing well? Is the poetry so good you can't get it cut of your head? Are the words true, and do they need saying? Does the music move you?

It's worth pointing out obvious differences between these songs and what we usually call "pop" songs:

1. They're often concerned with controversial subjects.
2. They may be short or long, or ignore the Big Beat and other time-honored jukebox requirements.

On the other hand, I'd guess that most of these songwriters are very glad if their songs make the top forty and are sung by all kinds of singers, as long as the songs are not massacred in the process. Whether or not the songs have this brief flash of lucrative notoriety, some of them are picked up by some of the millions of guitar pickers in our country, and the best will be handed on to future generations.

Then some professor can come along and collect them. He can call 'em folk songs then, if he wants. Our dust will not object.

POINTS TO CONSIDER

1. What does Seeger mean when he says that the "folk songs we love are masterpieces of composition"? Who composed them? How long did this composition take?

2. Describe the folk process. What elements are involved in the folk process that cannot be printed in a book? What relation does the folk process have to the commercial success of a given song?

3. What problems does the author have in defining "folk" music? How does he resolve these problems? Do you feel it is important to define "folk" music? Explain.

4. In what sense is "folk" music dying out? What sort of music is replacing it? Is this a "folk" process? Explain.

5. To what extent do you think that all art can be considered "process"?

Time, February 12, 1973

Life, metaphysicians of the record industry will tell you, is a super-monster smash; dig it. It is performed in an illogical world that is both flat and round, where 33⅓ r.p.m. exerts a fearful centrifugal force. The U.S., particularly that extensive tribe of its citizenry under 30, is electronically in thrall to the thrumming, incessant sound of music, a phenomenon that has branded the record business a supremely marketable mania. Every week, hundreds of records are poured into radio stations by promoters trying to crack the crucial list of Top 40 hits that get saturation air play. Every year, 5,000 new albums pile up on endless racks in drugstores and supermarkets, there to await the ready purses of Mom and her affluent children.

Last year those purses responded to the galactic, 16-track, monster-smash tune of nearly $2 billion in records and tapes ($3.3 billion world-wide), making music, for the first measurable time in history, the most popular form of entertainment in America. The television may drone on in the living room, but there is little that youth wants to hear from Archie Bunker or Marcus Welby—especially since it has found both relevance and escape in magical sound.

With such sales, no wonder the conglomerates are conglomerating in the record business. From film studios to breakfast-food makers to rent-a-car companies—everyone is trying to buy up a label and go from wax to riches. Even the moguls are falling in with the style, if not the substance, of rock culture. They are not necessarily above trying out guru beads, stack-heel boots, or an unmarked cigarette.

Your basic bopper on the beach, however, cannot see them for the stars. Today's pop-rock pantheon is the new Hollywood; its principal gods have filled the void left by the Harlows and Gables. Any number of the pop world's scores of superstars could serve to illustrate the process. Four who exemplify its various aspects as vividly as any are Balladeer Carole King, Hard-Rocker Ian Anderson, Pop-Jazz Songstress Roberta Flack and Fey Troubadour Harry Nilsson. Not exactly household names, they nevertheless enjoy more status with the young than a Newman or a Taylor. They are more lavishly remunerated than, say, Redford or MacGraw. Indeed, everything about the music industry of the '70s is reminiscent of Hollywood in the '30s and '40s: moguls, superstars and promoters operating in a world charged with sex and power and conspiring to sell slick, tuneful packages to a voracious public.

VAUDEVILLIANS

Fortunately, that public by and large insists upon a modicum of quality. Bizarre vaudevillians like Jethro Tull, the manic-impressive group for which Anderson is lead singer and flutist, are still artisans right down to their self-mocking codpieces and plaid jerkins. Singer-Composer King, 29, spins out her multitextured ballads with craft and sensitivity and raises her piano playing to something more than mere accompaniment. Nilsson, 31, blithe and winsome with his pen as well as his voice, first projected himself as a sort of sad-clown chronicler of Middle America *(Nobody Cares About the Railroads Anymore, Mr. Tinker),* now is a zany mod-rocker *(Coconut, Spaceman).* In the poised, warmly expressive style of Flack, 33, the earthy emotions of gospel *(Told Jesus)* mix with the more polished, sinuous phrasing of jazz *(Tryin' Times).*

The present pop market is so vast and varied that it seems able to accommodate a limitless range of recording styles. The names on the album covers alone denote the bewildering diversity. There are Mott the Hoople, Sly and the Family Stone, Aztec Two-Step, Five Pound Smile, Weather Report, Dr. Hook and the Medicine Show, Rasputin's Stash, Highway Robbery—old groups, new groups, weird groups, funny groups, groups never heard of before, groups never to be heard of again.

There are holdovers from the first wave of rock revolution in the '60s, like those satanic princes the Rolling Stones, who still sing a violent song of and for themselves with frenzied power. There are emergent personalities like Carly Simon,[1] 28, who epitomizes much that youth finds glamorous in the pop-rock world: daughter of Richard Simon, co-founder of Simon & Schuster, publishers, wife of Folk-Rock-Star James Taylor, exemplar of Sarah Lawrence[2] cerebral-voluptuary chic. *Aficionados*[2] all over the country are comparing notes on the possible lovers referred to in Carly's *You're So Vain,* a top-selling single. There are in-between figures like Elton John, 25, an established English performer who is still capable of breaking out with a monster like *Crocodile Rock.* In person, the ebullient John flings himself onstage in a cape that makes him look like Michael Pollard playing Captain Marvel, kicks away the piano stool and plays from a handstand position, among others.

Not only groups and individuals but also entire genres are swirling in wild profusion through today's pop-record scene. The most prevalent type these days is the solo troubadour who sings of quiet, simple joys, of lost loves and lonely roads; this strain encompasses such individual stylists as King, Simon, Nilsson and Taylor. Country rock is thriving with The Band (not to be confused with Nashville-based Country and Western, a separate universe); flower-power rock with The Grateful Dead. Progressive rock and jazz are teaming up in such potent combinations as Santana and the Mahavishnu Orchestra. Perhaps the hottest trend lies in the sweet soul of Flack and other black artists like Billy Paul *(Me and Mrs. Jones)* who are leading the field in the first large-scale cross-over of black performers into the pop mainstream and of black record buyers into traditionally white markets.

---

[1] *Time* suggests here that Carly Simon is a model example of a type of sophisticated, well-educated (Sarah Lawrence is an expensive women's college in New York) young person whose lifestyle emphasizes intellectual and artistic pursuits combined with a liberated sexuality.

[2] An *aficionado* is a person ardently devoted to a certain thing; in this case Carly Simon and her music.

Observes Columbia Records President Clive Davis, the most dynamic mover in the pop-rock groundswell: "One kind of music absorbed everything else in the '60s. In a sense it was a revolution. But now the universe of music has absorbed that, and is expanding on all fronts. You have the individual emerging again and artists coming from all areas of music. Beyond that, there are so many existing artists from the '60s who have maintained themselves that the market is much more scattered. There is not one sort of music that is dominating now."

As for the stars who are flourishing in this energetic eclecticism, many of them have come to learn, as did Garfield and Garland before them, that life at the top can be hard cheese. Record sales are highly volatile and the vaulting ascents and steep dives of pop reputations can give even hardy souls a severe case of the bends. As Rock Entrepreneur Bill Graham says, "What's it like to be 23 years old, sell a million records, own a boat, a car, a lot of real estate, and not have worked 20 years to get it?"

Many performers are what Publicist Gary Stromberg calls "gifted children—vulnerable, naive, spoiled, easily hurt. They can be brats, because the first time they ever got on a plane it was first-class." If the psychological pressures do not crush them, the physical rigors of touring, drugs and sex may. Two of the most incandescent of their number in the '60s, Janis Joplin and Jimi Hendrix, died a good 45 years too soon on the self-destructive road to that discovery.

Success may be hard to handle, but the decline that often follows is worse. "Those who don't plan ahead get into trouble," says Stromberg. "The group breaks up, and they aren't good at communicating in other ways than music. There is nothing left for them to do. So they keep on trying to put together a new group, and they keep on living in a dream world."

Even successful performers who can maintain their temperamental equilibrium are often painfully entangled in the coils of the record industry's machinery: the complexities of the recording studio, the insanities of promotional gimmicks, the potentially damaging imponderables of commercialism. The creative musicians among them dwell in a strained symbiosis with the moneymen. Says Guitarist Jerry Garcia of The Grateful Dead, one of Warner Bros.' top record sellers: "I resent being just another face in a corporate personality. There isn't even a Warner 'brother' to talk to. The music business and The Grateful Dead are in two different orbits, two different universes."

ASYLUM

Such strain produces a special effect on performers born of a highly sensitized generation that takes its own emotional pulse almost hourly. As Rock Singer Todd Rundgren describes it: "Your whole life becomes represented by what you do rather than what you are. To compensate for this you make a caricature of yourself, assert your own personality more than you would ordinarily need to. You dress louder, behave louder; your life becomes a performance, except when you are by yourself."

Many of the new breed of stars go to considerable lengths to be by themselves. Top groups are demanding autonomy in their recording activities, and sometimes acquire their own private recording studios, where they can be relatively free of the influence of their record companies. The asylum, as the record industry likes to designate itself, is increasingly being taken over by the inmates. Explains Jethro Tull's Anderson, 25, a former art student: "I moved away from painting because I wanted to remove myself from the influence of tutors and teachers. In being a rock musician, you should be left totally to your own devices. Any talent that emerges is something that comes from within you."

Anderson, the son of a Blackpool businessman, belies his bizarre appearance by eschewing drugs and cultivating an earnest strain of religious feeling. He originates most of the group's music through "just strumming a few lines on the guitar," and he admits that he picked up the flute one day "because it was the only instrument in the shop." He describes his onstage gyrations—twisting, hopping on one leg, hair flying—partly as "hamming it up" but also as a form of "conducting—you're actually another way of playing, another force."

Flack, who was trained as a classical soprano and later played piano in jazz clubs and taught music in public schools, has settled in a suburb of Washington, D.C. From there she directs her own Washington-based publishing firm, talent agency and production company in a characteristically slow, steady and thoughtful way.

SAMPLERS

Brooklyn-born King got her professional start in the hurly-burly of $50-a-week songwriting in Manhattan's Tin Pan Alley,[3] now lives an almost reclusive life with her husband and three children in Los Angeles' Laurel Canyon. As in her New York days, she slops around in nondescript clothes and talks rapidly when excited. But there is a new restraint and self-possession; she studies yoga, favors tea and Japanese-style raw fish and enjoys sewing samplers. She refuses all public appearances except infrequent concerts. This ploy provides a notable exception to the record-industry folk wisdom that touring and promotion are necessary to sell records. Without benefit of hoopla, King's 1971 album *Tapestry* has racked up a worldwide total of 9,000,000 sales, making it the biggest-selling LP by a single performer in recording history.

More than any other pop-record star, Nilsson has defined the boundaries of his professional activity by the four walls of the recording studio. His career is completely a product of recording technology, since he rarely gives any live performances at all. Brooklyn-born like King, he worked for a few years as a computer programmer in a Van Nuys, Calif., bank until one of the demonstration records that he was flogging to record companies on the side won him a contract. Friends suggest that part of his reluctance to perform comes from his shyness and engaging eccentricity. Nilsson insists that performing is "a separate occupation. I like concentrating my energies

[3] Tin Pan Alley is a term for New York City's popular music publishing industry.

in the studio and doing other things with the rest of my time." Among the other things: playing Ping Pong, reading science fiction and developing ideas for films and TV shows. Nilsson keeps a flat in London and often records there instead of the U.S.—a tribute to the London studios' more sophisticated electronic wizardry.

Some pop stars' isolationist tendencies are rooted in stark self-preservation. Take the bubble-gum idols, David Cassidy, 22, of *The Partridge Family,* and Donny Osmond, 15, of the Osmond Brothers. Their very lives are sometimes in peril. That is to be expected when the magazines that address themselves to their pubescent followers run features like "Take a Shower with David," inviting fans to send in bars of soap with love messages carved into them. David has discovered that you can lose a lot of shirts to clawing young crowds that way. Donny and his older brother Wayne once sneaked out of their hotel while on tour only to be mobbed in an electronics store. An exasperated Wayne asked the obvious: "Now how many 13-year-old girls would you expect to find in an electronics store?"

CRAVING

The answer is, of course, that you can find them hanging out in worshipful multitudes wherever their warbling royalty might chance to be. Not even the Sinatras or Monroes produced cults to rival those formed in the '60s and '70s. Says Joseph Smith, a former disk jockey who is co-chief of Warner Bros. Records: "Music is participatory now. You've got a generation buying it that has lived through ten years of craziness and crisis. The music has reflected every facet of that period." He adds: "Those kids need those albums. You can't separate it from their lives." Publicist Stromberg recalls the incident of a tearful, angry teen-ager screaming at a cop who had just ejected him from a Rolling Stones concert in Boston for scuffling. "You have no idea, *no idea at all,*" shouted the teen-ager, "what this concert means to me!"

Clearly the pop world has come a long way since the Crew-Cuts first sang *Sh-Boom.* When Elvis Presley twitched at the head of a pack of oil-gun-groomed Teen Angels, white youth abandoned the syrupy somnolence of Joni James and Patti Page to share, at a safe distance, the black experience expressed in rhythm and blues. In the late '50s, the sullen sounds of American rock gave way to the urban folk madrigals of the Kingston Trio. They and their imitators were in turn swept from the popular field by those definitive merry mercenaries the Beatles.

The British conquest of the American pop scene was total until 1967 and the storied Monterey Pop Festival. Indeed, the current health and wealth of the various record companies is a direct reflection of who tuned in to the festival and who did not. Most of today's successful moguls were there, contract-signing pens at the ready. At the time, the three top record companies were RCA, Capitol and Columbia. Joe Smith of Warner had pre-empted the pack by signing Jimi Hendrix before the festival. But the most enterprising of all was Columbia's Clive Davis, who in the wake of the festival signed Janis Joplin; Blood, Sweat and Tears; Santana; and Chicago. To their eventual sorrow, RCA and Capitol were still viewing such affairs—indeed, all of rock—as something of a passing fad. It was not; the war was on.

A brutal war it is, too, masterminded in the conference rooms of conglomerates and waged in the trenches where producers, promoters, distributors, program directors and disk jockeys all snap and claw at the big sound-dollar. The battle rages continually around one crucial question: Is it a hit (ding!) or a miss (thud)? Since only one record in 25 gets a serious shot at survival, the odds are long: simply to break even, a single must sell 25,000 copies, an album 85,000. But then it takes only a couple of hits to compensate for dozens of dogs. This is the era of the almighty album, and a monster single usually means not only a gold record (1,000,000 copies), but, when included on an LP, may even guarantee a gold album ($1,000,000).

SNOWBALL EFFECT

The selling of a record begins with the selling of the recording artist or group—first to the company, then to the public. Company scouts screen processions of talent—sometimes from managers, sometimes from the street, sometimes bearing impressive credits, sometimes clutching a tape recorded in their living room. Says Don Heckman, head of RCA's East Coast "contemporary" operation: "The top 10% of what is available to you is always cream. It doesn't take anything to recognize that someone like Carole King is a monster talent. It is the area between 90% and 40% that is the problem. The majority of artists that you bring in have to be worked with, and careers rise and fall on what happens with them."

When the board-room executives decide that a particular song or performer is ready, then the promotional wheels are put into action. A typical example is RCA's handling of one of its hot new properties: David Bowie, a spry English rock-vaudeville performer who flaunts his bisexuality.

Enter now the office of Stu Ginsburg, head of publicity for RCA's rock arm. His midtown Manhattan office is festooned with posters, cutouts, promotional T shirts, freaky record albums. Munching a chocolate cookie and propping his saddle shoes on a well-littered desk, Ginsburg explains: "You want to create a snowball effect. So you arrange live tours in patterned locations so that the radio and press coverage will overlap. You want to come into a city with advance air play, and you want to leave the city with press and more air play. It spreads. New York stations spread to Jersey, and so on."

Nowadays most record companies have taken over the role of tour agent. So when company executives decided to showcase Bowie, they first chartered a plane and flew a load of American rock writers to London, then arranged an American tour for Bowie. Local promoters, working in tandem with RCA, pushed Bowie's records at area rock stations, also offered interviews to local newspapers and FM disk jockeys.

NOT RATIONAL

As the Bowie caravan moved round the nation, RCA operatives at its center scrambled for more and more press attention. In some cities, Bowie sold well without much trouble; in others, local promoters filled seats by giving away tickets through organized radio contests. In many cases, RCA bought mounds of advertising at local stations and occasionally gave the station a piece of the concert action—thus ensuring air play of Bowie's records. All together, RCA laid $100,000 worth of promotion on Bowie's slender nose.

Although Carole King and Harry Nilsson have made it without going through the Bowie process, even King served her apprenticeship writing songs for other performers, and Nilsson arrived only with the help of the pop-cult film smash *Midnight Cowboy*. One of his early singles, *Everybody's Talkin'*, was released three times in two years with no visible means of support. Then the song was picked up for the Jon Voight-Dustin Hoffman movie. Shortly after the film came out, RCA Promoter Larry Douglas walked into the office of Program Director Walt Turner at WSAI in Cincinnati and threw the record on his desk. "Goddammit," he bellowed, "you're going to play that record!" Turner looked up in amusement. "Douglas," he asked softly, "are you still pushing that thing?" Turner finally agreed to let Douglas take him and his wife to see *Midnight Cowboy*. The record was played on WSAI the next day. Similar breakthroughs occurred all round the country, and eventually the single sold about 900,000 copies.

No, the promoter's lot is not a rational one. Clive Davis of Columbia, which led all other record companies last year with gross worldwide sales of around $340 million,[4] observes in explanation of his outfit's success: "There's no real difference between our operation and that of most other companies. You stand or fall with your list." Admits Stan Cornyn, Warner Bros.' vice president for creative services (meaning largely ads and promotion): "The reality is that if you have a good record, you can't kill it with a stick; if you have a terrible record, you cannot elect it Pope. If you have a middle-level record, it helps to have promotion."

A good promotion man must get radio play if his song is going to go anywhere on the charts. (An exception to the rule is the record, always an LP, that gains a following through exposure on FM stations, as many Jethro Tull albums have done.) This is really what all the planning and promotion is about. It is no easy task in these days when nearly all major radio stations play only the Top 40 current hits.

The Top 40 idea might charitably be called the brainchild of Los Angeles-based Program Director Bill Drake, who runs the action for RKO's 14 powerful pop-music stations. The concept is founded on the premise that the average radio audience changes every 30 minutes. Thus the notion is to keep repeating—over and over again—the same monster items that everyone wants to hear. In fact, Top 40 is an illusory designation; 25 is more like it. "Getting a record into air play," says Kal Rudman, publisher of an

---

[4] Runners-up: RCA ($203 million sales), Warner Communications ($180 million), Capitol ($130 million).

East Coast record tip sheet, "is tougher than getting a bill through Congress."

There are only three legitimate ways to get on the air. RCA Promotion Director Frank Mancini sums them up: "Hit the secondaries, hassle the Top 40 people, or do both." The likeliest route to success is through the secondaries—the hot stations in such medium-sized cities as Youngstown, Ohio; Hartford, Conn.; and San Diego, which tend to have more flexible program directors than the rigidly scheduled big-league stations. There are plenty of valid forms of blandishment, and some of them are quite inventive. One promo man in Cleveland dressed up in a Superman costume and climbed a fire escape to the third-floor window of a program director's office so that he could spring inside with his wares. Another managed to pose as a waiter in a program director's favorite restaurant, then served up his "push" single to the program director on a silver platter.

RCA's man on the West Coast, Lou Galliani, is the epitome of the new look in rising record-company executives, tricked out in velvet jeans, flowery shirts, shell beads around his neck and African trading beads around his wrist. He carries a leather shoulder bag and has a house near San Francisco that is decorated with animals, tropical fish and a delectable girl friend. Galliani sends the usual flowers and small gifts to radio-station employees (the bag limit is $25 by FCC law), procures the usual concert tickets and arranges the usual listener contests for trips to Hawaii with Elvis, or whatever. But he has been known to branch out from there. He once sent out tape cassettes containing "personalized" obscene telephone calls to several female radio-station employees. When the David Bowie entourage came to town, Galliani took out an ad in the personals column of *Rolling Stone:* "Desperate. Must have two tickets to see David Bowie performance in San Francisco, Oct. 28. Will pay up to $100 each. Call Clive or Ahmet." Meaning, of course, the rival potentates at Columbia and Atlantic.

There is also another, less frivolous way of winning favor. The term, coined during the Alan Freed scandal of the '50s, is payola. Its forms have changed, and in some areas it has been drastically reduced. Most radio formats now make it extremely difficult, if not impossible, for under-the-counter money to influence play lists. Top 40 jockeys no longer have control over their lists; program directors, in turn, are too tightly pressed by audience demand to fool around. Nonetheless, corruption persists.

BLOODSUCKER

"Payola is still the industry's little bastard," writes Roger Karshner, former vice president at Capitol, in his book *The Music Machine.* "No one will admit to him, but everybody pays child support, and the little devil keeps coming back for more—not openly of course, but quietly in sneakers. The greedy little bloodsucker has gone underground." That essentially means the burgeoning black radio stations. The going prices for air play these days range from an occasional $50 in some regional stations to as much as $1,000 for a week of concentrated play in the big city rhythm-and-blues stations. One industry attorney flatly asserts: "Nearly every black radio station in the U.S. is involved in payola."

A black executive of a major West Coast record company objects to such categorical accusations. "Hell," he says, "don't pin this on the black folk. White payola is still bigger; it always has been. The black cats get $50 to $100; the white guys get color-TV sets." The R. and B. stations do seem to be more susceptible to payola, thanks to more elastic formats and to the fact that pay scales for black DJs are lower. Payola takes on increasing importance in this area because of the growing number of sweet-soul cross-overs and the mounting influence of middle-class blacks (who can now afford albums) on the shape of the charts.

Industry executives are quick to note, defensively but with some point, that parties, junkets and the free use of facilities are acceptable in other businesses—why not in records? Yet the fact remains that record companies, at least indirectly, try to buy their way onto the air waves. One executive admits, "There's a lot of bread being passed around, man." Bread is rarely hard cash these days (too risky), but it often takes such forms as plane tickets, appliances and household renovation. There are grand old standbys (hard and soft women) and grisly new stratagems (hard and soft drugs). "Dope is a no-no," says one executive, "but some guys are passing it out."

It was probably inevitable that a $3 billion business would attract the omnivorous eye of the Mafia. Jukeboxes have always been a Mob staple; of the 58 gang chiefs arrested at the 1957 Apalachin, N.Y., underworld convention, nine had jukebox interests. The Mob also allegedly hit pay dirt recently by counterfeiting records at a New Jersey plant and bootlegging them in England and even Yugoslavia. According to reports, a summit conference of Mafia record bootleggers was held three months ago in Manhattan's Plaza Hotel. Deals were supposedly consummated in the hotel's genteel Palm Court, while near by, mink-wrapped dowagers spooned their strawberry parfaits.

Inside or outside the Mob, counterfeiting or pirating records is a lucrative adjunct to the legitimate record industry. Anybody who has access to modern taping or disk-pressing equipment can duplicate a record thousands of times over without paying royalties. Experts figure that pirates raked off nearly $200 million in profits last year. As one executive moans: "We are being penalized by technological progress."

FINGER POPPING

Still, such penalties are pittances compared with the bountiful legal profits to be made through old-fashioned executive ingenuity. Take Producer-Publisher Wes Farrell, who brought music to *The Partridge Family* and vice versa. One day he was watching the pilot for the family's television show and took an interest in David Cassidy, soon to become America's white-clad Aubrey Beardsley[5] faun. "I wondered," Farrell recalled, "why nobody

[5] Aubrey Beardsley was a nineteenth-century British illustrator famous, among other things, for elegant portrayals of handsome young male subjects.

had asked him if he could sing." As it turned out, David was not destined to be confused with Richard Tucker. No matter. Farrell called in 60 songwriters, who ground out some 300 tunes suitable for framing David. Within a year one of them, *I Think I Love You,* had sold 3.6 million copies.

Since most stars are bought and not made, money remains the deadliest weapon in a major company's arsenal. Witness a recent weekly singles meeting in the RCA board room. Gathered around a table piled high with cherry and pineapple Danish, 15 upbeat execs popped their fingers and wiggled their shoulders to the sounds being explained, then piped in, by Advertising and Merchandising Director Bil Keane. Soon Keane played "the Sneak of the Week," and everyone at the table was invited to guess who the newly acquired artist was. "Wilson Pickett!" someone shouted, and RCA President Rocco Laginestra confirmed that Pickett had been signed. "You stole him from Atlantic?" another executive was asked. "Right," came the answer. "How'd you do it?" The reply, this time accompanied by a blood-and-feathery grin: "Money."

In a similar singles meeting at Columbia Records recently, a fair portion of the session was dedicated to promoting an album by Cartoonist-Humorist Shel Silverstein. It seemed that a Seattle jockey had taken an interest in one routine about a rather septic young lady named Sylvia Stout, who for reasons of her own, refuses to take the garbage out. One idea struck the table like a bolt, and was promptly accepted: distribute little packets of garbage in Seattle supermarkets. Dynamite.

If the industry does have its share of garbage, there is less of it than was produced in myriad Hollywood film stinkeroos of the '30s and '40s. Indeed, the concept of artistic control that permeates the industry has produced an American pop-rock sound of increasingly high quality. As evidenced by the Beatles' *Sgt. Pepper,* for example, or the Beach Boys' *Surf's Up,* the freewheeling pop artists of the last decade, left to cavort in their electronic playpens, can produce sounds as aesthetically extraordinary as they are profitable. They have become casually expert in the manipulation of far-out electronic paraphernalia like the Moog synthesizer,[6] and they have learned to use the LP format in strikingly expressive new ways. Ian Anderson is preparing an album for Jethro Tull called *Passion Play,* which will use the recording medium to put across some of Anderson's religious ideas, as well as frame what he calls "a total theater trip."

QUADRAPHONIC

The future of the industry seems to be bounded only by Con Edison's[7] capacities. The widely heralded quadraphonic sound, which feeds four channels through separate speakers, is now a commercial reality, both in terms of recording techniques and home playing equipment. Experiments in tapes and cassettes are proceeding apace. The latest innovation: a video cassette that will show a live performance even as the music is being

[6] The Moog synthesizer is a device which can create a large variety of musical sounds electronically.

[7] Con Edison: an electric power company, meaning here electric power in general.

played. At the same time, more and more TV outlets are booking pop-record stars, opening up further possibilities for intermedia promotion; both ABC and NBC are experimenting with late-night programs featuring rock groups.

Though the increased sophistication of electronic gadgetry will continue to contribute immeasurably to the growth of the industry, the key to the business is still the writhing, undulating, switched-on men and women of music, the curve and contour of their artistry. Record executives, who live perpetually in the future, are watching, waiting, wondering: What will the next supermonster sound be? "If I knew what was coming," says Wes Farrell, "I would come into the office once a year and charge $100,000 a minute for my time. But the most exciting part of my life is that I don't know what's coming."

Whether what's coming is a West Texas farm boy playing Bach fugues on a cactus pear or the White House staff singing footlight favorites, you can bet your quadraphonic tape deck that Farrell and his competitors will be on hand, those contract-signing ballpoints at the ready; dig it.

■ OF FREAKS, INDIES AND BUBBLE GUM

Time, February 12, 1973

Whether tuning up a pitch in the studio or making one at a sales meeting, any would-be operator in the pop record business must know the lingo. A brief primer.

ARTIST—Any performer of whatever ability.

BOOGIE—To relax, kid around, do one's thing, take it easy.

BOP—To drink, smoke, pop pills, goof off or otherwise have a good time.

BREAK or BREAK OUT—To become a hit.

BUBBLE GUM—Rock for the pre-teeny-bopper set; the lowest common denominator in pop music.

DO ME A SOLID—Do me a favor.

FREAK—A rock performer with an attention-getting mannerism or physical handicap (e.g., albino Blues-Rocker Johnny Winter).

HYPE—False or exaggerated claims about a performer or record.

GOOD HYPE—Promotion or advertising that is, astoundingly enough, true.

INDIE—Independent producer or record company.

MONSTER—A superhit; also the creator of a superhit.

ON THE FARM—Woodshedding, or getting it all together, harks back to the not-so-distant days when rockers rented farms to do everything but farm on.

OUTRAGEOUS—Great.

PRODUCT—Records, as in "He puts out a lot of product."

RELEVANT—The kids will buy it.

STIFF—A record that does not sell.

STREET—The marketplace; also, the latest industry rumors, as in "The street says . . ."

TRIP—A cat's bag, style, anything he's got going down.

TURNTABLE HIT—A record that gets air play but does not sell.

UP FRONT—Having top priority.

WHIPPED—drunk.

POINTS TO CONSIDER

1. What, according to the article, is the most popular form of entertainment in America today? On what does the article base this claim? Do you agree? Explain why or why not.

2. In what ways does the article suggest that current popular music is similar to Hollywood of the thirties and forties? In what ways is it different?

3. What problems does success bring to recording stars? What are some of the ways performers attempt to deal with these problems?

4. What is the chief goal in the promotion of a song or album? What are some of the means used to attain this goal? What is payola? Where, according to the article, is it most likely to flourish?

5. What is meant by the statement in the article that popular music is "participatory"? Can you think of ways in which the current music is not participatory?

6. What does the article mean by "artistic control"? Why is this concept particularly important to popular music? How does the record industry's attitude toward artistic control differ from that of other media?

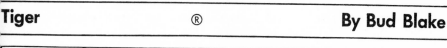

Tiger   ®   **By Bud Blake**

IDEAS FOR INVESTIGATION, DISCUSSION, AND WRITING

1.   What are some of the major varieties of popular music today? To what different kinds of listeners do they appeal? Which varieties seem to have the widest appeal and which the most limited? Why?

2.   What contributions have the following sources made to our current popular music:

    a.   baroque and classical music
    b.   Spanish and Portugese dance music
    c.   African music
    d.   Oriental music
    e.   folk music and ballads from the United States and other countries
    f.   U.S. jazz and blues
    g.   U.S. popular music of the 1920s–1950s
    h.   electronics and computers
    i.   psychedelic and "drug" art

Can you think of other influences? How do you account for this synthesis of such a variety of sources?

3.   How have the lyrics of popular songs changed significantly since the 1940s and the early 1950s? What influences do you think have helped to bring about this change? What relationship do you see between this change and the steady growth of interest in poetry by young people since 1955?

4.   How has the instrumentation of popular music changed in the past fifteen or twenty years to suit the changing nature of the music? What once popular instruments are seldom used now, and what different and new instruments have become popular? What do you make of the fact that much of today's popular music is affected in some way by electronics?

5.   Why do you think that much of today's popular music is meant to be heard very loud? What is the function or importance of this loudness? Is this a new phenomenon in popular music?

6.   To what extent have musical shows lagged behind or kept pace with the trends in popular music? Compare Broadway and film musicals to "off-Broadway" musicals and try to determine what accounts for the differences between them.

7.   How has popular music in the past fifteen or twenty years become increasingly significant as a social force or influence? What changes in our culture does this development reveal?

8.   Investigate the structure and function of ASCAP (American Society of Composers Artists and Publishers). What exactly is the organization supposed to do? How effective is it?

9.   Look into the mechanics of the recording industry. How are records produced? Who decides what records will be made? What processes are involved? What people? What are the costs?

10.   Make a similar investigation of the processes involved in copyrighting and publishing a song. How is a song copyrighted? What protection does the copyright afford the composer? What steps are necessary to publishing a song? What kind of market is there currently for sheet music?

11. Using either musical notation or a tape recorder, compare melodic lines of current songs with the melodies of an earlier era. Is there really that much difference between the popular music of today and that of twenty and thirty years ago? If so, wherein does the difference lie?

12. Find out who or what determines your local radio stations' "Top Forty" single recordings. Are the standings more or less legitimate indications of actual sales, or are there other factors involved? What problems do you encounter in trying to get information about this subject?

13. Listen to the range of different kinds of music broadcast by your local radio stations. What different kinds of music are played on which stations? Which kinds of music are played on the largest number of stations and which on the fewest? Why? How do the advertising and other kinds of programming on each station relate to the principal kind of music played on it?

14. Conduct a survey among various kinds of people in your community to determine who listens to which radio stations and with what frequency. Ask about their tastes in music to learn the connection between this factor and the stations that are listened to.

Part Eight

Education: Previews and Viewpoints

The various languages and media through which we communicate are not merely envelopes carrying any message indifferently. Rather, they are active processes which structure the way our senses report to us and the way our thoughts are shaped.

—John Culkin

Our churches and our schools have always been political arenas, despite the pretense of religious leaders and educators that they are not. Today's controversy over "filthy" English books is simply another move in the age-old power struggle for the control of children's minds.

—June Kirkhuff Edwards

If most had work to do that they liked, that used and rewarded much of their intelligence, skill, and judgment, work whose purposes they understood and shared and respected, and if they felt that what they thought, believed, wanted, said, and did made or might make a real difference, we would not be talking so much about learning. We would all be doing interesting things that mattered.

—John Holt

. . . Education can be just as relevant in preparing a person for creative and joyous living and for increased life expectancy as it is in preparing him to be an income producer and a solid citizen.

—Norman Cousins

Education

FROM FILM STUDIES TO MEDIA STUDIES

John Culkin   *Media and Methods*, December 1974

A tenth anniversary celebration is a proper time for bringing out some twelve-year-old Scotch and at least one 271-year-old aphorism. The potable is left to each person's devising. The quotable is supplied by one Andrew Fletcher of Saltoun (1655–1716). Back in 1703 he said, "Give me the making of the songs of a nation, and I care not who makes its laws."

For those of us working to have the schools deal with contemporary culture, Fletcher's remark is a reminder of how music, film, and television often bypass the meddling intellect to go directly to the emotions and feelings. It was this belief in the direct impact on the feeling level that got most of us caught up in film study back when *Media & Methods* was still in the loins of *School Paperback Journal.*

Unquestionably there is the need for a carefully annotated history of how we got from there to here. The growth of the film and media study movement has been closely associated with individuals and organizations whose stories merit telling in any complete review of how these ideas found their way into the schools and the lives of students. This brief essay can only hope to trace the history of an idea in a somewhat abstract fashion and to locate it within its current context of growth and assimilation. But the names, the faces, the meetings, the friendships, all the resonances of this small piece of educational history are very present and much cherished by those of us whose lives have been touched along the way.

We got wrapped up in motion pictures because they were emotion pictures. In an antiseptic atmosphere which had denied meaning to any life but that lived above the eyebrows, they opened up areas of feeling and relevance. For this reason, high schools tended to deal with "the film as experience" and to be less concerned with academic approaches presented by "the art and history of" courses.

The movement addressed itself primarily to high school English teachers, urging them to extend and enliven their study of literature by including the screening, discussion and analysis of features, documentaries and short films. Soon the students cajoled and pushed their way into the logical culmination: filmmaking. The overall result marked a sharp departure from the traditional audio-visual use of film and from the negative and fearful stance most school people took toward the popular culture.

Film study was an uncompromising beast in those heady days. It stressed the autonomy of film as a medium of communication and encouraged a respect for what film had to offer in humanistic education. It was not just another item in the curriculum, but a unique and privileged way of reaching students with experiences, emotions and styles of teaching that actually touched their lives.

Film study had reached what Alfred North Whitehead in *The Aims of Education* calls the "stage of romance"—a phase in which all the excitement, lure and unexplored potential of an area of knowledge are felt and stressed. In the total rhythm of learning, this exuberant stage yields inevitably, in Whitehead's terms, to a "stage of precision"—the exploration of the implications, structures and connections underlying the "stage of romance."

It is now time for some precision, reflection and re-evaluation. The years have taught us a lot: that the basic idea of film study is valid, that it yields to great variety in application, that it can and does enliven teaching, that it brings emotion and personal feeling into the classroom, that it can be integrated with the arts and humanities.

On the second go-around we should be guided by some reminders: that we still have much to learn about both media study itself and the needs of teachers, that there has been an unconscionable gap between the media teachers in the colleges and those in the secondary and elementary schools, that the majority of teachers probably still have not had the idea of media studies presented to them, that we cannot leave out the administrators, that there are media skills which all teachers should have, that the idea should be plugged into existing line-item budgets within the instructional media and library departments, that the development of regional resources and services is crucial, that exhortation is not enough unless it is accompanied by learning materials and teacher preparations. If all teachers and students need these new media skills, then we must look for the links within the schools which make them possible. The idea is too important to be left only to the enthusiasts and the experts.

In addition to sharing the past with others, there remains the ongoing task of grounding and relating what we already know. The media are not just connectors and conveyor belts between us and the environment. The various languages and media through which we communicate are not merely envelopes carrying any message indifferently. Rather, they are active processes which structure the way our senses report to us and the way our thoughts are shaped.

The distinctive thing about the human species is that we are symbol-making animals; every act of knowing involves the self acting on the environment through symbolic codes. It is this capacity to express thoughts and feelings which distinguishes us from the rest of living things. The canon of symbols includes words, images, gestures, cadences, sounds, and the entire range of art and media forms. In knowing more about these symbols, we know more about ourselves. The continued exploration of the forms leads us further into the probing of our own perceptual, sensory and cerebral activity. And that, brothers and sisters, is the bottom line for those of us involved in education.

Our efforts at making students their own television and film critics are now leading us to defining and staking out a new area of concentration: media studies. In its broadest formulation it integrates teaching about the new media with teaching about literature, drama and the fine arts, thereby creating an across-the-board and comprehensive approach to human symbols, codes, media and modes of communication. Each medium is studied in itself, and then enriched by meaningful comparisons and contrasts between it and other communication symbols. Together this adds up to a study of *homo signifex*—man the symbol-maker.

All this fancy and somewhat undigested talk about the media and the senses may seem like a long leap from the good old days when we sat around discussing *La Strada* and *High Noon*. But somehow it was all contained in that first step when most of us, having added one more medium to our repertoire, experienced a whole change of tone in our relations with each other and with our students. As extensions of our psychic and sensory powers, the media have a way of shaping us even as we shape them. Understanding media has a lot to do with understanding *me.*

Having said both too much and too little in this barbarously brief treatment of such a large swath of reality, I close with a quote from Susan Sontag who gets so much said so economically:

> Ours is a culture based on excess, on overproduction; the result is a steady loss of sharpness in our sensory experience. All the conditions of modern life—its material plentitude, its sheer crowdedness—conjoin to dull our sensory faculties . . . What is important now is to recover our senses. We must learn to *see* more, to *hear* more, to *feel* more.

POINTS TO CONSIDER

1. What was the initial appeal of film study in the classroom? How was this a "stage of romance"?

2. What is the "stage of precision"? How does this term apply to the development of film study into media study?

3. How does the author describe media? Do you think this is an adequate description? Explain.

4. What is *homo signifex?* Why is studying him important to us?

5. To what degree does our society and, therefore, our education tend to deny "meaning to any life but that lived above the eyebrows"? Discuss.

6. Do you feel, as the author implies in the choice of his final quotation, that media and the study of media are means of "recovering our senses," of seeing, hearing, and feeling more? Or do you think, as some people do, that media serve largely to increase sensory "crowdedness" and to dull or atrophy our senses instead of strengthening them? Explain.

MISS PEACH

By Mell Lazarus

Miss Peach by permission of Mel Lazarus and Field Newspaper Syndicate.

SCHOOL TEXTBOOK CONTROVERSIES

■ THE BOOK BANNERS

Newsweek, March 26, 1973

On the face of it, Ridgefield, Conn., is an unlikely setting for a pitched battle over academic freedom. Its stately colonial-style homes, rolling woodlands and quaint stone walls create a bucolic atmosphere that is surprising for a community of 20,000 people only 50 miles from New York City. But for three years now, Ridgefield has been seething over an effort to ban several controversial books used by the 6,000-pupil public school system. The dispute has pitted neighbor against neighbor, and has resulted in the abrupt dismissal of the town's moderately liberal school superintendent.

Book banning is not as much a thing of the past as most Americans might like to believe. The American Library Association reports more than 100 attempts to ban books from school libraries or curriculums last year in communities ranging from Dallas, Texas, to Hollidaysburg, Pa. "The general situation today is much worse than just five years ago," says ALA official Judith F. Krug. "People are worrying about things like drugs and crime. They are looking for easy solutions, and they think that if we can just get rid of this 'dirty' book or that 'subversive' book, our problems will go away."

"CATCHER"

Books are banned for nearly as many reasons as they are written. The most suppressed book in the country is J. D. Salinger's "Catcher in the Rye," a favorite of high-school English teachers that has been attacked for twenty years because of its four-letter words and disrespect for parental authority. Right behind "Catcher" on last year's censorship list was "The Inner City Mother Goose," which retells nursery rhymes in a bitter urban vernacular. Conservative whites have sought to ban Eldridge Cleaver's "Soul on Ice," while black activists have set out after "Huckleberry Finn." Other books frequently assailed include "1984," "Grapes of Wrath" and even "Gulliver's Travels."

Ridgefield typifies the stresses that have made scapegoats of schoolbooks in so many American communities. Despite its affluent setting, the town contains many lower-middle-class wage earners, as well as struggling young executives and hard-pressed older folks. Many residents are appalled at the town's pell-mell growth (the population has increased 150 per cent since 1960) and at the rising tax rate and the encroachment of "big-city problems." One early sign of political unrest was the fact that Ridgefield hired and fired four school superintendents in the six years that preceded the arrival of superintendent David Weingast from Newark, N.J., in 1966.

The long debate over books and the curriculum has left deep scars in Ridgefield. Norman Little charges that his children have been harassed in school. The local teachers' association complains of harassment from Little's allies and declares: "Fear is our constant companion in Ridgefield." One teacher claims that her family has been threatened. Last month, the feud came to a boil again when conservatives tried to ban "Soul on Ice" and another anti-Establishment book called "Police, Courts and the Ghetto." In a stormy meeting, the school board voted to retain the books. Then, when most of the audience had left, the board voted to withdraw the courses in which the books are used.

The bloodletting did not end there. At a subsequent meeting, the board decided not to renew Weingast's contract. A rumor soon spread that he had been fired for refusing to dismiss the high-school principal and the chairman of the social-studies department, both of whom had been branded as "too permissive." The leader of the conservative faction on the school board, Samuel DiMuzio, insists, "The decision about Dr. Weingast was made on the basis of his performance as an executive." But many other townspeople fear that the battle of Ridgefield has now turned from banning books to banning people.

◼ BURNING VONNEGUT

The Nation, December 3, 1973

Drake, N.D., population 700, would seem to have had only the slimmest chance of making the metropolitan dailies, but in democratic America no community should ever despair of achieving fame. Drake made it by burning three dozen copies of Kurt Vonnegut's *Slaughterhouse-Five.*

The town not only got an 8½-inch story in *The New York Times* (November 11) but its modest *auto-da-fé*[1] elicited an angry letter from Jerome Weidman, president of the Authors League of America, urging that copies of *Slaughterhouse-Five* be replaced in the school system and that the Drake board of education reconsider plans to burn James Dickey's *Deliverance* and an anthology of short stories by Hemingway, Faulkner and Steinbeck.

What happened, according to reports from Middle America, was that a high school sophomore complained that Vonnegut's novel was profane, or obscene, or both. Fearful that the girl's morals had been irremediably damaged, the board of education called a special meeting and decided to burn the book, the author not being available. The board also voted not to rehire an English teacher, Bruce Severy, 27, who had introduced Vonnegut to

[1] An *auto-da-fé* (act of the faith) was a public reading of the judgments of the courts of the Spanish Inquisition, very often accompanied by the public burning of condemned heretics.

Drake's children. Noting that none of the board members had read the controversial work, Mr. Severy declared that to condemn a book without reading it is "academically dishonest, anti-intellectual and irrational."

Just so. Equally pertinent is Franklin D. Roosevelt's remark, quoted by Mr. Weidman: "We all know that books burn—yet we have the greater knowledge that books cannot be killed by fire." Can Drake, N.D. expect to succeed where Hitler's Germany and Mussolini's Italy failed? To the contrary—a lot of Americans who missed *Slaughterhouse-Five* when it first came out will now borrow it from their libraries, or buy it in paperback.

■ THE BOOK BANNERS

Newsweek, September 30, 1974

"When the books go out, the children go in!" That slogan, pronounced by a fundamentalist minister and cheered by hundreds of protesting parents at a Labor Day rally, has now become a bitter battle cry in Kanawha County, W. Va. Conservative county residents charge that a number of the textbooks approved for use in their schools this year are "anti-religious, Communistic and pornographic"—and ever since last spring they have been trying to get the books removed from public-school curriculums. But from a simple plan to boycott schools until the books were banned, the Kanawha controversy escalated to a multi-county crisis that threatened to paralyze the entire industrial and mining area surrounding Charleston.

The trouble started last April, when school-board member Alice Moore, the wife of a fundamentalist Baptist minister, complained that textbooks the board had adopted encouraged disrespect for authority and religion and contained "filthy language." Drawing most of her fire were about a dozen textbooks, many of them designed as supplementary study for high-school students. Mrs. Moore singled out a work by black poet Gwendolyn Brooks as typical of the attack on religion ("I think it must be lonely to be God. / Nobody loves a master . . ."), and she found E. E. Cummings's poem "i like my body when it is with your body" just altogether too sexy. In "Communicating," a grammar-school series published by the D.C. Heath Co., Mrs. Moore unearthed an exercise she felt "subverted" youthful morals: "Most people think that cheating is wrong . . . Do you think there could ever be a time when it might be right?"

When a summer-long lobby failed to get the books excised from school lists, Mrs. Moore's supporters decided to try a boycott. The day school opened, they began picketing at local coal companies in an attempt to enlist the support of the area's 5,000 miners. They were successful; a number of the miners walked off their jobs in genuine sympathy with the conservatives' cause, others refused to cross any picket line on principle—a principle underscored by the fact that their contract expires in November.

Soon, virtually all of the county's mining operations were shut down, despite appeals from union officials.

VIOLENCE

Their ranks swelled by the wildcatting miners, the anti-textbook forces next moved to stop school buses and to block the entrances of the schools themselves. By the end of the second week of school, the protest had spread to nearby counties; in Kanawha one demonstrator had been shot, another severely beaten, and superintendent Kenneth Underwood closed the schools for fear of further violence.

Last week, the schools were reopened, and school-board officials started implementing a compromise plan approved by some of the conservatives. They removed the disputed textbooks from the classrooms and scheduled a 30-day review by a special committee of eighteen citizens. But the protests, now led by a coalition of preachers and parents—many of whom admit they have not even read the controversial texts—continued. Police in Charleston arrested a dozen demonstrators who had ignored court orders to limit all picketing to five persons. "If you think I've been tough now," warned a judge, after imposing stiff fines on the violators, "wait until next time."

ATTITUDE

Some critics of the boycott charge that the miners seized on the school issue as a pretext to strike—hoping thereby to reduce coal stockpiles and pressure their employers into raising their pay. But many of the protesting workers seem genuinely convinced that a "Communist influence" is governing the education of their children. "There are some leading phrases in these books that will change a person's attitude toward his family and his country," explains Joseph Tuemler, a picketing miner. "We're against that kind of stuff—we don't teach it at home and we don't want it in school."

School officials are at a loss as to how to counter such sentiments. But they are adamant about keeping the schools open—and maintaining the right of educators to choose the best textbooks for their classrooms. "Nothing has made me angrier than to see a group intimidate students to the point that they won't go to school," sighs Underwood. "If this is American, I guess I *am* anti-American."

■ DISPUTED BOOK OFF EBR LIST

Dick Wright   *Morning Advocate*, Baton Rouge, Louisiana, 1975

A classroom book that has been the center of a little publicized dispute since September is out of use for students in an English elective course offered at four East Baton Rouge Parish high schools.

The latest decision to remove the book came last week.

Whether the book is banned wasn't clear after a weekend check with a number of persons involved in the dispute. Critics of the book label it vulgar and immoral; a special committee read the book and recommended it be kept for classroom use among high school students.

"Mass Media and the Popular Arts," the book in question, was intended for a course on the news media, one of a number of courses students at the four schools may take to meet their English requirements. It got little use.

Early in the fall semester, a Baker High School girl who enrolled in the news media course complained to her mother about vulgarities as well as a couple of pictures (an advertisement and a magazine cover). The mother went to Baker principal Jerry Epperson. He took all copies of the book from the classroom of Mrs. Pinkie Sanders, the teacher.

From there the matter went to the central school system office. The book was withdrawn from use at the other schools and a review committee appointed.

A school board member, teachers, an assistant principal, students, a Parent-Teacher Association officer, a Chamber of Commerce representative and an employe of the state attorney general's office reviewed the contents and unanimously agreed it was fit and useful for high school students. The book, thereafter, was released for use again but some teachers didn't distribute it, some at least because they were nervous about what was taking place. The matter was far from settled.

Just before the Christmas holidays, the Baker student's mother and three or four other persons from Baker asked for a hearing before the school board. The hearing, in two parts, was in private and unofficial and members of the review committee attended.

The student's mother told the board she had trouble getting a copy of the book but she did have a list of the objectionable parts listed by page and paragraph. She referred the board members, who by now had copies of the book, to the instances she found objectionable. One of the men in the group told the board he found the book to be "filth."

At the second part of the hearing, a Baker minister attended and, telling the board "America is a Christian nation," called the book filth, garbage and said it was something people used to not allow in their backyards.

Dr. Helen Brown, supervisor of English, defended the book. She told the board and the Baker group that no child should ever be made to read a book he or she or a parent objected to, but she said theirs was the only complaint. She doubted whether one parent or a small group of people should be able to impose their standards on other parents and students.

Members of the committee joined her. They said young people see as much and worse in newspapers, magazines and on television. A student said the vulgarities are seen and heard in school hallways.

A copy of Time magazine showing a photograph of the goings on at Evil Knievel's big canyon jump was passed around. The photo showed a naked woman, front view, among the carousers.

After the hearing, the board decided the book could stay, provided it was used at the careful discretion of the teacher and only with juniors and seniors.

But the dispute continued.

Next, according to one teacher, the English teachers decided that if it would bring peace, they would mark out the vulgarities and cut out any offending pictures.

H. E. Aull, a school board member from Ward 1, has been against using the book ever since the dispute began. He wasn't for striking over words or cutting out pictures. "That's silly," he said Saturday. He wants the book banned.

Aull said the book is out of the schools and said he received word from Supt. Robert Aertker that it wouldn't be used again. Aull was planning to ask for a public hearing Thursday but he said in light of word the book has been removed for good, "We resolved it, and there's no need for a hearing now."

He said he was assured another book would be found for the course.

Aull said he's had numerous complaints about the book from the people in the Istrouma, Tara and Lee areas.

"I've worked very, very hard to get rid of it," he said, adding to that, "I held a lot of it (the complaining) down and tried to keep the matter in hand."

Mrs. Wallace F. Armstrong of Ward 1, a member of the review committee, said she hasn't received a single complaint. Neither was she aware of a decision to ban the book completely. "There hasn't been a vote," she said Saturday.

Some teachers quit using the book voluntarily, Mrs. Armstrong said. She felt most of the teachers backed off for fear of the publicity.

Mrs. Armstrong also questioned the wisdom of the board's removing a book under the present circumstances. She said, "You can object to anything."

Mrs. Nell Meriwether, the Tara teacher who wrote the course, said she looked at a number of books but couldn't find a book that was as good for the course as "Mass Media."

The intention of the course, she said, was to show the influence of mass media. "We're not trying to promote sex," she said, and a number of people have misconstrued the contents by taking them out of context.

"Mass Media" was only an additional source for the course, Mrs. Meriwether said, explaining that students also read magazines and newspapers and hear various speakers.

She said she doesn't care for the words either but she also said it is only reality to know that such words and pictures are used in the mass media. Mrs. Meriwether also teaches Biblical literature.

But the teacher is weary of the whole affair.

"I'm tired of it," she said, saying she felt the teachers' professional integrity has been tampered with.

Mrs. Meriwether said she's at the point that she would say just remove the book.

Commenting on recent statements from the governor and others criticizing teachers' performance, Mrs. Meriwether said, "Those of us who really try are those who get the punches."

■ THE TEXTBOOK CONTROVERSY / A POLITICAL CONFRONTATION

June Kirkhuff Edwards   *The Christian Century*, November 13, 1974

The strong protest being mounted in Virginia and West Virginia against textbooks used in English classes in the public high schools of those states strikes those of us of liberal persuasion as outrageous. Never will we let ultra-rightists dominate our schools, telling students what they may and may not read. We want our children to be broad-minded, to empathize with people of different backgrounds, and to experience vicariously some of the harsh realities of life that, we hope, they will never encounter themselves. As it happens, the textbooks in question (primarily the "Responding" series published by Ginn and Company) accord admirably with our views. They are relevant, ethnically inclusive and *interesting.* The students are "responding" to these books as never before, and they are loving what they read. And now come the diehard "Christians" trying to squelch all that is at last good in a high school English class, trying to bring back the "good old days" of censored classics, traditional teaching and sheer boredom. Can we, should we, let them succeed?

I

I suggest that this liberal reaction is overhasty, for in fact the controversy in the Virginias raises far more fundamental questions of ethics, politics and educational theory. The protest of these angry parents against the literature books has a legitimate, perhaps even healthy, base. Their concern over "dirty" words is only a focus for a much deeper concern: who shall control the education of their children? But this, surely, should be a concern of all of us, whatever our political and theological leanings.

If the protest were merely a matter of choosing "safe" books over "suggestive" ones, the case could be quickly closed. For what books could possibly be chosen that do not contain at least some objectionable words, allusions to sex, slurs about race, religion or gender, or graphic depictions of lives lived in cruel circumstances? Think now. Can you name even one?

Certainly not the Bible. Nor Shakespeare. Nor Chaucer. Nor Mark Twain with his use of "nigger" and his treatment of Injun Joe. Nor Louisa May Alcott with her goody girls behaving in traditional ways. No matter what book were chosen, someone somewhere would find it offensive. Clearly, choosing "safe" books is neither a realistic nor a possible solution.

Look more closely at the situation of our schools to see what the deeper problem really is. In the past 50 years our educational systems have grown from small one-room community centers to large and complex county or metropolitan bureaucracies. Time was when the teacher was a well-known local figure, directly accountable to the people he or she served. Today the walls of many schools are impregnably high. Often not even the teachers have a voice in determining curriculum or selecting textbooks. There is a semblance of "openness." PTA meetings sometimes *inform* parents about school decisions, but rarely are either parents or students allowed to share in policy-making, and rarely do parents insist that they be included. The textbook controversy in the Virginias is one of the few instances of open rebellion.

In an attempt to upgrade the quality of our schools, emphasis has shifted more and more toward professional expertise. Public school teachers and administrators have long envied the prestige enjoyed by physicians, lawyers and college professors, and have longed for the salaries that go with such recognition. It seems that the more esoteric the knowledge an individual possesses, the more the public is willing to pay him or her. The public schools' rebuttal to low salaries and low prestige has been to make the services they render more elusive, less easily observed. Just what do schools do these days? What books *are* the children reading? What ideas are they encountering daily in the classroom? Unless one is employed in a school or does volunteer work there, the answers are not easily come by. This is not to suggest that schools are any different—any better or any worse—than they have always been; it is simply to say that, bureaucratic as they are today, it is more difficult to find out what they are doing. The myth of "expertise" has all but taken over.

The Virginia fight against the English textbooks, then, is in reality a fight against the theory that professional educators have the right to control all decisions in a school system. It springs from the frustrated desire of parents to have some say about the education of their children—whether the parents' viewpoint be left, right or middle. In the case in question, people holding fundamentalist religious beliefs are rebelling against the more liberal-minded educators on the textbook selection committees. If these right-wingers have their way and force school boards to remove from classroom and library shelves all books they find objectionable, liberals and radicals will no doubt rebel in their turn, and for the same reason: to determine who has the right to control the schools.

II

The current controversy may die down, but it is not likely to die out, for the question it raises is fundamental to education in a democracy. If we are to find an answer, we shall have to consider making certain changes in public education.

First, the ethics of a compulsory school system in a supposedly free country must be dealt with. The law requires that every child attend school until age 16. Does that requirement endow educators with the right to control what each child reads and does every step of the way? Not, certainly, by standards of human decency. (Children *are* human, we tend to forget.)

It is true that a child who does not want to read a particular piece of poetry or fiction (or, usually, whose *parent* does not want him to read it) can normally be excused from doing so. But to a child, peer conformity is a force as compelling as is the law or the teacher. Hence being singled out embarrasses the child and can be psychologically detrimental to him. If compulsory school laws were repealed, or if the age were lowered as suggested by the Commission for the Reform of Secondary Education, parents who object to the books prescribed in the curriculum could at least have the choice of sending or not sending their children to school.

Yet if all citizens are to continue to be taxed for public education, perhaps this is not a fair solution. What parents are asking for is schooling *of their own choice.* This seems to me a legitimate request, and one that suggests another possibility. An educational system could provide within its jurisdiction alternative schools open to all students living in the area (within the limits set by overcrowding); in other words, a form of voucher system. For example, vocational-technical training could be emphasized in one or two schools, and traditional subjects and methods in one or two others. The open-concept school could be another. Parents and children would be free to choose the school which was most in line with their educational philosophy and career aspirations.

But this solution again has its unfair aspects, the primary problem being transportation. Busing children to the nearest school is headache enough; busing them to the school of their choice will be more troublesome. To make parents responsible for getting their children to schools not in their immediate area will not answer. It would penalize the poor and favor the well-to-do, since only the latter could afford the transportation costs that allowed their children to be mobile.

III

So I suggest a third solution, one that seems to me the most immediately practicable: namely, offering alternative courses within existing schools. This arrangement would necessitate a completely elective program, particularly for the areas most subject to controversy: English and social studies. It would perhaps mean an imbalance in teacher-pupil ratios. But just as in special education and compensatory programs, the needs of students do not fall neatly into 30-pupils-per-class divisions.

With regard to the controversy in the Virginias, I see ethical merit in setting up a class with a willing teacher for students of fundamentalist background who desire a particular type of textbook and method of teaching, even though they may be in the minority. As taxpaying citizens, as human beings in a democratic society, fundamentalist parents are entitled to the same consideration for their wishes as anyone else. And conversely, students who want to read books like the "Responding" series should have an equal right to enjoy a stimulating class without interference from people who personally object to these books. The majority should not rule in either case, nor the minority. All children and all parents have the right to demand that their interests, needs and desires be respected in the schools—especially since they have no choice about being there.

Our churches and our schools have always been political arenas, despite the pretense of religious leaders and educators that they are not. Today's controversy over "filthy" English books is simply another move in the age-old power struggle for the control of children's minds. The struggle will go on as long as each side insists on the triumph of its own views. The only ethical and politically practical answer to one group's manipulative domination of another is the establishment of alternatives in education and of freedom for students to choose their own direction.

■ **POINTS TO CONSIDER**

School Textbook Controversies

1. What specific charges are leveled at the books under attack? Do you think these charges are justified? Explain.
2. What psychological motivations do the articles suggest might lie behind the actions of the book banners? Do you agree? Explain.
3. How might the banning and burning of certain books have an effect exactly the opposite of that intended?
4. Do you believe that there are words, phrases, pictures, or ideas that are, in themselves, dangerous things capable of significantly harming someone? Explain.

The Textbook Controversy: A Political Confrontation

1. What, according to the author, is the essential concern behind the Virginia textbook protests? Do you agree?
2. Explain how the author feels that "expertise" has tended to isolate school systems from parents.
3. What possible solutions does the author present? With what advantages and disadvantages? Which solution seems most feasible to you? Why?

■ MASTERS OF MEDIOCRITY

Artist: Paul Coker, Jr.
Written by: Donald D. Shandler

Mad, March 1966

SUMMA CUM LAZY DEPT.

All around the country, college students are revolting (in more ways than usual) against what they consider to be an assembly-line educational system that grinds out graduates without teaching them anything. Yet, despite these protests, it is obvious that Higher Education will continue to reflect our nation's adult society . . . that more and more, college students will be trained to appreciate the positive aspects of getting lost in the shuffle and staying there . . . and that someday, we will be preparing our young people for an anonymous lifetime in a conforming apathetic world with . . .

COLLEGE PROGRAMS TO DEVELOP
MASTERS OF MEDIOCRITY

Megalopolis State University

COLLEGE OF DISILLUSION

CATALOGUE OF COURSES
FALL SEMESTER 1966

304. BASIC HYPOCRISY
3 Credits   T-W-Th
Room 180   Justifyette Hall   Mr. Lippservis

The advanced study of communicating on two levels is the core of this course. Students will learn that words and actions do not have to be consistent. Guest lecturers will include businessmen, politicians and educators who will demonstrate how their superficial ideas have not interfered with making a living.

305. ALL-PURPOSE OPINION FORMULATION
3 Credits   M-Th-F
Room 215   Patronizem Hall   Mr. Brownoze

Through concentrated training in the development of a total lack of enlightened opinion, firm conviction and ethical principles as they relate to the pressing issues of our time, this course is designed to pave the way for rapid advancement in later life by enabling the student to voice wholehearted agreement with all lunatic fringe views held by employers, wealthy prospective in-laws and other individuals who have something the student wants.

SENIOR COURSES

400. ADVANCED DISILLUSION
3 Credits   T-W-Th
Room 829   Faicet Hall   Dr. Know

A refresher course for the senior about to enter the cold, hard world. In addition to consoling the fourth year student for failing either to prepare himself for adult life or to drop out of school and get started on it, the course will help him develop the skills of goldbricking, social parasitism, ingratiating conformity, financial credit manipulation and income tax evasion.

401. CONTACT MAINTENANCE
3 Credits   M-W-F
Room 177   Potential Building   Miss Hughes

A frank seminar discussion of the importance of re-kindling and capitalizing on tenuous college relationships in later life. Emphasis will be placed on the selection of casual acquaintances most likely to succeed in order to weed out and discard potentially meaningless friends before it's too late. Attention also will be focused on the future fabricating of college reminiscences for the purpose of securing employment from and/or selling insurance to classmates you never actually met.

402. STUDIES IN EGOCENTRICITY
3 Credits   T-Th-F
Room 112   Ego Building   Prof. LeGate

Business administration students will find this course particularly advantageous in bulldozing their way into profitable endeavors for which they are unqualified. They will learn to overlook their inadequacies by becoming self-centered individuals with little regard for the person, dignity and property of others. Strong emphasis will be placed on the rude and the vulgar as a means of dominating those with less self-assurance.

404. PREPARATION FOR POST-GRADUATE APATHY
3 Credits   M-W-F
Room 390   Avoidit Hall   Mr. E. Lood

Offered for the first time during the present academic year, this course will aid the graduate in maintaining a solid foundation of self-centered dis-interest when confronted with the pressure to participate in suburban civic endeavors. Students will be taught the basic principles of begging off, indefinite postponement, quarrel-some behavior at planning sessions, and negative arguments against Little League baseball, the preservation of historical landmarks, the need for additional school crossing guards and expansion of facilities for anything.

405. FLAUNTING
2 Credits   W-F
Room 219   Regalem Hall   Mr. Bragg

Students will be encouraged to utilize their college degrees as symbols of superiority over more capable individuals who have been exposed to fewer years of formal schooling. Techniques will be stressed for dropping references to college days into conversations, for terminating arguments with inferiors by mis-quoting former professors, and for utilizing your educational background as an offsetting factor to explain away goofs on the job, all out of context.

406. INDEPENDENT STUDY
3 Credits   M-W-F
Room 300   Jon Hall   Miss Montez

Inserted into the curriculum for the benefit of seniors who otherwise would fall three units short of meeting the requirements for graduation. Special fee: $175, but well worth it to avoid being stuck here for another whole semester.

42

FRESHMAN COURSES

100A. INTRODUCTION TO APATHY

3 Credits   M-W-F
Room 2931   Chuckit Hall   Mr. D. Moralize

This survey course is geared to help the over-zealous freshman achieve the degree of apathy required on the college level. Lectures will concentrate on the futility of retaining such immature traits as ambition, ideals and a sense of school spirit.

100B. REMEDIAL INDIFFERENCE

2 Credits   Sat-Sun
Room 857   Over Hall   Mr. Whippinline

Prerequisite to INTRODUCTION TO APATHY for unusually difficult students who refuse to accept the status quo even after they have gained a fuller understanding of it.

101. BEGINNING DISILLUSION

3 Credits   M-T-Th
Room 77   Nohohpat Hall   Mr. C. Black

Designed to imbue the incoming student with a feeling of basic helplessness in regard to the more pressing problems confronting the world he lives in. Discussions will cover such topics as the inevitability of the Rotten Society, the insignificance of the individual in world affairs and the adoption of a realistic attitude that everything is bound to get a lot worse before it gets better, if ever.

102. UMBILICAL COORDINATION

3 Credits   T-W-F
Room 666   Navel Academy   Mother Wylie

This course will help to prevent the severing of the silver cord between a mother and her pampered child. It enables the overly-dependent freshman, away from home for the first time, to learn the advantages of continuing to lean on Mom throughout college, job-placement and marriage.

104. PARENTAL PRESSURE OPPOSITION

0 Credits   F-Sat-Sun
Room 803   Sickovit Hall   Mr. Offyurback

Students will learn to help their parents mature, by acquiring an over-all knowledge of methods helpful in decreasing family emphasis on academic success, choice of a career and general personality adjustment. Students will apply what they learn on weekends at home.

105. INTRODUCTORY NON-PARTICIPATION

3 Credits   M-W-Th
Room 1181   Rejectit Hall   Miss DeFunn

Especially designed to assist the naive freshman in conquering his immature desire to become involved in normal extra-curricular activities. Discussions will concentrate on loss of prestige, useless expenditure of energy and the lack of meaning in later life inherent in non-compulsory campus affairs. (Note: This course not open to students attending the University on athletic scholarships.)

106. FUNDAMENTALS OF KILLING LEISURE TIME

3 Credits   T-Th-F
Students Lounge   Downthe Hall   Mr. Goldbrick

Although specifically designed to assist the incoming student (who worked hard in high school preparing for college acceptance) to adjust to goofing off now that he's here, this course also lays the foundation for apathetic lolling after graduation. All aspects of unproductive leisure time activity will be examined with special emphasis on prolonged day dreaming.

SOPHOMORE COURSES

200. TECHNIQUES OF SCAPEGOATING

3 Credits   M-W-F
Room 701   Duckett Hall   Pastor Buck

Learning to blame teachers, parents, employers and society in general for personal shortcomings will be the student's objective in this course. Guest lecturers from the Department of Speech will assist with instruction in whining.

201. CONTEMPORARY SELF-ACCEPTANCE

3 Credits   T-W-Th
Room 59   Acceptit Hall   Mr. D. Lusion

For the second year student who has mastered the fundamentals of apathy, including the avoidance of responsibility and constructive participation, but who still experiences twinges of anxiety as to where his emerging lack of identity may lead him. This course enables the individual to drift with renewed confidence by pointing up how the growth of automation makes him increasingly unnecessary; the disintegrating world situation makes his future increasingly improbable, and the population explosion makes his inability to produce increasingly desirable.

202. PRINCIPLES AND METHODS OF CHEATING

3 Credits M-Th-F
Room 81 Cribbing Hall Miss DeMeanor

Areas covered to help students achieve better grades without studying or learning are microfilming techniques, trends in infra-red printing, skillful plagiarism and beating around the bush on final exams in 2,000 words or more.

202B. MEANINGLESS VOCABULARY-BUILDING

2 Credits T-F
Room 7922 Faykit Hall Dr. Papers

Vital to the student whose incompetence has developed to the point where he can't even learn to cheat. This course enables such individuals to prepare acceptable term and examination papers through the frequent insertion of impressive but meaningless words and phrases.

204. PRACTICAL MATERIALISM

3 Credits T-Th-F
Room 101 Amasset Hall Substitute Teachers

Naive college students will learn to replace love, faith, happiness and similar unprofitable emotions with chromium worldly goods: large homes, high-powered sports cars, color television sets, yachts, jewelry, self-defrosting refrigerators that make round ice cubes, etc.

205. HUMAN SELECTIVITY

3 Credits M-W-Th
Room 268 Contact Building Mr. Hooyuno

This course is constructed to teach the student to lean on others in order to survive. Experienced faculty members, long familiar with the cultivation of useful connections as opposed to meaningful relationships, will conduct seminars to assist under-graduates in the selection of rich, brainy, influential acquaintances who will do the student the most good after graduation.

205B. MARRYING FOR MONEY

3 Credits M-W-F
Room 242 Loveless Union Miss Alliance

Open only to students who have exhibited sufficient cunning to by-pass HUMAN SELECTIVITY. Instruction will concentrate on the choosing of a single member of the opposite sex to fulfill lifetime needs for wealth, job security, family position and a head start in career after graduation.

206. INTERMEDIATE DIS-ORIENTATION

2 Credits M-F
Room 187 Forgetit Hall Miss A. Ply

Now required of all sophomores. This course is designed to meet the needs of the second year student who, inadvertently, has seen a relationship between two or more facts he learned as a freshman and finds himself unable to be totally apathetic about it.

JUNIOR COURSES

301. DEVELOPMENT OF AESTHETIC DEPRECIATION

3 Credits T-Th-F
Room 111 DeBaysette Hall Miss Gyde

Students with little or no aesthetic awareness will receive guidance in producing a comfortable environment where their deficiencies can be maintained in later life. Instruction will include lectures in national park deforestation, rural stream pollution, proper placement of highway billboards, suburban split-level home selection, trashy book and motion picture enjoyment, and approved methodology in general littering.

302. PROGRESSIVE UNDERACHIEVEMENT

2 Credits W-F
Room 219 Connem Hall Miss Leed

Creating the impression that you are not performing up to capacity, and mistakenly leading professors to believe that you are an intelligent and worldly individual is the basis of this course. Emphasis will be placed on obscure name-dropping, thought-provoking question-asking, feigned appreciation of professorial witticisms, and carrying books above your class and age level.

303. UNPROGRESSIVE OVERACHIEVEMENT

2 Credits T-Th
Room 181 Impressum Hall Mr. Snow

Invaluable to the student who seeks a passing grade without ever completing a homework assignment. This course offers guidance in skimming through unassigned reading material to create the assumption that you are engrossed in the subject and are pursuing it beyond established requirements. Instruction also is given in embarrassing professors through the memorization and use of foreign phrases with no particular meaning, frequent reference to non-existent theorems, and scoring academic points by citing analogies that don't apply to the discussion topic.

1. Do you feel that colleges and universities do, in fact, train students to "appreciate the positive aspects of getting lost in the shuffle and staying there"? Does this also apply to high school? Explain, using, if you can, examples from your own experience.

2. Can you think of other courses that might be added to the catalog of the College of Disillusion?

3. What is satire, and what does it attempt to do? How is this article satirical?

4. In what ways do schools reflect the values of the societies which they serve? To what extent does this "catalog" satirize our society as a whole?

■ LEARNING BY DOING

John Holt   *East West Journal*

We hear much talk these days that the society of the future will be a learning society. Not long ago some of this talk put a thought in my mind about "learning." Suppose we were in the midst of a group of people, and found after a while that most of their talk was about breathing: "You are breathing very well today." "He breathes wonderfully, don't you agree?" "I am breathing better, but not as well as I should." "How can we all improve our breathing?" Would we not soon think that these people must all be sick, or just recovering from some trouble with their lungs? Otherwise, why make such a fuss about what healthy people do naturally?

If we could visit human societies in their most vigorous and creative periods, when most people were growing most rapidly in understanding, competence, and skill—say classical Greece, or 18th century New England—we would probably hear very little talk about "learning." People were learning a great deal because they were doing a great deal, because their lives made demands on, and opportunities and rewards for, their ingenuity and intelligence.

The best learning community I have ever known, in which most people were growing most rapidly in competence, skill, and judgment, was not meant to be a learning community at all. It was a U.S. submarine—the USS Barbero—in World War II. We were not in that sub to "learn about submarines," but to help fight the war. We never thought about learning. We were too busy running that complicated ship, trying to find and sink enemy ships, and trying to keep them from finding and sinking us, to have time to worry about learning.

Our present great concern about learning, and all the time, talk, and money we spend on it, seems to me a sign—one of many—that something is very wrong with modern society—*all* modern societies. If most had work to do that they liked, that used and rewarded much of their intelligence, skill, and judgment, work whose purposes they understood and shared and respected, and if they felt that what they thought, believed, wanted, said and did made or might make a real difference, we would not be talking so much about learning. We would all be busy doing interesting things that mattered.

In recent months I have been spending many hours a day playing the cello, which I have only just begun to play, and which I mean someday to play well. Most people would say I was "learning to play the cello." But this implies that there are two processes: (1) learning to play the cello (2) playing it, and that after doing the first for a while I will stop and begin doing the second. This is, of course, nonsense. There are not two processes, but one. We learn to play the cello, like anything else, by doing it. At first, we don't do it well. Later, if we have good models, and perhaps some good advice, if we play often, and always play as well as we can, we play better. There is no other way.

It now seems to me vitally important that we understand that this process, which some call learning but I call "doing," is very different from and indeed *the opposite of* the process we call "education." By "doing" I mean the things people do in their own time and their own way, for their own reasons, purposes, and satisfaction, with no more help than they want to ask for, to explore the world around them (in time as well as space) so as to gain more understanding, competence, freedom, control, and joy within it. By "education" I mean a process in which some people decide that *other* people ought to be made to know, believe, and want certain things, and try to find ways to do this. I mean, in short, a process in which some people set out to *shape* other people. I am wholly against this process, however carried out, and the system of credentials and compulsory schooling, carrots and sticks, which we use to carry it out. Education and compulsory schooling seem to me among the most authoritarian of all the inventions of man, and the deepest foundations of the slave state we are so busy making. And I am afraid that this learning society that everyone talks about will in fact be an "education" society, and that unless we take steps to prevent it the people-shapers will find ways to keep shaping us all through our lives.

I do not believe that this process of education, which in rival societies we quite rightly call brainwashing, can be wisely and humanely carried out.

It must in the long run lead to invidious comparisons, judgments, pseudo-diagnoses and predictions, humiliation, threat, punishment and cruelty. Nor do I think that schools, as long as they are run by and work for educators rather than do-ers, can be made into places that are good for people, young or old. The only "educational reform" that seems to me serious is the task of taking the schools away from the educators and putting them at the service of the do-ers. This is not a task that can be done *within* schools, though some people can and should help to do it. It is a political task, and one of the most urgent of our time. I hope we may soon get to work on it.

■ **POINTS TO CONSIDER**

1. What does the author describe as the relationship between learning and doing? In what kinds of situations does he feel people learn best? Agree or disagree, using examples from your own experience.

2. How does the author contrast learning or "doing" with "education"? Do you agree with his statement that "education" is one of the "most authoritarian of all the inventions of man"? Explain.

3. What is the "educational reform" the author suggests? Why is this reform a "political task"?

4. Do you think it is possible, or feasible, for people to learn everything they need or want to know "by doing"? Explain.

■ SCIENCE, EDUCATION AND THE ENJOYMENT OF LIVING

Norman Cousins   *Saturday Review,* April 20, 1968

Let me show my hand at once. I contend that science tends to lengthen life, and education to shorten it; that science has the effect of freeing man for leisure, and that education has the effect of deflecting him from the enjoyment of living.

What seems to me most significant about the gap between the two cultures, starkly lamented by C. P. Snow, is not so much a difference in background or ambience[1] as the fact of paradoxical effect. The dominant tendency in contemporary education is to teach man how to do things rather than how to exercise creative options. The dominant tendency of science is to emancipate man from doing things, enabling him to preside over more open time then he has known since ancient Greece. The combined result is that man has wondrous new options he is not prepared to recognize or enjoy.

Putting it differently, education trains men to perform. It doesn't put nearly so much effort or imagination into the process of self-discovery and creative development, without which freedom tends to be somewhat circumscribed, even brittle. What we have on parallel tracks, then, is science carrying man in the direction of greater freedom—or at least in a direction that gives him access to options he has never known before—while education carries him in a direction that enables him to be functional rather than resourceful. Thus is produced the most poignant of all questions: What happens to a man when he chronically lives under his productive capacity?

The most costly disease in America is not cancer or coronaries. The

[1] Ambience is cultural environment

most costly disease is boredom—costly for both individual and society. The dominant types of boredom in modern civilization, of course, are directly related to shorter work weeks, shorter work days, earlier retirement, and increased life expectancy. The cause is surging technology, rodent control, conquest of microbes, muscular unionism, and adroit politics.

Leisure time in the contemporary world is potentially man's greatest gift to himself; actually, it is a problem of ghastly dimensions. It has thrown man out of joint. People have more time on their hands than their knowledge, interests, or aptitudes can accommodate. Few things are more terrifying in this world for some persons than an open hour if the TV set is out of order. Their relaxation reflexes have been conditioned by the turning of knobs. If the knob does not produce an image, the result is akin to personal disaster.

Even without respect to the pacifying characteristics of the TV screen, however, a whole new world of potential leisure has sprung up for which people are unprepared. The shorter work week may produce premature retirement symptoms rather than a condition of creative liberation. That is, available new hours are more likely to lead to helplessness and floundering than to active discovery of exciting new options. Retirement, supposed to be a chance to join the winner's circle, has turned out to be more dangerous than automobiles or LSD. Retirement for most people is literal consignment to no-man's land. It is the chance to do everything that leads to nothing. It is the gleaming brass ring that unhorses the rider.

My concern about education, to repeat, is that it tends to shy away from the requirements of the creative process and therefore from the enjoyment of living. In this sense, it is somewhat indifferent to the possibilities inherent in the prolongation of life. It has yet to develop the techniques that can make it richly relevant to new opportunities for leisure. It is not sufficiently enthralled by the mysteries of the inner universe of the individual and therefore it has little to say to him about the essential encounter with the abstract or the uses of the abstract in giving him an enlarged sense of what is joyously fulfilling. It tends to allow difficulties in defining purpose to obstruct the pursuit of purpose. Such a pursuit may not always be either informed or successful, but it is occasionally exhilarating. It may also lead to a greater sense of what is integral; it can provide nourishment for the subconscious.

There is no objective way of determining whether it is good or bad to have increased leisure time during those years when one is not required or even permitted to be part of the accredited community of producers. My judgment—and, if I am lucky, it will have some basis in abstract thought and not just in observation—is that leisure is an option in freedom and that freedom is good, and that there is no impassable distance between the option of freedom and the full exercise of it.

I do not regard the school as the sole means for making man aware of these options or enabling him to use them. Education transcends the school—or should, if the school is any good. But the school must not become an illusion. It must never assume that the world stands ready to do everything it does not. And one of the most important jobs before the school is to educate for a fuller life and a larger one.

Consider the school's introverted attitude toward nonschool hours. It doesn't adequately use these hours to prepare the individual for doing things productively and enjoyably. The student should be encouraged to turn to leisure-time pursuits that need careful cultivation in a world in which the dominant part of an individual's life will consist of free time.

The school's business, quite properly, consists largely of problem-solving. But the school makes a mistake in chasing the student with problem-solving right into his home. Homework ought to be the means for educating a student in the enjoyment of living, not for hammering home the day's lessons. And the place to begin is early in grade school.

There are intimations of Calvinism[2] in the reluctance of many schools to encourage the student to develop creative leisure-time interests. I see nothing subversive or shattering about giving a student an evening assignment to attend a good motion picture or concert, or read a good novel, or see something worthwhile on TV, or listen to some recordings in classical music, pop, or jazz. This kind of homework can lead to exciting classroom discussion. Good talk is one of the most stimulating and rarest experiences on this planet. The school has an opportunity to make it somewhat less rare. Going even further: the community could do worse than to subsidize a boy of modest means to an evening date with his girl friend on the town, including a visit to the theater and perhaps even some after-theater entertainment.

What I am suggesting is that education can be just as relevant in preparing a person for creative and joyous living and for increased life expectancy as it is in preparing him to be an income-producer and a solid citizen. The will to live and everything that goes with it are indigenous[3] parts of the liberal arts. It is in this direction that education may find its greatest energy and widest area of service. The relationship between the good life and the good society remains the most insistent item on the joint agenda of education and the nation.

■ **POINTS TO CONSIDER**

1. How does science lengthen life? According to Cousins, how does education turn people from the enjoyment of life? How does this "shorten life"?
2. In what way is leisure in our present society like LSD or "the brass ring that unhorses the rider"?
3. What does Cousins mean when he says that education "tends to allow difficulties in defining purposes to obstruct the pursuit of purpose"?
4. How does Cousins think a school should deal with the problem of utilizing leisure time?
5. What is Cousins's attitude toward homework? How does homework

[2] Calvinism is the puritanical religious philosophy which embodies the outlook that toil is good for the soul and that leisure leads to spiritual corruption.

[3] Indigenous means natural and inborn.

conflict with educating people in ways to employ their leisure time? What alternative to homework does he offer?

6. To what extent is Cousins's feeling about the "disease" of boredom in our society similar to Fromm's feeling in "Personality Packages" (p. 17) about a person's transformation into a commodity?

"NO COMMENT."

Courtesy of Publishers-Hall Syndicate, Inc.

■ IDEAS FOR INVESTIGATION, DISCUSSION, AND WRITING

1.   In what sense can public education be considered a mass communication medium like the movies, newspapers, magazines, or television? What do school systems have in common with the other media as means of communication? To what extent are they different? What do these similarities and differences reveal about the function which public education serves in our society? What is your opinion of this function?

2.   Write an essay comparing the U.S. education system with that of another country. Do the two systems seem to be attempting to create different kinds of people? How? Which system is the more standardized? Why? What effects, good and bad, does this have on the quality of education? How do fundamental approaches differ? What effects do these differences have?

3.   Write an essay discussing the statement: "There is no teaching; there is only learning." To what extent is the statement true? How might this statement be applied to actual teaching situations?

4.   After an investigation of several sources write a summary of what psychology tells us about the process of learning. To what extent are these principles being applied in school today? To what extent are they being ignored? Cite examples in each case. Can you give suggestions as to how they might be put into practice in certain educational situations?

5.   Investigate and discuss in a report the principles and applications of programmed learning. To what subjects has the programmed approach been applied? To which subjects does it seem the approach lends itself most readily? To which least readily? What advantages does this method offer? What disadvantages?

6.   In an essay describe what you would consider to be the ideal grade school, high school, or college. Give as complete a picture of the school as possible, including its enrollment, location, physical structure, courses, rules (if any), and resources. Indicate how many teachers there would be and in what manner they would teach. As you describe the various facets of your school, explain and justify them where you feel it necessary.

7.   Discuss in an essay the following statement by Paul Goodman:

University education—liberal arts and the principles of the professions—is for adults who know something, who have something to philosophize. Otherwise, as Plato pointed out, it is just verbalization.

What does this statement imply about the present system of education in this country? Do you agree? Why?

8.   Investigate and report on the problems of college admission. To what extent is it true that "only the rich go to college"? What sources of financial aid are available to the student? What are quota systems? Where and how are they used? Do black students have a harder time getting into college than their white peers? Or, is it easier for them? Why?

9.　After consulting several authorities, discuss in an essay the question of what should be the role of a college or university. What role should it play in society? Should it train philosophers or accountants or both? Should it seclude itself from politics and government, or should it serve the government?

10.　Discuss Jerry Farber's assertion that in education the medium is the message and the medium is regimentation: desks in straight rows, raising one's hand to ask to leave the room, hall passes, and so forth.

11.　Make a study of teaching machines and their role in education as a mass medium. Will the machines and their prepackaged programs further standardize curricula? What arguments can be advanced for and against the large-scale use of teaching machines in modern education?

12.　Investigate the effects of the large standardized tests such as the College Entrance Examination Board tests and others on the education system. What effects if any have these tests had on high school teaching and curricula? What effects have they had on admissions procedures in major colleges and universities?

13.　Gather all the data possible on the size and extent of education as an industry. How many people are employed in education? What percentage of the national wealth is used for education? What does it cost to educate a single pupil at various levels? How does education compare with other industries with respect to size and efficiency of service? On the basis of these observations what conclusions or recommendations could be made?

14.　Make a study of the principles of the "new education" as found in the books of such authors as A. S. Neil, John Holt, Jerry Farber, Herbert Kohl, and others. What are the major premises of their beliefs? What changes do they suggest in the present system?

15.　Investigate the recent phenomenon of the "free school." What exactly is a free school? What are its goals? How is it financed? How is it run? What alternatives do these schools attempt to offer to the traditional schools? How well do they succeed?

■ A SELECTED BIBLIOGRAPHY

I. Periodicals

A. General Periodicals: These popular publications of news and cultural features regularly contain articles and editorials on the mass media and popular arts and offer reviews of books, films, and television shows as well as good cartoons, photography, and advertising.

Atlantic Monthly, Atlantic Monthly, Inc., 8 Arlington St., Boston, MA 02116.
Commentary, American Jewish Committee, 165 East 56th St., New York, NY 10022.
Commonweal, Commonweal Publishing Co., Inc., 23 Madison Ave., New York, NY 10016.
Ebony, 1820 South Michigan Ave., Chicago, IL 60016.
Esquire, Esquire, Inc., 488 Madison Ave., New York, NY 10022.
Harper's, Harper's Magazine, Inc., 2 Park Avenue, New York, NY 10016.
Hudson Review, Hudson Review, Inc., 65 East 55th St., New York, NY 10022.
Kaiser News, Kaiser Aluminum and Chemical Corp., Kaiser Center, 300 Lakeside Drive, Oakland, CA 90012.
Mad Magazine, E.C. Publications, Inc., 485 Madison Ave., New York, NY 10022.
McCalls, McCall Corp., 230 Park Avenue, New York, NY 10017.
Ms. Ms. Magazine Corp., 370 Lexington Avenue, New York, NY 10017.
Nation, Nation Co., Inc., 333 Sixth Avenue, New York, NY 10014.
New Republic, Robert J. Myers, 1244 19th Street, NW, Washington, D.C. 20036.
Newsweek, Newsweek, Inc., 444 Madison Avenue, New York, NY 10022.
New York, N.Y.M. (New York Magazine) Corp., 755 Second Avenue, New York, NY 10017.
New York Review of Books, NYREV, Inc., 250 West 57th Street, New York, NY 10019.
New York Times Magazine (section of the *New York Times* Sunday edition), New York Times Co., 229 West 43d Street, New York, NY 10036.
New Yorker, New Yorker Magazine, Inc., 23 West 43d Street, New York, NY 10036.
Playboy, HMH Publishing Co., Inc., 919 North Michigan Avenue, Chicago, IL 60611.
Ramparts, Noah's Ark, Inc., 2749 Hyde Street, San Francisco, CA 94109.
Saturday Review, Saturday Review, Inc., 380 Madison Avenue, New York, NY 10017.
Time, Time, Inc., 541 North Fairbanks Court, Chicago, IL 60611.
Village Voice, 80 University Street, New York, NY 10003.

B. Special Interest Periodicals: The following publications focus particularly on one or a few of the mass media or popular arts.

Advertising Age, Crain Communications, Inc., 740 Rush Street, Chicago, IL 60611.

American Education, U.S. Department of Health, Education, and Welfare, U.S. Office of Education, 400 Maryland Avenue, SW, Washington, DC 20202.

American Film: Journal of the Film and Television Arts, American Film Institute, John F. Kennedy Center for the Performing Arts, Washington, DC 20566.

Audio-visual Communications, United Business Publishers, Inc., 750 Third Avenue, New York, NY 10017.

A-V Communication Review, Association for Educational Communications and Technology, 1201 16th Street, NW, Washington, DC 20036.

Billboard, Billboard Publications, Inc., 9000 Sunset Boulevard, Los Angeles, CA 90069.

Broadcasting, Broadcasting Publications, Inc., 1735 De Sales Street, NW, Washington, DC 20036.

Cineaste: A Magazine for the Film Student, Cineaste Magazine, 333 Sixth Avenue, New York, NY 10014.

Close-up: Quarterly Magazine of the Popular Arts, Views and Reviews Publications, Inc., 424 East Wisconsin Avenue, Milwaukee, WI 53202.

Columbia Journalism Review, Columbia University, Graduate School of Journalism, New York, NY 10027.

Contemporary Music, Burton Publications, Inc., 103 Park Avenue, New York, NY 10017.

Country Music, K.B.O. Publishers, Inc., 475 Park Avenue, Suite 1102, New York, NY 10022.

Crawdaddy: A Magazine of Rock, Crawdaddy Publishing Co., 72 Fifth Avenue, New York, NY 10011.

Down Beat, Maher Publishers, Inc., 222 West Adams Street, Chicago, IL 60606.

Education Digest, Prakken Publishers, Inc., P.O. Box 623, 416 Longshore Drive, Ann Arbor, MI 48107.

Educational Forum, J. Richard McElhewy, P.O. Box A, West Lafayette, IN 47906.

Educational Record, American Council on Education, 1785 Massachusetts Avenue, NW, Washington, DC 20036.

Educational Screen and Audio-visual Guide, Trade Periodicals, Inc., 434 South Wabash Street, Chicago, IL 60605.

Educational and Industrial Television, C.S. Tepfer Publishing Co., 607 Main Street, Ridgefield, CT 06877.

Film Quarterly, University of California Press, Berkeley, CA 94720.

Film Society Review, American Federation of Film Societies, 144 Bleeker Street, New York, NY 10012.

Films in Review, National Board of Review of Motion Pictures, Inc., 31 Union Square, New York, NY 10003.

High Fidelity / Musical America, Billboard Publications, Inc., 130 East 59th Street, New York, NY 10022.

Improving College and University Teaching, 101 Waldo Hall, Oregon State University, Corvallis, OR 97331.

Journal of Advertising Research, Advertising Research Foundation, 3 East 54th Street, New York, NY 10022.

Journal of Broadcasting, Broadcast Education Association, Temple University, Philadelphia, PA 19122.

Journal of Popular Culture, Popular Culture Association, Bowling Green State University, Bowling Green, OH 43403.

Journal of Popular Film, Popular Press, 101 University Hall, Bowling Green State University, Bowling Green, OH 43403.

Journalism Quarterly, Association for Education in Journalism, School of Journalism, University of Minnesota, Minneapolis, MN 55455.

Media and Methods, Media and Methods Institute, 134 North 13th Street, Philadelphia, PA 19107.

Modern Photography, 130 East 59th Street, New York, NY 10022.

PMI (Photo Methods for Industry), Gellert Publishing Corp., 33 West 60th Street, New York, NY 10023.

Popular Photography, Ziff-Davis Publishing Co., One Park Avenue, New York, NY 10016.

Publisher's Weekly, R. R. Bowker Co., 1180 Avenue of the Americas, New York, NY 10036.

Rolling Stone, Straight Arrow Publishers, 625 Third Street, San Francisco, CA 94107.

Sight and Sound: The International Film Quarterly, 155 West 15th Street, New York, NY 10001.

Stereo Review, Ziff-Davis Publishing Co., One Park Avenue, New York, NY 10016.

Television Quarterly, National Academy of Television Arts and Sciences, 54 West 40th Street, New York, NY 10018.

TV Guide, Triangle Publications, Inc., P.O. Box 400, Radnor, PA 19088.

TV-Radio Mirror, McFadden-Bartell Corp., 205 East 42d Street, New York, NY 10017.

Today's Education (Journal of the N.E.A.), National Education Association of the United States, 1201 16th Street, NW, Washington, DC 20036.

Underground Press Revue, Grape Press, Box 26, Village Station, New York, NY 10014.

II. Books

The following books focus upon one or more of the mass media and popular arts. Although some older volumes are included, the emphasis is on books published in the past five to fifteen years.

A. Mass Media, Popular Arts, and Popular Culture in General

Allen, Donn, *The Electric Humanities: Patterns for Teaching Mass Media and Popular Culture.* Dayton, Ohio: Pflaum, 1971.

Berger, Arthur Asa, *Pop Culture.* Dayton, Ohio: Pflaum, 1973.

Browne, Ray B., Marshall Fishwick, and Michael T. Marsden, eds., *Heros of Popular Culture.* Bowling Green, Ohio: Popular Press, 1972.

Casty, Alan, ed., *Mass Media and Mass Man,* 2d ed. New York: Holt, Rinehart & Winston, 1973.

Davison, W. Phillips, and Frederick T. C. Yu, eds., *Mass Communication Research: Major Issues and Future Directions.* New York: Praeger Special Studies, 1974.

Emery, Edwin, Phillip H. Ault, and Warren K. Agee, *Introduction to Mass Communications,* 4th ed. New York: Dodd, Mead, 1973.

Emery, Michael C., and Ted Curtis Smythe, eds., *Readings in Mass Communication: Concepts and Issues in the Mass Media,* 2d ed. Dubuque, Iowa: Wm. C. Brown, 1974.

Fishwick, Marshall, and Ray B. Browne, eds., *Icons of Popular Culture.* Bowling Green, Ohio: Popular Press, 1970.

Glessing, Robert J., and William P. White, eds., *Mass Media: The Invisible Resource.* Chicago: Science Research Associates, 1973.

Hall, James B., and Barry Ulanov, eds., *Modern Culture and the Arts,* 2d ed. New York: McGraw-Hill, 1972.

Hammel, William M., ed., *The Popular Arts in America: A Reader.* New York: Harcourt Brace Jovanovich, 1972.

Hiebert, Ray Eldon, Donald F. Ungerait, and Thomas W. Bohn, *Mass Media: An Introduction to Modern Communication.* New York: McKay, 1974.

Kirschner, Allen, and Linda Kirschner, eds., *Readings in the Mass Media* (three volumes). New York: Odyssey, 1971.

Lutz, William D., ed., *The Age of Communication.* Pacific Palisades, Calif.: Goodyear Publishing Co., 1974.

McLuhan, H. Marshall, *Counterblast.* New York: Harcourt, Brace & World, 1969.

————, *Culture Is Our Business.* New York: McGraw-Hill, 1970.

————, *The Gutenberg Galaxy: The Making of Typographic Man.* Toronto: University of Toronto Press, 1962.

————, *The Mechanical Bride: Folklore of Industrial Man.* Boston: Beacon Press, 1967.

———— and Quentin Fiore, *The Medium Is the Massage: An Inventory of Effects.* New York: Bantam Books, 1967.

————, *Understanding Media: The Extensions of Man.* New York: McGraw-Hill, 1964.

Nye, Russell B. *The Unembarrassed Muse: The Popular Arts in America.* New York: Dial Press, 1970.

Pember, Don R., *Mass Media in America.* Chicago: Science Research Associates, 1974.

Rivers, William L., Theodore Peterson, and Jay W. Jensen, *The Mass Media in Modern Society,* 2d ed. San Francisco: Rinehart, 1971.

Rosenberg, Bernard, and David Manning White, eds., *Mass Culture Revisited.* New York: Van Nostrand, Rinehold, 1971.

Sandman, Peter M., David M. Rubin, and David B. Sachman, *Media: An Introductory Analysis of American Mass Communications.* Englewood Cliffs, N.J.: Prentice-Hall, 1972.

Schramm, Wilbur, *Men, Messages, and Media: A Look at Human Communication.* New York: Harper & Row, 1973.

——— and Donald F. Roberts, eds., *The Process and Effects of Mass Communication,* 2d ed. Urbana: University of Illinois Press, 1971.

Servan-Schreiber, J. J., *The Power To Inform; Media: The Information Business.* New York: McGraw-Hill, 1974.

Strainchamps, Ethel, ed., *Rooms with No View: A Woman's Guide to the Man's World of the Media.* New York: Harper & Row, 1974.

Tucker, Nicholas, *Understanding the Mass Media; A Practical Approach to Teaching.* Cambridge, Mass.: Harvard University Press, 1966.

Valdes, Joan, and Jeanne Crow, *The Media Works.* Dayton, Ohio: Pflaum, 1973.

Voelker, Francis H., and Ludmila A. Voelker, *Mass Media: Forces in Our Society,* 2d ed. New York: Harcourt Brace Jovanovich, 1975.

Wells, Alan, ed., *Mass Media and Society.* Palo Alto, Calif.: National Press Books, 1972.

B. Advertising

Backman, Jules, *Advertising and Competition.* New York: New York University Press, 1967.

Bernstein, David, *Creative Advertising.* London: Longman, 1974.

Bogart, Leo, *Strategy in Advertising.* New York: Harcourt, Brace & World, 1967.

Buzzi, Giancarlo, *Advertising: Its Cultural and Political Effects.* Tr. B. David Garmize. Minneapolis: University of Minnesota Press, 1967.

Cohen, Dorothy, *Advertising.* New York: Wiley, 1972.

Della Femina, Jerry. *From Those Wonderful Folks Who Gave You Pearl Harbor: Front Line Dispatches from the Advertising War.* New York: Simon and Schuster, 1970.

Fochs, Arnold, *Advertising That Won Elections.* Duluth, Minn.: A. J. Publishing Company, 1974.

Foster, G. Allen, *Advertising: Ancient Market Place to Television.* New York: Criterion Books, 1967.

Glatzer, Robert, *The New Advertising: The Great Campaigns from Avis to Volkswagen.* New York: Citadel Press, 1970.

Goulart, Ronald, *Assault on Childhood.* Los Angeles: Shelborne Press, 1969.

Inglis, Fred, *The Imagery of Power: A Critique of Advertising.* London: Heinemann, 1972.

Key, Wilson Bryan, *Subliminal Seduction: Ad Media's Subliminal Manipulation of a Not So Innocent America.* Englewood Cliffs, N.J.: Prentice-Hall, 1973.

Kleppner, Otto, *Advertising Procedure,* 5th ed. Englewood Cliffs, N.J.: Prentice-Hall, 1966.

Kuhns, William, *Waysteps to Eden: Ads and Commercials.* New York: Herder and Herder, 1970.

Langholz Leymore, Varda, *Hidden Myth: Structure and Symbolism in Advertising.* London: Heinemann, 1975.

Lyon, David G., *Off Madison Avenue.* New York: Putnam, 1966.

Nicosia, Francesco M., ed., *Advertising, Management, and Society.* New York: McGraw-Hill, 1974.

Ogilvy, David, *Confessions of an Advertising Man.* New York: Atheneum Press, 1963.

Packard, Vance, *The Hidden Persuaders.* New York: McKay, 1957.

Seldin, Joseph J., *The Golden Fleece: Selling the Good Life to Americans.* New York: Macmillan, 1963.

Simon, Julian L., *Issues in the Economics of Advertising.* Urbana: University of Illinois Press, 1970.

Stevens, Paul, *I Can Sell You Anything.* New York: Ballantine Books, 1972.

Thorelli, Hans B., Helmutt Becker, and Jack Engledow, *The Information Seekers: An International Study of Consumer Information and Advertising Image.* Cambridge, Mass.: Ballinger Publishing Company, 1975.

Wight, Robin, *The Day the Pigs Refused to Be Driven to Market: Advertising and the Consumer Revolution.* New York: Random House, 1974.

Wright, John S., Daniel S. Warner, and Willis L. Winter. *Advertising.* New York: McGraw-Hill, 1971.

C. Journalism, Cartoons, Publishing, and Popular Print

Agee, Warren K., ed., *The Press and the Public Interest.* Washington, D.C.: Public Affairs Press, 1968.

Babb, Laura Langley, *Of the Press, by the Press, for the Press (and Others Too).* Washington, D.C.: Washington *Post,* 1974.

Bailey, Herbert Smith. *The Art and Science of Book Publishing.* New York: Harper & Row, 1970.

Barron, Jerome A., *Freedom of the Press for Whom? The Right of Access to the Media.* Bloomington: Indiana University Press, 1973.

Berger, Arthur A., *The Comic Stripped American: What Dick Tracy, Blondie, Daddy Warbucks, and Charlie Brown Tell Us about Ourselves.* New York: Walker, 1973.

Bradley, Duane, *The Newspaper: Its Place in a Democracy.* New York: Van Nostrand-Reinhold, 1965.

Brucker, Herbert, *Communication Is Power; Unchanging Values in American Journalism.* New York: Oxford University Press, 1973.

Cook, Fred J., *The Muckrakers: Crusading Journalists Who Changed America.* Garden City, N.Y.: Doubleday, 1972.

Couperie, Pierre, *A History of the Comic Strip.* New York: Crown Publishers, 1968.

Daly, Charles U., *The Media and the Cities.* Chicago: University of Chicago Press, 1968.

Daniels, Leslie, *Comix: A History of Comic Books in America.* New York: E. P. Dutton, 1971.

Dembner, S. Arthur, and William E. Massee, *Modern Circulation Methods.* New York: McGraw-Hill, 1968.

Dennis, Everette E., and William L. Rivers, *Other Voices: The New Journalism in America.* San Francisco: Canfield Press, 1974.

Doig, Ivan, and Carol Doig, *News: A Consumer's Guide.* Englewood Cliffs, N.J.: Prentice-Hall, 1972.

Edwards, Verne E., Jr., *Journalism in a Free Society.* Dubuque, Iowa: Wm. C. Brown, 1970.

Efron, Edith, *The News Twisters.* Los Angeles: Nash, 1971.

Emery, Edwin, *The Press and America: An Interpretative History of the Mass Media.* Englewood Cliffs, N.J.: Prentice-Hall, 1972.

Feiffer, Jules, *The Great Comic Book Heroes.* New York: Dial Press, 1965.

Freeman, Gillian, *The Undergrowth of Literature.* London: Nelson, 1967.

Gerald, J. Edward, *The Social Responsibility of the Press.* Minneapolis: University of Minnesota Press, 1963.

Glessing, Robert J., *The Underground Press in America.* Bloomington: Indiana University Press, 1970.

Griffith, Thomas, *How True: A Skeptic's Guide to Believing the News.* Boston: Little, Brown, 1974.

Gunther, Max, *Writing the Modern Magazine Article.* Boston: The Writer, Inc., 1968.

Hynds, Ernest C., *American Newspapers in the 1970's.* New York: Hastings House, 1975.

Johnson, Michael L., *The New Journalism: The Underground Press, the Artists of Non-Fiction, and Changes in the Established Media.* Lawrence: University Press of Kansas, 1971.

Kennedy, Bruce M., *Community Journalism: A Way of Life.* Ames: Iowa State University Press, 1974.

Kobre, Sidney, *The Development of American Journalism.* Dubuque, Iowa: Wm. C. Brown, 1969.

Lee, Stan, *Origins of Marvel Comics.* New York: Simon and Schuster, 1974.

Lowenthal, Leo, *Literature, Popular Culture, and Society.* Palo Alto, Calif.: Pacific Books, 1968.

MacDougall, Curtis D., *Interpretative Reporting.* New York: Macmillan, 1972.

————, *The Press and Its Problems.* Dubuque, Iowa: Wm. C. Brown, 1964.

Madison, Charles Allan, *Book Publishing in America.* New York: McGraw-Hill, 1967.

McGaffin, William, and Erwin Knoll, *Anything but the Truth: The Credibility Gap.* New York: Putnam, 1968.

McLean, Ruari, *Magazine Design.* New York: Oxford University Press, 1969.

Merill, John Calhoun, *The Elite Press: Great Newspapers of the World.* New York: Pitman Publishing Corporation, 1968.

Mills, Nicolaus, ed., *The New Journalism: A Historical Anthology.* New York: McGraw-Hill, 1974.

Rivers, William L., *The Adversaries: Politics and the Press.* Boston: Beacon Press, 1970.

Robinson, Jerry, *Comics: An Illustrated History of Comic Strip Art.* New York: Putnam, 1974.

Rothstein, Arthur, *Photojournalism: Pictures for Magazines and Newspapers.* New York: American Photographic Book Publishing Co., 1965.

Rucker, Frank W., and Herbert Lee Williams, *Newspaper Organization and Management.* Ames: Iowa State University Press, 1965.

Schuneman, R. Smith, *Photographic Communication: Principles Problems and Challenges of Photojournalism.* New York: Hastings House, 1972.

Short, Robert L., *The Gospel According to Peanuts.* Richmond, Va.: John Knox Press, 1965.

————, *Parables of Peanuts.* New York: Harper & Row, 1968.

Smith, Donald, *The New Freedom to Publish: Trends in Libel and Privacy Laws.* New York: Magazine Publishers Association, 1969.

Tebbel, John, *The American Magazine: A Compact History.* New York: Hawthorne Books, 1969.

Wolfe, Tom, *The New Journalism* (with an anthology edited by Tom Wolfe and E. W. Johnson). New York: Harper & Row, 1973.

Wolseley, Roland E., *Black Press, U.S.A.* Ames: Iowa State University Press, 1971.

————, *Understanding Magazines.* Ames: Iowa State University Press, 1965.

Woodward, Bob, and Carl Bernstein, *All the President's Men.* New York: Simon and Schuster, 1974.

————, *The Final Days.* New York: Simon and Schuster, 1976.

D. Radio and Television

Anderson, Chuck, *The Electronic Journalist: An Introduction to Video.* New York: Praeger, 1973.

Arlen, Michael J., *The Living Room War.* New York: Viking Press, 1969.

Arons, Leon, and Mark A. May. *Television and Human Behavior: Tomorrow's Research in Mass Communication.* New York: Appleton-Century-Crofts, 1963.

Barnouw, Erik, *A History of Broadcasting in the United States.* New York: Oxford University Press, 1966.

Bluem, A. William, *Documentary in American Television.* New York: Hastings House, 1965.

————, *Television in the Public Interest.* New York: Hastings House, 1961.

Blumler, Jay G., *Television in Politics.* Chicago: University of Chicago Press, 1969.

Bogart, Leo, *The Age of Television,* 3d ed. New York: Frederick Ungar Publishing Company, 1972.

Bower, Robert T., *Television and the Public.* New York: Holt, Rinehart & Winston, 1973.

Brown, Les, *Television: The Business behind the Box.* New York: Harcourt Brace Jovanovich, 1971.

Chester, Edward W., *Radio, Television, and American Politics.* New York: Sheed and Ward, 1969.

Chester, Giraud, Garnet R. Garrison, and Edgar Willis, *Television and Radio.* New York: Appleton-Century-Crofts, 1970.

Cole, Barry G., ed., *Television: A Selection of Readings from TV Guide Magazine.* New York: The Free Press, 1970.

Comstock, George A., *Television and Human Behavior: The Key Studies.* Santa Monica, Calif.: Rand, 1975.

Dizard, Wilson P., *Television—A World View.* Syracuse, N.Y.: Syracuse University Press, 1966.

Emery, Walter B., *Broadcasting and Government: Responsibilities and Regulations.* East Lansing: Michigan State University Press, 1971.

————, *National and International Systems of Television Broadcasting: Their History, Operation, and Control.* East Lansing: Michigan State University Press, 1969.

Friendly, Fred W., *Due to Circumstances beyond Our Control.* New York: Random House, 1967.

Gattegno, Caleb, *Towards a Visual Culture.* New York: Guterbridge and Diensfrey, 1969.

Green, Maury, *Television News: Anatomy and Process.* Belmont, Calif.: Wadsworth Publishing Co., 1969.

Green, Timothy, *The Universal Eye: The World of Television.* New York: Stein and Day, 1972.

Hall, Mark W., *Broadcast Journalism: An Introduction to News Writing.* New York: Hastings House, 1971.

Head, Sidney W., *Broadcasting in America.* Boston: Houghton Mifflin, 1972.

Hilliard, Robert L., *Radio Broadcasting.* New York: Hastings House, 1967.

Hodgkinson, A. W., *Screen Education: Teaching a Critical Approach to Cinema and Television.* Paris: UNESCO, 1964.

Johnson, Nicholas, *How to Talk Back to Your Television Set.* New York: Bantam Books, 1970.

————, *Test Pattern for Living.* New York: Bantam Books, 1972.

Klavan, Eugene, *Turn That Damned Thing Off: An Irreverent Look at TV's Impact on the American Scene.* Indianapolis: Bobbs-Merrill, 1972.

Koenig, Allen, and Ruane B. Hill, *The Farther Vision: Educational Television Today.* Madison: University of Wisconsin Press, 1967.

Krasnow, Erwin G., and Laurence D. Longley, *The Politics of Broadcast Regulation.* New York: St. Martin's Press, 1973.

Kuhns, William, *The Electronic Gospel.* New York: Herder and Herder, 1969.

Madsen, Roy, *The Impact of Film: How Ideas Are Communicated through Cinema and Television.* New York: Macmillan, 1973.

Mayer, Martin, *About Television.* New York: Harper & Row, 1972.

McGinniss, Joe, *The Selling of the President 1968*. New York: Trident Press, 1968.

Melody, William H., *Children's Television: The Economics of Exploitation*. New Haven: Yale University Press, 1973.

Morris, Norman S., *Television's Child*. Boston: Little, Brown, 1971.

Newcomb, Horace, *TV: The Most Popular Art*. Garden City, N.Y.: Anchor Press/Doubleday, 1974.

Park, Rolla Edward, *Cable Television and UHF Broadcasting*. Santa Monica, Calif.: Rand, 1971.

Polsky, Richard M., *Getting to Sesame Street: Origin of the Children's Television Workshop*. New York: Praeger, 1974.

Schiller, Herbert I., *Mass Communications and American Empire*. New York: A. M. Kelley, 1969.

Scornia, Harry J., *Problems and Controversies in Television and Radio*. Palo Alto, Calif.: Pacific Books, 1968.

———, *Television and the News*. Palo Alto, Calif.: Pacific Books, 1968.

———, *Television and Society: An Inquest and Agenda for Improvement*. New York: McGraw-Hill, 1965.

Shomberg, Michael, *Guerilla Television*. New York: Holt, Rinehart & Winston, 1971.

Shulman, Milton, *The Ravenous Eye: The Impact of the Fifth Factor*. London: Cassell, 1973.

Steiner, Gary A., *People Look at Television*. New York: Alfred A. Knopf, 1963.

Ward, Scott, *Effects of Television Advertising on Children and Adolescents*. Cambridge, Mass.: Marketing Science Institute, 1971.

Weinberg, Meyer, *TV in America: The Morality of Hard Cash*. New York: Ballantine Books, 1962.

White, David Manning, and Richard Averson, *Sight, Sound, and Society: Motion Pictures and Television in America*. Boston: Beacon Press, 1968.

Wood, William Almon, *Electronic Journalism*. New York: Columbia University Press, 1967.

E. Photography

Braive, Michel F., *The Photograph: A Social History*. New York: McGraw-Hill, 1966.

Brandt, Bill, *Shadow of Light*. New York: Viking Press, 1966.

Capa, Cornell, ed., *The Concerned Photographer*. New York: Grossman, 1968.

Cartier-Bresson, Henri, *The World of Henri Cartier-Bresson*. New York: Viking Press, 1968.

Coffin, Charles Henry, *Photography as a Fine Art*. New York: Amphoto, 1972.

Cousteau, Jacques Yves, *The Living Sea*. New York: Harper & Row, 1963.

Craven, George M., *Object and Image: An Introduction to Photography*. Englewood Cliffs, N.J.: Prentice-Hall, 1975.

Eisenstaedt, Alfred, *Witness to Our Time*. New York: Viking Press, 1966.

Evans, Walker, *American Photographs*. New York: Doubleday for the Museum of Modern Art, 1961.

Feininger, Andreas, *The Complete Photographer*. Englewood Cliffs, N.J.: Prentice-Hall, 1965.

———, *Photographic Seeing*. Englewood Cliffs, N.J.: Prentice-Hall, 1973.

Germar, Herb, *The Student Journalist and Photojournalism*. New York: Rosen Press, 1967.

Hymers, Robert P., *The Professional Photographer in Practice*. London: Fountain Press, 1964.

Karsh, Yousuf, *Karsh Portfolio*. London: Nelson, 1967.

Larmore, Lewis, *Introduction to Photographic Principles*. New York: Dover Publications, 1965.

Lyons, Nathan, ed., *Photographers on Photography*. Englewood Cliffs, N.J.: Prentice-Hall, 1966.

Miller, Thomas H., and Wyatt Brummitt, *This Is Photography, Its Means and Its Ends*. Rochester, N.Y.: The Case-Hoyt Corporation/Doubleday, 1963.

Newhall, Beaumont, *The History of Photography from 1839 to the Present Day*. New York: Doubleday for the Museum of Modern Art, 1964.

Photojournalism. New York: Time-Life Books, 1971.

Steichen, Edward, ed., *The Family of Man*. New York: MACO for the Museum of Modern Art, 1955.

Szarkowski, John, *Looking at Photographs*. New York: Doubleday for the Museum of Modern Art, 1973.

———, *The Photographer's Eye*. New York: Doubleday for the Museum of Modern Art, 1966.

F. Films

Bazin, André, *What Is Cinema?* Tr. Hugh Gray. Two volumes. Berkeley: University of California Press; vol. 1, 1967; vol. 2, 1971.

Bobker, Lee R., *Elements of Film*, 2d ed. New York: Harcourt Brace Jovanovich: 1974.

Bogle, Donald, *Toms, Coons, Mulattoes, Mammies, & Bucks: An Interpretive History of Blacks in American Films*. New York: Viking Press, 1973.

Burch, Noel, *Theory of Film Practice*. Tr. Helen R. Lane. New York: Praeger, 1973.

Carmen, Ira H., *Movies, Censorship, and the Law*. Ann Arbor: University of Michigan Press, 1966.

Carvie, Peter, *Seventy Years of Cinema*. South Brunswick, N.J.: A. S. Barnes, 1969.

Chase, Donald, *Film Making: The Collaborative Art*. Boston: Little, Brown, 1975.

DeNitto, Dennis, and William Herman, *Film and the Critical Eye*. New York: Macmillan, 1975.

Farber, Stephen, *The Movie Rating Game*. Washington, D.C.: Public Affairs Press, 1972.

Fell, John L., *Film: An Introduction*. New York: Praeger, 1975.

Feyen, Sharon, and Donald Wigal, eds., *Screen Experience: An Approach to Film.* Dayton, Ohio: Pflaum, 1969.

Geduld, Harry M., ed., *Film Makers on Film Making.* Bloomington: Indiana University Press, 1967.

Gianetti, Louis D., *Understanding Movies,* 2d ed. Englewood Cliffs, N.J.: Prentice-Hall, 1976.

Hall, Ben M., *The Best Remaining Seats: The Story of the Golden Age of the Movie Palace.* New York: C. N. Potter, 1961.

Haskell, Molly, *From Reverence to Rape: The Treatment of Women in the Movies.* New York: Holt, Rinehart & Winston, 1972.

Heraldson, Donald, *Creators of Life: A History of Animation.* New York: Drake Publishers, 1975.

Jacobs, Lewis, *The Emergence of Film Art.* New York: Hopkinson and Blake, 1969.

Kael, Paulene, *Deeper into Movies.* Boston: Atlantic/Little, Brown, 1973.

————, *Going Steady.* Boston: Atlantic/Little, Brown, 1970.

Kauffmann, Stanley, *Figures of Light.* New York: Harper & Row, 1971.

————, *Living Images: Film Comment and Criticism.* New York: Harper & Row, 1975.

Knight, Arthur, *The Liveliest Art,* 2d ed. New York: New American Library, 1971.

Lawson, John H., *Film: The Creative Process.* New York: Hill and Wang, 1967.

MacCann, Richard Dyer, *Film: A Montage of Theories.* New York: E. P. Dutton, 1966.

Macgowan, Kenneth, *Behind the Screen: The History and Techniques of the Motion Picture.* New York: Delacorte Press, 1965.

Madsen, Axel, *The New Hollywood: American Movies in the '70's.* New York: Crowell, 1975.

Mallery, David, *The School and the Art of Motion Pictures.* Boston: National Association of Independent Schools, 1966.

Mamber, Stephen, *Cinema Verité in America: Studies in Uncontrolled Documentary.* Cambridge, Mass.: M.I.T. Press, 1974.

Mascelli, Joseph U., *The Five C's of Cinematography: Motion Picture Filming Techniques Simplified.* Hollywood, Calif.: Cine/Grafic Publications, 1965.

Mast, Gerald, *A Short History of the Movies.* Indianapolis: Bobbs-Merrill, 1971.

McClelland, C. Kirk, *On Making a Movie: Brewster McCloud.* Nancy Hardin, ed. New York: New American Library, 1971.

McClure, Arthur F., ed., *The Movies: An American Idiom: Readings in the Social History of the American Motion Picture.* Rutherford, N.J.: Farleigh-Dickenson University Press, 1971.

Mellen, Joan, *Women and Their Sexuality in the New Film.* New York: Horizon Press, 1973.

Mekas, Jonas, *Movie Journal: The Rise of the New American Cinema 1959–1971.* New York: Macmillan, 1972.

Montagu, Ivor, *Film World: A Guide to Cinema.* Baltimore: Pelican Books, 1968.

Murray, James, *To Find an Image: Black Films from Uncle Tom to Super Fly.* Indianapolis: Bobbs-Merrill, 1973.

Nobile, Philip, ed., *Favorite Movies: Critics' Choice.* New York: Macmillan, 1973.

Perkins, V. F., *Film as Film.* New York: Pelican/Penguin, 1972.

Piper, James, *Personal Filmmaking.* Reston, Va.: Reston Publishing Co./ Prentice-Hall, 1975.

Randall, Richard, *Censorship of the Movies.* Madison: University of Wisconsin Press, 1968.

Renan, Sheldon, *An Introduction to the American Underground Film.* New York: E. P. Dutton, 1967.

Rosen, Marjorie, *Popcorn Venus: Women, Movies, and the American Dream.* New York: Coward, McCann, and Geoghegan, 1973.

Rosenthal, Alan, *The New Documentary in Action: A Casebook in Filmmaking.* Berkeley: University of California Press, 1971.

Sarris, Andrew, *The Primal Screen: Essays on Film and Related Subjects.* New York: Simon and Schuster, 1973.

Scott, James, *Film: The Medium and the Maker.* New York: Holt, Rinehart & Winston, 1975.

Stedman, Raymond William, *The Serials and Drama by Installment.* Norman: University of Oklahoma Press, 1971.

Stephenson, Ralph, and J. R. Debrix, *Cinema as Art.* Baltimore: Penguin Books, 1967.

Stewart, David, ed., *Film Study in Higher Education.* Washington, D.C.: American Council on Education, 1966.

Taylor, John Russell, *Cinema Eye, Cinema Ear: Some Key Film Makers of the Sixties.* New York: Hill and Wang, 1964.

Turan, Kenneth, and Stephen F. Zito, *Sinema: American Pornographic Films and the People Who Make Them.* New York: Praeger, 1974.

Youngblood, Gene, *Expanded Cinema.* New York: E. P. Dutton, 1970.

G. Popular Music

Artis, Bob, *Bluegrass.* New York: Hawthorne Books, 1975.

Baez, Joan, *Daybreak.* New York: Dial Press, 1968.

Boeckman, Charles, *And the Beat Goes On.* New York: Robert B. Luce, 1972.

Brown, Duane, *Toward a Theory of Popular Culture: The Sociology and History of American Music and Dance 1920–1968.* Ann Arbor, Mich.: Ann Arbor Publishers, 1969.

Cohn, Nik, *Rock from the Beginning.* New York: Stein and Day, 1969.

Cone, James H., *The Spirituals and the Blues: An Interpretation.* New York: The Seabury Press, 1972.

Courtlander, Harold, *Negro Folk Music.* New York: Columbia University Press, 1963.

Dolan, Robert Emmett, *Music in Modern Media.* New York: G. Schirmer, 1967.

Eisen, Jonathan, ed., *The Age of Rock: Sounds of the American Cultural Revolution.* New York: Random House, 1969.

Engel, Lehman, *American Theatre Music*. New York: Macmillan, 1967.

Ewen, David Wark, ed., *American Popular Songs from the Revolutionary War to the Present*. New York: Random House, 1966.

———, *Great Men of American Popular Song*. Englewood Cliffs, N.J.: Prentice-Hall, 1972.

Gahr, David, and Robert Shelton. *The Face of Folk*. New York: Citadel Press, 1968.

Garland, Phyl, *The Sound of Soul*. Chicago: H. Regnery, 1969.

Gillett, Charlie, *Making Tracks: Atlantic Records and the Growth of the Multi-billion Dollar Industry*. New York: E. P. Dutton, 1974.

Glazer, Tom, ed., *Songs of Peace, Freedom, & Protest*. New York: McKay, 1970.

Greenway, John, *American Folksongs of Protest*. New York: Octagon Books, 1970.

Hellbut, Tony, *The Gospel Sound: Good News and Bad Times*. New York: Simon and Schuster, 1971.

Hemphill, Paul, *The Nashville Sound: Bright Lights and Country Music*. New York: Simon and Schuster, 1970.

Hopkins, Jerry, *The Rock Story*. New York: New American Library, 1970.

Jahn, Mike, *The Story of Rock from Elvis Presley to the Rolling Stones*. New York: Quadrangle/The New York Times Book Co., 1973.

Jones, Leroi, *Black Music*. New York: W. Morrow, 1967.

———, *Blues People: Negro Music in White America*. New York: W. Morrow, 1963.

Lawless, Ray M., *Folksingers and Folksongs in America*, 2d ed. New York: Duell, Sloan & Pearce; 1965.

Lovell, John, Jr., *Black Song: The Forge and the Flame*. New York: Macmillan, 1972.

Mahey, Richard, *The Pop Process*. London: Hutchinson, 1969.

Malone, Bill C., *Country Music U.S.A.: A Fifty Year History*. Austin: University of Texas Press, 1968.

Marks, J., *Rock and Other Four Letter Words: Music of the Electric Generation*. New York: Bantam Books, 1968.

Meltzer, R., *The Aesthetics of Rock*. New York: Something Else Press, 1970.

Price, Stephen D., *Take Me Home: The Rise of Country and Western Music*. New York: Praeger, 1974.

Rublowsky, John, *Popular Music*. New York: Basic Books, 1967.

Seeger, Pete, *The Incompleat Folk Singer*. New York: Simon and Schuster, 1972.

Shaw, Arnold, *The World of Soul: Black America's Contribution to the Pop Music Scene*. New York: Cowles Book Co., 1970.

Shemel, Sidney, *More about This Business of Music*. New York: Billboard Publishing Co., 1967.

———, *This Business of Music*. New York: Billboard Publishing Co., 1964.

Sinclair, John, and Robert Levin, *Music and Politics*. New York: World Publishing Co., 1971.

Stambler, Irwin, ed., *Encyclopedia of Pop, Rock, and Soul*. New York: St. Martin's Press, 1974.

———, *Encyclopedia of Popular Music*. New York: St. Martin's Press, 1965.

Swanwick, Kieth, *Popular Music and the Teacher*. New York: Pergamon Press, 1968.

Ulanov, Barry, *A History of Jazz in America*. New York: Viking Press, 1952.

H. Education

Farber, Jerry, *The Student as Nigger*. North Hollywood, Calif.: Contact Books, 1969.

Gillis, Don, *The Art of Media Instruction*. Dallas: Crescendo Book Publications, 1973.

Goodman, Paul, *Compulsory Miseducation and the Community of Scholars*. New York: Vintage Books, 1966.

Gross, Ronald, and Beatrice Gross, eds., *Radical School Reform*. New York: Simon and Schuster, 1969.

Herndon, James, *The Way It Spozed to Be*. New York: Simon and Schuster, 1968.

Holt, John, *Escape from Childhood*. New York: E. P. Dutton, 1974.

————, *Freedom and Beyond*. New York: E. P. Dutton, 1972.

————, *How Children Fail*. New York: Dell Publishing, 1964.

————, *How Children Learn*. New York: Pitman Publishing Corp., 1967.

Illich, Ivan, *Deschooling Society*. New York: Harper & Row, 1970.

Keats, John, *The Sheepskin Psychosis*. Philadelphia: Lippincott, 1965.

Kozol, Jonathan, *Free Schools*. Boston: Houghton Mifflin, 1972.

Leonard, George B., *Education and Ecstasy*. New York: Delacorte Press, 1968.

Martin, John Henry, and Charles H. Harrison, *Free to Learn: Unlocking and Ungrading American Education*. Englewood Cliffs, N.J.: Prentice-Hall, 1972.

Martin, Warren B., *Alternative to Irrelevance*. Nashville: Abingdon Press, 1968.

Mahew, Lewis B., *Higher Education in the Revolutionary Decades*. Berkeley: McCutchan Publishing Co., 1967.

Neill, A. S., *Freedom—Not License!* New York: Hart Publishing Co., 1966.

————, *Summerhill: A Radical Approach to Child Rearing*. New York: Hart Publishing Co., 1960.

Postman, Neil, and Charles Weingartner, *Teaching as a Subversive Activity*. New York: Delacorte Press, 1969.

Riesman, David, Joseph Gusfield, and Zelda Gamson, *Academic Values and Mass Education*. Garden City, N.Y.: Doubleday, 1970.

Silberman, Charles E., *Crisis in the Classroom*. New York: Random House, 1970.

Sowell, Thomas, *Black Education: Myths and Tragedies*. New York: David McKay Co., 1972.

Taylor, Harold, *Students without Teachers*. New York: McGraw-Hill, 1969.

Thornton, James W., *New Media and College Teaching*. Washington, D.C.: National Education Association, 1968.

Tonsor, Stephen J., *Tradition and Reform in Education*. La Salle, Ill.: Open Court Publishing Co., 1974.

Vermilye, Dyckman W., ed., *The Expanded Campus.* San Francisco: Jossey-Bass, Inc., 1972.

Wiseman, T. Jan, and Molly J. Wiseman, *Creative Communications: Teaching Mass Media.* Minneapolis: National Scholastic Press Association/University of Minnesota, 1974.

Woodring, Paul, *The Higher Learning in America: A Reassessment.* New York: McGraw-Hill, 1968.

■ SOURCES OF MEDIA FOR THE CLASSROOM

Here is a partial listing of organizations which sell or rent films, filmstrips, records, audiotapes, and other audiovisual materials. Most will send catalogs of their audiovisual holdings upon request.

Ad-Tapes Catalog
PO Box 66
Palos Verdes Estates
California 90274

Agency for Instructional Television
Box A
Bloomington, Ind. 47401

Argo Sight and Sound
London Records, Inc.
539 West 25th Street
New York, N.Y. 10001

Associated Educational Materials, Inc.
Glenwood at Hillsboro St.
Raleigh, N.C. 27602

Audio/Brandon Film Center
34 MacQuesten Parkway South
Mount Vernon, N.Y. 10550

AudioVisual Market Place
Collier Macmillan School and Library Services
866 Third Avenue
New York, N.Y. 10022

BFA Educational Media
2211 Michigan Avenue
Santa Monica, Calif. 90404

Blackhawk Films
Eastin-Phelan Corporation
Davenport, Iowa 52808

Caedmon Recordings of the Spoken Word
D. C. Heath and Company
2700 N. Richardt Avenue
Indianapolis, Ind. 46219

Caedmon Records
505 Eighth Avenue
New York, N.Y. 10018

Carousel Films, Inc.
1501 Broadway
New York, N.Y. 10036

CCM Films, Inc.
866 Third Avenue
New York, N.Y. 10022

Center for Mass Communications
Columbia University Press
440 West 110th Street
New York, N.Y. 10036

Churchill Films
622 North Robertson Blvd.
Los Angeles, Calif. 90069

Cinema 16/Grove Press
80 University Place
New York, N.Y. 10003

Columbia Cinematique
711 Fifth Avenue
New York, N.Y. 10022

Columbia Special Products
51 West 52d Street
New York, N.Y. 10019

Contemporary Films
828 Custer Avenue
Evanston, Ill. 60602

Contemporary Films/McGraw-Hill
1221 Avenue of the Americas
New York, N.Y. 10020

Continental 16
241 East 34th Street
New York, N.Y. 10016

Coronet Films
65 East South Water Street
Chicago, Ill. 60601

Creative Learning Center
108 St. John's Road
Baltimore, Md. 21210

Current Affairs
527 Madison Avenue
New York, N.Y. 10022

Decca Records
445 Park Avenue
New York, N.Y. 10022

Doubleday MultiMedia
1376 Reynolds Avenue
Santa Ana, Calif. 92705

EAV (Educational Audio Visual)
29 Marble Avenue
Pleasantville, N.Y. 10570

Educational Corporation of America
984 Livernois Road
Troy, Mich. 48084

EMC Corporation
Educational Materials Division
180 East Sixth Street
St. Paul, Minn. 55101

Encyclopaedia Britannica Educational Corp.
425 North Michigan Ave.
Chicago, Ill. 60611

Film Images
1034 Lake Street
Oak Park, Ill. 60301

Films Incorporated
4420 Oakton Street
Skokie, Ill. 60076

Folkway Records, Inc.
165 West 46th Street
New York, N.Y. 10036

Harper & Row, Publishers
Audiovisual Materials
10 East 53d Street
New York, N.Y. 10022

Houghton Mifflin
Multimedia
110 Tremont Street
Boston, Mass. 02107

Indiana University
Audio-Visual Center
Bloomington, Ind. 47405

International Film Bureau
322 South Michigan Avenue
Chicago, Ill. 60604

Janus Films
24 West 58th Street
New York, N.Y. 10023

Lansford Publishing Co.
2516 Lansford Avenue
San Jose, Calif. 95125

Learning Arts
PO Box 917
Wichita, Kans. 67201

Learning Corporation of America
711 Fifth Avenue
New York, N.Y. 10022

Library Record and Tape Service
14940 Calvert Street
Van Nuys, Calif. 91401

Listening Library
1 Park Avenue
Old Greenwich, Conn. 06870

London Records, Inc.
539 West 25th Street
New York, N.Y. 10001

Mass Communications, Inc.
25 Sylvan Road South
Westport, Conn. 06880

Mass Media Ministries
2116 North Charles Street
Baltimore, Md. 21218

McGraw-Hill Films/Contemporary
McGraw-Hill Sound Seminars
1221 Avenue of the Americas
New York, N.Y. 10020

McIntyre Productions, Inc.
Box 16031
Kansas City, Mo. 64112

Media Research and Development
Arizona State University
Tempe, Ariz. 85281

Motion Picture Enterprises Publications, Inc.
Audiovisual Source Directory
Tarrytown, N.Y. 10591

Multimedia Publications, Inc.
P.O. Box 5097
Stanford, Calif. 94305

Museum of Modern Art
Department of Film
11 East 53d Street
New York, N.Y. 10019

National Audiovisual Center
General Service Administration
National Archives and Record Service
Washington, D.C. 20409

National Center for Audio Tapes
University of Colorado
348 Stadium Building
Boulder, Colo. 80302

National Information Center for Educational Media
University of Southern California
University Park
Los Angeles, Calif. 90007

NBC Educational Enterprises
30 Rockefeller Plaza
New York, N.Y. 10020

Nonesuch Records
15 Columbus Circle
New York, N.Y. 10023

Prentice-Hall Media, Inc.
150 White Plains Road
Tarrytown, N.Y. 10591

Pyramid Films
P.O. Box 1048
Santa Monica, Calif. 90406

Quad Films
P.O. Box 2986
St. Louis, Mo. 63130

Rose Discount Records
214 South Wabash Avenue
Chicago, Ill. 60604

Schwann
137 Newbury Street
Boston, Mass. 02116

Spoken Arts, Inc.
New Rochelle, N.Y. 10801

Sterling Educational Films
241 East 34th Street
New York, N.Y. 10016

Swank Motion Pictures
201 South Jefferson Avenue
St. Louis, Mo. 63166

Teaching Films Custodians
25 West 43d Street
New York, N.Y. 10016

Time-Life Multimedia
Time and Life Building
New York, N.Y. 10020

20th Century-Fox Films
1417 North Western
Los Angeles, Calif. 90027

Twyman Films, Inc.
329 Salem Avenue
Dayton, Ohio 45401

United Artists
729 Seventh Avenue
New York, N.Y. 10019

University of California
Extension Media Center
2223 Fulton Street
Berkeley, Calif. 95720

University of Illinois

Visual Aids Service
Div. of University Extension
704 South Sixth Street
Champaign, Ill. 61820

University of Iowa
Audiovisual Center
Iowa City, Iowa 52240

University of Michigan
Audio-Visual Education Center
416 Fourth Street
Ann Arbor, Mich. 48104

Warner Brothers, Inc.
4000 Warner Blvd.
Burbank, Calif. 91505

■ ACKNOWLEDGMENTS

Hollis Alpert, "In Answer to Dr. Greenson," from *Saturday Review,* June 15, 1974. Reprinted by permission.

Michael J. Arlen, "You'll Laugh! You'll Cry! You'll Watch Them Die," from *Playboy,* May 1972. Originally appeared in *Playboy Magazine.* Copyright © 1972 by Michael J. Arlen. Reprinted by permission of Candida Donadio and Associates, Inc.

Herman Badillo and James Ryan, "Rep. Herman Badillo's Account of His Harrowing Three Days Inside Attica State Prison," in *New York News,* September 13, 1971. Copyright © 1971 New York News, Inc. Reprinted by permission.

Marilyn Bailey, "Wives Will Run It Down to the People," from the *Rochester Democrat and Chronicle,* September 13, 1971. Reprinted by permission.

Jerome A. Barron, "Freedom of the Press for Whom? The Right of Access to Mass Media." Copyright © 1973 by Indiana University Press, Bloomington. Reprinted by permission of the publisher.

Duane Bradley, "What Is News?" from *The Newspaper: Its Place in a Democracy,* published by Van Nostrand Reinhold Company, 1966. Copyright 1966 by Litton Educational Publishing, Inc. Reprinted by permission.

Marjorie Burns, "The Advertiser's Bag of Tricks," from *Scholastic Voice,* November 8, 1973. Copyright © 1973 by Scholastic Magazine, Inc. Reprinted by permission from Scholastic Voice.

Bob Buyer and Ray Hill, "Attica Death Toll Rises to 41: Transfer Start," from *Buffalo Evening News,* September 14, 1971. Reprinted by permission.

Cincinnati Horizons, "Television: What Public? Whose Interest?" vol. 3, no. 7, July 1974. Reprinted by permission.

Norman Cousins, "Science, Education, and the Enjoyment of Living," from "Art, Adrenalin, and the Enjoyment of Living," in *Saturday Review,* April 20, 1968. Copyright 1968 by Saturday Review, Inc. Reprinted by permission.

Harvey Cox, "The Playboy and Miss America," from *The Secular City,* 1966. Copyright © by Harvey Cox 1965, 1966. Reprinted with permission of The Macmillan Company.

Bosley Crowther, "Magic, Myth, and Monotony," from *Mass Media in a Free Society,* 1969. Reprinted by permission.

John Culkin, "From Film Studies to Media Studies," from *Media and Methods,* December, 1974. Reprinted by permission.

June Kirkhuff Edwards, "The Textbook Controversy: A Political Confrontation," from *The Christian Century,* November 13, 1974. Copyright 1974 Christian Century Foundation. Reprinted by permission from The Christian Century.

Edith Efron, "Is Television Making a Mockery of the American Woman?" from *TV Guide Magazine,* August 8, 1970. Copyright © 1970 by Triangle Publications, Inc., Radnor, Pennsylvania. Reprinted with permission from TV Guide ® Magazine.

David Elliott, "What Has Happened to Movie Audiences?" from *Chicago Daily News,* October 27, 1971. Reprinted with permission from the Chicago Daily News.

William Federici, "I Saw Seven Throats Cut," from *New York News,* September 14, 1971. Copyright 1971 New York News, Inc. Reprinted by permission.

Erich Fromm, "Personality Packages," in *The Art of Loving* by Erich Fromm. Copyright © 1956 by Erich Fromm. Reprinted by permission of Harper & Row, Publishers, Inc.

David Gahr and Robert Shelton, "The Big Sound from the Country," from *The Face of Folk Music,* 1968. Reprinted by permission of Citadel Press, Inc.

Ralph Greenson, "A Psychoanalyst's Indictment of 'The Exorcist,'" from *Saturday Review,* June 15, 1974. Reprinted by permission.

August Gribbin, "The Maestro of Motivational Research," from *The National Observer,* November 13, 1971. Reprinted by permission.

Nancy Hardin, "For Paperback Houses, There's No Business Like Show Tie-In Business," in *Publishers Weekly,* February 17, 1975. Courtesy of Nancy Hardin.

Robert Hatch, "The Exorcist," from *The Nation,* February 2, 1974. Reprinted by permission.

John Holt, "Learning by Doing," from "The Learning Society." Originally published in the *Christian Science Monitor,* April 8, 1974. Copyright © 1974 by John Holt. Reprinted by permission of the Robert Lescher Literary Agency.

Emmet John Hughes, "The Impact of TV on American Politics," from "52,000,000 TV Sets: How Many Votes?" in *New York Times,* November 11, 1968. Copyright © 1968 by The New York Times Company. Reprinted by permission.

Morton M. Hunt, "Love According to Madison Avenue," from *Horizon,* November 1959. Copyright © 1959 by Morton M. Hunt.

Nicholas Johnson, "Communications and the Year 2000," from *How to Talk Back to Your Television Set* by Nicholas Johnson. Copyright © 1967, 1968, 1969, 1970 by Nicholas Johnson. Reprinted by permission of Little, Brown, and Company in association with the Atlantic Monthly Press.

Pauline Kael, "Marketing the Movies," and "Movies on TV," excerpts from "On the Future of Movies," in *The New Yorker,* August 5, 1974. Copyright © 1974 The New Yorker Magazine, Inc. Reprinted by permission.

Stanley Kauffmann, "The Exorcist" (including "Postscript"), February 9, 1974, in *Living Images: Film Comment and Criticism.* Copyright © 1974 by Stanley Kauffmann. By permission of Harper & Row, Publishers, Inc.

Francine Klagsrun, "How Ms. Magazine Got Started," in *The First Ms. Reader,* Appendix 1, 1973. Reprinted by permission of Warner Books, Inc.

Jerzy Kosinski, "TV As Babysitter," from *TV-NBC-Comment,* vol. 2, no. 30 by Jerzy Kosinski, September 3, 1972. Reprinted with permission of Jerzy Kosinski.

Dawn Ann Kurth, "Bugs Bunny Says They're Yummy," from *The New York Times,* July 2, 1972. Copyright © 1972 by The New York Times Company. Reprinted by permission.

W. T. Lhamon, Jr., "Rock: The Unspeakable Mix," from *The New Republic,* March 2, 1974. Reprinted by permission of The New Republic, © 1974, The New Republic, Inc.

McCalls, "Your Soap-Opera Sitter," May 1974. Reprinted by permission.

Joe McGinniss, "Selling the President on TV," from *The Selling of the President, 1969.* Copyright © 1969 by Joe Mac, Inc. Reprinted by permission of Simon and Schuster.

William C. Martin, "The God-Hucksters of Radio," from *The Atlantic,* June 1970. Reprinted by permission.

Thomas H. Middleton, "On Shooting First," from *Saturday Review,* September 25, 1973. Reprinted by permission of Thomas H. Middleton.

The Midwest Motorist, "Elements of Persuasion and Techniques of Propaganda," December 1971. Reprinted by permission.

John G. Morris, "This We Remember: The Pictures That Make Vietnam Unforgettable," *Harper's Magazine,* September 1972. Used with the permission of John G. Morris.

James P, Murray, "To Find an Image: Movies and Life and Black People," from *To Find an Image,* 1973. Copyright © 1973 by James P. Murray. Reprinted by permission of the publisher, The Bobbs-Merrill Company, Inc.

The Nation, "Burning Vonnegut," December 3, 1973. Copyright by The Nation. Reprinted by permission.

National Review, "Exploiting Attica," from *National Review,* October 8, 1971. Reprinted by permission of National Review.

Robert F. Nelson, "Making the Dial Volkswagen Commercial," from *Exploring Television,* by William Kuhns, 1975. Reprinted by permission of Robert F. Nelson.

Newsweek, "The Book Banners," from *Newsweek,* March 26, 1973, and September 30, 1974. Copyright © 1973 and 1974 Newsweek, Inc. Reprinted by permission.

The New Republic, "Dead End at Attica," September 25, 1971. Copyright © 1971, The New Republic, Inc. Reprinted by permission of The New Republic.

New York News, "The Prisoners' Demands," September 12, 1971. Copyright 1971 New York News, Inc. Reprinted by permission.

New Yorker, "The Best-Sellers List," from "Notes and Comments," from *The New Yorker Magazine,* December 8, 1962. Copyright © 1962 The New Yorker Magazine, Inc. Reprinted by permission.

Patricia O'Brien, "Housewife Image Tarnished on TV," from *Chicago Sun-Times,* October 1964. Reprinted by permission.

David Ogilvy, "Should Advertising Be Abolished?" from *Confessions of an Advertising Man,* 1963. Copyright © 1963 by David Ogilvy, Trustee. Reprinted by permission of Atheneum Publishers.

Allan Parachini, "Doonesbury: Social Protest Hits the Comic Pages." Reprinted from the *Columbia Journalism Review,* November/December 1974 ©.

William S. Pechter, " 'The Exorcist' and Its Audience," from *Commentary,* March 1974. Copyright © 1974 by the American Jewish Committee. Reprinted from *Commentary* by permission.

Pete Seeger, "The Folk Process," from *The Incomplete Folk Singer,* 1972. Copyright © 1972 by Pete Seeger. Reprinted by permission of Simon and Schuster.

Diane K. Shah, "Secret Urges on Her Mind," from *National Observer,* June 7, 1975. Reprinted by permission.

Donald D. Shandler and Paul Coker, Jr., "Masters of Mediocrity," in *Mad,* no. 101, March 1966. Copyright © 1966 by E. C. Publications, Inc. Reprinted by permission.

David Shaw, "Violent Movies Create Violent Kids," from *Today's Health,* October 1974. Reprinted by permission.

Robert Lewis Shayon, "No Exit," from *Saturday Review,* August 7, 1965. By permission of Saturday Review, Inc., and the author.

Alton Slagle, "Rocky Rejects Deal with Attica Cons: A Massacre Feared by Negotiators," in *New York News,* September 13, 1971. Copyright 1971 New York News Inc. Reprinted by permission.

Susan Sontag, "The Imagination of Disaster," from *Against Interpretation* by Susan Sontag. Copyright © 1961, 1962, 1963, 1964, 1965, 1966 by Susan Sontag. Reprinted with the permission of Farrar, Straus, & Giroux, Inc.

John Szarkowski, "The Photographer's Eye," from *The Photographer's Eye* by John Szarkowski. Copyright © 1966 The Museum of Modern Art, New York. All rights reserved. Reprinted by permission of the publisher.

Time, "A Bible Buyer's Catalogue," December 20, 1975. Copyright © 1975 by Time, Inc. Reprinted by permission from Time, The Weekly Newsmagazine.

Time, "Soul: Singing It Like It Is," June 28, 1968. Copyright © 1968 by Time, Inc. Reprinted by permission from Time, The Weekly Newsmagazine.

Time, "Pop Records: Moguls, Money, and Monsters," February 12, 1973. Copyright © 1973 by Time, Inc. Reprinted by permission from Time, The Weekly Newsmagazine.

Today's Health, "The Town Meeting Is Not Dead—It's Alive and Well on Radio," June 1970. Reprinted by permission.

U.S. News and World Report, "What TV Is Doing to America," April 15, 1974. Copyright 1974 U.S. News and World Report, Inc. Reprinted by permission from U.S. News and World Report.

U.S. News and World Report, "Why U.S. Prisons Are Exploding," September 27, 1971. Reprinted by permission from *U.S. News and World Report.* Copyright 1971 U.S. News and World Report, Inc.

Kurt Vonnegut, Jr., ". . . But Words Can Never Hurt Me." From the volume *Wampeters, Foma and Granfalloons,* by Kurt Vonnegut, Jr. Copyright © 1965–1970, 1972–1974. A Delacorte Press/Seymour Laurence book, used by permission of the publisher.

Tom Wicker, "The Animals at Attica," in *The New York Times,* September 16, 1971. Copyright © 1971 by The New York Times Company. Reprinted by permission.

Ed Wilks, "The Cartoon Is an Old Art Form," from the *St. Louis Post-Dispatch,* May 4, 1972. Reprinted by permission.

Tom Wolfe, "Why They Aren't Writing the Great American Novel Anymore," from *Esquire Magazine,* December 1972. Copyright © 1972 by Esquire Magazine. Reprinted by permission of International Creative Management.

Roland E. Wolseley, "Is There a Black Press?" Copyright © 1974 by Iowa State University Press, Ames, Iowa. Reprinted by permission from *The Black Press, U.S.A.*

Dick Wright, "Disputed Book off EBR List," in *Sunday Morning Advocate,* January 12, 1975. Reprinted by permission of Morning Advocate, Baton Rouge, Louisiana.

INDEX OF NAMES, SUBJECTS, AND SOURCES

■ INDEX OF NAMES, SUBJECTS, AND SOURCES

Names in this index are cited as subjects and not as authors of the selections. Page numbers in *italic* following names of publications indicate selections from these publications; other citations represent the publications as subjects.